NEURAL COMPUTING
ARCHITECTURES

NEURAL COMPUTING ARCHITECTURES

THE DESIGN OF BRAIN-LIKE MACHINES

EDITED BY IGOR ALEKSANDER

The MIT Press
Cambridge, Massachusetts

First MIT Press edition, 1989

© 1989 North Oxford Academic Publishers Ltd and named contributors

Printed and bound in Great Britain.
First published in Great Britain 1989
by North Oxford Academic Publishers Ltd,
a subsidiary of Kogan Page Ltd,
120 Pentonville Road, London N1 9JN

Library of Congress Cataloging-in-Publication Data
Neural computing architectures: the design of brain-like machines/
    edited by Igor Aleksander.
        p. cm
    Includes index.
    ISBN 0–262–01110–7
    1. Neural computers. 2. Computer architecture. I. Aleksander,
Igor.
QA76.5.N426 1989
006.3- -dc19   88-38352
                                                                    CIP

Contents

Contents

PART I
The Classical Perspective

1 Why neural computing? a personal view

I. Aleksander

Department of Electrical Engineering, Imperial College of Science and Technology, London, UK

Abstract

The sudden growth of interest in neural computing is a remarkable phenomenon that will be seen by future historians of computer science as marking the 1980s in much the same way as research into artificial intelligence (AI) has been the trademark of the 1970s. There is one major difference, however: in contrast with AI, which was largely an outlet for a minority of computer scientists, neural computing unites a very broad community: physicists, statisticians, parallel processing experts, optical technologists, neurophysiologists and experimental biologists. The focus of this new paradigm is rather simple. It rests on the recognition by this diverse community that the brain 'computes' in a very different way from the conventional computer.

This is quite contrary to the focus of the AI paradigm, which is based on the premise that an understanding of what the brain does represents a true understanding only if it can be explicitly expressed as a set of rules that, in turn, can be run on a computer which subsequently performs artificially intelligent tasks. Those who contribute to neural computing believe that the brain, given sensors and a body, builds up its own hidden rules through what is usually called 'experience'. When a person activates his muscles in complex sequences driven by signals from his eyes, from sensory receptors in his muscles and even from his ears when performing an every-day act such as getting on a bus, or when he notices a 'polite chill' in a colleague's voice, these are examples of large numbers of implicit rules at work in a simultaneous and coordinated fashion in the brain. In neural computing it is believed that the cellular structures within which such rules can grow and be executed are the focus of important study as opposed to the AI concern of trying to extract the rules in order to run them on a computer.

Neural computing is thus concerned with a class of machines that compute by absorbing experience, and in that sense is a class which includes the brain, but may include other forms with similar properties. It is for reasons of extending interest to these other forms that we have chosen to use the word *architectures* in the title of this book. Its authors are not latter-day Frankensteins in the business of *making brains*. They are, however, united in trying to *understand* computing structures that are brain-like in the sense that they acquire knowledge through experience rather than preprogramming. So, *Neural Computing Architectures* is not about the details of mimicking the neurons of the brain and their interconnections, but more about the nature of the broad class of machines which behave in brain-like ways and, through this, adding to both our armoury of knowledge in computing and to our ability to apply such knowledge through the design of novel machinery.

Perhaps, from all this it may be possible to draw out a definition of neural computing:

> *Neural computing is the study of cellular networks that have a natural propensity for storing experiential knowledge. Such systems bear a resemblance to the brain in the sense that knowledge is acquired through training rather than programming and is retained due to changes in node functions. The knowledge takes the form of stable states or cycles of states in the operation of the net. A central property of such nets is to recall these states or cycles in response to the presentation of cues.*

1. Origins

There is undoubtedly a certain degree of hype associated with this field. Phrases such as 'the dawn of a new era' are used by conference organizers, and the press talks of 'new computers that are built like the brain and really think for themselves'. But there is nothing new about neural computing: it is as fundamental as the more conventional or 'algorithmic' mode. Norbert Wiener in his 1947 book *Cybernetics* writes:

> *Mr. Pitts had the good fortune to come under Dr. McCulloch's influence (in 1943) and the two began working quite early on problems concerning the union of nerve fibres by synapses into systems with given overall properties... They added elements suggested by the ideas of Turing in 1936: the consideration of nets containing cycles.*[1]

So some of the discussions that fill the pages of this book and echo in the auditoria of conferences were begun more than ten years before the invention of the computer that we know and love. The McCulloch and Pitts model of the neuron is still the basis for most neural node models, and Turing's concern about nets and cycles is the very stuff of neural computing. Indeed, the 1960s were most productive in this area. The work of Rosenblatt of Cornell University on 'perceptrons' is well known, as is the destruction of its credibility in 1969 by Minsky and Papert of MIT which led to a halt to such work in the USA.[2] More detailed reference to these events may be found in other parts of this book. It is as a reaction to this mistaken criticism that the current revival started in 1983 with analyses that are summarized in Part IV of this book.

But in Europe, neural net researches were not as prone to the winds of change that blew from the direction of MIT as their colleagues in the USA. Eduardo Caianiello in Italy and Teuvo Kohonen in Finland continued to develop an understanding of neural computers to great depth and elegance. I am pleased to have been able to include their contributions in this book. I, too, largely due to a fascination with how well and fast the brain performs tasks of pattern recognition using components much slower than those found in computers, continued designing machines based on the neuron models that I first defined in 1965. These are characterized by the fact that they are easily implemented in electronics and can be understood using formal logic. Part II of this book is concerned with this approach, which has led to the commercialization of practical systems and which points to new high-performance systems for the future.

While this approach is not new, there is no doubt that the work of the 'Parallel Distributed Processing' (PDP) group in the USA has been fundamental in nailing down both the language and the targets of the current paradigm, and it is for this reason that Part IV of this book is an extended review of the pair of books generated by this group under the PDP banner (Rumelhart & McClelland, 1986).[3] But what do the rapidly expanding band of workers in neural computing hope to achieve?

2. Four promises

There appear to be four major reasons for developing neural computing methods, the first of which is a rebuttal of the Minsky and Papert criticism. Although this is not the place to debate the technical issues, it is helpful to note that the criticism was founded on a demonstration that there are simple pattern recognition tasks that neural nets appeared not to be able to accomplish. It is now clear that this conclusion was mistaken because it was founded only on a restricted class of neural system. In fact, the first promise of neural computing is that it is *computationally complete*. This means that, given an appropriate neural structure, and appropriate training, there are no computational tasks that are not available to neural nets. This does not mean that a neural net is as efficient at performing certain tasks as a conventional computer. For example, in order to perform multiplications, the net may have to learn multiplication tables in the way that a human being does, and it can be easily outperformed by a fast arithmetic unit in a conventional computer. But there are tasks for which the neural net not only outperforms the conventional computer but is the *only* way of performing the task.

This leads to the second promise: *functional use of experiential knowledge*. It is here that the neural net can perform functions beyond the capability of rule-based, conventional systems. Typical are the Achilles' heels of artificial intelligence: speech, language and scene understanding. The problem with conventional approaches to these tasks is either that rules are difficult to find, or the number of such rules explodes alarmingly even for simple problems. Imagine having to distinguish between the faces of two people. What information should be extracted? What should be measured in this information? How can we be sure that what we measure will distinguish between the faces? Although a considerable amount of study may provide the answers to some of these questions and, when compiled into a program, may actually differentiate between the faces in question, there is no guarantee that the same measures can be applied to another pair of faces. In contrast, 20 seconds of exposure to a neurally based system such as the WISARD (Aleksander *et al.*, 1984) will allow the net to select among a vast number of rules (node functions) in a very short time in order to provide the best discriminators between the images in question.

The third promise is *performance*: rapid solutions to problems which in conventional computers would take a long time. For example it has been possible to solve the 'travelling salesman problem'* in many fewer steps than by conventional (exhaustive) algorithm.

But there is a snag to the exploitation of this performance: neural systems have actually to be built or run on general purpose *parallel* machines. It is worth pointing out that machines such as the connection machine (Hillis, 1986) are not neural systems. They are general purpose parallel systems that require programs as much as any conventional machine. But the program could be the structure of a neural net, that is, an emulation which, due to the parallelism of the host machine, exploits the speed with which the neural system is capable of solving some problems. Indeed, several 'neural computers' that are appearing on the market are emulations of this type. A useful function that they perform is to provide a tutorial vehicle that gives their users experience in the way such systems work. The first serious neural computer capable of solving real-life problems in real time is still to be built. Although this book

---

*The travelling salesman problem concerns the finding of the shortest route between geographically scattered points. This is traditionally difficult for conventional machines because it relies on the testing of an astronomically large number of paths. The neural computer, by performing local operations in parallel and then allowing these to interact, finds solutions very rapidly.

4

contains no specific designs from which such a system might emerge, it does contain information that may be important for anyone wishing to embark on the design of such a machine. There are many opportunities open for the design of the neural node (eg by optical means, conventional memory chips or special very large scale integrated systems (VLIS)).

The fourth and final promise of neural computing is the provision of an *insight into the computational characteristics of the brain*. This is very much the stated aim of the authors of the PDP books, but is not emphasized strongly in the structure of *Neural Computing Architectures*. In fact, it is becoming apparent that the nature of the research that one does in neural computing will differ according to whether one is concerned with (1) the understanding of principles and the design of machines on one hand, or with (2) brain modelling on the other.

In (1) above, general structures are investigated, while in (2) certain structure characteristics may be ruled out of court should they not conform to what is known of the brain, even if such structures may be computationally highly competent. But this book does not completely ignore an interest in brain modelling: in Part I, some concern is shown for the mechanisms of language understanding in humans which may contribute both to the creation of novel machinery as well as providing a deeper analysis of what may be happening in the brain when it is 'understanding' language.

3. About this book

As already stated, the aims of this book are to provide a guide to architectural issues that arise in neural computing. We see these as being complementary to those of the PDP volumes which are subtitled 'Explorations in the microstructure of cognition'. Clearly, a better understanding of the subject matter constituting cognition in humans is of common concern, but in this book it is the influence of physical structure which unites the authors. The book also aims to present a view (by no means exhaustive) of concerns in Europe, while the PDP books represent the work of researchers in the USA.

In Part I, 'The Classical Perspective', some of the longest-standing European contributors make their statements alongside some related work from more recent arrivals. This perspective is not only fundamental in its own right, but also adds substantially to understanding in a way that is complementary to similar work in the USA.

Part II, 'The Logical Perspective', represents lesser known work in which the neuron is modelled as a logic truth function which can be implemented in a direct way as a silicon read-only-memory. However, it is not only the implementability that is significant in this perspective, but also the fact that neural computing is seen from the mathematical perspective of logic, automata theory and probability theory. This too is seen as being complementary to the favoured approaches in the PDP style which use statistical mechanics as the analytic substrate, the two approaches together forming a more solid pillar for the understanding of neural computing than either of the methodologies on their own.

Part III, 'Analysis and Implementation', presents new material both in the form of analytical tools and models, as well as a suggestion for implementation in optical form.

Part IV, 'The PDP Perspective', is a single extended chapter that summarizes the considerable wealth of theory, application and speculation represented by researchers in the USA. This is not intended to be a replacement for reading the PDP volumes: it is included for completeness so that the authors of *Neural Computing Architectures* can make reference to this work without leaving the reader in the dark, until such time as he can get around to reading the PDP work.

4. The future?

The considerable hype surrounding much current work on neural computing is by no means constructive, but it is at least self-defeating. Many laboratories new to neural computing are discovering that it is not fruitful to cobble together *any* simulation of a neural net, and then hope that it will compute the first thought-of task. This quickly diverts the thrust towards the need to understand what can and cannot be expected of a particular net, and the way the parameters of a net are optimized. The aim of the authors of this book is to contribute to such understanding, which is the best way of fighting the exaggeration.

So what is the ultimate neural computing architecture of the future likely to be? This is an area on which the authors may differ, mainly due to their dedication to the understanding of specific approaches. But one thing does seem to be evident. Neural computing of the future is not likely to be a *replacement* of conventional computing and AI programs, but, rather, is likely to form a complementary technology. It would border on the silly to create with difficulty neural computations that can be performed with ease through conventional methods. The key issue, however, is that the two methods must be able to exist under the same roof (or metal box). So the ultimate challenge for experts in computer architecture is to exploit the two technologies within the box, while presenting a single, flexible interface to the user.

References

1. Wiener, N. *Cybernetics* (Cambridge Mass: MIT Press, 1947).
2. Minsky, M. & Papert, S. *Perceptrons: An Introduction to Computational Geometry* (Boston: MIT Press, 1969).
3. Rumelhart, D. E. & McClelland, J. L. (eds.) *Parallel Distributed Processing*, Vols. 1 and 2 (Cambridge Mass: MIT Press, 1986).

2 A theory of neural networks

Eduardo R. Caianiello

Dipartimento di Fisica Teorica, Università di Salerno–1–84081
Baronissi (SA)

Abstract

This chapter describes the writer's past contribution in developing McCulloch's models of neural activity. Central to this was the creation of an algebraic formulation called 'Neuronic Equations' (NE). This both advanced and generalized McCulloch's treatment, liberating the discussion to include time behaviour, learning, and the intellectual framework for what might constitute a 'thinking machine'. Much work has been done since this was first published in the *Journal of Theoretical Biology* in April 1961, leading to a variety of quantitative results. Amongst other things, it was found that NEs could be solved *exactly* as an inverse problem: given a prescribed behaviour, determine the net that generates it. Such explicit solutions include the class of NE that describe cellular automata and a precise specification of behaviour in terms of cycles, transients and singularities. The results thus obtained, provide a natural framework for the discussion of contemporary concerns in neural computing. The Appendix directs the reader (through a bibliography) towards discussions of application to linguistics, pattern recognition and the mature multilevel structures.

1. Introduction: the 1961 model

I owe my first contact with cybernetics (a term that I use in Norbert Wiener's sense, as it is used in the USSR or Germany, but not in the USA) to *The Living Brain* by Grey Walter. I read the book in 1955, in Copenhagen, where I was the Italian representative at CERN, then located at Niels Bohr's Institute. It was love at first sight. The following year, having been offered the Chair of Theoretical Physics in Naples, I started a group funded by modest but vital US Air Force and US Army support. The subsequent research included some neuroanatomy and electronics directed towards the study of the brain. Here is a sketch of the situation as it looked then.

My colleagues openly doubted my sanity: five years were to pass

8

before I could obtain a meagre allowance of Italian money. In the meantime, in the USSR cybernetics was an unfavoured word, almost a synonym for capitalism. But, ironically, Gel'fand and the Nobel prize-winner, Tamms, succeeded in launching a major effort in the field, only because, as I learned later from Tsetlin, they drew attention to the existence of my little group in Italy, which had hardly any connection with 'capital'. From those pioneering days I remember with gratitude my long association with Norbert Wiener, who was our guest for a year and a half in Naples, and Warren McCulloch, a most frequent visitor who radiated a constant stream of ideas and human warmth. In 1960 Wiener was the first to read, and comment most encouragingly on, the manuscript of my first work in the subject, which appeared in April 1961. McCulloch who was chairing the 1966 meeting at Wright Patterson Air Force Base, was generous enough to proclaim my quantitative analysis of cycles in neural nets as the first breakthrough on the subject. I feel it due and appropriate that, before giving an account of my own efforts, I should express here my profound indebtedness to and admiration of those two giants, whose acquaintance has so much enriched my life.

'Outline of a theory of thought processes and thinking machines' was the title of the work I have just mentioned. I still consider it as descriptive of the subject at hand, and feel that I have nothing to recant in relation to it. I must leave it to the interested reader to compare its content with the present outburst of papers on parallel processing, connectionism etc. Here I can only mention briefly some of the points of the model and comment, just as briefly, on points of difference with some of today's approaches.

McCulloch's aim was to model the brain's activity: binary decision elements were neurons, which, when assembled into nets with appropriate interconnections, were proved isomorphic with finite automata. Some logical reasoning could thus be attributed to them; the language and technique were those of standard two-valued logic. My own model was also based on the crucial idea of the binary neuron, but the language was that of algebra: neuronic equations (NE) were written in terms of Boolean response functions for a frozen net (which was taken to be synchronous, in view both of realistic interpretations or of permissible micro-quantizations of time intervals). It thus became possible to study the long-range behaviour, cycles, transients and conditions of nets that would ensure that no cycle exceeded some prescribed duration. The structure of the net could change with some specific laws, if required. These changes were controlled by mnemonic equations (ME), of which an example was given to prove that nets with structures evolving according to some form of such equations would be capable of learning and forgetting (which should be considered important); they are also

9

capable of recognizing patterns, associating them, forming hierarchies of them, etc. Such nets required control organs (such as exist in the brain), they were shown to need periods of 'sleep', and might possibly be psychoanalysed. Two extreme types of learning were envisaged: positive, by reinforcement of connections; or negative, by partial obliteration of them. Only the first was explicitly treated, since the second required exactly the same mathematics. Further, the need for specific time scales was emphasized, and (in the language of a physicist), were called the 'Adiabatic learning hypothesis' (ALH). All key points were studied, both theoretically and through the use of computer simulations, by many authors, notably the Japanese Ishihara, Nagumo, Sato, Amari, Kitagawa and many others, and of course by my own group Lauria, de Luca, Ricciardi and others, with satisfactory results.

All our work was done on a strictly deterministic basis. Here, perhaps, lies the main difference between our approach and many recent approaches to the subject. A comment on this would not go amiss. In my work on quantum field theory I had been lucky enough to discover that the rather unfamiliar 'Pfaffian' algorithm was the key to the then rather crucial problem of understanding the structure and combinatorics of Feynman diagrams. Pfaffians were soon shown to answer many otherwise unapproachable questions related to spin systems, in particular the Ising model. This was between 1952 and 1954. What could have been easier for a physicist, well aware of the obvious analogies between spins and formal neurons, than to apply to this his own techniques, known at the time to a very small community. This was fertile ground for a transfer of plentiful know-how on the subject. Here I take the step of quoting from my own paper: 'A dynamical interpretation ... would indeed be quite natural ...; we deem it more meritorious, at this stage, to resist the temptation of adapting the available quantum-field-theoretical knowledge to these problems than to yield to it'.

I still feel much the same way after a quarter of a century, particularly when I see that so many are claiming that problems are almost solved, even though basic questions cannot yet be properly formulated or even guessed at. To put it plainly: my view is that before studying the statistics of a telephone network, it would be better to make sure that two phones can actually communicate.

Any statistical theory has to introduce additional parameters, such as a temperature or a Hamiltonian; notions quite foreign to neural networks which present problems of a different, or possibly greater, magnitude; information entropies of many kinds are natural to this way of thinking. On the other hand, Hamiltonian and standard stochastic techniques may curtail our vision and blind us to the real extent of the subject. Of course, for the solution of specific problems, such as certain forms of associative memories or pattern recognition, the situation can be very different, in the sense that the techniques I have mentioned provide some real solutions to technical problems. Therefore what I have written is not intended to be a criticism. However, as far as neural computers are concerned, the real game has not yet started; though I do believe that the work I have carried out over the past fifteen years would be useful with respect to these more restricted practical aims.

The major technical problem was posed by the neuronic equations, which I have mentioned above, as a result of their total non-linearity. It turned out, however, that it is this very feature that permits their exact solution, as I shall explain below.

One can define and solve an inverse problem: given any sequence of states, arbitrarily prescribed *a priori*, it is possible to determine the net that will perform such a sequence exactly. The formalism contains, as will be seen, cellular automata as a particular case. It also provides an appropriate framework for studying statistical problems of several sorts. The purpose of this paper is therefore to restate some old things, limiting the discussion to neuronic equations (NE) (ME and ALH will not be discussed). This is done from the perspective of recent developments and allows me to comment on possible further developments that accord with these newer approaches.

2. Linear separable neuronic equations

2.1 The problem

The main challenge was presented by the neuronic equations. The study of mnemonic equations and the Adiabatic learning hypothesis (when needed) is goal oriented, and one must take different technical aspects if one wants to model a brain, or an associative memory, or some parallel machine.

An NE expresses at time $t + \tau$ (τ a constant delay) the state of the net as determined by its situation at time t. According to the problem at hand, it may be convenient to use values 0,1 or $-1,1$ to denote the two allowed states of a neuron. We take thus the Heaviside or signum functions of real functions of binary variables: the *discontinuous* and the *continuous* aspect tied together in an essential way; their interplay is fundamental to NE, whatever the system, neural or not, described by them.

Its full understanding was possible as a result of a lucky circumstance. Many authors have preferred non-linearities of smoother types, eg sigmoid or quadratic forms, so as to use the mathematics of continuum— that is, standard calculus. It was just our taking the opposite approach— that is, using consistently totally discontinuous functions—that permitted

11

the exact solution of our neuronic equations and all the problems connected with them, as will be outlined below. The breakthrough came about in a most elementary manner, from the obvious property

$$\text{sgn } xy = \text{sgn } x \times \text{sgn } y,$$

which may be said to express a full measure of the properties of linear functions. It is well to emphasize that any general model of neural activity, including ours, can only express the *laws* of a neural medium, and certainly cannot express the behaviour of a brain or a robot. Likewise, physics provides laws, not automobiles or TVs. For these, rules have to be found or invented. Our search for appropriate rules, (which at another level will again become laws) had led us to different paths (see bibliographical Appendix).

The exact solvability of neuronal equations puts them on the same footing as linear equations for the study of exact or approximate models of general systems. In this report, I shall focus attention exclusively on this point. I wish to note that the application of so crude a model to biological situations, (where a real neuron may be simulated as a VLSI module based on our mathematical analysis), gave results far exceeding our expectations.[2, 3]

2.2 Notation

The 'neuron' is a binary decision element whose states may be better described as $x = (0.1)$ or $\xi = (-1.1)$, according to the specific purpose in hand of course

$$x = 1/2(1 + \xi)$$

The net has N neurons, whose interconnections determine its structure. We are not concerned here with specific structures; the NE describe thus a general net as if it were a physical medium of which the NE describe the laws. Denote with

$$x \equiv \mathbf{x} \equiv \{x^1, x^2, \ldots, x^N\}; \qquad x^h = 0, 1$$
$$\xi \equiv \boldsymbol{\xi} \equiv \{\xi^1, \xi^2, \ldots, \xi^N\}; \qquad \xi^h = \pm 1$$

variables, vectors, or one-column matrices, whose components have values as specified. Let $F(\xi)$, $\Phi(x)$ be any real functions subject only to the condition

$$F(\xi) \neq 0; \qquad \Phi(x) \neq 0$$

for any choice of variables ξ^h, x^h.

This requirement (which is not in fact a restriction) will simplify our discussion remarkably. Let

$$1[\Phi] = \begin{cases} 1 \text{ for } \Phi > 0 \\ 0 \text{ for } \Phi < 0 \end{cases} \text{(Heaviside step function)}$$

$$\sigma[F] \equiv \text{sgn}\,[F] = \begin{cases} 1 \text{ for } F > 0 \\ -1 \text{ for } F < 0 \end{cases} \quad \text{(signum)}$$

Define

$$\langle F(\xi) \rangle = \frac{1}{2^N} \sum_{(\xi^1 = \pm 1, \ldots, \xi^N = \pm 1)} F(\xi^1, \xi^2, \ldots, \xi^N) \qquad \text{(trace)}$$

The tensor powers of ξ have 2^N components:

$$\eta^\alpha = \begin{cases} 1 \equiv \xi^0 \\ \vdots \\ \xi^h \\ \vdots \\ \xi^{h_1} \xi^{h_2}, \ldots, \xi^{h_k} \\ \vdots \\ \xi^1 \xi^2, \ldots, \xi^N \end{cases} \quad \begin{array}{l} h = 1, 2, \ldots, N \text{ (linear terms)} \\ \alpha = h_1, h_2, \ldots, h_k \text{ (non-linear terms)} \end{array}$$

$\eta \equiv \boldsymbol{\eta} \equiv \{\eta^\alpha\}$ is thus a vector in 2^N dimensions, $\eta^\alpha = \pm 1$; the α-ordering of the indices $0, 1, \ldots, 2^N - 1$ may be arranged to suit particular needs; we choose here

$$\boldsymbol{\eta} = \begin{bmatrix} 1 \\ \xi^N \end{bmatrix} \times \begin{bmatrix} 1 \\ \xi^{N-1} \end{bmatrix} \times \cdots \times \begin{bmatrix} 1 \\ \xi^1 \end{bmatrix} = \begin{bmatrix} 1 \\ \xi^1 \\ \xi^2 \\ \xi^1 \xi^2 \\ \xi^3 \\ \vdots \\ \xi^1 \ldots \xi^N \end{bmatrix}$$

Then, all the properties of Boolean functions needed here can be readily derived from the evident ones

$$(\sigma[F])^2 = +1; \quad \sigma(\sigma[F]) = \sigma[F]; \quad \sigma[FG] = \sigma[F]\sigma[G].$$

In particular, one has the η-expansion

$$\sigma[F(\xi)] = \sum_{\alpha = 0}^{2^N - 1} f_\alpha \eta^\alpha \equiv f^T \eta,$$

where

$$f_\alpha = \langle \eta^\alpha \sigma[F(\xi)] \rangle = \langle \sigma[\eta^\alpha F(\xi)] \rangle$$

13

If one wishes to use the (0, 1) Heaviside functions, posing

$$\chi \equiv \chi \equiv \begin{bmatrix} 1 \\ x^1 \\ x^2 \\ x^1 x^2 \\ \vdots \\ x^1 x^2 \dots x^N \end{bmatrix},$$

one finds easily

$$x = C\eta,$$

with

$$C = \begin{bmatrix} 1 & 0 \\ \frac{1}{2} & \frac{1}{2} \end{bmatrix} \times \begin{bmatrix} 1 & 0 \\ \frac{1}{2} & \frac{1}{2} \end{bmatrix} \times \dots \times \begin{bmatrix} 1 & 0 \\ \frac{1}{2} & \frac{1}{2} \end{bmatrix},$$

(*N* times)

so that the connection between the η- and the X-expansion is given by

$$1(\Phi[\chi]) = g^T \chi = g^T C\eta = \tfrac{1}{2}(1 + \sigma[\Phi]) + \tfrac{1}{2} f^T \eta$$

or, with

$$\bar{f}_0 = 1 + f_0, \qquad \bar{f}_\alpha = f_\alpha \quad (\alpha > 0),$$

by

$$g = \tfrac{1}{2}(C^T)^{-1}\bar{f}; \qquad \bar{f} = 2C^T g.$$

The X-expansion is less suited than the η-expansion for algebraic manipulations, though more directly related to logic and probabilistic considerations.

2.3 Some properties of linear separable NE

Our first work considered only linear functions $\Phi(x)$ or $F(\xi)$, hence l.s. Boolean functions $1[\Phi(x)]$ and $\sigma[F(\xi)]$. It is instructive to consider this case first. The NE of [1] (we write $u_h \equiv x_h = (0, 1)$ for consistency with the notation used there)

(Form I) $\qquad u_h(t+\tau) = 1 \left[\displaystyle\sum_{\substack{h=1,\dots,N \\ r=1,\dots,L}} a_{hk}^{(r)} u_k(t-r\tau) - s_h \right].$ $\qquad$ (1)

Equation (1) thus takes into account delayed actions of neurons of the net [$a_{hk}^{(r)} > 0$ excitation, $a_{hk}^{(r)} < 0$ inhibition, $a_{hk}^{(r)}$ loop of self-excitation or inhibition, s_h threshold]. NE written as in Equation (1), which we may call *First Form*, describe the state of the net at time $t+\tau$: they are *state equations*. They can equivalently be written as *excitation equations*, in the *Second Form*

(Form II)
$$w_h(t+\tau) = \sum a_{hk}^{(r)} 1[w_k(t-r\tau)] - s_h. \tag{2}$$

It can be shown[4] that Equations (1) and (2) can be written as well, by enlarging the number of neurons from N to NL, as if without delays $[a_{kh}^{(r)} \rightarrow a_{hk}^{(0)} \equiv a_{hk}]$. In matricial notation, setting $(NL \rightarrow N)$

$$u_h(m\tau) = u_{h,m}; \quad \mathbf{u}_m \equiv \begin{bmatrix} u_{1,m} \\ u_{2,m} \\ \vdots \\ u_{N,m} \end{bmatrix}; \quad A \equiv \{a_{hk}\},$$

we find

(Form I)
$$\mathbf{u}_{m+1} = 1[A\mathbf{u}_m - \mathbf{s}] \tag{3}$$

(Form II)
$$\mathbf{w}_{m+1} = A1[\mathbf{w}_m] - \mathbf{s}. \tag{4}$$

Multivalued logic

Equations (1) or (3) describe a net with binary decision elements, ie 2-valued logic. Equations (2) or (4) can be constructed with suitable A and $\mathbf{s}$ so as to give any wanted number k of values at each element (k need not be the same for all elements); *they describe therefore as well a net working with some k-valued logic*; Equations (1) or (3) show the connection with binary nets.

Constants of motion

Let γ_r be vectors, and form from Equation (4) the scalar products

$$\gamma_r \cdot \mathbf{w}_{m+1} = \gamma_r \cdot A1[\mathbf{w}_m] - \gamma_r \cdot \mathbf{s}.$$

If

$$A^T \gamma = 0$$

we find

$$\gamma_r \cdot \mathbf{w}(\tau) = -\gamma_r \cdot \mathbf{s} = \text{constant.} \tag{5}$$

If A is of order N and rank R, there are $N-R$ vectors satisfying Equation (5) and as many linear constants of motion in the net. They can be utilized eg as failure detectors; nets may be computed so as to have prescribed constants of motion and no limitation on couplings within rank R. It is also possible, of course, to obtain quadratic constants, etc.

Self-dual nets

We pass now to the signum representation. A particular condition appears then to simplify remarkably the form of Equations (3) and (4):

$$A\mathbf{I} = 2s;$$

this means *self-duality*, and if it holds Equations (3) and (4) become $(A \rightarrow \frac{1}{2}A)$:

$$\mathbf{u}_{m+1} = \sigma[A\mathbf{u}_m] \qquad (6)$$

$$\mathbf{w}_{m+1} = A\sigma[\mathbf{w}_m]. \qquad (7)$$

Equations (6) and (7) reduce immediately in turn to the form Equations (3) and (4) by keeping fixed the state of some given neuron ($N-1$ neurons are then free). The self-dual form of NE simplifies many computations.

2.4 Expansions of linear separable functions

For self-dual functions the η-expansion has only odd terms:

$$\sigma\left[\sum_{h=1}^{N} a_h \xi^h\right] = \sum_{h=1}^{N} f_h \xi^h + \sum_{h_1 < h_2 < h_3}^{1,\ldots,N} f_{h_1 h_2 h_3} \xi^{h_1} \xi^{h_2} \xi^{h_3}$$

$$+ \ldots + f_{1,2,\ldots,N} \xi^1 \xi^2 \ldots \xi^N.$$

Assume, to begin with, that

$$a_1 \geqslant a_2 \geqslant \ldots \geqslant a_N > 0$$

so that one readily has

$$f_1 \geqslant f_2 \geqslant \ldots \geqslant f_N \geqslant 0.$$

These restrictions are easily removed (see later); they serve only to simplify our discussion. We shall be concerned in particular with the relevant case

$$F(\xi) = \sum_{h=1}^{2n+1} \xi^h \qquad (8)$$

where of course, $f_1 = f_2 = \ldots = f_N$. Clearly, this $F(\xi) \neq 0$ always.

As an illustration (remembering that $a_1 \geqslant a_2 \geqslant a_3 > 0$):

$$\sigma[a_1 \xi^1 + a_2 \xi^2 + a_3 \xi^3] = \tfrac{1}{2}\xi^1 + \tfrac{1}{2}\xi^2 + \tfrac{1}{2}\xi^3 - \tfrac{1}{2}\xi^1 \xi^2 \xi^3$$

if a_1, a_2, a_3 can be the sides of a triangle,

$$\sigma[a_1 \xi^1 + a_2 \xi^2 + a_3 \xi^3] = \xi^1$$

if $a_1 > a_2 + a_3$. The extension of this 'triangular inequality' to higher N has been done[5] it accounts in particular for the coefficient $-\frac{1}{2}$ of $\xi_1 \xi_2 \xi_3$, and leads to 'polygonal inequalities' that generalize the standard triangular one. One finds, in particular, the remarkable expansion of the signum of Equation (8):

$$\sigma\left[\sum_{h=1}^{2n+1} \xi^h\right] = f_{(1)}\sum \xi^h + f_{(3)} \sum_{h_1 < h_2 < h_3} \xi^{h_1}\xi^{h_2}\xi^{h_3}$$

$$+ \ldots + f_{(2n+1)}\xi^1\xi^2,\ldots,\xi^{2n+1} \quad (9)$$

where the coefficients $f_{(1)}, f_{(3)}, \ldots$, are given by

$$f_{(2h+1)} = \frac{(-1)^h(2h-1)!!}{(2n-1)(2n-3)\cdots(2n-2h+1)} f_{(1)}$$

$$= (-1)^h \frac{(2n-2h-1)!!(2h-1)!!}{2n!!}.$$

and

$$f_{(k)} = (-1)^{n+1} f_{(2n+2-k)}.$$

As an example, with $2n+1 = 19$, only 5 of the 2^{19} coefficients of the η-expansion differ in modulus; they are:

$$f_{(1)} = -f_{(19)} = \frac{1}{2^{18}} 48\,620,$$

$$f_{(3)} = -f_{(17)} = \frac{-1}{2^{18}} 2860,$$

$$f_{(5)} = -f_{(15)} = \frac{1}{2^{18}} 572,$$

$$f_{(7)} = -f_{(13)} = \frac{1}{2^{18}} 220,$$

$$f_{(9)} = -f_{(11)} = \frac{1}{2^{18}} 140.$$

Identification of the variables $\xi^1, \ldots, \xi^{2n+1}$ in groups:

$$\xi^1 \equiv \xi^2 \equiv \ldots \equiv \xi^{m_1}; \ldots; \xi^{2n+1-N} \equiv \ldots \equiv \xi^{2n+1} \equiv \xi^N$$

yields the expansion of

$$\sigma\left[\sum_{h=1}^{N} m_h \xi^h\right] \qquad (m_h \text{ integer} > 0)$$

and hence of any l.s. function with given *real* coefficients $a_h{}^5$.

17

2.5 Continuous vs. discontinuous behaviour: transitions

We have considered linear arguments $\sum_{h=1}^{N} a_h \xi^h$ with the condition

$$a_1 \geqslant a_2 \geqslant \ldots \geqslant a_N > 0$$

that is, the canonical form of a self-dual l.s. function (threshold = 0). All these conditions are most easily removed, as is well known:

(1) Putting in the function and in its η-expansion $\xi^h = +1$ or -1 changes a_h into a threshold.

(2) A permutation of the variables $\xi^1, \ldots, \xi^N$ changes the original η-expansion into that of the permuted ones.

(3) Only positivity remains: this is removed by a change of sign of any wanted set of variables, accompanied by a change of $f_{j_1, j_2 \ldots j_n}$ into $(-1)^{r_h} f_{j_1, \ldots, j_n}$, where r_h is the number of indices among $j_1, \ldots, j_h$ corresponding to variables ξ^1 that have changed sign. To every canonical l.s. function correspond therefore

$$\Omega_N = \frac{2^N N!}{2^Z \Pi s_i!} \begin{cases} z \text{ number of } f_i = 0 \\ s_i \text{ number of } f_j = f_k = \ldots = f_i \end{cases} \tag{10}$$

different l.s. functions, whose η-expansions are immediately deducible from the canonical η-expansion by the operations β) and γ) above; thresholds, and even terms, by α).

We find here the most remarkable property of such functions; we can indeed regard the operations β) and γ) as defining *different sectors* in N space of a same function, α) as a restriction to *a semi-space in a given sector*. Hence, dynamical behaviour (change of a_h) will consist in jumps, or transitions, across sectors; as long as one stays within a sector, changes are irrelevant. *The continuum of real numbers reduces thus, in a perfectly defined way, to the discontinuous behaviour of l.s. functions.* Since any Boolean function is reducible to a net of l.s. functions, and in the finite and discrete any function is expressible through Boolean functions, the claim that the study of l.s. NE describes the most general nonlinear behaviours is already substantiated.

3. General Boolean neuronic equations and cellular automata: the inverse problem

3.1 Linearization in tensor space

We suppress here the restriction that the arguments of our NE be linear, so that the most general Boolean functions are allowed into them.

It is convenient here to work directly with the tensorial signum expansion. If each neuron h of the net has as excitation function the real function $f^{(h)} = f^{(h)}(\xi^1, \xi^2, \ldots, \xi^N)$, we can write the NE for a general net as

$$\xi^h_{m+1} = \sigma[f^h(\xi^1_m, \ldots, \xi^N_m)] = \sum_\alpha f^h_\alpha \eta^\alpha_m = f^{hT}\eta_m. \tag{11}$$

We consider now the normalized ξ-state matrix of the net $\varphi_{(N)}$; with $N = 3$, eg it is

$$\varphi_{(3)} = 2^{-3/2} \begin{bmatrix} 1 & -1 & 1 & -1 & 1 & -1 & 1 & -1 \\ 1 & 1 & -1 & -1 & 1 & 1 & -1 & -1 \\ 1 & 1 & 1 & 1 & -1 & -1 & -1 & -1 \end{bmatrix}$$

We can augment the $N \times 2^N$ ξ-matrix $\varphi_{(N)}$ to the $2^N \times 2^N$ η-state matrix, from

$$\eta = \begin{bmatrix} 1 \\ \xi_N \end{bmatrix} \times \ldots \times \begin{bmatrix} 1 \\ \xi_1 \end{bmatrix}$$

as follows:

$$\Phi_{(N)} = \begin{bmatrix} \frac{1}{2} & \frac{1}{2} \\ \frac{1}{2} & -\frac{1}{2} \end{bmatrix} \times \ldots \times \begin{bmatrix} \frac{1}{2} & \frac{1}{2} \\ \frac{1}{2} & -\frac{1}{2} \end{bmatrix} \qquad (N \text{ times}).$$

$\Phi_{(N)} \equiv \Phi$ is an Hermite matrix such that

$$\Phi = \Phi^T, \Phi^2 = 1, \Phi = \Phi^{-1}, \det(\Phi_N) = (-1)^N.$$

We can thus also augment the N ξ-state NE to the 2^N η-state form

$$\eta_{m+1} = F\eta_m,$$

in which F is a $2^N \times 2^N$ matrix whose first row has all elements $= 1$; the N 'linear' rows have the linear coefficients at r.h.s. (11), and the remaining ones are given by tensor multiplication.

We obtain thus the *central result*, that passage from ξ- to η-space *linearizes* the NE. Thus:

$$\eta_m = F\eta_{m-1} = \ldots = F^m\eta_0. \tag{12}$$

That passage to functional space should linearize the NE is of course not surprising; the relevant feature is that 2^N is (of course) *finite*, and from now on standard matrix algebra can be used.

3.2 Cellular automata

Cellular automata are presented as arrays (for simplicity, linear, finite and closed topologically into a ring) of N cells, or 'sites', the situation of each of which is described by an integer number whose value depends on those of the cells at the previous (discretized) time. This integer is assumed to belong to a ring R_h; h is mostly taken $= 2$ (*any other case can be reduced to this*). The 'dynamics' of the automaton are fixed by taking for all cells the same nearest neighbours connections, and the ensuing evolution is observed on the computer; the results have given rise to a fast growing literature, because of their stimulating analogies with many phenomena typical of non-linear systems of the most varied kinds. No generality is lost by taking $h = 2$; but then, it is trivially seen that they can be treated as special nets ruled by Boolean NE of type (11).[6] Their evolution is linearized by Equation (12). Hence the treatment is identical for nets and automata; results specific to the latter will be reported without proofs (which are in Caianiello & Marinaro (1986)[6]).

3.3 The direct and the inverse problem

By applying Equation (12) to each column of the Φ matrix (ie to all 2^N states of the net) we obtain the *next-state* matrix

$$\Phi_{m+1} = F\Phi_m, \quad \text{with} \quad \Phi_0 \equiv \Phi.$$

We remark now that the effect of F on Φ_m is to *permute* its columns, or to *suppress* some column and bring one of the remaining ones to its place (*degeneration*). That is,

$$F\Phi = \Phi P, \tag{13}$$

whence

$$P = \Phi F \Phi \tag{14}$$

P tells *what* the net does at the next time state (synchronicity need not be assumed for many of the considerations that follow); F tells *how* it does it.

All this is done, by putting the dynamics, ie F, on computers, is the computation of P: this we call the 'direct problem'.

But (14) yields also at once:

$$F = \Phi P \Phi \tag{15}$$

and (the N 'linear' rows of) F complete the exact Boolean expansion of neuron, or automaton cell, of the function required by each neuron (or site) in order that the evolution, arbitrarily prescribed by us with assignment of P, take place. This we call the 'inverse problem', and (15) solves it completely.

3.4 Transients and cycles

The two peculiar properties of the evolution of a finite net or cellular automaton:

(1) the existence of transient states (possible configurations which die after one or more steps);

(2) the evolution into cycles, in which a sequence of states repeats itself indefinitely;

are simply expressed in terms of the eigenvalues of the P matrix.

In fact, since clearly P is a permutation matrix, its eigenvalues are zero or roots of the unit. The eigenvalues zero denote degeneration and corresponds to transient states; the roots of the unit to cycles.

These features appear in the characteristic equation of the permutation matrix P which is

$$\lambda^{n_0} \sum_i (\lambda^{l_i} i - 1)^{n_i} = 0 \qquad (16)$$

where n_0 gives the total number of transient states (the fraction of the 2^N possible states which die in the evolution); n_i is the number of cycles of length l_i. The sum is over all the possible cycles ($l_1 = 1$ is a steady state).

The integer parameters n_0, l_i and n_i depend on N and on the evolution rule; they are connected by the relation

$$n_0 + \sum_i n_i l_i = 2^N.$$

All possible states are either transient states or enter into a cycle. Relevant information on the global behaviour for $t \to \infty$ obtains from the computation of the parameters n_0, l_i, and n_i.

If one considers the limit $N \to \infty$ the parameter n_0 is directly connected with the 'set dimension'[6] or fractal dimension through the relation

$$d = \lim_{N \to \infty} (1/N) \log_2 (2^N - n_0) \qquad (0 \le d \le 1)$$

The multiplicity n_i of a cycle of length l_i is given by

$$n_i = (T_r(P_N)^{l_i} - \sum T_r(P_N)^{l_j}) 1/l_i$$

where l_j are divisors of l_i and T_r indicates the trace operation.

Additional information about the evolution, step by step, can be obtained by looking at the structure of the P matrix.

Clearly, F satisfies the identical characteristic equation (16) as P.

3.5 Normal modes

NE exhibit *normal modes*, just as linear ones, though more complex than the simple periodic sequences typical of linearity in N-space; they intertwine into 'reverberations'[7] since they stem from linearity in 2^N-space. Their interpretation is in principle the same as that expressed by Eigen and Schuster[8] for 'quasispecies' in their classic discussion of hypercycles (for which NE might be an apt tool).

Let the matrix Δ, det $(\Delta) \neq 0$, diagonalize F:

$$F\Delta = \Delta\Lambda \qquad (\Lambda \text{ diagonal})$$

Then

$$P \cdot \Phi\Delta = \Phi\Delta \cdot \Lambda,$$

ie $\Phi\Delta$ diagonalizes P.
   If we set

$$\eta_m = \Delta\chi_m$$

the NE read

$$\Delta\chi_{m+1} = F\Delta\chi_m = \Delta\Lambda\chi_m$$

so that

$$\chi_{m+1} = \Lambda\chi_m$$

or

$$\chi_{\alpha, m+1} = \lambda_\alpha \chi_{\alpha, m}$$

express the wanted normal modes.

3.6 Additive cellular automata

This denomination is given in the literature to automata whose evolution rule guarantees the existence of a 'superposition principle'. We have shown[6] that 'additivity' is fully equivalent to an evolution law (ie NE) (11) which consists of a single *monomial* connecting neighbouring cells (of same type for each cell): hence, a typically *non-separable* function. The typical example[6]

$$x^k_{t+\tau} = x_t^{k-1} + x_t^{k+1} \pmod 2$$

becomes in our formalism[6]

$$\zeta^k_{t+\tau} = -\zeta_t^{k-1} \zeta_t^{k+1}$$

and all standard results are readily derived by the most elementary means.

4. Remarks and perspectives

4.1 Synthesis of nets

The synthesis of a net (or automaton) is described by Equation (15), ie by the solution of the inverse problem.
   Working with permutation matrices P is far simpler than using F. If

we request that the net be Boolean, it is immediately feasible. If, instead, we require that the net be linear separable, or of some other special type, we have to start with F:

$$P = \Phi F \Phi$$

since the condition for a matrix P to describe a linear separable net is not yet known (it is actually easy to see that matrices P satisfying a same Equation (14) may give rise, depending upon the phase relations one chooses for cycles, to separable or to non-separable nets).

Nor does working with this matricial notation, ie with η-expansions, bring to light a main feature of the NE, the close relation between the continuous and discontinuous aspects of the theory. This point, discussed in [7] is essential for any concrete application of the formalism to adaptive or learning devices, or just for reliable design.

The synthesis of l.s. NE is, however, of high interest, for example because they are taken as prototypes for associative memories. This problem has been exactly formulated[8] and it appears to be amenable to a neat mathematical solution, on which we hope to be able to report in the near future.

4.2 Statistics

In physics, resort to statistics is made in order to take into account the imperfection of our knowledge of initial conditions; not certainly of basic equations.

In this specific sense, our 2^N-dimensional formalism can be utilized, with steps which we cannot discuss here, so as to yield results similar to those wanted in physics.

Nets pose however a greater variety of problems: malfunctions of several types and noise, which become particularly relevant when learning or adaptation take place.

Here too, one is forced to work in 2^N-space; our formalism is a natural preliminary to the study of master equations or other techniques, as may be required.

References

1. 'Outline of a Theory of Thought-Processes and Thinking Machines', *J. Theor. Biol.* **2**, 204 (1961).
2. 'Decision Equation for Binary Systems—Application to Neural Behaviour' (in coll. with A. De Luca), *Kybernetik 3 Band, 1 Heft*, 33–40 (1966).
3. 'Il sistema nervoso centrale', *Atti Conv. Med. Eur.*, 1st. Angelis (1970).
4. 'Synthesis of Boolean Nets and Time-behaviour of a General Mathematical Neuron' (in coll. with E. Grimson), *Biol. Cybernetics* **18**, 111–117 (1975).
5. 'Polygonal Inequalities as a Key to Neuronic Equations' (in coll. with G. Simoncelli), *Biol. Cybernetics* **41**, 203–209 (1981).

6. 'Linearization and Synthesis of Cellular Automata. The additive case' (in coll. with M. Marinaro), *Physica Scripta* **34**, 444 (1986). 'The inverse problem of neural nets and cellular automata' (in coll. with M. Marinaro), Computer Simulation in Brain Science, Cambridge University (1987).
7. 'Neuronic Equations Revisited and Completely Solved' in 'rain Theory' Eds. G. Palm, A. Aertsen, Springer, Berlin (1986).
8. Eigen, M., Schuster, P.: 'The hypercycle—principle of natural self-organization'. Springer Verlag, Berlin (1979).
9. 'The inverse problem for linear boolean nets' (in coll. with M. Marinaro and R. Tagliaferri), Neural Computers, Springer Verlag (1988). 'Associative Memories as Neural Networks' (in coll. with M. Marinaro and R. Tagliaferri), Proceedings Ninth European Meeting on Cybernetics and Syste Research, Vienna (1988).

Bibliographical Appendix (additional to references)

—FROM W. McCULLOCH'S LOGICAL NETS TO ALGEBRAIC EQUATIONS: 'THOUGHT' AS A DYNAMICAL COLLECTIVE PROCESS

'Mathematical and Physical Problems in the study of Brain Models', Symposium on Neural Theory and Modelling, Ojai Valley, December (1962).
'Non-linear Problems Posed by Decision Equations', Proceedings of International Summer School, Ravello (1965), Academic Press, N. York.
'Decision Equation and Reverberations', *Kybernetik 3 Band,3 Heft*, 33 (1966).
'A study of Neural Networks and Reverberations', Wright Patterson Air Force Base Conference, Dayton, Ohio (1966).
'Reverberations and Control of Neural Networks (in coll. with L. M. Ricciardi and A. De Luca), *Kybernetik* **4**, 10 (1967).
'Reverberations, Constant of Motion, General Behaviour' (in coll. with A. De Luca and L. M. Ricciardi), Proceedings Neural Networks, Ravello, Springer Verlag (1968).
'Synthesis of Reverberating Neural Networks' (in coll. with A. Aiello and E. Burattini), *Kybernetic Band 7, Heft* **5**, 191 (1970).
'Encyclopaedic Dict. of Mathematics', MIT Press (1974).
'Neural Nets: A Brief Survey', Proceedings NATO School on New Concepts and Technologies in Parallel Information Processing, Capri Noordhoff Publishing, Series E9, 265 (1975).
'Methods of Analysis of Neural Nets' (in coll. with E. Grimson), *Biol. Cybernetics* **21**, 1–6 (1976).
'Normal Modes in Neural Nets' (in coll. with G. Simoncelli), in Cybernetics Systems ...' Ed. E. R. Caianiello, G. Musso, Research Studies Press, Letchworth (1984).
'From Neuronic Equations to Spin Systems'—'Progress in Quantum Field Theory'—Eds. H. Ezawa, S. Kamefuchi—North Holland, Amsterdam (1986).

—ON BOOLEAN FUNCTIONS (L. S. AND NOT)

'Some Remarks on the Tensorial Linearization of General and Linearly separable Boolean Functions', *Kybernetik* **12**, 90–93 (1973).
'Tensorial Linearization of Threshold Functions'—Proc. NATO School on New Concepts and Technologies in Parallel Information Processing, Capri Noordhoff Publishing Series E9, 313 (1975).
'On Boolean Functions and Nets'—Atti Accademia Lincei, Tomo **11**, 501–507 (1976).

—ON NATURAL LANGUAGES, STRUCTURE AND ORGANIZATION

'On the Analysis of Natural Languages', Proceedings of the 3rd All Union Conference on Cybernetics, Odessa, SSR, (1965).

'The Procrustes Program for the Analysis of Natural Languages', Proceedings Int. School on Automatic Interpretation and Classification of Images, Tirrenia—Academic Press, (1969).

'On Form and Language: the Procrustes Algorithm for Feature Extraction' (in coll. with R. Capocelli), *Kybernetik* **8**, 223–233 (1971).

'Neural Nets and Natural Languages', Proceedings, Tokyo JITA Conference, (1972)

'Some Remarks on Organization and Structure', *Biol. Cybernetics* **26**, 3 (1977).

'Sulla legge di distribuzione delle monete' (in coll. with G. Scarpetta, G. Simoncelli), *Rassegna Economica* **44**, 771–794 (1980).

'A Systematic Study of Monetary Systems' (in coll. with G. Scarpetta, G. Simoncelli), *J. General Systems* **8**, 81–2 (1982).

'Structure and modularity in self-organizing complex systems' (in coll. with M. Marinaro, G. Scarpetta, and G. Simoncelli), Topics in the General Theory of Structures, Reidel Publ. Comp. **5** (1987).

—ON C-CALCULUS: ARITHMETICS OF (COMPOSITE) STRINGS OF (SIMPLE) SETS

'A Calculus of Hierarchical Systems', Proceedings 1st Int. Congress on Pattern Processing IEEE, 73CHO 821-9C ppl e 2 (1973).

'A Model for C-Calculus' (in coll. with A. G. S. Ventre), *Int. J. of Gen. Systems* (1975).

'A New Approach to Some Problems of Pattern Analysis' (in coll. with A. Apostolico and S. Vitulano), *Proceedings of Informatics* **76**, p. 104 (1976) Bled, Lugoslavia.

'Structural Analysis of Hierarchical Systems' (in oll. with R. Capocelli), 3rd J.P.R. Conference, Coronado, California, (1976).

'C-Calculus: An Elementary Approach to Some Problems in Pattern Recognition' (in coll. with A. Apostolico, E. Fischetti, S, Vitulano), Pattern Recognition (1978).

'A New Approach to Some Problems of Cell Motion Analysis Based on C-Calculus' (in coll. with L. Huimin), Topics in the general theory of structures, Reidel Publ. Comp. (1987).

'On Some Analytic Aspects of C-Calculus' (in coll. with A. G. S. Ventre), Topics in the general theory of structures, Reidel Publ. Comp. 175 (1987).

'Implementation of the C-Calculus' (in coll. with P. E. Eklund and A. G. S. Ventre) (in print).

—OTHER

'An Algorithm for Feature Classification and Structural Memorization' (in coll. with A. Aiello, E. Burattini, A. Massarotti), *Kybernetik* **12**, 145–153 (1973).

'Comparison of Two Unsupervised Learning Algorithms' (in coll. with L. Bobrowski), *Biol. Cybernetics* **37**, 1–7 (1980).

'Energetics Versus Communication in the Nervous System' in coll. with E. Di Giulio), *Cybernetics and Systems* **13**, 187–196 (1982).

'A Geometrical View of Quantum and Information Theories'—Theoretical Physics Meeting E.S.I. (1983).

'Entropy, Information and Quantum Geometry'—Proc. of Santa Fè Int. Conference on Non-Linear Phenomena, July 1984. Lecture delivered at the NATO A.S.I. 'Non Equilibrium Quantum Statistical Physics', Santa Fè, New Mexico (1984).

'Systems and Uncertainty: A Geometrical Approach'—Topics in the general theory of structures, Reidel Publ. Co. (1987).

25

3 Speech recognition based on topology-preserving neural maps

Teuvo Kohonen

Helsinki University of Technology, Laboratory of Computer and Information Science, Rakentajanaukio 2 C, SF-02150 Espoo, Finland

Abstract

Artificial neural networks can effectively be applied to the processing of natural sensory signals, in particular to the recognition of phonemes by a speech recognizer where an exacting statistical analysis is needed. It is known that the biological brain contains various topographically ordered 'maps', such that different neural cells respond optimally to different signal qualities. Some time ago, this author discovered a self-organizing process by which such an optimal topographical mapping of the signal space is constructed which yields a reasonably high accuracy in recognition tasks. A 'neural network' processor has already been implemented. We have been able to produce a raw transcription of unlimited Finnish and Japanese dictation with an accuracy of up to 90% (referring to the correct orthography of these languages). Most errors that occur at this stage are caused by coarticulation effects, and the majority of the remaining errors can be corrected by means of an automatically constructed grammar. Thus, without any 'language models', which would be computationally heavy, we have implemented a *phonetic typewriter* for unlimited text. The output, correct up to 92–97%, is obtained in real time.

1. Introduction

Speech recognition belongs to the broader category of pattern recognition tasks for which, during the past tens of years, many methods have been tried. While progress in many other fields of technology has been astoundingly rapid, the investments into the studies of such 'natural' tasks have not yet ripened into adequate dividends.

Since the brain has already implemented the speech recognition function and many other functions, too, a recent straightforward conclusion has been that artificial 'neural networks', the models of which have been studied since the early 1940s, should be able to do the same. Before then, however, it will be necessary to understand in detail those principles of signal processing that are being applied in the neural networks. Also, pattern recognition, ie, artificial perception, obviously needs a reference frame in which tokens of earlier sensory experiences are stored. This framework is somewhat loosely called 'memory'; more formally it might be termed 'internal representation' of sensory knowledge. One of the first problems seems to be to reveal its physical structure.

Some hints about the 'internal representations' are obtained from the fact that the cortex of the biological (especially mammalian) brain is essentially a two-dimensional sheet, and many of its areas are specialized to different sensory modalities. In these areas, first of all in the primary sensory areas, the various cells seem to respond to many abstract qualities of the sensory stimuli in an orderly fashion. For instance, in the auditory areas there is a 'scale' for different acoustic frequencies, and in the visual areas one can find a 'colour map', maps for orientation of line segments, etc. In some animals for which hearing is an important means of orientation (eg owls) maps have been found of the acoustic space. Bats have coordinate systems relating to echo delays on their cortex, etc. It seems as if two-dimensional geometric mapping or abstract 'imaging' of sensory feature dimensions were one of the most central principles for the organization of the 'internal representations' in the brain.

Some years ago this author introduced a 'neural' mapping principle[1] which is able to extract automatically a few (usually two) of the most important feature dimensions of a multi-dimensional signal space and to display the input vectors in such a low-dimensional coordinate system, ie, a two-dimensional 'map'. In contrast to the well-known Fukunaga–Koonz method,[2] the selected feature dimensions are not the same for the whole pattern space, but optimal feature dimensions for every region of the pattern space are determined dynamically: the dimensionality-reducing mapping is thus non-linear but nonetheless continuous, and it is mainly the *local topology*, rather than the global metric, which is preserved in the map. This method has a bearing on Sammon,[3] non-linear mapping which also aims at two-dimensional representation of high-dimensional pattern spaces. The most important difference between our method and that of Sammon is that whereas the latter is restricted to a mathematical algorithm which maps a set of *a priori* given patterns on a two-dimensional (continuous) plane, the maps in our method are formed on a network of discrete physical elements which are able to average over an indefinite number of input patterns. They are also able to produce immediate output responses to new patterns, this implementing the pattern recognition operation physically.

The present method can thus be used for direct identification of input objects. In the work in presentation we have applied it to the visualization of continuous speech, and to phonemic labelling and segmentation of speech waveforms. We will call these and related representations *phonotopic maps*. They may bear some similarity to the various feature maps that exist in the biological brain.

2. General thoughts about automatic speech recognition

One of the conventional approaches in speech recognition has been to consider words as integral acoustic patterns, and their spectrograms (frequency spectra vs. time) have directly been compared with stored spectrograms. Isolated-word recognition, however, cannot be a very ambitious goal for speech understanding. Also, when the size of the vocabulary increases, the comparison computations become heavy. It would therefore seem more reasonable to divide the words into smaller acoustic sub-units, eg, phonemes, and compare strings of their symbolic representations.

We have mostly worked with Finnish and Japanese, the phonemes of which are easily distinguishable by stationary spectral properties. Furthermore, the orthographies of Finnish and romanized Japanese are almost completely phonemic. These two facts supported the selection of phonemes as the basic phonological units for our design.

The so-called phonetic typewriters for English may be based on the recognition of words from a large vocabulary. The plural and genitive forms, etc, can be regarded as separate words. This is not possible in many other languages, such as Finnish and Japanese, which have numerous inflexions and endings. In the latter case, every phoneme must be recognized separately. Major difficulties are caused by the coarticulation effects. Due to these, it is not sufficient to improve the recognition of individual phonemes alone; the syntactic rules of speech must also be taken into account.

The above-mentioned facts have motivated us to choose the following two-stage system configuration. First, based on the above-mentioned phonotopic maps, the acoustic processor module produces a phonemic transcription of uttered speech. Possible errors in the transcriptions (due to coarticulation effects and variations in speech) are then corrected at the post-processing stage, which applies a new grammatical method called '*dynamically expanding context*'.[4] This method automatically derives a large number of production rules from samples of natural speech data, which are then used to transform the erroneous strings into orthographically edited text.

A microprocessor-based real-time speech recognition system which implements these principles is also described in this presentation. The equipment is able to produce orthographic transcriptions for arbitrary words or phrases uttered in Finnish or Japanese. It can also be used as a large-vocabulary isolated-word recognizer, discussion of which we shall, however, omit here.

3. Acoustic preprocessing of the speech signal

Before speaking of 'neural networks', one should actually have already taken into account the physiological facts about the sensory organs which underlie hearing. The main operation carried out by the external, middle, and inner ear is a frequency analysis, centrally based on the resonances of the basilar membrane. The spectral decomposition of the speech signal is transmitted to the brain through the auditory nerves. To be quite exact, each peak of the pressure wave gives rise to separate bursts of neural impulses: thus some kind of time–domain information, in addition to the amplitude spectrum, is also transmitted by the ear. To put it another way, synchronization of neural impulses to the acoustic signals seems to take place, conveying phase information. One might therefore stipulate that the first stages in speech recognition should already contain detectors which simulate the operation of the sensory receptors as fully as possible.

Biological neural networks are also able to adapt to signal transients in a fast, non-linear way; this knowledge has been taken into account in many physical 'ear models' which describe both mechanical properties of the inner ear, and chemical transmission in its hair cells.[5]

Although we were aware about these physiological facts, we decided to apply the conventional frequency analysis techniques to the pre-processing of speech. The reason for this was that digital Fourier analysis is both accurate and fast, and the fundamentals of digital filtering are well understood. Digital signal processing is a standard method in acoustic engineering and telecommunication. Our decision was thus a typical engineering choice. We also hold the view that the self-organizing neural network described below can accept many alternative kinds of pre-processing and is able to compensate for modest imperfections, as long as they are not inconsistent. Several experimental results have justified this: for instance, no large differences have remained in the recognition accuracies for stationary and transient phonemes, which need different kind of dynamical signal sampling.

The microphone signal must first be prepared for the pattern-recognition algorithm. Roughly corresponding to the physical properties of the inner ear, some enhancement operations are first performed, after which the speech signal is analysed into short-time spectra. Since the different frequencies produced by the speech apparatus are mutually dependent, one-third-octave resolution in the spectral decomposition seems to be sufficient to distinguish the different phonemes; a compromise between recognition accuracy and computing load seems to be to have 15 frequency channels distributed over the scale of the audible tones.

The technical details of the acoustic preprocessing stage are, briefly, the following: (1) 5.3 kHz low-pass switched-capacitor filter; (2) 12-bit A/D-converter with 13.02 kHz sampling rate; (3) 256-point FFT every 9.83 ms using Hamming window; (4) logarithmization and smoothing of the power spectrum; (5) placing 15 components into a spectral vector from the frequency range 200 Hz–5 kHz; (6) subtraction of the average from the components; and (7) normalization of the pattern vectors. Except for steps (1) and (2), an integrated-circuit signal processor TMS32010 is used for computations.

4. The algorithm which forms the sensory maps

Several algorithms or system models are able to form the kinds of sensory map discussed in the Introduction.[6] The present study is restricted to a computationally simple version, a short-cut formulation of the more 'physical' neural network behaviour, which generally produces very reliable maps. This algorithm is also easily amenable to parallel computation. Its fundamentals and mathematical theory have been discussed at length in the references.[7-11]

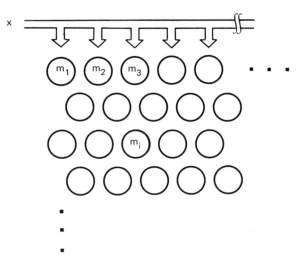

Figure 1   *Neural array for self-organizing maps.*

Assume a two-dimensional array of units of 'neurons' which are arranged in a hexagonal lattice (Fig. 1). To every node i of it we assign a time-variable *weight vector* $\mathbf{m}_i(t) \in \mathbb{R}^n$, $t = 0, 1, 2, \ldots$. The initial values $\mathbf{m}_i(0)$ can be chosen as random vectors. Assume that an *input pattern vector* $\mathbf{x}(t) \in \mathbb{R}^n$ is broadcast to and concurrently compared with all the $\mathbf{m}_i(t)$. The following two rules define a process in which the above mapping is formed by self-organization when a sufficient number of statistically distributed input vectors are applied.

Rule 1
Find unit c whose weight vector $\mathbf{m}(t)$ has the *best match* with $\mathbf{x}(t)$, a sample vector:

$$\|\mathbf{x}(t) - \mathbf{m}_c(t)\| = \min_i \{\|\mathbf{x}(t) - \mathbf{m}_i(t)\|\}. \tag{1}$$

Unit c is thereby said to respond to $\mathbf{x}(t)$. (In the simplest case, Euclidean norms are used. The algorithm seems to be rather insensitive to different norms.)

Rule 2
Modify the weight vectors of unit c and its *topological neighbours*: the topological neighbourhood $\mathbf{N}_c$, illustrated in Fig. 2, refers to the lattice of nodes and is usually a function of time. The adaptation law in this model reads

$$\left.\begin{aligned}
\mathbf{m}_i(t+1) &= \mathbf{m}_i(t) + \alpha(t)[\mathbf{x}(t) - \mathbf{m}_i(t)] && \text{for } i \in \mathbf{N}_c, \\
\mathbf{m}_i(t+1) &= m_i(t) && \text{for } i \notin \mathbf{N}_c.
\end{aligned}\right\} \tag{2}$$

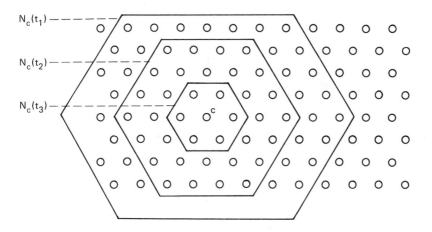

Figure 2   *Definition of the neighbourhood set* $\mathbf{N}_c(t)$ $(t_1 < t_2 < t_3)$.

In Equation (2), $\alpha(t)$ is a real, positive scalar parameter, the *adaptation gain* which is a slowly decreasing function of time ($0 < \alpha(t) < 1$). This has a bearing on the gain factors used in the well-known Robbins–Monro stochastic approximation.[12] Assuming that the process contains t_2 steps, a simple practical choice for $\alpha(t)$ might be: for $0 \leqslant t \leqslant t_1$, $\alpha(t) = k_1(1 - t/t_1)$, and for $t_1 < t \leqslant t_2$, $\alpha(t) = k_2(1 - t/t_2)$. Here t_1 and t_2 depend on the dimensions of the array, not on the dimensionality of $\mathbf{x}(t)$, and in the experiments reported below we had $k_1 = 0.1$, $k_2 = 0.008$, $t_1 = 10\,000$, $t_2 = 90\,000$. The radius of $\mathbf{N}_c$ decreased linearly from 12 to 1 during $0 \leqslant t \leqslant t_1$ after which it remained constant.

The mathematical proof of this process is lengthy and has only been carried out completely in the one-dimensional case.[8,10] One may qualitatively understand something of it by considering that the weight vectors $\mathbf{m}_i$ within $\mathbf{N}_c$ adaptively tend to follow up the input signals x. In other words, these neurons start to *become selectively sensitized* to the prevailing input pattern. This, however, *only occurs around the best-matching 'neuron'*. For another input, the neighbourhood encompasses other neurons which then become sensitized to that input. In this way different parts of the network are automatically 'tuned' to different inputs.

The network will indeed be 'tuned' to different inputs *in an ordered fashion, as if a continuous map of the signal space were formed over the network*. Continuity of this mapping already follows from the simple fact that the vectors $\mathbf{m}_i$ of contiguous units are modified in the same direction, whereby during the course of the process, the neighbouring values become smoothed. *Ordering* of these values, however, is a very subtle phenomenon, the proof or complete explanation of which is mathematically very sophisticated, and cannot be given here.

5. Phoneme maps

The simplest type of phonotopic maps formed by self-organization is called the *phoneme map*.[13] There are 21 phonemes in Finnish: /u,o,a,æ,ø,y,e,i,s,m,n,ŋ,l,r,j,v,h,d,k,p,t/. For their representation we used *short-time spectra* as the input patterns $\mathbf{x}(t)$. The spectra were evaluated every 9.83 ms. They were computed by the 256-point FFT, from which a 15-component spectral vector was formed by proper grouping of the channels.

In the present study all the spectral samples, even those from the transitory regions, were employed and presented to the algorithm in the natural order of their utterance. The maps in this paper thus represent the true statistics of natural speech waveforms. During adaptation, the

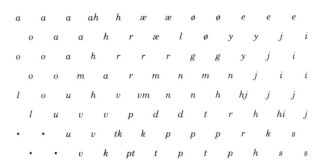

a	a	a	ah	h	æ	æ	ø	ø	e	e	e
	o	a	a	h	r	æ	l	ø	y	y	j	i
o		o	a	h	r	r	r	g	g	y	j	i
	o	o	a	m	a	r	m	n	m	n	j	i	i
l	o	u	h	υ	υm	n	n	h	hj	j	j
	l	u	υ	υ	p	d	d	t	r	h	hi	j
.	.	u	υ	tk	k	p	p	p	r	k	s
.	.	υ	k	pt	t	p	t	p	h	s	s

Figure 3   *Calibrated phoneme map. The double labels show which neurons respond to two phonemes. Distinction of /k,p,t/ from this map is not reliable and needs the analysis of their transient spectra by an auxiliary map. In the Japanese version there are auxiliary maps for /k,p,t/, /b,d,g/, and /m,n,ŋ/ for their more accurate analysis.*

spectra were not segmented or labelled in any way: any features whatsoever present in the speech waveform contributed to the self-organized map. After adaptation, the map was calibrated using known stationary phonemes (Fig. 3). This map resembles the well-known *formant maps* used in phonetics; the main difference is that in our maps *complete spectra*, not just two of their resonant frequencies, are used to define similarity relations between points in the map. It is not possible, however, to say explixcitly which the two feature dimensions are that are reflected in the map. This map may be regarded as a *similarity graph* in which the distance between two images is approximately proportional to the dissimilarity of the original spectra, in terms of their Euclidean distance.

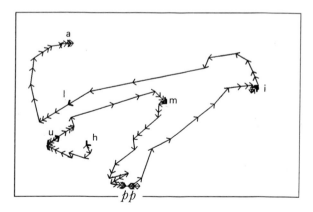

Figure 4   *Trajectory of the responses of the Finnish word /humppila/ over the map. A moving average of the sequential locations was computed in order to make the curves smoother.*

Any sequence of responses, or their trajectory on the map, for utterances of speech segments, can also be visualized. Fig. 4 shows such a trajectory with a timescale (at 9.83-ms intervals) marked on the curve by arrowheads.

Recognition of the phonemes is a decision-making process in which the final accuracy only depends on the rate of misclassification errors. It is therefore necessary to try to minimize them by a decision-controlled (supervised) learning scheme, using a training set of speech spectra with known classification. In practice, to fine-tune the map in this way, it will be sufficient to dictate 100 words which are then analysed by an automatic segmentation method.[14] The latter picks up the training spectra that are then applied in the supervised learning algorithm shown below. Since this process also needs an appreciable number of steps to converge to the asymptotic state, the training spectra must be repeated in the algorithm cyclically, or in a randomly permuted order.

Assume that the map is already formed, and our aim is to fine-tune the vectors $\mathbf{m}_i$. The new training inputs $\mathbf{x}(t)$ are again compared with each $\mathbf{m}_i$ in a sequence, but this time only the 'winner', indexed by c, is identified at each step. The $\mathbf{m}_i$ are then updated recursively according to the following rule:

$$\left.\begin{aligned}
\mathbf{m}_c(t+1) &= \mathbf{m}_c(t) + \alpha(t)(\mathbf{x}(t) - \mathbf{m}_c(t)), && \text{classes of } \mathbf{x}(t) \text{ and } \mathbf{m}_c(t) \text{ agree,} \\
\mathbf{m}_c(t+1) &= \mathbf{m}_c(t) - \alpha(t)(\mathbf{x}(t) - \mathbf{m}_c(t)), && \text{classes of } \mathbf{x}(t) \text{ and } \mathbf{m}_c(t) \text{ disagree,} \\
\mathbf{m}_i(t+1) &= \mathbf{m}_i(t) \quad \text{for } i \neq c.
\end{aligned}\right\}$$

$$(3)$$

Here $\{\alpha(t)\}$ is a similar decreasing sequence of 'gain parameters' as before.

After training, the $\mathbf{m}_i$ will have acquired such values that classification by the 'nearest neighbour' principle, by comparison of $\mathbf{x}$ with the $\mathbf{m}_i$, very closely complies with that of the Bayes classifier. The decision surface defined by this *learning vector quantization (LVQ)* classifier[15] (see also 2nd edn[7]) is piecewise linear.

6. Special problems with transient phonemes

Generally, the spectral properties of consonants behave more dynamically than those of vowels, and also the stationary intervals of many consonants are short. On the other hand, the stationary parameters of certain consonants are very similar. It seems advantageous to pay attention to the plosive burst and transient region between a consonant and the subsequent vowel to identify the consonant. In our system transient information is coded in additional phonotopic maps (called *transient maps*) and they are trained by using transient spectral samples alone, to describe the dynamic features with higher resolution. Our system was in fact developed in two versions: one for Finnish, one for Japanese.

In the Japanese version, four transient maps have been constructed to distinguish the following cases:

(a) voiceless stops /k, p, t/ and glottal stop (vowel at the beginning of utterance);
(b) voiceless stops /k, p, t/ without comparison to the glottal stop;
(c) voiced stops /b, d, g/;
(d) nasals /m, n, η/.

Only one transient map has been adopted in the Finnish version, accomplishing the distinction between /k, p, t/ and the glottal stop (/b/ and /g/ do not exist in original Finnish).

In spectral labelling, the stationary map is used by default to produce a tentative quasiphoneme sequence. Detecting a consonant-vowel combination in the resulting phonemic transcription activates the corresponding transient map by which the consonant segment is labelled more accurately.

The distinction accuracy of the cases in the due transient maps is as high as about 90%, on average. Utilization of the transient maps improves the overall recognition accuracy by 6–7% (cf. performance below).

7. Compensation for coarticulation effects

On account of coarticulation effects, ie, transformation of the speech spectra due to neighbouring phonemes, systematic errors appear in phonemic transcriptions. For instance, the Finnish word *hauki* (meaning pike) is almost always recognized as phoneme string /haouki/ by our acoustic processor. One may then suggest that if a transformation rule /aou/ → /au/ is introduced, this error is corrected. The context effects, however, may extend over several phonemes.

In the following, we shall use a formal notation $x(A)y \rightarrow (B)$ which means that segment A will be replaced by segment B in the context $x(.)y$. Consequently, the above transformation rule may be rewritten as $a(o)u \rightarrow (\ )$.

One might also imagine that it is possible to list down and take into account all such variations. However, there may be hundreds of different frames or contexts of neighbouring phonemes in which a particular phoneme may occur. In order to find them automatically, this author has developed a method called *Dynamically Expanding Context*[4] which constructs such a grammar. Its rules or productions can be used to transform erroneous symbol strings into correct ones. The rules are context-dependent and as general as possible.

To construct the rule set, each correct string T must first be aligned with the corresponding incorrect phonemic transcription S produced by the acoustic processor. It may be sufficient to mention here briefly, that dynamic programming is used for this purpose. Here is an example of the result:

$$S = \text{"-elsinkhi"}$$
$$T = \text{"helsink-i"}$$

The hyphens mean simply a skip in the letter position. Context-independent productions are first obtained by comparison of the pieces of S and T. The productions can be formed phoneme by phoneme, or, eg, by grouping subsequent vowels and consonants. Examples of both follow in which the top-row entries denote the left-hand sides of the rules, and the bottom-row entries the corresponding right-hand sides of the rules, respectively:

Production by phonemes:	Productions by vowel and consonant groups:
e l s i n k h i	e ls i nkh i
he l s i n k i	he ls i nk i

When several examples of erroneous strings, corresponding to the same correct string, are collected and processed, there may occur plenty of conflicts in the sense that the same *A* would be transformed into different *B*. Such conflicting cases must then be resolved by creating new production rules with expanded context. Expansion of context is made gradually, symbol by symbol.

The practical implementation of this principle is based on the following concept of *Dynamically Expanding Context*. The central idea underlying it is that for any segment *A* we first define a series of stepwise expanding frames, each frame, eg, consisting of an increasing number of symbol positions on either or both sides of *A*. The *n*th frame in this series is then said to correspond to the *nth level of context*. The due level is determined for each production automatically, as explained below. Consider, for instance, the string 'eisinki' (erroneous form of 'helsinki'), and the phoneme (s) in it. A possible definition of frames and contextual levels around (s) is exemplified in Table 1. We have used contexts of this type up to the eighth level.

Table 1. *Exemplification of contextual levels*

Level	Context	
0	—	(context-free)
1	i (.)	
2	i (.) i	
3	ei (.) i	
4	ei (.) in	

It may have become clear from the above that we do not know *a priori* how wide a context is necessary to resolve all conflicts; it must be determined experimentally, after all data have been collected. To this end we have to construct a series of tentative productions, starting at the lowest contextual level, and proceeding higher upon need. All the tentative productions $x(a)y \to (B)$ are stored in memory in the form of ordered sets $(xAy, B, \text{conflict bit})$, where xAy is simply the concatenation of x, A, and y, and a *conflict bit* is further associated with each set. This bit is 0 initially, and as long as the rule is valid. If it becomes necessary to invalidate a rule, the conflict bit is set equal to 1. The rule must not be deleted completely from memory, because it is needed in the hierarchical search were the final contextual level is determined automatically. So the rules, with dynamically expanding context, are logically represented as a tree structure in memory.

During application of these rules (editing), each segment A (eg, a phoneme) of the erroneous string is operated in turn, starting from the left end. If the conflict bit was set (the rule was invalidated), the context of that segment must be expanded one level up, and a new search initiated. This is repeated until a valid matching rule is found whose conflict bit is off. Then the right-hand side of the rule (B) is the corrected segment, which is concatenated to the string corrected so far.

If, during expansion of the context, a strange context $x(A)y$ in the new (erroneous) string was encountered, one must back up to the next lower contextual level, at which conflicting cases exist (and the context bit is one). In spite of unresolved conflicts, one may still resort to an 'educated guess', or an estimation procedure to find the most probable (corrected) production. One may, when performing the searches relating to a particular segment A, tentatively store all the Bs which are encountered during context expansion. A majority voting over the set of Bs found for this A (for the different xAy) is then the best guess. Also more complicated estimates exist.

The correction procedure can also be iterated, ie, a (partially) corrected string may once again be transformed by the grammar.

In reality, the algorithm is rather detailed, and the reader is advised to consult the original publication.

8. Microprocessor implementation of the system

This speech recognition system has been implemented on an IBM PC/AT and two auxiliary processor boards.[16] One board is dedicated to preprocessing, and the other, the main board, to phonemic recognition (Fig. 5). Currently, the post-processing methods are realized on the personal computer, but the main board has enough capacity to take care of post-processing, too, once the progress code for it has been finished.

The neural network implementation actually only exists 'virtually', because the signal processing operations are computed by an array processor principle based on the TMS32010 signal processor. At the recognition phase, the TMS32010 computes all the responses of the 'neurons' to the pattern vector. The weight vectors of the map are represented in in-line program code of the TMS32010 by the so-called immediate multiply instructions (MPYK) with double precision which in this case means 25 bits. The program code is generated automatically by the personal computer and then loaded into the RAM of TMS32010. Currently, also the self-organized computation of the weight vectors m_i, ie, learning is made in the host computer, but in coming versions, the learning process too will be implemented on the processor board.

The 80186 'host' processor, among other tasks, performs the segmentation of the quasiphoneme sequence, and the detected phonemes are immediately transferred to the personal computer. Still, only a small

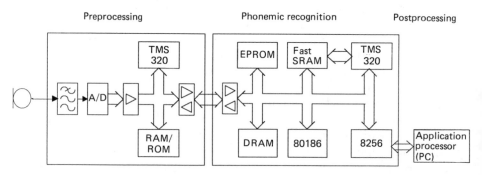

Figure 5   *Block scheme of the microprocessor implementation. A/D: analogue-to-digital converter. TMS320: Texas Instruments 32010 signal processor chip. RAM/ROM: 4-kword random-access memory, 256-word programmable read-only memory. EPROM: 64-kbyte electrically erasable read-only memory. DRAM: 512-kbyte dual-port random-access memory. SRAM: 96-kbyte paged dual-port random-access memory. 80186: The Intel microprocessor CPU. 8256: parallel interface.*

fraction of the computing capacity of the 80186 processor is utilized. The post-processing methods could be programmed for the 80186 processor to build a complete stand-alone speech recognition unit. For example, a sample set of 5000 words produces about 11 000 production rules, corresponding to a memory space of about 300 kB.

9. Performance

The system is speaker-adaptive: the phoneme maps are computed reasonably fast, which means that revising a standard map for a new speaker requires only 100 word samples, and the computation takes 10 minutes on a personal computer. The updating algorithm is based on the learning vector quantization. A fast automatic segmentation program has also been developed to pick the phonemic prototypes from word samples.

The combined segmentation and labelling accuracy of the acoustic processor for raw phonemes varies between 80% and 90%, depending on speaker and the phonetic complexity of the text. The final accuracy of the orthographically corrected and edited text varies between 92% and 97%, referring to individual letters. This accuracy depends on the speaker and the amount and content of speech encoded into rules.

When producing orthographically corrected text, the mean correction time of the present system is about 300 ms per average word, and the recognition process almost completely overlaps the pronounciation. Newer designs will have roughly five times higher speed.

New grammatical rules for post-processing can easily be added on-line, first pronouncing a word or a phrase, and then entering the correct written form via the keyboard.

10. Conclusions

The 'neural' speech recognition discussed above is only one application of our 20-year long research into neural computing principles. This system also contains technical, non-neural solutions. Selection of this practical objective, however, has taught us a valuable lesson that many sophisticated network models may be able to respond correctly to and classify artificial data, whereas the difficulties start to soar when natural, stochastic signals are applied. The natural representations are usually not clustered into disjoint sets, so the most important problem is then to minimize the misclassification errors. The importance of this problem does not become obvious before the 'neural networks' are made to interact with the real world.

References

1. Kohonen, T. In *Proc. 2nd Scand. Conf. on Image Analysis*, pp. 214–220 (Suomen Hahmontunnistustutkimuksen Seura r.y., Helsinki, Finland, 1981).
2. Fukunaga, K. & Koontz, W. L. G. *IEEE TC* **19**, 311–318 (1970).
3. Sammon, J. W. *IEEE TC* **18**, 401–409 (1969).
4. Kohonen, T. In *Proc. 8th Int. Conf. on Pattern Recognition*, pp. 1148–1151 (IEEE Computer Society Press, Washington, DC, 1986).
5. Meddis, R. *J. Acoust. Soc. Am.* **79**, 703–711 (1986).
6. Kohonen, T. *Biol. Cyb.* **43**, 59–69 (1982).
7. Kohonen, T. *Self-Organization and Associative Memory* (Springer Verlag, Heidelberg, 1984; 2nd edn 1988).
8. Kohonen, T. *Biol. Cyb.* **44**, 135–140 (1982).
9. Kohonen, T. In *Proc. 6th Int. Conf. on Pattern Recognition*, pp. 114–128 (IEEE Computer Society Press, Washington, DC, 1982).
10. Cottrell, M. & Fort, J. C. *Ann. Inst. Henri Poincaré* **23**, 1–20 (1987).
11. Ritter, H. & Schulten, K. *Biol. Cyb.* **54**, 99–106 (1986).
12. Robbins, H. & Monro, S. *Ann. Math. Statistics* **22**, 400–407 (1951).
13. Kohonen, T., Mäkisara, K. & Saramäki, T. In *Proc. 7th Int. Conf. on Pattern Recognition*, pp. 182–185 (IEEE Computer Society Press, Silver Spring, 1984).
14. Torkkola, K. Automatic alignment of speech with phonetic transcriptions in real time, to be published in *Proc. 1988 IEEE ICASSP* (New York, Apr. 11–14, 1988).
15. Kohonen, T. An introduction to neural computing, to be published in *Neural Networks* (January 1988 issue); also in Kohonen, T. *Learning Vector Quantization* (Helsinki University of Technology Report TKK-F-A601, 1986).
16. Kohonen, T., Torkkola, K., Shozakai, M., Kangas, J. & Ventä, O. In *Proc. European Conference on Speech Technology*, pp. 377–380 (CEP Consultants Ltd, Edinburgh, 1987).

4 Neural map applications

G. Tattersall

School of Information Systems, University of East Anglia, UK

Abstract

For several years it has been known that a self-organizing array of neural elements with modifiable synaptic weights is capable of forming a topologically ordered map of data to which it has been exposed. Neural maps are useful when the *perceptual* relationship between stimuli is reflected in the pattern space from which they are drawn. When patterns with this type of natural structure are applied to a neural map they cause neural firings whose spatial positions correspond to the perceptual relationship between the patterns. For example, if the neural array is exposed to spectral vectors which represent different speech sounds, particularly the vowel sounds, different neural elements in the array become atuned to different types of sound. The relative positions of neural elements which are excited by different speech sounds reflect the phonetic relationship between the same set of sounds. This property, originally discovered by Kohonen,[1] has been exploited to make speech recognition systems using neural maps and is described in more detail later in the chapter.

In this chapter we explore ways in which pattern recognition and feature extraction may be obtained using neural mapping techniques. In particular, the difference between supervised and unsupervised neural learning systems is considered and it is shown that important pattern processing properties are obtainable using unsupervised systems.

1. Processing patterns with neural systems

The ideas proposed here are built around a central hypothesis:

Stimuli which we find perceptually significant have natural structure. Furthermore, it is suggested that our brains have an architecture which is matched to this natural structure and that any machine that we build for pattern understanding should try to emulate this structure.

41

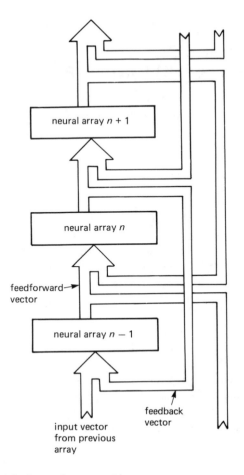

Figure 1   *General stacked neural array architecture.*

The principle architectural features suggested for the neural processing system is a stack of topologically ordered neural arrays with feedforward and feedback connections between different levels of the stack, as shown in Fig. 1.

Fig. 2 shows the model for each element, which is assumed to produce an output which is a function of the weighted sum of its inputs via the synaptic weights. A key feature, which will be justified later, is that the magnitude of the synaptic weight vector associated with each element is assumed to have a constant value regardless of the modification of each individual weight. Alternatively, an adaptive gain factor is made to operate on the outputs of all the neurons in the array such that the magnitude of the vector of output excitations is always a constant.

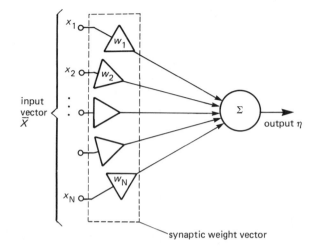

Figure 2   *Model of a neural element.*

The properties of this architecture will be studied in some detail later in this chapter, but to start, it is worth exploring the fundamental differences between the *unsupervised* neural mapping approach suggested here and the more common *supervised* learning schemes for neural processors.

2. Explicit supervision and clustering

Neural maps are generated by a process of self-organization. In other words, the neural map is generated by applying input patterns to the neural array without a human supervisor commanding the machine to assign the patterns to any particular class which the supervisor finds significant. This is unusual, and to understand its significance we first examine the role of supervision in learning.

In supervised learning a human supervisor examines each training pattern before it is applied to the learning machine, and assigns a class label to that pattern. To be of any use, the class label must have some perceptual significance to the human supervisor. The minimal task of the learning machine, after it has been trained, is to accept any one of the previous training patterns and produce a flag denoting the class which was attached to that pattern by the human supervisor. Of course, in practice, we require the machine to do more than just recognize members of the training set. The machine should be capable of assigning the correct class flag to an input pattern which is only *approximately* like one

43

of the training set. It should be noted that for this to happen there must be some natural structure in the input data such that patterns which have the same perceptual significance to the human supervisor are clustered in the pattern space. It is quite permissible for there to be several clusters associated with a single class, but it is nonsensical to suppose that a perceptually distinct class would have members spread homogeneously over the pattern space. This is an important point: it suggests that all pattern processing systems, whether supervised or unsupervised, require natural structure in the input data. Any type of explicitly supervised pattern recognition machine can be thought of as an association system, as shown in Fig. 3, which is trained to associate class labels, C, with input patterns, X.

Is supervision really necessary? Superficial examination of human behaviour suggests not. We are all familiar with what we consider to be supervised human learning: for example, we may say to a child, 'Look! There is an egg', while we point to a chicken egg. On another occasion we may point to a duck egg and say 'Look! There is an egg.' The visual patterns presented by these two examples of the class 'egg' are quite different in some ways. The rule of the supervised training has been to link these two examples into the single class called 'egg'. However, it is hard to believe that the child, faced with these two examples of the same

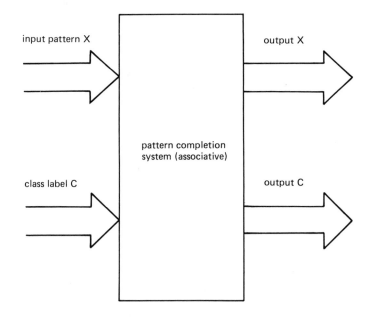

Figure 3   *Supervised associative mapping system.*

class, would not have recognized their similarity and associated them in its mind. If this were the case, all that the supervised learning has achieved is to cause the word 'egg' to be associated with these two examples of what is already a naturally distinct class in the mind of the observer.

Such a class would be naturally distinct if the description of its members in some feature space were much closer together than to any other image. This suggests that any group of patterns that is worthy of a distinct class label in our perception will form a distinct cluster in a naturally ocurring feature space in our brains.

This example of human supervised learning suggests that supervision is unnecessary other than as a means of associating a particular word or label with a natural class cluster. However, now consider the situation in which the child is shown many examples of different types of table. Every time a different table is produced the teacher or supervisor points to the object and says 'table'. In this example the shapes of the tables vary widely and it is unlikely that they form a natural cluster in the raw pattern space, even allowing for such things as rotation, translation and scale invariant transformations.

It is in this situation that the proponents of supervised learning claim that supervision is essential in order that the child recognize all these different objects as belonging to the same class. In neural computing terms the word 'table', or its physical associations, is the target output that must be activated when the child is stimulated with the image of any one of the wide variety of table types.

The role of explicit supervision in this situation is to generate a mapping between any pattern space description of a table and a single-target output. This mapping should be sensitive only to the essence of 'tableness' rather than to the specific details of a particular table. Notice that the mapping is learnt and that it converts the poorly clustered descriptions of 'tables' in the raw pattern space to a tight, ideally single-point, cluster in a new feature space, as shown in Fig. 4.

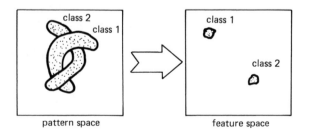

Figure 4   *Learnt mapping from pattern to feature space.*

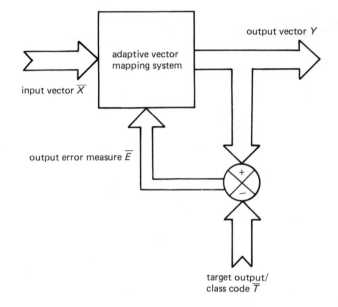

input vector $\overline{X}$

adaptive vector mapping system

output vector Y

output error measure $\overline{E}$

target output/
class code $\overline{T}$

Figure 5   *Supervised adaptive mapping system.*

Any supervised learning systems which learns pattern to feature space transformations can be represented diagrammatically, as in Fig. 5 which shows an adaptive vector transformer which maps a pattern space vector **X** to a feature space vector **Y**. The learning or adaption is controlled by an error vector **E** which is generated by taking the difference between the target vector **T**, supplied by the supervision, and the actual output **Y**. Adaption for the coefficients of the transformation matrix is commonly done by some form of the steepest descent algorithm.

The usual neural implementations of this system are the simple and multi-layer perceptrons[2] shown in Figs. 6 and 7, in which synaptic weights are slowly modified until the desired mappings are learnt. It is well known that the multi-layer perceptron is capable of mapping a class whose members form several separate clusters in the pattern space to a simple cluster in the learnt feature space, whereas the simple perceptron can do no more than 'tighten' single-class clusters.

Clearly, the supervised learning of mappings would be unnecessary if the elements of the necessary mapping functions were already embodied in the architecture of our brains. If progressively higher orders of feature were abstracted from the input patterns and the form of these features was determined by the brain architecture, rather than detailed synaptic weight values, then we would expect any group of patterns that we perceive as belonging to a single class to form a single natural cluster at

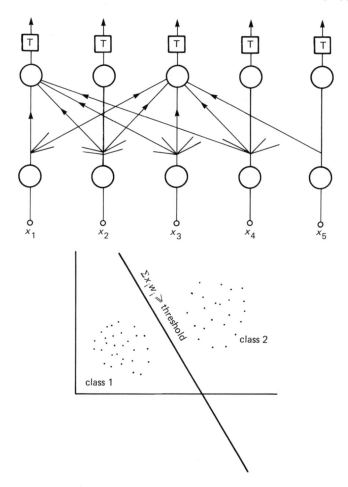

Figure 6   *Simple perceptron linearly dissects the pattern space.*

some level of representation in the brain. For example returning to the example of tables, a feature space might exist at some level of abstraction in which images are reduced to the ordering of a set of corner points from the original image. In this feature space all tables might be reduced to the same description, regardless of the detailed design of the actual table being viewed. The size, aspect ratio and viewing angle of the table would not affect its feature space description and all tables would be forced to lie in a *single* natural cluster regardless of their form. If certain forms of feature abstraction are embodied in our brain architecture, supervised learning becomes unnecessary except that it causes an explicit flag or label to be attached to each of the natural class clusters.

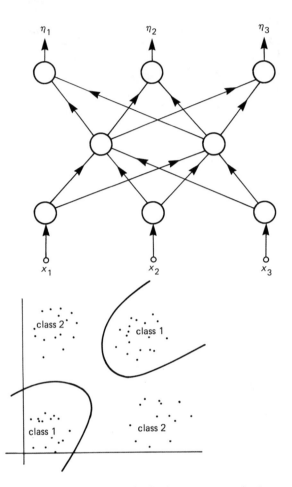

Figure 7   *Multi-layer perceptron maps multiple clusters to a single cluster.*

However, it is arguable that even the labelling function of explicit supervision is unnecessary to either human or mechanical learning systems. If a specific neural firing pattern is always initiated in a neural machine or a biological brain by a particular external stimulus, then it is unnecessary to attach an explicit label to that firing pattern because the firing pattern is itself acting as the label. Moreover, if the firing pattern is *consistent* with the firing patterns produced by other stimuli, its meaning is defined by its mutually consistent relationships to other possible firing patterns.

In other words, we first postulate that all stimuli derived from the physical world have meaning due to their self consistent, stable relation-

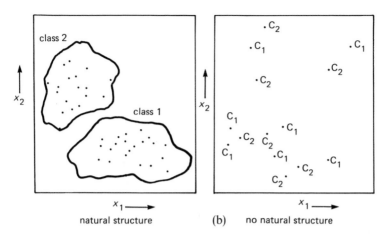

Figure 8   *Neural pattern structure: perceptual similarity.*

ship. If the neural system encodes these stimuli by particular firing patterns, the firing patterns must themselves have meaning within the system whether it be biological or mechanical.

3. Natural structure in patterns

The expression 'natural structure' has been used rather freely in the preceding section and thus we will now examine this idea in more detail. The simplest type of natural pattern structure occurs when the perceptual similarity between patterns is mirrored by their pattern space similarity. This is illustrated in Fig. 8(a) in which two perceptually distinct classes form two well-separated clusters in the pattern space. A counterexample of patterns exhibiting no obvious natural structure is shown in Fig. 8(b)

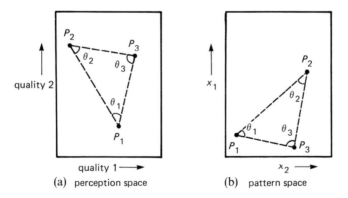

Figure 9   *Natural pattern structure of perceptual topology mirrored in pattern space.*

49

in which patterns corresponding to two perceptual classes are mixed homogeneously within the pattern space with no distinct class clusters.

A more interesting extension of the idea of natural pattern structure is illustrated in Fig. 9. In this case the topology of the patterns in their perceptual space is mirrored by their relative positions in the pattern space. Imagine a perception space in which three patterns, P_1, P_2, and P_3 exist with some mutual orientation, as depicted in Fig. 9(*a*). These patterns have natural structure if their perceptual topology is mirrored in their pattern space, as shown in Fig. 9(*b*).

A good example of this type of natural pattern structure is contained in speech vowel sounds. If the cardinal vowels are represented by spectral vectors derived, for example, by a 16 channel filterbank analysis of the speech, then it is found that the topological relationship between the vowel sounds depicted in the 16-dimensional pattern space is mirrored in a two-dimensional perceptual quality space whose dimensions are related to tongue height and retraction.

The next type of natural pattern structure is rather different to the preceding two. Many patterns are found to have limited dimensional freedom due to correlation between the elements of the pattern. This is illustrated by the very simple example of Fig. 10(*a*) which depicts a mechanical system consisting of two pivoted arms, the upper arm being constrained to move only up or down along the guide rail. The state of the system might be described by a two-dimensional vector whose elements are the angles θ_1 and θ_2 of the two pivot arms. However, it is obvious that this system only has one degree of freedom because θ_1 and θ_2 are completely correlated. Fig. 10(*b*) shows a pattern space description of the possible states which are clearly shown to be inherently one-dimensional.

This is a very common type of natural structure: the *inherent dimensionality* of a set of patterns may be much less than the number of

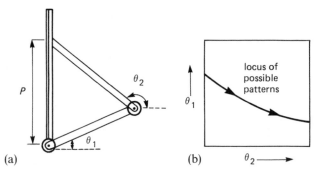

Figure 10   *Natural pattern structure: constrained freedom.*

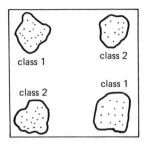

Figure 11   *Hidden natural pattern structure.*

dimensions in their pattern space. Again, an example of this structure is found in the context of speech vowel sounds; 16-dimensional spectral vectors representing the vowel sounds are found in fact to have an inherent dimensionality of only 2 corresponding approximately to the positions of 2-formant frequency peaks.

The final example of a type of natural pattern structure is shown in Fig. 11. In this case it is seen that more than one distinct cluster is associated with each of the two classes. In this particular example, class 1 patterns are defined as the fuzzy exclusive OR-ing of two pattern variables and class 2 patterns as the exclusive NOR-ing of the same variables. Although the natural structure of the classes is broken in their pattern space description there is a simple logical function underlying the two classes. For this reason such patterns are said to have hidden structure and, in general, unsupervised learning systems cannot associate multiple clusters within a single class unless the architecture of the system forces such an association.

It is our contention that if a class of patterns is perceptually distinct to us, and yet its members are only linked by hidden structure, then that hidden structure must be matched to our brain architecture such that separated clusters within the class are associated with a single meaning. The often-quoted example of classes defined by odd or even parity, in other words the exclusive OR operation, are not perceptually distinct classes according to common sense. In order to see these patterns as a single class we need to resort to formal logic techniques.

4. Operation of the self-organizing neural array

The principles of the self-organizing neural array have been extensively described by Kohonen,[1] so only a brief description will be given here.

The basic array consists of a large number of neural elements laid out in a line, rectangle or cuboid for one-, two- or three-dimensional arrays as required. Every neuron has N inputs which are supplied with the same N-dimensional input pattern vector $\bar{\mathbf{X}}$. The output η_i, of the ith neuron in the array is a function, f, of the similarity, S, between the input pattern $\bar{\mathbf{X}}$ and a prototype vector, $\bar{\mathbf{W}}_i$, uniquely associated with the neuron:

$$\eta_i = f\{S(\bar{\mathbf{X}}, \bar{\mathbf{W}}_i)\}.$$

5. Specific algorithms: the metric

The arrangement of a one-dimensional array is shown in Fig. 12 by way of example. At the commencement of training, the prototype weight vectors $\bar{\mathbf{W}}_i$ are usually initialized with random angular values. Training then proceeds by drawing an input vector $\bar{\mathbf{X}}$ from the training set and applying it to the array, causing a peak of excitation at some position in the array. A spatial neighbourhood is next defined around the most excited element and the prototype vectors of all elements lying within the neighbourhood are modified so that they become incrementally more similar, using metric S, to the current input vector:

$$\bar{\mathbf{W}}_i^{n+1} = g\{\bar{\mathbf{W}}_i^n + k \cdot \bar{X}\}.$$

This process is typically repeated for many thousands of different input vectors, starting with a large spatial neighbourhood which shrinks as training progresses. On completion of training, application of an input vector to the array will cause all elements to be excited to some extent. However, a clear peak in excitation should occur at one position in the array and this position will be related to the region in pattern space from which the input vector was drawn. The array will be globally ordered only if the inherent dimensionality of the input data does not exceed the physical dimensionality of the array. If this constraint is not obeyed, the map will be topologically correct when viewed locally, but not ordered globally.

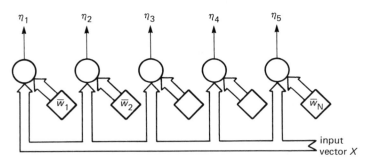

Figure 12   *A one-dimensional neural array.*

In our work, we have used the scalar product of **X** and **W**$_i$ as the similarity metric, S. This metric seems to have many advantages over other metrics, particularly in the speech recognition applications. This is because the ranking of the excitations of the neural element is unchanged by a change in magnitude of **X̄** and consequently neural maps become ordered in terms of the profiles of input patterns alone and are not affected, for example, by the loudness of a particular sound.

Use of the scalar product as a similarity metric is also attractive because it corresponds directly to the long standing physical model of a neural element shown in Fig. 2 in which the neural output is related to the weighted sum of the input pattern vector elements, where the weighting factors are the elements of the prototype vector **W̄**$_i$, ie:

$$\eta_i = \sum_{i=1}^{N} w_{ji} \cdot x_j$$

or

$$\eta_i = \bar{\mathbf{W}}_i \cdot \bar{X}.$$

A disadvantage of using the scalar product metric is that the similarity value varies cosinusoidally with the angle, θ, between **X** and **W**$_i$ and this causes the excitation to also vary cosinusoidally across the array, ie:

$$S = |\mathbf{X}| \cdot |\mathbf{W}_i| \cos \theta.$$

The cosine term leads to poor discrimination by the array between input patterns which may be very different in a perceptual sense but which happen not to have a very large angular difference.

6. Specific algorithms: synaptic weight modification

The weight vectors are modified so that they become more similar to the current input vector. However, as we desire the map to be ordered in terms of pattern profile but not magnitude, the synaptic weight vectors must be modified in direction but not magnitude. In fact, the magnitude of every neuron's synaptic weight vector must be made identical otherwise a neuron with a particularly large weight vector could give a large neural output even if the angle between it and the current input vector were small.

The update algorithm complying with this requirement is:

$$\bar{\mathbf{W}}_i'^{n+1} = \bar{\mathbf{W}}_i^n + k \cdot \bar{\mathbf{X}},$$

$$\bar{\mathbf{W}}_i^{n+1} = \frac{\bar{\mathbf{W}}_i'^{n+1}}{|\bar{\mathbf{W}}_i'^{n+1}|}.$$

53

An intuitively appealing side effect of this particular form of synaptic weight modification algorithm is that the magnitude of each incremental change in $\bar{\mathbf{W}}_i$ depends on the magnitude of $\bar{\mathbf{X}}$. The greater the magnitude of $\mathbf{X}$, the greater its effect on the learning process.

7. Specific algorithms: the spatial neighbourhood

The usual self-organizing algorithm requires a sequential search for the excitation peak in the array, followed by the definition of a spatial neighbourhood around the excitation peak. If the neighbourhood is made wide, say half the width of the array, ordering is obtained but full convergence is never achieved. This is because most neural elements lie within the current neighbourhood most of the time and their weight vectors are thus subject, over time, to incremental steps towards all regions of the data space as successive input vectors are applied to the array. The net result is that the weight vectors take on values which tend to match the *mean* value of all the pattern vectors applied.

At the other extreme, definition of a very small neighbourhood destroys the coupling between the elements and ordering cannot be obtained even though the weight vectors spread to match data from all regions of the data space.

The solution proposed by Kohonen[1] is to start training with a large neighbourhood, obtain ordering, and then reduce the neighbourhood until full convergence is obtained. This process is rather inelegant, firstly because it involves a sequential search which does not fit well with the concept of a parallel distributed processing system, and secondly because the shrinking of the neighbourhood presupposes a finite amount of training and knowledge of how many training patterns will be used.

We have considered two different approaches to the coupling of the neural elements so that both ordering and convergence are obtained. Both methods are inherently parallel processes and are therefore more attractive than the shrinking neighbourhood technique.

In the first of the new methods, all neurons are modified every time a new input pattern is applied, regardless of the stage of training. However, in this case, the value of the weight vector update step size, k, is made a function, $L(x)$ of the physical distance of the particular neuron from the most excited neuron in the array. The form of $L(x)$ is shown in Fig. 13 where it can be seen that the function assigns positive step sizes to neurons near the position of the excitation peak, negative step sizes to neurons some distance from the peak and very weak positive step sizes to neurons which are very distant from the peak.

The rationale behind this function is that the fairly wide positive step

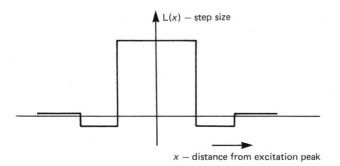

Figure 13 *Step-sized function used with non-shrinking neighbourhood.*

size neighbourhood provides strong coupling between the neural elements so that global ordering is obtained. The region of negative step size counteracts the tendency of the large positive neighbourhood to confine the weight vectors to a small central region of the data space, since on average neurons are subject to both attraction and repulsion from each region of the data space. The weak excitory region at large distances is important as it acts as a safety net which prevents neuron weight vectors being pushed totally out of the input data space and thereby rendering the neuron useless.

Unfortunately, this approach is not very robust. Small changes in the ratio of magnitudes and widths of the positive and negative neighbourhoods, or a change in the distributions of the input data, can cause the system to become unstable.

An alternative approach, which has been used with success, is to give the weight vectors of the array an initial but *arbitrary* order. For example, if a two-dimensional array is being used, the four corner neurons' weight vectors are initially set to match data from four extremities of the data space. The weight vectors of all other neurons are then set by linear interpolation to intermediate values between the extremities.

A fixed but small positive update neighbourhood is used during subsequent training. A refinement of the technique which avoids a search for the position of the excitation peak in the array is to update all neurons' weight vectors, but by an amount proportional to the excitation of each neuron such that:

$$\bar{\mathbf{W}}_i^{\prime n+1} = \bar{\mathbf{W}}_i^n + k \cdot \eta_i \cdot \bar{\mathbf{X}},$$

$$\bar{\mathbf{W}}_i^{n+1} = \frac{\bar{\mathbf{W}}_i^{\prime n+1}}{|\bar{\mathbf{W}}_i^{n+1}|}.$$

8. A neural architecture to perform feature extraction

It was argued earlier that a mapping system is required between the pattern space in which stimuli are initially defined, and the feature space in which perceptually distinct classes of stimuli form very tight clusters. Such mappings can be generated using supervised learning. However, we are searching for a neural architecture which can learn without supervision and in which suitable mappings are implicit.

Before looking at the detail of specific architectures to perform this function it is necessary to examine the fundamental process involved in feature extraction.

Feature extraction always involves the destruction of some information about the original pattern. The whole point of the process is to find some features of a pattern which are characteristic of the pattern's perceptual class and to ignore or throw away information which is specific only to an individual pattern but not general to the entire class.

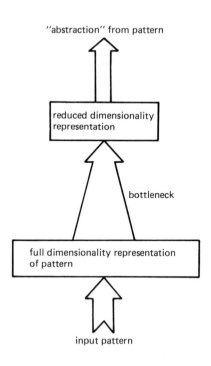

Figure 14   *The representation bottleneck.*

9. The representation bottleneck

Consideration of the basic nature of feature extraction provides a guide as to the form of neural architecture required: since a pattern's feature space description always contains less information than the pattern space description, a method of forcing feature extraction is to pass the pattern vectors through some form of representation bottleneck, as shown in Fig. 14. Assuming that signal value quantization is not used, the bottleneck must be a reduction in the number of dimensions available to represent the pattern.

Applying this idea to a neural array system leads to the general

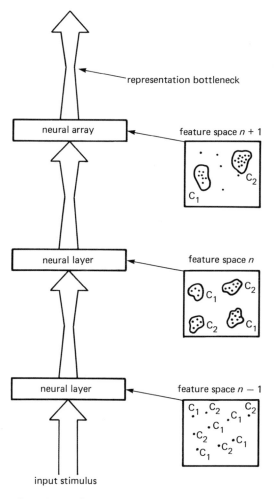

Figure 15   *Forcing class clusters by representation bottlenecks.*

structure of Fig. 15, in which self-organizing neural arrays are placed in a stack. Data from the output of one array is conceptually passed through a representation bottleneck before being applied to the next array. In practice, the bottleneck may be implicit and integrated with the array.

The desired function of the systems is also depicted in Fig. 15. Perceptually distinct classes of pattern C_1 and C_2 which do not cluster in feature space $n-1$, eventually form distinct clusters in feature space $n+1$. The succession of feature spaces are mapped onto each of the neural arrays and so patterns from class 1 cause excitation peaks in one localized area of array $n+1$, whereas patterns from class 2 cause excitation in a different area and are therefore distinct within the machine's 'perception'.

9.1 Types of representation bottleneck

The representation bottlenecks must have a form which leads to the extraction of useful features. At first sight there appear to be limitless possibilities. However, we will consider just three types which appear to be both biologically plausible and to have interesting properties.

10. Pattern magnitude bottleneck

This bottleneck arises naturally within the neural array when the scalar product similarity measure is used along with the constraint that all neurons' weight vectors have the same magnitude.

Fig. 16 illustrates the operation of the bottleneck by means of a 'toy'

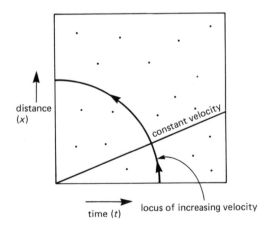

Figure 16   *Magnitude bottleneck operation.*

example in which journeys are represented by a two-dimensional pattern vector consisting of the distance covered and the elapsed time. On a large number of different journeys one might expect a distribution of vectors, represented by dots, over the pattern space $x - t$.

This data is basically two-dimensional; however, a one-dimensional feature underlying the data is the speed of a particular journey, x/t. Journeys of the same speed obviously lie along a radial line from the origin of the pattern space with an angle which increases with speed. However, as already discussed, neural arrays using the scalar product metric become ordered in terms of the profiles or direction of the applied pattern vectors and the positions of the excitation peak in the array is not affected by the magnitude of the pattern vector. Thus, application of the two-dimensional $[\mathbf{x}, \mathbf{t}]$ vectors to one-dimensional array will cause the array to order and respond to the speed feature and not to specific values of x and t.

10.1 Single peak position sensing using magnitude bottleneck

A less trivial application of this type of bottleneck is to make a neural array order and respond to the *position* of a peak in an input vector. For example, a pattern vector may consist of the magnitudes of the discrete Fourier transform coefficients of a signal having a single spectral peak of a variable frequency and indeterminate amplitude. Applying this type of pattern vector to a one-dimensional neural array can cause an excitation peak at a physical position within the array which is directly related to the position of the spectral peak coded by the input vector.

The reason for this behaviour can be understood from Figs. 17(*a*) and (*b*) which shows the form of pattern vector being applied to the array and their positions as points in pattern space. In our simulation of this system we have generally used 100-dimensional pattern vectors, but for

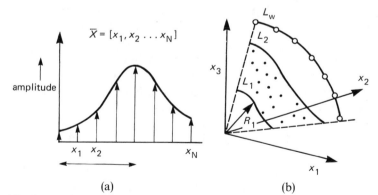

(a)   (b)

Figure 17   *Vector form of the spectral peak.*

obvious reasons we only show the patterns in a three-dimensional space in this example. Imagine to start that the spectral peak is of constant low amplitude, R_1, and that many pattern vectors are generated with their peaks covering the entire range of possible frequencies. The pattern space positions of these vectors will lie on the locus L_1, shown in Fig. 17(b), which winds through the dimensions of the space but always at a radius of R_1.

A one-dimensional neural array will order on this data such that its synaptic weight vectors lie on a locus L_w which maintains a constant radius R_w from the origin and lines up with the origin and the locus L_1. A pattern which lies at one end of the locus L_1 angularly matches the weight vector of a neural element at one end of the array and so would produce an excitation peak at that point in the array.

Now consider the effect of changing the magnitude of the spectral peaks. The loci, L_1 and L_2 define a curly surface in the space and changing the magnitude merely shifts the pattern vector point to a different radius but keeps the point within the $L_1 - L_w$ surface. Thus, change in magnitude does not change the position of the most excited neuron in the array.

Notice that if the spectral peak is very sharp, the points will tend to jump from dimension to dimension and a continuous locus will not be obtained. A neural array cannot order on this type of disjointed data because there are many possible paths between the separate pattern points. Seen from the neural array's point of view, the data has as high inherent dimensionality as the pattern space.

10.2 Double peak position sensing using magnitude bottleneck

An extension of the previous idea is to see if a two-dimensional neural array will order when it is trained with pattern vectors containing pairs of peaks of variable, uncorrelated position and variable magnitude, as shown in Fig. 18(a). This is particularly relevant to the mapping of spectral vectors produced by speech vowel sounds which can be characterized by the frequencies of the first two formant peaks.

If it is assumed that the peaks do not cross over, it is reasonable to visualize each peak as occupying a separate sub-space within the pattern space. Variation of each peak's position and magnitude generates a curvy surface within the subspace which always passes through the origin, as shown in Fig. 18(b). Since the two sub-spaces are orthogonal, the two surfaces together define a three-dimensional volume within the pattern space.

Applying a wide range of double peak vectors to a two-dimensional array using scalar product metric and constant magnitude weight vectors causes the array to order such that its weight vectors lie on the

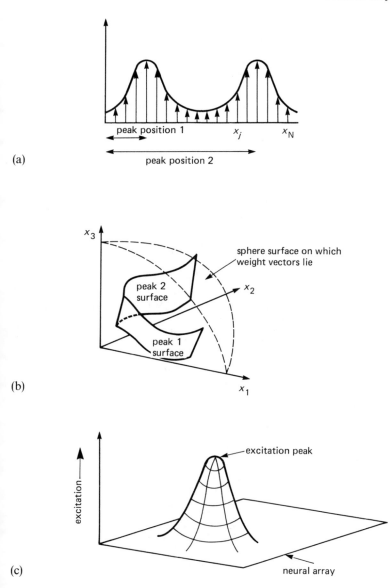

Figure 18   (a) *Vector form of the double peak.* (b) *Volume defined by the individual peak sub-spaces.* (c) *a neural array response double peak.*

surface of a sphere containing the three-dimensional volume occupied by the data. A pattern vector causes a peak of excitation in the array at the neuron whose weight vector most closely matches the pattern vectors **angle**. Examination of Fig. 18(*b*) makes it clear that changing the position

61

of either peak in the pattern vector causes the coordinates of the neuron with the best matching weight vector to change in an ordered manner. However, although changing the magnitude of either peak moves the point representing the pattern within the three-dimensional volume, it does not change the position of its projection onto the weight vector sphere and therefore does not effect the position of the excitation peak within the neural array.

This result has been confirmed by simulation using a 10×10 neural array and 64-dimensional pattern vectors containing pairs of gaussian shaped peaks. The simulation exhibits array ordering in which the coordinates of the array excitation peak map directly from the positions of the two peaks in the input vector.

11. Array dimension bottleneck

We now consider a second type of representation bottleneck which may force the generation of useful features. What happens if the vector of neural excitations from a two-dimensional array is applied to the input of a one-dimensional array? How is data from the two-dimensional array represented by the one-dimensional array? Before examining this question in detail, it is necessary to understand that the inherent dimensionality of the vector of neural excitation from a two-dimensional

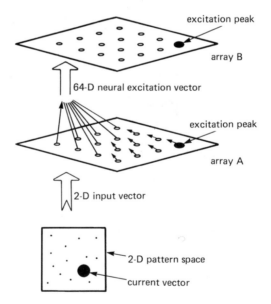

Figure 19   *Neural excitation vector from array **A** applied to the input of array **B**.*

array is actually only two. This can be verified by the simulation outlined in Fig. 19 in which a two-dimensional array, **A**, is first trained on two element vectors uniformly distributed across their two-dimensional space. After sufficient training, array **A**, produces a neural excitation peak at a position in the array which directly maps to the point in the two-dimensional space from which the input pattern was drawn. We wish to prove that the vector of neural array outputs representing this peak, is itself inherently two-dimensional.

In our simulation, array **A** contained 64 neural elements in an 8×8 formation. The outputs of all these elements are gathered together into a single 64-dimensional vector which is applied to the input of a second two-dimensional 8×8 neural array, **B**, in which every neuron has 64 inputs. If the 64-dimensional vector from array **A** is really two-dimensional, then array **B** should eventually order such that application of a 64-dimensional neural excitation vector from array **A** causes a single excitation peak in array **B**. The position of the peak should directly map to the position of the excitation peak in array **A**, and hence to the position of the original input vector in its two-dimensional pattern space. All these propositions have been verified by simulation, in which single, distinct excitation peaks were produced in array **B**.

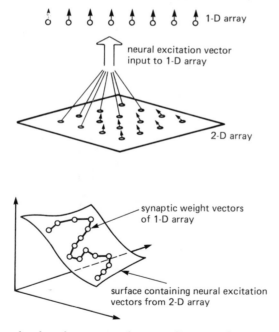

Figure 20   *Array bottleneck: output of a two-dimensional array applied to a one dimensional array.*

Having confirmed that the vector of neural excitations from a two-dimensional array is inherently two-dimensional, we return to the question of what happens when such a vector is applied to a one-dimensional rather than a two-dimensional array. The bottleneck is illustrated in Fig. 20 which shows the expected result when the weight vectors of the one-dimensional array arrange themselves on the surface of a sphere and attempt to match all the vector angles taken up by the output from the two-dimensional neural array. Since the variation in these angles has two degrees of freedom, the one-dimensional array is unable to map its input data consistently.

However, this problem can be overcome in the following way. Consider the effect of first projecting the two-dimensional array output vectors onto a plane passing through the origin. If the magnitude variation of the vector projections is ignored (which will be the case if they are applied to a neural array which uses scalar product metric), then these vectors are inherently one-dimensional and when applied to a one-dimensional array will cause it to order globally, placing its weight vectors on a circle lying within the plane and centred on the origin, as shown in Fig. 21. The one-dimensional array will, therefore, form a map which is ordered in terms of a **new feature**. This feature represents the angular bearing of the excitation peak caused by the input vector to the two-dimensional array, as seen from the position of the mean of all excitation peaks.

At this stage this may seem rather contrived and pointless. However, we will try to show both that this type of feature is useful and that its generation is plausible in a neural sense. First consider how the output vectors from a neural array might be projected onto a surface passing through the origin. This is simply achieved by using an intermediate

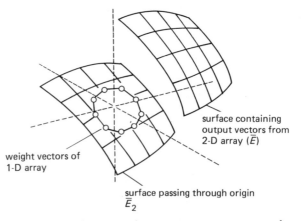

weight vectors of
1-D array

surface containing
output vectors from
2-D array $(\bar{E})$

surface passing through origin
$\bar{E}_2$

Figure 21   *Projection of two-dimensional array output vectors onto the surface through the origin.*

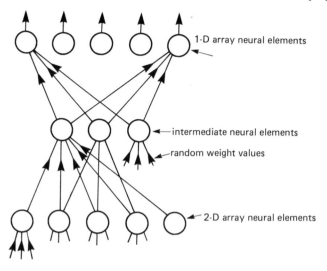

Figure 22   *System implementation of vector projection.*

layer of neural elements with both positive and negative random synaptic weight values. This layer processes the output vector from the two-dimensional array before it passes in to the input of the one-dimensional array, as shown in Fig. 22. The qth neuron in the intermediate layer has a synaptic weight vector:

$$\bar{\mathbf{V}}_q = \alpha_{q_1}\bar{i} + \alpha_{q_2}\bar{j} + \dots .$$

The set of weight vectors of all the intermediate neurons, therefore, define a surface which passes through the origin. The output of the qth intermediate neuron is produced by the scalar product of the intermediate neuron weight vector and the output excitation, vector $\bar{\mathbf{E}}_1$, from the two-dimensional array, so:

$$\eta_q = \bar{\mathbf{V}}_q \cdot \bar{E}_1,$$

and, the outputs of all the intermediate neurons form a new excitation vector $\bar{\mathbf{E}}_2$:

$$\mathbf{E}_2 = [\eta_1 \dots \eta_q \dots \eta_M],$$

where $\bar{\mathbf{E}}_2$ is the required projection of $\mathbf{E}_1$, onto the surface through the origin.

11.1 Applications of the array dimension bottleneck to speaker independent vowel maps

The work on bottlenecks was originally prompted by the desire to generate speaker independent neural maps of speech sounds. One relatively speaker-independent representation of vowel sounds is the ratio of the first two format peaks in the spectrum of the sound. In principle it seems that the bottleneck could provide such maps, although this has yet to be confirmed with real speech data. For example, if spectral vectors derived from speech are applied to a two-dimensional array, it will eventually order such that the position of its excitation peak has coordinates related to the formant peak values F_1 and F_2. Passing the output excitation vector of the two-dimensional array through the bottleneck should cause the one-dimensional array to become organized in terms of the 'angular bearing' of the F_1, F_2 coordinate of the sound. This is crudely related to the required formant frequency ratio.

11.2 Line angle and position extraction

Another application of the bottleneck which has been investigated by simulation is to obtain a neural map coding of the translation of a line in an image field independent of its angle and, vice-versa, a neural map coding of the line's angle, independent of translation.

In the simulation straight lines of variable position, P, and the angle, θ, are defined within a 10×10 pixel field. The 100-dimensional vector derived from the image element outputs are inherently two-dimensional since they have only two degrees of freedom, P and θ. Consequently, application of a large number of the image vectors to a two-dimensional array should cause it to order so that its output excitation peak has coordinates related directly to P and θ, as shown in Fig. 23.

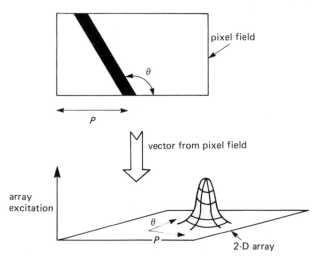

Figure 23   *Two-dimensional array ordering on image of line at variable angle and position.*

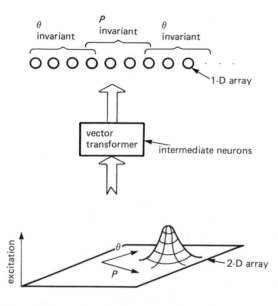

Figure 24 *Partial translation and angle invariance obtained using an array bottleneck.*

This has been confirmed by simulation, although care must be taken to 'blurr' the line slightly otherwise ordering will not occur. The reason for this has already been fully explained in the context of peak position mapping and is because the vector representing the image must move smoothly through its space as P or θ varies and not 'jump' from dimension to dimension.

Approximate translation and angular invariant mappings of the line can now be obtained by passing the output of the two-dimensional array through a layer of intermediate neurons acting as a transformer and then

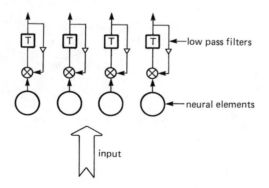

Figure 25 *Bandwidth bottleneck.*

applying the transformed vector to a one-dimensional array which becomes ordered in terms of the angular bearing of the P, θ coordinates of the line. Examination of Fig. 24 shows that some parts of the array are sensitive to P but relatively insensitive to θ while in other regions of the array, the reverse is true.

12. The bandwidth bottleneck

Frequently it is necessary to extract some features which are characteristic of a particular *temporal sequence* of patterns. For example, in the context of speech recognition, it is sometimes desirable to recognize a particular sequence of spectral vectors as characteristic of a particular phoneme. Such spectral vectors are usually obtained by sampling the short-term spectrum of the speech at about 10-ms intervals which corresponds to the Nyquist sampling rate, given a maximum articulation frequency of about 50 Hz.

Characteristic features of this type of sequence are very simply produced on a neural map by the introduction of a bandwidth bottleneck

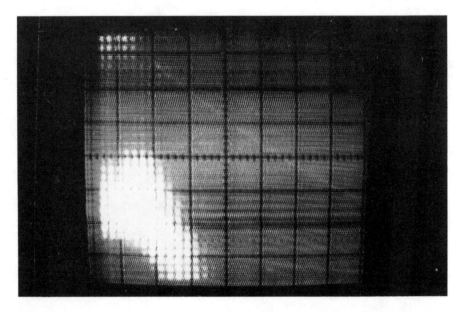

(a)

Figure 26 (*a*) *Excitation due to 'EE' as in 'bead'.* (*b*) *Excitation due to 'E' as in 'bed'.* (*c*) *Excitation due to 'AA' as in 'cat'.* (*d*) *Excitation due to 'UU' as in 'good'.* (*e*) *Excitation due to 'AR' as in 'car'.*

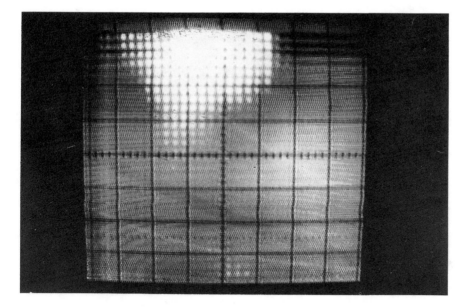

(b)

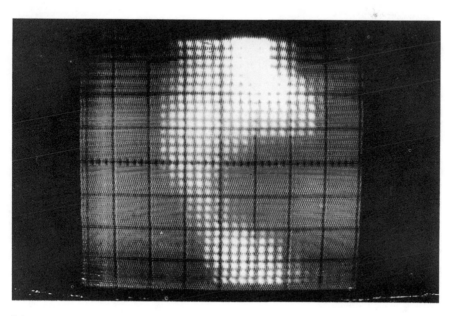

(c)

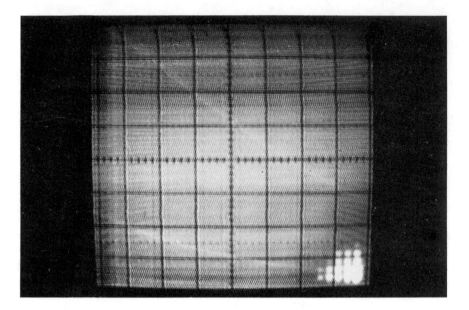

(d)

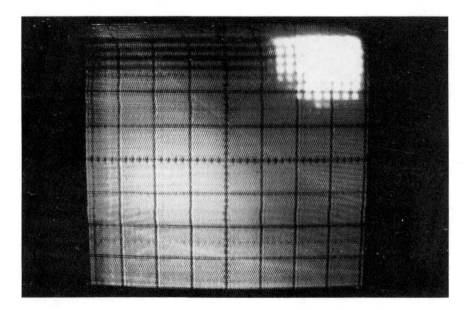

(e)

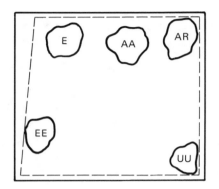

Figure 27   *Plot of vowel positions in array.*

in the array. The bandlimiting is achieved by making the output excitation of each neural element persist with exponential decay, even after the input has ceased. In essence, each neural element produces an output which is passed through a first-order low pass filter, as shown in Fig. 25.

The effect of the filters can be seen by looking at Fig. 26 which shows the output excitations of a 29 × 29 neural array which has self-organized on large amounts of natural speech. The excitation patterns correspond to a number of different vowel sounds. Each different sound is spectrally analysed and applied to the array at 10-ms intervals. The region of the array which is excited by each sound is plotted in Fig. 27, which shows that the neural map reflects the phonetic relationship between them.

Now say that we want to generate an output excitation vector which is characteristic of the vowel transaction. In the absence of the excitation persistence in each neural element, a series of distinct excitation peaks would be produced in the array at 10-ms intervals as the time-varying spectrum of the vowel transition is sampled. At any instant the output excitation of the array would only contain information about the instantaneous sound and none about the sound sequence.

Fig. 28 shows the effect of including excitation persistence. The output excitations in the array after completion of several transitions are shown and clearly information about the nature of the sequence has been coded in the shape of the excitation trajectory. The single output excitation vector produced by the array is characteristic of the entire sequence, covering a time roughly equal to the time constant of the persistence.

Several points should be noted. Firstly this system actually needs to be over-sampled relative to the Nyquist rate such that successive input vectors only change by a small amount and, therefore, cause the array excitation peak to move incrementally across the array and form a

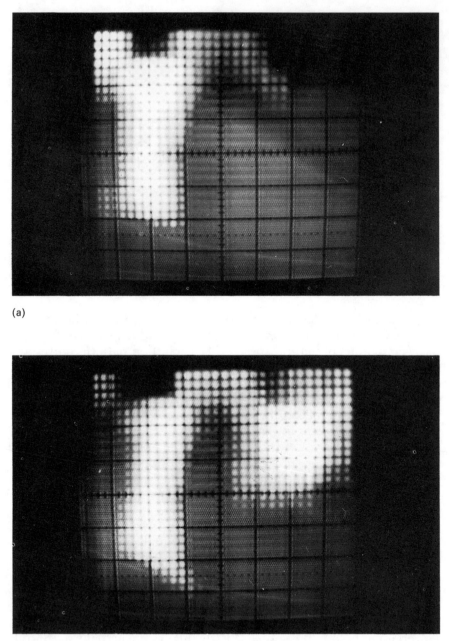

(a)

(b)

Figure 28   (a) *Trajectory due to transition 'AA–EE'.* (b) *Trajectory due to transition 'EE–AA'.* (c) *Trajectory due to transition 'EE–AA–UU'.*

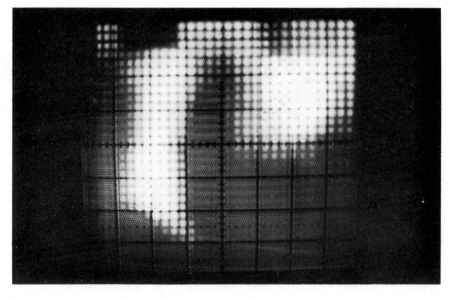

(c)

continuous trajectory. In the context of speech recognition we believe that an interval of 2–4 ms is optimal. Secondly, this sytem could not work in an array which was not topologically ordered: incremental changes in the input vector could cause the excitation peak to jump over the array, again leading to non-continuous trajectories. Lastly, the time constant of the persistence needs to be chosen with care. If it is made too short then only a very short sequence can be encoded by the single output excitation vector. If it is made too long, different sequences will not be discriminable because all neurons will be stimulated at some time and will remain excited. This leads to a final excitation vector which is virtually the same regardless of the order of the sequence.

References

1. Kohonen, T. *Self Organisation and Associative Memory* (Springer Verlag, 1982).
2. Rumelhart, D. E. & Hinton, G. *Learning Internal Representations by Error Propagation* ICS Report 8506, University of California, September 1985.

5 Backpropagation in non-feedforward networks

Luís B. Almeida

Institute of Computer Systems, University of Lisbon, Rua Alves Redol 9
Lisbon, Portugal

Abstract

Backpropagation is a powerful supervised learning rule for networks with hidden units. However, as originally introduced, and as described in Chapter 4, it is limited to feedforward networks. In this chapter we derive the generalization of backpropagation to non-feedforward networks. This generalization happens to take a very simple form: the error propagation network can be obtained simply by linearizing, and then transposing, the network to be trained.

Networks with feedback necessarily raise the problem of stability. We prove that the error propagation network is always stable when training is performed. We also derive a sufficient condition for the stability of the non-feedforward neural network, and we discuss the problem of the possible existence of multiple stable states. Finally, we present some experimental results on the use of backpropagation in non-feedforward networks.

1. Introduction

Backpropagation, as originally introduced[1-3] (see also Chapter 4) is a learning technique for feedforward networks, ie, networks in which the interconnections form no feedback loops.* The main topic of this chapter is the extension of backpropagation to non-feedforward networks, ie, the elimination of the restriction that there be no loops in the network. We will see that the resulting learning procedure is a natural extension of the original backpropagation technique, though its derivation is somewhat more involved. We will then address the problem of network stability, which necessarily arises when one considers a network with feedback loops, and we will present some experimental results on non-feedforward

---

*We will also call these networks *multi-layer perceptrons*, since they can be considered as a generalization of the single-layer perceptron of Rosenblatt.[14]

74

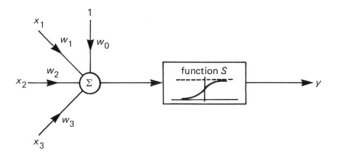

Figure 1   *Structure of a network unit.*

networks. Finally, relationships of these networks with other structures, namely Hopfield networks[4,5] and Boltzmann machines[6] (see also Chapter 4) are discussed. The work presented in this chapter was first reported by the author in Almeida 1987(a) and Almeida 1987(b) an independent, somewhat different derivation of the same learning rule was presented by Pineda.[9]

Before proceeding to the derivation of the learning procedure, it is important to clarify the context that we are assuming. We will consider a network of units of the type depicted in Fig. 1, ie, in which a weighted sum of the inputs is performed (including a bias term $\mathbf{w}_0$), the result of this sum (also called the *activation level* of the unit) being fed through a non-linear element, with a differentiable input–output function S.

We will assume that we present each input pattern to the network long enough for it to reach stable equilibrium, and only then do we observe its outputs, and compare them to the desired ones (the issue of whether the network is guaranteed to reach stability will be addressed later, in Section 3). Finally, we will assume that the function to be learned by the network is combinatorial, ie, that the desired outputs depend only on the present inputs, and not on past ones. Note that a different class of non-feedforward networks was considered in Rumelhart *et al.*, 1986; in these networks, a sample-and-hold operation was assumed to be per-formed synchronously at the outputs of all units, and the function to be learned was sequential, ie, desired outputs depended both on present and past inputs. The existence of the synchronous sample-and-hold effectively breaks the feedback loops, allowing the network to be transformed into an equivalent feedforward one, as had already been suggested by Minsky and Papert.[10]

2. Derivation of the learning rule

Let us consider a network with N units, whose outputs we designate by y_n ($n = 1, \ldots, N$), and with external inputs x_k ($k = 1, \ldots, K$). Denote by $\mathbf{a}_{ni}$

the weight in the interconnection from unit n to unit i, by $\mathbf{b}_{ki}$ the weight in the interconnection from external input k to unit i, and by $\mathbf{c}_i$ the bias term of unit i. The activation levels of the units are then given by:

$$s_i = \sum_{n=1}^{N} \mathbf{a}_{ni} y_n + \sum_{k=1}^{K} \mathbf{b}_{ki} x_k + \mathbf{c}_i \qquad (i = 1, \ldots, N), \qquad (1)$$

and the unit outputs by:

$$y_i = S_i(s_i) \qquad (i = 1, \ldots, N), \qquad (2)$$

where S_i is the non-linear function in unit i (this function may vary from one unit to another). Sigmoids are the most frequently used functions S_i, in backpropagation experiments. However, any other continuously differentiable functions are also acceptable from a theoretical viewpoint. If we designate by O the set of units that produce the external outputs of the network, these outputs are given by:

$$o_p = y_p. \qquad (p \in O). \qquad (3)$$

Given a specific input vector $[x_k]$, the solutions of equations (1–3) are the equilibrium states of the network. A network implemented in analogue hardware would find a solution 'automatically' (assuming that no unstability occurred). In computer simulations, the solution can only be found by iterative techniques, because of the non-linearity of the functions S_i and of the existence of feedback. This, however, does not affect in any way the reasonings that follow.

In feedforward perceptrons, the units can be numbered in such a way that the matrix $[\mathbf{a}_{ni}]$ is triangular with a null diagonal, and Equations (1–3) yield the equilibrium state of the network in a straightforward manner. If we denote by d_p the desired values of the outputs for the specific input vector being considered, the output errors are given by

$$e_p = o_p - d_p \qquad (p \in O), \qquad (4)$$

and the total squared error for that input vector is

$$E = \sum_{p \in O} e_p^2. \qquad (5)$$

Backpropagation is a learning rule that corresponds to gradient minimization of the average of E (this average is computed over all input vectors in a specific training set). The essential point of this learning rule is that in feedforward perceptrons the partial derivatives of E relative to the interconnection weights can be computed through a simple backward propagation of the output errors e_p. We will see that this backward propagation procedure can be formulated in terms of simple operations (linearization and transposition) performed on the perceptron network.

Consider again a general perceptron (feedforward or not). A new network can be obtained by linearization of the perceptron around an equilibrium state. Denoting its variables by a prime, the equations of the linearized network are:

$$s'_i = \sum_{n=1}^{N} \mathbf{a}_{ni} y'_n + \sum_{k=1}^{K} \mathbf{b}_{ki} x'_k \qquad (i = 1, \ldots, N), \qquad (6)$$

$$y'_i = D_i(s_i)s'_i \qquad (i = 1, \ldots, N), \qquad (7)$$

$$o_p = y_p \qquad (p \in O), \qquad (8)$$

where s_i is the activation level of unit i of the perceptron in the equilibrium state, and D_i is the derivative of S_i. Note that in terms of the linearized network, $D(s_i)$ is just a constant coefficient.

In Fig. 2(a), an example of a simple feedforward perceptron is given, and in Fig. 2(b) we show the corresponding linearized network. Fig. 2(b) is drawn in graph notation. The important convention of this notation is that, whenever two or more branches converge at a certain node, the value present at that node is the sum of the outputs of all branches that converge into it. This convention eliminates the need for explicitly representing summations.

An important concept in the theory of linear networks is the concept of transposition.[11] It is most easily expressed in terms of graph notation:

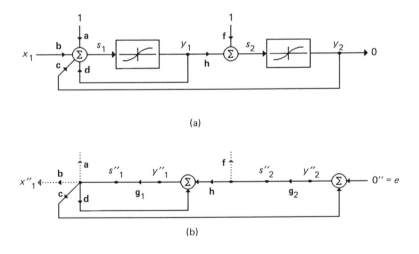

(a)

(b)

Figure 2 *Illustration of backpropagation in a non-feedforward network. (a) A simple non-feedforward network. (b) The corresponding error propagation network, obtained by linearization and transposition (the dotted parts are not needed for error propagation). Italic characters denote network variables, bold characters denote weights,* $\mathbf{g}_i = D_i(s_i)$.

the transpose of a network is obtained simply by reversing the direction of flow in all branches of the corresponding graph, while keeping the weights unchanged. Of course, this implies that the inputs of the initial network now become outputs, and vice-versa. As an example, the transpose of the network of Fig. 2(*b*) is shown in Fig. 2(*c*). The equations of the transpose of the linearized perceptron network are (using double primed variables for this new network):

$$
y''_i = \begin{cases} \displaystyle\sum_{n=1}^{N} \mathbf{a}_{in}s''_n + o''_i & (\text{if } i \in O) \\[2mm] \displaystyle\sum_{n=1}^{N} \mathbf{a}_{in}s''_n & (\text{if } i \notin O). \end{cases} \tag{9}
$$

$$
s''_i = D_i(s_i)y''_i \qquad (i = 1, \ldots, N). \tag{10}
$$

$$
x''_k = \sum_{n=i}^{N} \mathbf{b}_{kn}s''_n \qquad (k = 1, \ldots, K). \tag{11}
$$

The inputs of this network are o''_i ($i \in O$), and its outputs are x''_k ($k = 1, \ldots, N$).

Backpropagation in a feedforward perceptron can be easily formulated in terms of this transposed, linearized network. In fact, it is easy to see that if we apply the errors e_i at the inputs o''_i, ie, if we make $o''_i = e_i$ ($i \in O$), Equations (9 and 10) are exactly the correct equations for backward propagation of the error. Consequently,

$$
\frac{\partial E}{\partial \mathbf{a}_{qr}} = 2y_q s''_r \qquad (q, r = 1, \ldots, N). \tag{12}
$$

$$
\frac{\partial E}{\partial \mathbf{b}_{qr}} = 2x_q s''_r \qquad (q = 1, \ldots, K; \quad r = 1, \ldots, N). \tag{13}
$$

$$
\frac{\partial E}{\partial c_r} = 2s''_r \qquad (r = 1, \ldots, N). \tag{14}
$$

This is an interestingly simple result: in a feedforward perceptron, the appropriate network for backward error propagation is just the transpose of the linearized perceptron. And given its simplicity, one is immediately led to wonder whether this result will also apply to non-feedforward perceptrons. We will now prove that it does.

Consider again a non-feedforward perceptron. The partial derivative of the total error E relative to a weight $\mathbf{a}_{qr}$ is:

$$
\dot{E} = \sum_{p \in O} \frac{\partial E}{\partial o_p} \dot{o}_p = 2 \sum_{p \in O} e_p \dot{o}_p, \tag{15}
$$

where we have denoted by a dot the differentiation relative to $\mathbf{a}_{qr}$, for simplicity. If we differentiate Equations (9–11) relative to this weight, we will obtain

$$\dot{s}_i = \begin{cases} \displaystyle\sum_{n=1}^{N} \mathbf{a}_{ni}\dot{y}_i + y_q & (\text{if } i = r) \\ \displaystyle\sum_{n=1}^{N} \mathbf{a}_{ni}\dot{y}_i & (\text{if } i \neq r). \end{cases} \tag{16}$$

$$\dot{y}_i = D_i(s_i)\dot{s}_i. \tag{17}$$

$$\dot{o}_p = \dot{y}_p. \tag{18}$$

But these are just the equations of the linearized perceptron, Equations (6–8), with a single input y_q applied at node s'_r (with a unit weight). Since this network is linear and has a single input, its outputs will be proportional to this input:

$$\dot{o}_p = y_q t'_{rp} \qquad (p \in O, \quad q, r = 1, \ldots, N). \tag{19}$$

We will call t'_{rp} the *transfer ratio* of the linearized perceptron from node s'_r to output o'_p. An important theorem of network theory, the *transposition theorem*,[11] tells us that the transfer ratio between s'_r and o'_p in this network is equal to the transfer ratio t''_{pr} from o''_p to s''_r in its transpose:

$$\dot{o}_p = y_q t''_{pr} \qquad (p \in O, \quad q, r = 1, \ldots, N). \tag{20}$$

Replacing in (15), we obtain:

$$\dot{E} = 2y_q \sum_{p \in O} e_p t''_{pr} \qquad (q, r = 1, \ldots, N). \tag{21}$$

But since the transposed network is linear, the sum on the right-hand side of this equation is just the value that we will obtain at node s''_r if we apply the errors e_p at the respective inputs o''_p:

$$\frac{\partial E}{\partial \mathbf{a}_{qr}} = 2y_q s''_r \qquad (q, r = 1, \ldots, N), \tag{22}$$

which is exactly the same as Equation (12). Similar derivations could be given for Equations (13) and (14), completing the proof that the transpose of the linearized perceptron is still the appropriate error propagation network, in the case of non-feedforward systems.

Fig. 3(*a*) shows an example of a perceptron with feedback, and in Fig. 3(*b*) is the corresponding error propagation network. The preceding results mean that, for example:

$$\frac{\partial E}{\partial c} = 2y_2 s''_1. \tag{23}$$

79

$$\frac{\partial E}{\partial h} = 2y_1 s''_2. \tag{24}$$

These results mean that training of a non-feedforward network through backpropagation can be done in much the same way as for a feedforward network. We apply a pattern at the input, and find the corresponding outputs. We then compute the output errors, which we apply at the

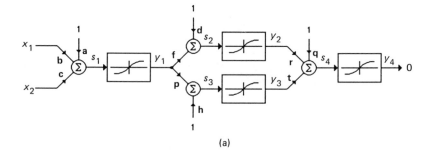

(a)

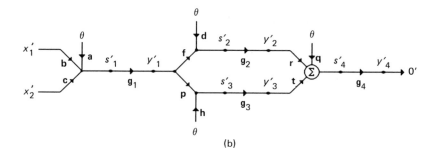

(b)

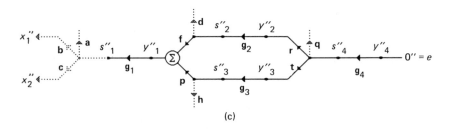

(c)

Figure 3 *Illustration of backpropagation in a feedforward network. (a) A simple feedforward network. (b) The corresponding linearized network, drawn in graph notation. (c) The transpose of (b): this is the error propagation network (dotted parts are not needed for error propagation). Italic characters denote network variables, bold characters denote weights,* $\mathbf{g}_i = D_i(s_i)$, D_i *being the derivative of* S_i.

inputs of the error propagation network. Equations (12–14) then give us the components of the gradient of E relative to the weights, from which the weight updates can be computed. The only important difference relative to feedforward networks consists of the fact that we now must let the perceptron network reach equilibrium before observing its outputs, and we must also let the error propagation network reach equilibrium before observing the values s''_r, for use in Equations (12–14). As mentioned in the introduction, the issues of whether the perceptron and the error propagation network are stable or not, will be dealt with in Section 3.

An important property of backpropagation, both in feedforward and non-feedforward networks, is that it is local: if we consider a hardware implementation of a perceptron together with the corresponding error propagation network, and if the two networks are implemented side by side, the circuitry for weight update will only need short local inter-connections. A non-local learning rule would make hardware imple-mentation of a reasonably sized network very difficult because of the enormous number of long interconnections that would be needed.

3. Stability

In this section we will address some stability issues that arise in perceptrons with feedback. First of all, the problem of whether the error propagation network is stable or not will be discussed. We will then derive a sufficient condition for the stability of the perceptron network, and finally we will examine the possibility of the existence of multiple stable states for the same input vector.

3.1 Stability of the error propagation network

As noted in the preceding section, we must let the error propagation network reach equilibrium before observing its node variables, s''_r. Therefore, it is most desirable that this network be stable. An unstable error propagation network might still have some interest in theoretical terms, but it would be difficult to use in practical applications. Fortunately, it is easy to show that, when error propagation is performed, the error propagation network is always stable, if some precautions are taken. In fact, it is a well-known result from the theory of dynamical systems[12] that the stability of a network at an equilibrium state is equivalent to the stability of the network obtained through linearization around that state (except in some boundary situations that we shall not detail here, but which occur with essentially zero probability). On the other hand, the stability of a linear network depends on the eigenvalues of its system matrix, and these eigenvalues are not affected by transposition of this matrix (network transposition, in dynamical terms, corresponds to the transposition of the system matrix). Therefore, the stability of the linearized network is equivalent to the stability of its transpose. Finally, this means that if the perceptron network is stable, the error propagation network also is, and since we have assumed that we always let the perceptron reach stability before observing the outputs and propagating the errors, stability of the error propagation network is guaranteed.

One should note that in this reasoning there was an implicit assumption which should be made clear: in fact, Equations (6–8) and (9–11), which were used for the linearized network and its transpose, respectively, in the derivation of the learning rule, concerned only the static behaviour of these networks. However, in the above reasoning about stability, it was assumed that these networks are the linearized perceptron and its transpose, respectively, not only in static but also in dynamical terms. In practice, this means that for stability of the error propagation network to be guaranteed, the dynamical properties of the error propagation network should closely match those of the perceptron.

3.2 Stability of the perceptron network

While stability of the error propagation network was relatively easy to deal with, the issue of the stability of the perceptron itself is much more difficult. Up to now we have assumed that some time after presentation of an input vector, which is held constant, the network would reach equilibrium. However, the perceptron being a non-linear system with feedback, other situations may arise: it can oscillate, or even exhibit chaotic behaviour; if the functions S_i are unbounded, it can also diverge toward infinity.

We do not know of any useful necessary and sufficient condition for stability of such a network. However, at least two sufficient conditions for stability of neural networks exist: the Cohen–Grossberg criterion[13] and Hopfield's weight symmetry condition[4,5] (the latter is a particularly simple special case of the former). Here, we shall derive a sufficient condition for stability which is a generalization of weight symmetry, while still being a special case of the Cohen–Grossberg criterion.

Before deriving this condition, let us note that while the equilibrium states of the perceptron network depend only on the static characteristics of its units, stability of these states depends on the dynamical properties of the units, too. Therefore, Equations (1–3), which were adequate for defining the equilibrium states of the perceptron, tell us nothing about the stability of those states. For studying stability, we have to make some assumptions about the dynamical properties of the units.

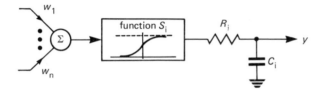

Figure 4   *A model of the assumed dynamical behaviour of the network units.*

If an implementation of the perceptron in analogue hardware is envisaged, it is quite natural to consider the units as exhibiting a low-pass behaviour (even if their maximum operating frequency is very high). Therefore a simple, plausible dynamical model for the units is the one depicted in Fig. 4, where the input summation and the non-linear element are assumed to be instantaneous, and the latter is also assumed to have zero output impedance. The subscript i in the resistor and the capacitor indicates that their values can vary from one unit to another.

In passing from the static Equations (1–3) to the dynamical ones, we must replace Equation (2) by:

$$\frac{dy_i}{dt} = \frac{1}{R_i C_i}[S_i(s_i) - y_i] = \tau_i^{-1}[S_i(s_i) - y_i], \tag{25}$$

where $\tau_i = R_i C_i$. Therefore,

$$\frac{dy_i}{dt} = \tau_i^{-1}\left[S_i\left(\sum_{n=1}^{N} a_{ni} y_n + \sum_{k=1}^{K} b_{ki} x_k + c_i\right) - y_i\right]. \tag{26}$$

We shall prove that a sufficient condition for the stability of the network is that the S_i be strictly increasing and bounded, and that there exist positive coefficients μ_i such that:

$$\mu_i a_{ni} = \mu_n a_{in} \qquad (i, n = 1, \ldots, N). \tag{27}$$

For this pupose, let us consider the *energy function:*[*]

$$W = -\frac{1}{2}\sum_{n=1}^{N}\sum_{i=1}^{N} \mu_i a_{ni} y_n y_i - \sum_{k=1}^{K}\sum_{i=1}^{N} \mu_i b_{ki} x_k y_i - \sum_{i=1}^{N} \mu_i c_i y_i + \sum_{i=1}^{N} \mu_i U_i(y_i), \tag{28}$$

where U_i is a primitive of S_i^{-1} (the functions S_i are invertible, since they are strictly monotonic). In dynamical system nomenclature, W would be called a *Liapunov function.*[12] Note that if S_i are sigmoids, the U_i are

---

[*] A very similar energy function was used by Hopfield (1984) in a network of analogue-valued units, which are slightly different from those of Fig. 4.

83

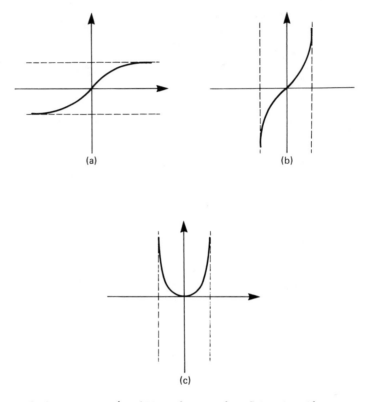

Figure 5   *The function S_i, S_i^{-1} and U_i, in the case where S_i is a sigmoid.*

U-shaped functions (Fig. 5).

Differentiating W with respect to time, we obtain:

$$\frac{dW}{dt} = \sum_{n=1}^{N} \frac{\partial W}{\partial y_n} \frac{dy_n}{dt},$$

(29)

with

$$\frac{\partial W}{\partial y_n} = -\frac{1}{2} \sum_{i=1}^{N} (\mu_n \mathbf{a}_{in} + \mu_i \mathbf{a}_{ni}) y_i - \sum_{k=1}^{K} \mu_n \mathbf{b}_{kn} x_k - \mu_n \mathbf{c}_n + \mu_n S_n^{-1}(y_n).$$

$$(n = 1, \dots, N). \quad (30)$$

But using (27) and defining $z_n = S_n^{-1}(y_n)$:

$$\frac{\partial W}{\partial y_n} = -\mu_n \left[\left(\sum_{i=1}^{N} \mathbf{a}_{in} y_i + \sum_{k=1}^{K} \mathbf{b}_{kn} x_k + \mathbf{c}_n \right) - z_n \right].$$

(31)

On the other hand, (26) becomes:

$$\frac{dy_n}{dt} = \tau_n^{-1} \left[S_n \left(\sum_{i=1}^{N} \mathbf{a}_{in} y_i + \sum_{k=1}^{K} \mathbf{b}_{kn} x_k + \mathbf{c}_n \right) - S_n(z_n) \right]. \tag{32}$$

One can readily see that, since S_n is strictly increasing, and μ_n and τ_n are positive, $\partial W / \partial y_n$ and dy_n/dt are always of opposite signs (or both equal to zero). Therefore, W can only decrease with time (or be constant, in which case the system will be at an equilibrium state). This shows that the network cannot oscillate, or have a chaotic behaviour. If the S_n are sigmoid (or otherwise bounded) the network also cannot diverge toward infinity, and therefore it must converge towards some equilibrium state. In terms of the function W, the network must always descend towards some local minimum, corresponding to a stable equilibrium state. Theoretically, it could also stop at a saddle point (or even at a local maximum, if initialized there), but residual noise, which always exists in analogue implementations, will move it away from there; in digital implementations and in computer simulations, a small amount of noise can be added, for the same effect. Since we always train the network at stable states, training through backpropagation can be viewed as moving these states (the minima of W) towards positions in which they produce outputs closer to the desired ones.

By making all the $\mu_i = 1$ in the condition for stability, Equation (27), we can see that this condition encompasses weight symmetry as a special case. Weight symmetry is important both because it has been used in various neural network structures (eg in Hopfield networks and Boltzmann machines), and because it is easy to enforce in combination with backpropagation: we simply have to use the same initial value for both weights $\mathbf{a}_{ni}$ and $\mathbf{a}_{in}$, and to update them both by the average of the updates $\Delta \mathbf{a}_{ni}$ and $\Delta \mathbf{a}_{in}$ that would normally be used for each of them. Enforcing Equation (27) in its general form is somewhat more complex.

As a final remark on this section, we should note that in the experiments that we have performed with perceptrons with feedback, unstable situations arose only very infrequently, when weight symmetry was not enforced. In the three experiments given in the following sections they never arise at all.

3.3 Multi-stability

A non-linear network with feedback can have more than one stable state, for the same input vector. These multiple stable states can give rise to a sequential behaviour, which could be useful for sequential applications, if a learning rule for these conditions were known. For the combinatorial applications that concern us here, multiple stable states are regarded as inconvenient, and a criterion guaranteeing the existence of a single stable state per input vector would be useful. No such criterion is known to the author. However, it is possible to draw some intuitive conclusions on this matter, as we will see below.

There is one special kind of multi-stable situation which has no disadvantages: this is the case where, of all the stable states that exist for a given input vector, the same single one is visited in actual operating conditions, whenever that vector arises at the input. In this case the network will behave as if the other states did not exist, and multi-stability will not be a problem.

For the other, more common, cases, an intuitive reasoning can convince us that the problem may not be too serious. In fact if, for the same input vector, multiple stable states are visited during the training procedure, learning will tend to move these states towards positions in which they produce similar outputs, which are close to the desired output values. Therefore, these states may merge, or if they stay separate they will probably come to produce similar outputs after training is complete, and the network will behave almost as if it had a single stable state per input vector. The author's experience, with the simulation of a number of small-sized perceptrons with feedback (up to about 20 units) suggests that multi-stability is not, in fact, a serious problem.

4. Experimental results

Three experiments with non-feedforward perceptrons will be reported here. The first is an example of a problem in which existence of feedback does not bring any great advantage. The other two are examples of cases in which existence of feedback is quite advantageous. In all the experiments reported here, the networks were fully interconnected, except for the restriction of being feedforward, where mentioned. The arctangent function was used for the S_i, rather than the more usual $S_i(s) = 1/(1 + e^{-s})$, but this is probably rather unessential in what concerns the performance obtained by the various networks. However, it is important for the correct interpretation of the weight values given in Table 2.

The first example consisted of a very simple problem: the network had

Table 1. *Results for $d = x^2$, $x \in [-1, 1]$*

Structure	No. of weights	Average RMS error
2 units, feedforward	5	0.25
2 units, feedback	8	0.17
3 units, feedforward	9	0.11

Table 2. *Results for the 'largest of 3 inputs' problem*

Structure	No. of independent weights	Average error rate per output (%)
3 units, feedforward	15	5.9
4 units, feedforward	22	5.5
5 units, feedforward	30	3.5
6 units, feedforward	39	3.6
3 units, feedback, unconstrained	21	1.7
3 units, feedback, symmetrical	18	1.4

an analogue input x, which could take any value between -1 and 1. There was a single output, and the desired value of that output was $d = x^2$. Both feedforward and non-feedforward networks were tried on this problem, each of them with ten randomly chosen sets of initial weight values. The results are summarized in Table 1. One can see that the existence of feedback actually improved the performance of the two-unit network somewhat, but at the cost of using extra weights. A three-unit feedforward network, with just one more weight, yielded a still better performance, appearing to make better use of its degrees of freedom. Similar results were obtained in other problems of the same kind (eg, $d = x^2$ with $x \in [0, 1]$, and $d = x_1 x_2$ with $x_1, x_2 \in [-1, 1]$).

In the second experiment, which we shall call the 'largest of three inputs' problem, the network had three analogue inputs $x_1, x_2, x_3 \in [-1, 1]$ and three outputs o_1, o_2, o_3. The outputs were desired to indicate which of the inputs was largest. For example, if x_2 was larger than x_1 and x_3, o_2 should have a high value, and o_1 and o_3 should be low.

Table 2 summarizes the results obtained with ten different random initializations for each structure. One can see that the use of feedback

Table 3. *Example of a set of weights obtained in the 'largest of three inputs' problem*

Source	Destination		
	Unit 1	Unit 2	Unit 3
Bias	-7.0	-6.9	-7.0
x_1	7.8	-3.4	-3.6
x_2	-4.7	6.2	-4.8
x_3	-4.0	-3.8	6.7
Unit 1	-3.0	-3.7	-3.8
Unit 2	-3.3	-2.4	-3.4
Unit 3	-3.7	-3.6	-2.5

resulted in considerable improvement: three-unit networks with feedback yielded less than half the error rate of even five- or six-unit feedforward systems, while having a significantly lower number of weights. The networks with feedback developed strong negative weights between each unit and the other two, in a kind of 'lateral inhibition' scheme (see Table 3). With these weights, when one unit became slightly more active than the other two, it tended to shut them down, and this in turn would allow that unit to become more activated still. This kind of positive feedback allowed the network to perform much better than feedforward networks.

When weight symmetry was imposed as a means of guaranteeing the stability of the networks, the performance still showed a slight improvement. This is not surprising, since the problem to be solved is symmetrical. Imposing weight symmetry actually forces the network in this case to be closer to optimality. And in fact, the weights developed when symmetry was not imposed were always almost symmetrical, as shown in Table 3.

The last example concerns a pattern completion problem. Ten random binary vectors, each having ten components, were generated. These vectors stayed fixed throughout the test, forming the patterns to be learned (since the patterns were generated at random, this was a worst-case situation, in a certain sense). When each pattern was presented to the network, only eight components of the vector were given, the network being required to guess the other two. The missing components were independently and randomly chosen for each new presentation.

Networks with feedback are much better suited for pattern completion problems than feedforward ones. In fact, in structures with feedback, one unit can be made to correspond to each of the pattern components; the outputs of the units corresponding to known components are then simply clamped to the known values, while the others are left free. When equilibrium is reached, the outputs of the free units represent the network's guesses about the values of the corresponding components. In this situation one can interpret interconnection weights between units as representing constraints between the components they represent, much in the same manner as is done in Boltzmann machines.[6] Of course, the network can have extra (hidden) units that do not correspond to any component.

As described above, structures with feedback are better suited to pattern completion problems because their units can be used interchangeably as inputs and outputs. Feedforward structures, with their rigidly defined inputs and outputs, are not so well adapted. We did, however, also experiment with feedforward perceptrons, for comparison purposes. We used a ten-input, ten-output structure, and in the inputs corresponding to missing components we applied a value midway

Table 4. *Results of pattern completion problem*

Structure	No. of independent weights	Average error rate per missing component (%)
10 units, feedforward	155	4.50
10 units, feedback, unconstrained	110	0.89
10 units, feedback, symmetrical	65	0.86

between 'low' and 'high'. Of the ten outputs, only those corresponding to missing components were observed, and only the corresponding errors were propagated. Table 4 shows the results of this experiment, where once again each structure was tested with ten randomly generated sets of initial weight values.

We can see that structures with feedback performed much better than those with feedforward, showing that they are in fact much better adapted to the problem. This better performance was achieved while at the same time decreasing the number of weights, because in this application the non-feedforward structures do not have any external inputs, in the sense used in preceding sections.

The symmetrical networks performed slightly better than the unconstrained ones. We do not know whether this difference is significant, or whether it is due to statistical fluctuations. It is not obvious, in this case, that optimal solutions should be symmetrical (though the interpretation of weights as mutual constraints, mentioned above, might suggest that they should be so). But what is certainly significant is that the symmetry constraint did not bring about any large impairment in the network's performance.

The above results, while still few in number, suggest two conclusions:

(1) One should not expect a major increase in the performance of a perceptron in every situation, just by 'throwing in' feedback. In most cases, the best network structures will probably turn out to have feedback only in some groups of units, just as layered feedforward structures are often preferable to fully connected ones in feedforward systems.

(2) Weight symmetry, as a means of guaranteeing stability, will probably not impair the network's performance significantly in many situations.

5. Concluding remarks

In this chapter we have presented a generalization of the backpropagation learning rule to non-feedforward networks. The resulting learning rule is a direct extension of backpropagation, if viewed in terms of network theory. The error propagation network was shown to be stable when error propagation is performed, and a sufficient condition for the stability of the perceptron network was derived. Finally, some experimental results involving networks with feedback were presented.

Of course, much remains to be done in this area. The problem of perceptron stability is still not sufficiently solved, since the stability condition we have derived is very restrictive. For example, feedforward networks, which are always stable, do not obey that condition. Acceleration of learning is also an important issue—backpropagation is a slow learning procedure, both for feedforward and non-feedforward networks.

Another important problem to be solved is which kinds of network topologies are best suited for given applications (layered or non-layered structures, feedback within layers or among them, feedback in all layers or in just a few of them, etc.). Answers to this problem will most probably come from the accumulation of experience with these networks: general theoretical results relating to topologies may be hard to find.

Implementation is also an important issue. Digital implementations are more complex for non-feedforward networks than for feedforward ones, since a loop must be included in the former to achieve convergence towards equilibrium. On the other hand, this convergence will be 'automatic' in analogue implementations. However, some care must be taken in these implementations to match the dynamical properties of the perceptron and the error propagation network, as noted in the discussion on stability.

Finally, an intriguing relationship exists between perceptrons with feedback and other structures, namely Hopfield networks[4,5] and Boltzmann machines:[6] if we make the interconnection weights symmetrical in a non-feedforward perceptron, and if we take the functions S_i as sigmoids that we make progressively steeper, approaching step functions, the energy function W defined in Equation (28) becomes equal, in the limit, to the energy functions of Hopfield networks and Boltzmann machines. This fact may help to unify concepts relating to these three network structures. For example, it is quite possible that backpropagation, seen as a means for moving energy minima, can be used to train Hopfield networks and Boltzmann machines.

References

1. Werbos, P. Beyond regression: new tools for prediction and analysis in behavioral sciences (PhD thesis in applied mathematics Harvard University, August 1984).
2. Parker, D. *Learning-Logic: Casting the Cortex of the Human Brain in Silicon*

(Tech. Report TR-47, Center for Computational Research in Economics and Management Science, MIT, Cambridge, Mass: MIT Press, February 1985).

3. Rumelhart, D., Hinton, G. & Williams, R. Learning internal representations by error propagation. In Rumelhart, D. E. & McClelland, J. L. (eds.), *Parallel Distributed Processing: Explorations in the Microstructure of Cognition* (Cambridge, Mass: MIT Press, 1986).

4. Hopfield, J. Neural networks and physical systems with emergent collective computational abilities, *Proc. Nat. Acad. Sci. USA* **79**, 141–152 (1985).

5. Hopfield, J. Neurons with graded response have collective computational properties like those of two-state neurons, *Proc. Nat. Acad. Sci. USA* **81**, 3088–3092 (May 1984).

6. Hinton, G., Sejnowski, T. & Ackley, D. *Boltzmann Machines: Constraint Satisfaction Networks that Learn* (Tech. Report CMU-CS-84-119, Carnegie-Mellon University, Pittsburgh, PA, 1984).

7. Almeida, L. A learning rule for asynchronous perceptrons with feedback in a combinatorial environment, *Proceedings of the 1987 IEEE First Annual International Conference on Neural Networks, S. Diego, CA USA, June 1987* (NY: IEEE, 1987).

8. Almeida, L. Backpropagation in perceptrons with feedback. In *Neural Computers, Proceedings of the NATO ARW on Neural Computers, Düsseldorf, September/October 1987* (Heidelberg: Springer Verlag, 1987).

9. Pineda, J. Generalization of backpropagation to recurrent neural networks, *Proceedings of the IEEE Conf. on Neural Information Processing Systems—Natural and Synthetic, Boulder, CO, USA, Nov. 1987* (NY: IEEE, 1987).

10. Minsky, M. & Papert, S. *Perceptrons: An Introduction to Computational Geometry* (Cambridge, Mass: MIT Press, 1969).

11. Oppenheim, A. & Schafer, R. *Digital Signal Processing* (Englewood Cliffs, NJ: Prentice-Hall, 1975).

12. Willems, J. *Stability Theory of Dynamical Systems* (London: Thomas Nelson and Sons Ltd, 1970).

13. Cohen, M. & Grossberg, S. Absolute stability of global pattern formation and parallel memory storage by competitive neural networks, *IEEE Trans. Sys. Man and Cybern.*, vol. SMC-13, no. 5, pp. 815–826 (September/October 1983).

14. Rosenblatt, F. *Principles of Neurodynamics: Perceptrons and the Theory of Brain Mechanisms* (New York: Spartan Books, 1962).

6 A PDP learning approach to natural language understanding

N. E. Sharkey

Centre for Connection Science, Department of Computer Science, University of Exeter, Exeter EX4 4PX, UK

Abstract

A parallel distributed schema applier is presented here which can be used to paraphrase schema-based texts. It has three integrated components, a network of actions, a network of scenes, and a paraphraser/sequencer. The system takes as input simple vignettes consisting of routine actions such as *go into the bank, write a cheque, give the cheque to the bank teller, receive the money, count the money, and leave the bank.* In the simulations reported here the system learns to associate 72 such actions with 25 general scenes. It then learns to collate these scenes into self-organizing schemata by installing coalitions of scenes as attractors in the scene memory network. All of the schemata share at least one scene and some share as many as four. The behaviour of the system is compared with psychological evidence from memory and reading studies.

Two of the innovations presented here are how to represent schemata with shared units as memory attractors, and how to move from one schemata to the next as the text evolves. Another important innovation in this system is that it reflects the centrality or importance of actions within a schema. During learning, some classes of action are seen by the system more often than others. We experimented with three frequency classes. The higher the frequency the more central or important the action. Once sufficient learning had occurrred, the system could be used to 'infer' the routine knowledge implied in vignettes. This was done as follows. An input action activated a scene unit which in turn acted to assemble a schema. When the schema was assembled it fed back activation to the action units. The activation levels reflected the degree of confidence that an action had occurred in the vignette. It turned out that the activation level on an action unit was greater the more central the action. This was what was needed for the paraphraser.

A difficulty encountered for paraphrasing was that the action units and the scene units were temporally unordered (as in any PDP system). A paraphrase must take into account the sequential nature of schemata.

We developed a least mean squares sequencer and found it to be very effective at learning to generate sequences of actions from the schemata. The sequencer was keyed by a contextual memory which consisted of the scenes that made up the schemata. Thus when a given set of scenes which formed one of the schemata were presented to the sequencer, it would output the actions of that schemata in their normal temporal order.

One useful point of this system is that access to the sequencer was through action predicates. These could activate a schema which would both complete the action level activations and act as a context for the sequencer. The sequencer could then output directly onto the action units. This meant that centrality was also reflected in the sequencer. Using a global threshold the memory output could be long, medium, short, or accurate. In this way the paraphraser could be used for inferencing at different levels depending on the required degree of informativeness.

1. Introduction

The focus of this chapter is on techniques for modelling the representation, acquisition, application and retrieval of routine human knowledge for use during text understanding. Other PDP research on language has mainly concentrated on issues of syntactic parsing,[1-3] case assignment,[4] and word sense disambiguation.[5] While these investigations are important, we also need to go beyond them and consider questions about how humans use their knowledge about everyday events and their knowledge of the intentions of others in order to understand language. It is only then that we will be able to build a natural language understanding device.

The research reported here is motivated by the assumption that texts written by humans for humans often contain only partial patterns of the information they are intended to convey. The reader is left to complete the missing information. Think how boring it would be if this were not the case. For example, supposing a friend told us the following tale:

I went to a restaurant last night. When I got there I turned the handle and opened the door. Then I went inside and looked around for an empty table to sit at. When I found one I sat down. A person came up to me and asked me what I would like to eat. They wrote down my order. Then they went away again. Later they brought me some food. I ate it and asked for the bill. When it came, I went up to the cashier and paid. Then I left the restaurant and went home.

In this example, much of what we already know is said explicitly. Usually, people assume that we know such things about restaurants and do not bore us with the details. These are normally left in the background to highlight other more interesting statements such as, 'it took us an hour to get served', or 'when the food finally came it was cold'.

Because people leave out so much in what they say it is very difficult to build machines that can understand human language. One 'traditional' artificial intelligence (AI) solution (or partial solution) to this problem has been to use schemata or scripts.[6] These are essentially pre-formed packages of information about social settings such as *catching a train, going to a wedding, or eating in a restaurant.* The idea is that particular cues in a text activate this information in memory and guide our comprehension. Psychological research over the last decade has supported a number of AI intuitions. Research using many tasks such as free recall, recognition, reading-time, and verification time has uncovered a number of stable findings. For example, there are strong indications that routine knowledge is *automatically* activated to fill in missing information. Automaticity contrasts with the idea that comprehenders wait until they *need* such information and then they retrieve it. In one series of experiments, Bower, Black, & Turner conducted a normative study in which they asked people to generate the routine actions for stereotypical situations such as *eating in a restaurant.*[7] They generated normative scripts from the most frequently mentioned actions and then used them to write short stories. Experimental subjects read these stories and, after a 20-minute delay, were asked to recall them freely. It turned out that many events that had not been mentioned in the stories were intruded into the free recalls. Importantly, these intrusions were, in the main, observed in the normative scripts on which the stories were based. Furthermore in related studies Bower *et al.* and Graesser, Gordon & Sawyer[8] gave people stories to read and then tested them on their recognition of certain actions in the texts. They found a higher likelihood of 'false recognition' for events that had appeared in the normative scripts than for other actions. The point is that people's interpretation of texts is coloured by their knowledge about routine events. They fill in missing information automatically.

One technique used in my laboratory to find out what is active in memory at a given time is the lexical decision task. In this task, people read a letter string on a computer screen (eg rabbits or assintart) and then decide as quickly as possible whether or not it forms an English word. When they have decided they press either a 'yes' or a 'no' button accordingly. Sometimes the decisions are preceded by textual indications of the appropriateness of a routine knowledge schema such as, 'the children's birthday party was going quite well'. Typically, we find that when people read a text containing such indications, they make faster decisions about words which had occurred in the normative scripts than other words.[9] We have used this technique widely and have made a number of discoveries about the automatic nature of routine knowledge access. In a recent study (Sharkey & Sharkey, in preparation), we found that even the mention of a place such as a restaurant (as in 'Bill and Harry argued as they walked past a restaurant') was enough to activate the restaurant schema in memory. Furthermore, we have found that sentences containing words from the underlying norms are read faster than similar sentences containing control words.[10,11]

We have attempted to model the above research (and others) by 'teaching' the systems some of the mundane knowledge that so readily comes to mind for the human. Earlier work on routines did not have a learning component,[12] and other research along similar lines has centred around a large symbolic component.[13,14] Work by Golden[15] is closer to our own and will be discussed later. In the remainder of this chapter I will describe some of the simulations that highlight the importance of some PDP techniques for use in AI. This research also represents several steps in the development of a computational model of the psychological processes involved in text comprehension.

2. Simulation 1: dynamic memory and movement through schemata

Dynamic memory
Schank and Abelson's routine knowledge schemata or scripts are divided into two levels: actions and scenes.[6] Each scene is made up of a group of actions. For example, a *restaurant* script consists of scenes such as *entering, finding a seat, ordering food, eating,* and *paying.* Each of these scenes governs a number of actions such as *reading the menu, calling the waiting person, asking for food,* etc. This scene–action hierarchy has received support in a number of psychological studies.[7] A further interesting finding concerning the internal organization of knowledge structures comes from Bower *et al.* Their experimental subjects read a number of stories, each based on a different script. Some of these stories were based on similar scripts, eg *a visit to a doctor* and *a visit to a dentist.* These are scripts that have certain scenes in common. Bower *et al.* found that when the subjects were asked to recall the stories (20 minutes after reading), they tended to intrude events from one story to another when the stories were based on scripts that shared scenes.[7]

These intrusion findings lead to a model of human knowledge structure in which scenes are shared between schemata. That is, instead of each schema being pre-compiled as a single unit, it is collated from shared units. Schank[16] responded to the Bower *et al.* data with a dynamic memory model: 'Script-like structures (corresponding to what we have called scenes or even parts of scenes) are constructed from higher-level general structures as *needed* by consulting rules about the particular situation...' Schank proposed abstract memory structures in situation memory, called memory organization packets (MOPs), which are used to organize episodic memory into scripts.

The same general view is taken here about dynamic memory and the compilation of scenes into routine knowledge schemata. However, the style of implementation and representation of our dynamic memory is radically different from Schank's. We use a parallel distributed representation in which there are no abstract organizers, such as MOPs, and no rules to consult. In the model presented here, schemata are self-organizing and result from a particular learning algorithm. The system's knowledge exists as connection strengths among a network of units. And a particular schema is represented as a pattern of activity over a set of units.

Content addressable memory

Our starting point was to treat the problem of scene assembly as one involving pattern completion. Each scene may be treated as a single bit in a binary vector—when a scene is active it adopts a $+1$ state and a 0 state otherwise. A system, when presented with a partial pattern (one or two scenes of a routine knowledge schema) would be required to complete the pattern, ie activate all of the other appropriate scenes. This idea appears to mesh well with Hopfield's work on content addressable memory.[17] Hopfield developed a 'one-shot' weight setting scheme rather like the outer product or Hebbian learning rule (cf Sharkey[18, 19]). The change in weight is given by

$$\Delta \mathbf{w}_{ij} = \begin{cases} s_i s_j, & i \neq j \\ 0, & \text{otherwise} \end{cases}$$

where s_i is the activation on the ith unit, and $\mathbf{w}_{ij}$ is the weight from the ith to the jth unit. Hopfield's procedure operates by installing the memory structures as minima of the energy function:

$$E = \frac{1}{2} \sum_{i \neq j} s_i \mathbf{w}_{ij} s_j + \sum_j s_j \theta, \tag{1}$$

where θ is a threshold (note that by setting the threshold to zero, we can remove the second summation term).

Once installed, each memory may be accessed from partial information by an iterative retrieval scheme which is a form of gradient descent in the energy function. An interesting property of Hopfield's scheme is that the contribution of a change in a unit, from -1 to 1 or vice-versa, to the total energy can be computed locally for each unit. The units are updated randomly and asynchronously by computing a potential change in energy:

$$\Delta E_j = \sum_i s_i w_{ij} - \theta \qquad (2)$$

If the energy change is positive, the unit adopts a $+1$ state or if it is negative a -1 (or in some systems 0) state.

One problem with Hopfield networks is that they only work effectively in conditions where the storage patterns are orthogonal to one another. Since the whole point of our exercise is to retrieve patterns with shared elements (scenes), this is a serious weakness. Hopfield's way around this was to use vectors of very high dimension. However, this gives the network a very limited storage capacity of approximately 0.15 bits per weight. We developed quite a different solution which will be discussed below.

A second problem with Hopfield networks is that if too many patterns are installed, there will be spurious minima in which the system can get stuck. Since the system can only descend in energy, it will never be able to get out of unwanted minima. Hopfield's answer to this problem was to set the initial state of the system a shorter Hamming distance away from the desired minimum than from any other minima. However, Hopfield did not provide a means to ensure the correct starting state.

An alternative method which avoids spurious local minima is the Boltzmann machine. Unlike Hopfield's deterministic unit updating, the Boltzmann machine updates the units stochastically. The probability that a unit i will be in a state $+1$ after being updated is given by

$$P_i = \frac{1}{1 + e^{-\Delta E_j \backslash T}} \qquad (3)$$

where T is the 'temperature'. The system works by means of an annealing schedule. A partial pattern is 'clamped' on the input vector (this means it is held unchanged throughout), then the temperature T is raised and then gradually reduced. At high temperatures the probability of a unit coming on is random and as T approaches 0 the system's behaviour approximates to a deterministic machine. By raising the temperature in this way and letting it cool gradually, the system is efficient at finding the appropriate local minimum.

Nonetheless, when we implemented a dynamic memory scheme based on the Boltzmann machine, we encountered a number of difficulties. The most salient arose when attempting to model movement through a text. Only the very simplest of stories involve the use of one knowledge structure; most stories necessitate access to several—one after another.

To see why this is a problem, let us consider a memory network consisting of six units: A, B, C, D, E, F. Imagine that two schemata are installed in this memory. The first consists of scenes A, C, E and the second consists of scenes B, D, F. Now in order to test the system, we clamp scene A and run the annealing schedule so that the memory relaxes on the appropriate A, C, E schema. This is easy, but what about subsequent inputs? What if the next input activated scene C? This scene is already active and so it seems highly implausible to release the clamp from A, put it on C and run the annealing schedule again (and this would run counter to priming findings[9]). On the other hand, if the new input was B, it would be necessary to clamp B and anneal in order to replace the A, C, E memory with the, now more appropriate, B, D, F schema. In order to model the empirical findings, these systems would have to *know* whether a new input belonged to an already active schema or to a new one. (Incidentally, a similar criticism obtains for the Rumelhart *et al.* schema model[20].)

The pulse-net
Our first solution to the problem of movement through schemata was the Binary and Continuous Activation System (BACAS).[21] We used a modified version of Hopfield's weight setting scheme which ensured that all scenes which never co-occurred were negatively connected. Then by analogy with an electronic device we developed the pulse mechanism which is now described.

To understand the pulse mechanism, imagine a set of hardware units arranged in a network so that each is connected to all the others. Each unit is an electronic device such that if it is in a $+1$ state, it will transmit either a positive or negative charge to its neighbours depending on the sign of their connections. If it is in a 0 state it will have no effect on the network. Imagine, further that, in any time slice, one of these units is selected for update—ie if switching it on leads to a decrease in energy, as described in Equation (2), then it will adopt the $+1$ state. In the pulse net, whenever a unit adopts the $+1$ state it generates a power surge or (square wave). This has the effect of switching all of its negatively connected neighbours to the *off* state. More formally, if a unit s_i adopts a state $+1$ during update then $s_j = 0$, if $\mathbf{w}_{ij} < 0$, otherwise there is no change until the next update.

The pulse has the effect of getting rid of unwanted knowledge structures and leaving the system a shorter Hamming distance away from the appropriate minimum than any other minima. If a scene belongs to the currently active memory then it will effect no change in the system since it will be positively connected to all the active units. Thus we have supplied the system with *knowledge*, in its connections, about whether or not an input belongs to the currently active knowledge structure.

An interesting property of the BACAS system is that no annealing schedule is required. The pulse mechanism leaves the system closer to the appropriate minimum than other minima (in Hamming distance), and so we can effectively use Hopfield's gradient descent method.

The trick is to get the correct weight settings. One of the main purposes of the network was to utilize sharedness. A problem with using Hopfield's weight scheme is that sometimes schemata with shared elements would have negative connections to and from those elements. This means that, with the pulse mechanism, some appropriate scenes could not co-exist. In BACAS we used a modification of the Hopfield weight setting scheme to ensure that each of the schemata was a local minimum and that they were connected to their shared scenes by small positive coefficients. In essence, we set the weights by hand (see Sharkey, Sutcliffe & Wobcke for details).[21]

Table 1. *A list of the five routine knowledge schemata and the 25 scenes used in the simulation. The shared scenes are marked with a +. Note that each schema shares at least one scene with at least three other schemata*

Cashing a cheque	*Taking the subway*
Enter the bank	Go into the subway
Write the cheque	Buy a ticket +
Stand in line +	Go to the trains
Transact with the teller	Find a seat +
Get the money	Get off the train
	Show the ticket +
Going to see a film	Leave the subway
Choose a film	
Go to the cinema	*Shopping in a supermarket*
Stand in line +	Enter the supermarket
Buy a ticket +	Collect the items
Show the ticket +	Stand in line +
Find a seat +	Pay for the items
Be in the cinema	Leave the supermarket
Leave the cinema	
Catching a plane	
Buy a ticket +	
Pack	
Go to the airport	
Check in	
Go to the plane	
Show the ticket +	
Find a seat +	
Fly	

In the current version of the model pulse mechanism with an incremental least mean squares (LMS) or delta rule learning technique to install the routine knowledge schemata as memory attractors.

Method

Materials

Five routine knowledge schemata were selected. All of these were based on the Galambos norms.[22] However, Galambos gives only a list of actions for each schema so we had to devise a reasonable set of scenes to govern the actions (the actions themselves are used in Simulation 2). A complete list of the routine knowledge schemata and scenes is given in Table 1.

The 25 scenes each had a corresponding bit in a 25-element input vector. When the bit corresponding to a scene was in the $+1$ state, that scene was said to be active. Three intercorrelated measures were used to specify the relationships between the states of the network. (i) The *Hamming distance* between one vector and another is the number of bits between two vectors eg the vectors $\langle 0\,1\,1 \rangle$ and $\langle 1\,0\,0 \rangle$ have a Hamming distance of 3. (ii) The *Euclidian distance* between the state of the system at time (t) and the state of the system at time $(t+1)$ is measured in terms of the distance between two points representing the respective states of the system in n-dimensional space. The distance between two vectors $\mathbf{v}_1$ and $\mathbf{v}_2$ in $\mathbf{R}^n$ is given as the length of the first vector minus the second vector, $\|\mathbf{v}_1 - \mathbf{v}_2\|$, where length $\|\mathbf{v}\| = \mathbf{v} \cdot \mathbf{v}$. (iii) The *angle* between two states of the system is given by $arccos\ \mathbf{v}_1 \cdot \mathbf{v}_2 / \|\mathbf{v}_1\|\,\|\mathbf{v}_2\|$. These measures were used to calculate the relative distances and angles between the schemata in the network, as shown in Table 2. The mean Hamming distance between the ten combinations of patterns was 10.8 (range 8–13; standard deviation $= 1.75$).

Procedure and architecture

The architecture is simple. There are 25 interconnected scene units and 25 input units. The weights between these units are initially set to small negative random values between -1 and 0. The learning was carried out as follows:

(1) A given knowledge structure was selected and appropriate bits in the input vector were set to the $+1$ state.

(2) The input units activated the scene units one at a time using the squash function:

$$s_j = \frac{1}{1+e^{-x}}, \tag{4}$$

where $x = \sum_i i_i w_{ij}$, where s_j is the jth scene unit and w_{ij} is the weight

Table 2. *Measures of the pairwise inter-correlations among the five routine knowledge schemata. Three different metrics are used: the angle in degrees, the Euclidian distance and the Hamming distance (see text for details)*

—	—	S1	S2	S3	S4	S5
S1	Angle	0	80.90	90.00	90.00	78.46
—	Euclidian	0	3.32	3.60	3.46	2.83
—	Hamming	0	11.00	13.00	12.00	8.00
S2	Angle	80.90	0	67.98	66.37	80.9
—	Euclidian	3.32	0	3.16	3.00	3.32
—	Hamming	11.00	0	10.00	9.00	11.00
S3	Angle	90.00	67.98	0	66.37	90.00
—	Euclidian	3.60	3.16	0	3.00	3.60
—	Hamming	13.00	10.00	0	9.00	11.00
S4	Angle	90.00	67.98	66.37	0	90.00
—	Euclidian	3.46	3.00	3.00	0	3.46
—	Hamming	12.00	9.00	9.00	0	12.00
S5	Angle	78.46	80.90	90.00	90.00	0
—	Euclidian	2.83	3.32	3.60	3.46	0
—	Hamming	8.00	11.00	11.00	12.00	0

between the ith input unit and the jth scene unit. As each unit came *on* the pulse mechanism deactivated all negatively connected scenes.

(3) The gradient descent algorithm (Equation (2)) was run for one cycle of random updates with the pulse mechanism operating every time a new unit came on.

(4) The scene unit values were compared with the input unit values and the LMS technique (delta rule) was applied. The actual input was

used as the *teacher*. This is a form of auto-association. The weight change for each unit is given by:

$$\Delta w_{ij} = \eta \delta_i s_i, \tag{5}$$

where η is the learning rate parameter ($\eta = 0.1$ in the current simulation), Δw_{ij} is the weight increment/decrement, s_i is the binary value of the ith scene unit and $\delta_i = (i_i - s_i)$, where i_i is the activation on the ith input unit.

(5) Another knowledge structure was selected and the procedure was repeated until the sum squared error $= 0$.

Results and discussion

Using the above procedure with $\eta = 0.1$, the system learned the five schemata to a criterion value of sum squared error $= 0$ in 19 learning cycles (considerably less learning is required when the schemata are less densely interconnected). After learning, the five knowledge structures were minima of the energy function E (Equation (1)). The energy values for each of the memory attractors were as follows: *cashing a cheque* $= -3.80$; *going to see a film* $= -15.74$; *catching a plane* $= -15.52$; *taking the subway* $= -13.24$; *shopping in a supermarket* $= -3.53$. There appears to be a direct relationship between the number of shared scenes in a schema and its energy value. The more scenes that a schema shares with other schema, the lower is its energy value.

After learning, the system was tested by starting it off with one of the stored schemata. Then a scene not in the current schemata was chosen and set to the $+1$ state. This initiated the pulse mechanism and the system was standardly given four asynchronous random update cycles to settle in the appropriate minimum. (When the updates were not random, ie the scene vector elements were updated in order from 0 to n only one update cycle was needed. However, this seemed less plausible for a truly parallel system than the random update.) The state of the system in two time slices is reported here: (i) immediately after the first initiation of the pulse mechanism; and (ii) after the fourth update.

For each of the two time slices, the following observation held for every simulation of moving from one routine knowledge schemata to another. The simulations exhausted all possibilities of the system being relaxed in one schemata and then moving to another. In state (i) after the initial pulse, the system always (a) *leapt* to a higher energy value; (b) deactivated all scenes in the *old* schema except those which were shared with the *new* one; and (c) moved the state of the system a shorter Euclidian and Hamming distance and a smaller angle from the desired attractor than from any of the other attractors. In one example, when the system was relaxed in the *catching a plane* minimum, the scene *go to the cinema* was set to $+1$. The result was that all of the units were pulsed to the *off* state with the exception of the newly activated scene and the shared scenes: *find a seat*, *buy a ticket*, and *show the ticket*. The new state of the system was a shorter Hamming distance from the target schema attractor *going to see a film* than any of the other schemata. In state (2) after four random asynchronous updates the system always stabilized on the desired energy minimum, ie the appropriate schema.

3. Simulation 2: centrality and schema completion

In Simulation 1, we were concerned only with the assembly of scenes. However, as was mentioned earlier, evidence suggests that routine knowledge schemata have at least two levels: scenes and actions. In Simulation 2 the interaction between the two levels was considered. The upper level consisted of the scene units and is described in Simulation 1. The lower level consisted of action predicates such as *get onto the train*.

Once the scene schemata had been installed as attractors in the network (as in Simulation 1), the next step was to attach the routine action predicates to their appropriate scenes. The idea was that activation would be input to action units from a text. The action unit would, in turn, activate the scene units until one of them exceeded the threshold and adopted the $+1$ state. The pulse mechanism and gradient descent would then come into operation and *complete* an appropriate schema at the scene level. Activation would then be passed down from the scene units to the appropriate action units. Thus the schema would also be *completed* at the action level.

In constructing this part of the simulation, an important psychological property, *centrality*, was incorporated into the system. Centrality refers to the importance of an action to a routine knowledge schemata. For example, the most central action of the *restaurant* schemata would be *eating the food*. The psychological validity of this notion was provided in a series of experiments by Galambos & Rips.[22] They found that the time to decide if an action belonged to a routine knowledge schemata was shorter if the action was more central. Of course if an action is central to a schema it will occur more frequently. In the simulation that follows we build in centrality by presenting the system with some items more frequently than others during the learning phase. The hope was that, after pattern completion, the more central actions would be more active that the others. In this way, the activity level of an action unit is thought to represent the degree of confidence of the system that the action had been present.

Method

Materials
The same five routine knowledge schemata were used as in the previous

simulation. However, this time the 72 actions were used as well as the 25 scenes. The actions were divided into three frequency groups. For the high-frequency group, one central action was chosen for each scene. The medium-frequency group had a second action for each scene and the low-frequency group consisted of all the actions that were left over. Thus there were 25 high, 24 medium (because one of the scenes consisted of only one action), and 23 low frequency actions.

Procedure
The LMS technique was applied to learn the connections between the actions and their appropriate scene units.

(1) Vignettes of action predicates were presented to the system one at a time. Each vignette consisted of either a single-action predicate or a small group. The actions in a vignette were always from the same scene. Each action was represented in the input vector by a single bit set to $+1$. The high-frequency actions appeared in every appropriate vignette; the medium-frequency actions appeared in one in three appropriate vignettes; and the low-frequency actions appeared in only one in six appropriate vignettes.

(2) Activation from the input vector was summated on the elements of the output vector. Each element of the output vector represented a scene unit. Unlike the preceding simulation the squash function was not used. Rather, activation from the lower level was simply summed on the upper-level units. The reason for this is that the links were to be bi-directional. That is, activation from the action units was to activate the scene units and then the scene units were to activate the appropriate missing action units. In a pilot study the squash function was used and the initial inputs to the scene units were all 0.5. This meant that negative weights grew between the actions of one scene and all the other scene units (including those from the same schema). Thus when the scenes sent activation back to the actions they cancelled each other out. However, when activation was a linear sum of the inputs, there were no connections from the actions from one scene and other scene units.

(3) The activity on the output (scene) units was compared to a target vector. This always had one bit set to $+1$ for the appropriate scene unit. The delta rule (Equation (5)) was then applied to learn the connections between the action(s) and the corresponding scene unit. Both tests were carried out with all actions.

After learning, two tests were carried out on the simulation. The first consisted of presenting an action to the system and then if a scene unit came on (had activation above zero) it was set to the $+1$ state and activation was passed back down to the action units. The second test began as the first one, except that when the scene unit adopted the $+1$ state the pulse mechanism came into operation and gradient descent was used as in Simulation 1. The weights between the scene units were those learned in Simulation 1.

Results and discussion

With $\eta = 0.1$, the system learned the patterns in 18 cycles. The learning was said to have been completed if there were no errors when each scene was presented with all of its corresponding actions. This meant that the high-frequency actions were presented 18 times, the medium-frequency six times, and the low-frequency three times.

Test 1

When an action was presented to the system the appropriate scene unit always adopted the $+1$ state. No other scene unit came on. Furthermore, when activation was fed back from scene units in the $+1$ state, only the appropriate actions were ever activated. These results held for the presentation of all actions in turn.

Test 2

Like test 1, when an action was presented to the system the appropriate scene unit always came on. This time, however, the pulse mechanism came into operation and the gradient descent algorithm was run as in Simulation 1. Since the same between-scene weights were used here, the system always successfully collated the appropriate routine knowledge schemata (see the results of Simulation 1 above). The crucial test was how the action units would behave when activation was fed back to them from the scene level. In this case all and only the appropriate actions were activated. This happened in all cases except when the first scene to be activated was a shared scene. This ambiguity led the system into an unpredicted schemata.

Centrality

It was suggested that the idea of centrality could be recreated in the simulation by controlling the frequency with which particular actions

Table 3. *The average activation on the different frequency classes of action units after action completion. These values reflect the centrality of the actions. Higher activation means more central actions*

High freq.	Medium freq.	Low freq.
0.74	0.22	0.07

were presented to the system during learning. The object was to find out that, if we presented three different frequency classes to the system during learning, there would be a difference in the activation levels of the actions after the action completion phase. This was successful. Table 3 shows the average activations of action units in the three frequency classes after a scene unit adopted the $+1$ state and sent activation back down to the action units.

In summary, combining the results from the first two simulations, a schemata access system has been built which takes action predicates as inputs and then fills in the routine knowledge required for understanding. This system has benefits over more traditional AI systems in that (i) it has fast parallel access to its schemata; (ii) the schemata are self-organizing, ie they are assembled dynamically; (iii) the system has been based on psychological data and thus moves some way towards a processing account of how humans use their routine knowledge during language comprehension.

In the next two simulations we examine a technique to get appropriate serial behaviour from schemata actions and then we see how this can be combined with the results of the schemata system just described.

4. Simulation 3: sequential movement through a schema

Human data indicates that whenever people read a story based on routine knowledge schemata with the actions out of *normal* order, they tend to recall the story in a normalized order.[7, 23] However, the networks we have discussed so far are temporally unordered. That is, when the system relaxes on a particular routine knowledge schemata, it knows which elements of memory are active but it has no idea which order they occur in. Clearly, humans have the ability to recall information, to a great extent in terms of how it was originally ordered. For our purposes, it is vitally important to have a system that can temporally order its memory so as to produce even the simplest paraphrase of a text.

However, eliciting serial behaviour from a neural network has long been regarded as a difficult task.[20, 24, 25] Of course, it would be a simple matter to say that sequence is an emergent property of the neural network and thus we only have to model it with something like a LISP list structure. However, this begs the question as to how sequential memory retrieval emerges from a neural-like system. Furthermore, it is important to use the same style of learning rules throughout a number of different domains if we are to make general scientific claims. Consequently the sequences discussed here are all based on parallel architectures and processes.

The first sequencer that we developed was a simple loop construct which moved a $+1$ along a binary vector. We used the output of one element of the sequence as the input for the next element and so on. A set of input/output pairs for a simple loop sequence is shown below.

$$
i_1 = \begin{bmatrix} 1 \\ 0 \\ 0 \\ 0 \\ 0 \end{bmatrix} \quad
o_1 = \begin{bmatrix} 0 \\ 1 \\ 0 \\ 0 \\ 0 \end{bmatrix} \quad
i_2 = \begin{bmatrix} 0 \\ 1 \\ 0 \\ 0 \\ 0 \end{bmatrix} \quad
o_2 = \begin{bmatrix} 0 \\ 0 \\ 1 \\ 0 \\ 0 \end{bmatrix}
$$

$$
i_3 = \begin{bmatrix} 0 \\ 0 \\ 1 \\ 0 \\ 0 \end{bmatrix} \quad
o_3 = \begin{bmatrix} 0 \\ 0 \\ 0 \\ 1 \\ 0 \end{bmatrix} \quad
i_4 = \begin{bmatrix} 0 \\ 0 \\ 0 \\ 1 \\ 0 \end{bmatrix} \quad
o_4 = \begin{bmatrix} 0 \\ 0 \\ 0 \\ 0 \\ 1 \end{bmatrix}
$$

Note that each of the outputs o is the input i on the next cycle. The output o_5 will be the same as i_1. The outer product learning rule was used (where $\Delta w_{ij} = \sum_i s_i s_j$) (see Sharkey[18]) to associate the input–output pairs. When these associations are learned, the system will cycle through the sequence until stopped. This technique is very effective to learn a sequence in 'one shot'. However, its one major drawback is that all of the sequences must be orthogonal to one another. And, as already pointed out, our target domain—the knowledge schemata—contain many shared elements.

At first thought, it seemed that it would be relatively straightforward to use the *last-output–next-input* technique in combination with the LMS procedure to learn sequences with shared elements. However, life is not so easy! The problem is that when the sequencer arrives at output actions which are shared with another sequence, it doesn't know which way to go. It sometimes runs off the rails into the wrong schema and then continues with the wrong sequence. For example, consider two sequences: *abcfxyz* and *defuvw*. Both sequences share the element *f*. Now suppose we start the sequencer off at *a*. It will produce *abcf* with no problem, but now it has a choice of *xyz* or *uvw*. The system may respond correctly but it has no way of making the correct choice. This is because it does not have a memory of which sequence it has been traversing.

One way around the choice problem, developed by Golden,[15] is to have the system output more than one action at a time. Golden's sequencer moves through the sequence with output triples. This works well as long as *all* three elements in any triple are not shared with any other sequence. If three or more are, then Golden's system will derail at critical choice points, as explained above. One of our schemata has four shared scenes and 13 shared actions—so Golden's sequencer would not fulfill our purposes here.

We needed a sequencer where we did not have to specify the sharedness limit for any given set of patterns. Our solution was to provide the sequencer with a contextual memory. Since schemata are usually activated by contextual information, we divided the input vector into two fields: a *context* field and a *sequence* field. Each sequence had its own context field and this served to disambiguate the sequence at choice points. The input to a context field was the group of scene units making up the schema of the sequence to be learned. This acted as a key to initiate the appropriate sequence of actions.

Method

Materials
The same five routine knowledge schemata were used here as in the preceding simulations. Each sequence consisted of an ordered list of all of the actions in a given routine knowledge schema. The actions were represented by a single bit in the input vector and a single bit in the output vector. Each sequence had a corresponding context field. This consisted of the scenes which made up the schemata. Each scene was represented by a single bit in the context field of the input vector.

Procedure and architecture
The sequencer consists of two layers of units (input and output) and one layer of weights. There were 97 input units divided into 72 units in the sequence field and 25 units in the context field. The procedure was as follows.

(1) The scene units of the target schema were input into the context field.

(2) The output layer was activated by the input layer using the squashing function (Equation (4)).

(3) The LMS technique was applied (see Equation (5)) with the first action of the sequence used as the target.

(4) The output of the sequence was then fed back into the sequence field of the input vector and the context field was held constant.

(5) The LMS technique was again applied with the next action in the sequence as the target.

(6) Steps 4 and 5 were repeatedly applied until the sequence was exhausted. Then the scene units of the next target schema were input into the context field and the procedure was carried on from Step 2.

Results and discussion

There are two sets of results to report here. The first is for the initial element of each sequence and the second is for the non-initial portion of each sequence. With an $\eta = 0.75$, the initial element of each sequence took around 300 learning cycles to reach an output criteria of 0.9. The rate of learning depended on the correlations among the context field patterns. These are the scene patterns described in Table 2. The more inter-correlated a pattern was the longer its initial sequence took to be learned. This is because the system has a tendency to generalize across similar context patterns and the unlearning of the generalizations increases learning time. To see the scale of this increase, the non-initial portions of the sequences were learned to the same criteria within only 50 cycles.

On this particular learning task, our sequencer was superior to the Jordan sequencer.[24] The Jordan sequencer is very good at learning strings with several repetitions, eg *aabacccd*. Our system would find such examples impossible. However, the Jordan sequencer is severely restricted by the length of the sequences. When we used it to learn our five routine knowledge schemata it produced some odd results. When the majority of actions were at the 0.9 criteria, several were around 0.9e−5. Despite repeated learning trials, there was little further improvement. In particular, the last three actions of the *catching a plane* schema stayed close to zero. This was the longest schema, with 23 actions. Jordan's solution to this problem would be to split the sequences into smaller chunks— these could be the scenes—and then two sequencers. The first would output the scenes in order and the second would run through the actions of each scene as it was output by the first. For the current learning task our sequencer was much simpler and far faster, with one layer of weights, than a system that would need four layers.

5. Simulation 4: memory retrieval, paraphrase and sequential access

We now examine how the three simulations reported above can be combined to form a memory retrieval system and a simple paraphraser. There is no further learning in this simulation. In the sequencer described above, the contextual input to initiate a given sequence consisted of the scene units from one of the five routine knowledge schemata. In other words the scene vector is one and the same as the context field for the sequencer. Thus the input to initiate the sequencer can be taken directly from the output of the scene collation process (Simulation 1). This is very straightforward. The new part of this simulation concerns how to combine the level of activation in the action network with the sequencer. Recall that in Simulation 2, after schema completion, the action units were in states of activity which reflected both their centrality and whether or not they had been actually mentioned. Clearly, in a paraphrase or a memory output we would like this information to be reflected. For example, in a short paraphrase we would want the actions actually presented to be mentioned along with those which were most central to the active schema.

In order to obtain a reflection of 'actual mention' and centrality, the output from the sequencer was input to the action network. As each action was output from the sequencer, its activation (always $+1$) was summed with the activation on the corresponding unit in the action network. In this way the most active unit would be the one that had been explicitly mentioned, the next most active would be the most central, and so on. The idea was that as each output from the sequencer was input to the action network, the appropriate action would be output if and only if its unit exceeded an output threshold. Each of the units in the memory net has the same output threshold. This threshold can be set globally to reflect desired degrees of accuracy. For instance in short paraphrase mode the system is at its most accurate. With the addition of the sequencer activation, the actual actions in the text just presented are recalled along with only the highly central ones. By reducing the output threshold we can achieve different degrees of memory distortion with less central actions intruding more and more.

Method

Procedure and architecture
The architecture of the system consisted of interacting parts: the scene–action network and the sequencer. These parts are joined in two ways. First, the scene vector acts as the context field for the sequencer; and second, the sequencer outputs are input to the action vector. The procedure is essentially a combination of the procedures of the simulations up to this point without the learning component. All the weights which were learned in the previous simulations are used again here.

(1) One or more actions were input to the action vector (ie the corresponding bits were set to $+1$) and this activation was summed on the scene units.

(2) When a scene unit exceeded the 0 threshold, it adopted the $+1$ state and the pulse mechanism came into operation (all scene unit negatively connected to the threshold unit were set to the 0 state).

(3) The gradient descent algorithm was applied for four cycles of

random updates. This set the state of the scene net to a minimum of the energy function (Equation (1)).

(4) Activation from the scene vector was summed back on the action vector across the same weights. This resulted in pattern completion of the schema at the action level. The level of activation on the action units reflected their centrality and whether or not they had been actually mentioned.

(5) The system waited for a prompt so say whether an actual, short, medium, or long paraphrase was required.

(6) The scene vector (in its role as context field) activated the sequencer and the output of the sequencer was fed back into the input field to produce *t* the next output in the sequence.

(7) At the same time as 6, the sequencer output activated the corresponding action in the action vector. If the activation on an action unit exceeded the output threshold (actual = 1.0, short = 0.7, medium = 0.2, long = 0), that action was output from memory.

Results

The simulation can be thought of as occurring in five stages: text input and activation, pulse operation, scene collation, action completion, and memory output. A trace of a two sample runs is given below along with different length paraphrases.

Input text: (go to the bank, give cheque to bank teller, leave the bank)

*********** pulse operating ***************

active scenes: enter bank

*********** pulse operating ***************

active scenes: enter bank, transact with bank teller

*********** pulse operating ***************

active scenes: enter bank, transact with bank teller, get money

*********** collating scenes ***************

stand in line
enter bank
write cheque
transact with bank teller
get money

*********** action completion ***************
⟨These are unordered but arbitrarily printed out reading from left to right along the action vector. The activation values are shown in parentheses.⟩

go to the back of the line (0.22)
stand in line (0.75)
move forward (0.07)
go to the bank (1.00)
go into the bank (0.23)
write down the amount of money on the cheque (0.74)
write down the date on the cheque (0.06)
write signature on the cheque (0.21)
record the amount of money on the cheque (0.06)
go to the teller's window (0.21)
endorse the back of the cheque (0.06)
give the cheque to the teller (1.00)
show identification (0.06)
receive the money (0.75)
count the money (0.22)
leave the bank (1.00)

************ sequencer activated ***************

paraphrase—long, medium, short, or accurate? → long

go to the back of the line
stand in line
move forward
go to the bank
go into the bank
write down the amount of money on the cheque
write down the date on the cheque
write signature on the cheque
record the amount of money on the cheque
go to the teller's window
endorse the back of the cheque
give the cheque to the teller
show identification
receive the money
leave the bank

paraphrase—long, medium, short, or accurate? → medium

go to the bank
go into the bank
write down the amount of money on the cheque
write signature on the cheque
go to the back of the line
stand in line

go to the teller's window
give the cheque to the teller
receive the money
count the money
leave the bank

paraphrase—long, medium, short, or accurate? → short

go to the bank
write down the amount of money on the cheque
stand in line
give the cheque to the teller
receive the money
leave the bank

There is also an accurate paraphrase mode which outputs only those actions which were actually mentioned. This output is not a special example of the operation of the system, but is typical of the output of the system.

6. General discussion and conclusions

The purpose of research reported here was to develop a parallel distributed schema applier for use as one part of a natural language understanding system. The aim was to base the schema applier, as far as possible, on data from psychology experiments with humans. To this end, four simulations were presented here. In the first, the problem of dynamic assembly of scenes into schemata was tackled. Unlike previous work in AI, the scenes in the simulation organized themselves into schemata under the direction of the text. In line with data from Bower et al.,[7] each schema had at least one shared scene with at least one other schema. An LMS learning technique was used in combination with the pulse mechanism to install each of the schema as attractors in the memory net. After learning, the system worked as desired. Turning one unambiguous scene *on* was sufficient to attract the state of the system to the appropriate schema. Furthermore, the operation of the pulse mechanism enabled the system to move from one schema to another under the direction of the text.

Simulation 2 was an extension of Simulation 1 to the action predicate level. The LMS technique was again used to associate a set of actions with each of the schemata. There were two main objectives to this association. The first was to provide a means of accessing the schemata from the text at the action level. The result was that when action predicates were input to the system they activated a scene or scenes. This

113

in turn set off the pulse mechanism and the gradient descent in energy collated the scenes into a schemata. The second objective was to complete the pattern of activation at the action level—to make the mundane inferences as it were. Psychological data suggested that actions should have differential activation according to their centrality in the scene to which they belonged. Centrality was modelled here by presenting the system with three different frequency classes of action predicates during learning. The most frequently presented items were those that were most central. In the simulation, after the scenes were collated, activation was passed down the same links that had been used for associating the actions with the scene units. It turned out that there was a marked centrality effect as reflected in relative activation values on the action units.

The third simulation was concerned with the sequential nature of the schemata. In the previous simulations the actions and scenes were not temporally ordered. In this simulation we tested an LMS sequencer and found it to be very effective at learning to generate sequences of actions from the knowledge structures. The sequencer was keyed by a contextual memory which consisted of the scene that made up the schemata. Thus when a given set of scenes which formed one of the schemata were presented to the sequencer, it would output the actions of that schemata in their normal temporal order.

The final simulation put all the pieces from the other simulations together to form a unified schema application system. One very useful point of this system is that access to the sequencer was through action predicates. These could activate a schema which would both complete the action level activations and act as a context for the sequencer. The sequencer could then output directly onto the action units. This meant that centrality was also reflected in the sequencer. Using a global threshold the memory output could be long, medium, short, or accurate. In this way the paraphraser could be used for inferencing at different levels depending on the desired degree of informativeness required. Furthermore, the memory output could now easily be seen to model the pattern of intrusions found in memory experiments.

The system described here is part of an ongoing project on the construction of a natural language understanding system based on connectionist principles. Amanda Sharkey has been refining some of the psychological work on how activation effects understanding of sentences. Richard Sutcliffe has been working on question-answering, and Nick Reeves has had some success with a back propagation verb disambiguator. The latter two have used microfeatural representation rather than the single bit representations used here. Using microfeatural representations would increase the scope of the current system and allow similarities of meaning to be taken into account. This is planned for the near future.

I have also built a computational model of action understanding using the goals of a character. This has been shown to fit well with human data on a goal–action decision task.[19,26,27] The Sharkey[19] version of the model provides a means of binding characters to goals in such a way that actions associated with the goals have the same bindings. This system has been designed so that it is compatible with the system described in current chapter. I plan to combine them in the next phase of the project. This will enable (a) actions to activate goals; (b) character binding on the actions; (c) decisions about goal and plan relationships; and (d) the generation of sequences of actions from goals (ie canned planning).

In sum, we have gone some way toward developing a model which demonstrates how some of the routine knowledge needed for language understanding could be automatically activated, deactivated and controlled by textual input. There is no central processor with an instruction set in the system. Furthermore, various learning techniques for installing routine schemata and action sequences have been demonstrated which could have general applicability in AI.

Acknowledgements

I would like to thank the Economic and Social Research Council (Grant No. C 08 25 0015) for supporting this research.

References

1. Waltz, D. L. & Pollack, J. B. Massively parallel parsing: a strongly interactive model of natural language comprehension. *Cognitive Science* (1985).
2. Selman, B. *Rule-based Processing in a Connectionist System for Natural Language Understanding* (TR CSRI-168. Computer Systems Research Institute, University of Toronto, 1985).
3. Fanty, M. *Context Free Parsing in Connectionist Networks* (TR174, Department of Computer Science, Rochester, 1987).
4. McClelland, J. L. & Kawamoto, A. H. Mechanisms of sentence processing: assigning roles to constituents. In McClelland, J. L. & Rumelhart, D. E. (eds.) *PDP*, Vol. II, pp. 272–326 (Cambridge MA: MIT Press, 1986).
5. Cottrell, G. W. *A Connectionist Approach to Word Sense Disambiguation* (TR154, Department of Computer Science, Rochester, 1985).
6. Schank, R. C. & Abelson, R. P. *Scripts, Plans, Goals and Understanding* (NJ: Lawrence Erlbaum, 1977).
7. Bower, G. H., Black, J. B. & Turner, T. J. Scripts in memory for text. *Cognitive Psychology* **11**, 177–220 (1979).
8. Graesser, A. C., Gordon, S. E. & Sawyer, J. D. Recognition memory for typical and atypical actions in scripted activities: tests of a script pointer +tag hypothesis. *Journal of Verbal Learning and Verbal Behavior* **18**, 319–332 (1979).
9. Sharkey, N. E. & Mitchell, D. C. Word recognition in a functional context: the use of scripts in reading. *Journal of Memory and Language* **24**, 253–270 (1985).

10. Sharkey, N. E. & Sharkey, A. J. C. KAN: a knowledge access network model. In Reilly, R. (ed.) *Communication failure in Dialogue and Discourse* (Amsterdam: Elsevier, North Holland, 1987*a*).
11. Sharkey, N. E. & Sharkey, A. J. C. What is the point of integration? The loci of knowledge-based facilitation in sentence processing. *Journal of Memory and Language* **26**, 255–276 (1987*b*).
12. Shastri, L. & Feldman, J. A. Neural nets, routines, and semantic networks. In Sharkey, N. E. (ed.) *Advances in Cognitive Science*, Vol. 1 (Chichester: Ellis Horwood, 1986).
13. Chun, H. W. & Mimo, A. A massively parallel model of schema selection. *Proceedings of the First Annual International Conference on Neural Networks*, San Diego (1987).
14. Dolan, C. P. & Dyer, M. G. Symbolic schemata, role binding, and the evolution of structure in connectionist memories. *Proceedings of the First Annual International Conference on Neural Networks*, San Diego (1987).
15. Golden, R. M. Modelling causal schemata in human memory: a connectionist approach (unpublished PhD thesis, Brown University, 1987).
16. Schank, R. C. *Dynamic Memory* (Cambridge: Cambridge University Press, 1983).
17. Hopfield, J. J. Neural networks and physical systems with emergent collective computational abilities. *Proceedings of the National Academy of Sciences, USA* **79**, 2554–2558 (1982).
18. Sharkey, N. E. Neural network learning techniques. In McTear, M. (ed.) *An Introduction to Cognitive Science* (Chichester: Ellis Horwood, 1988*a*).
19. Sharkey, N. E. A PDP system for goal-plan decisions. *Proceedings of the Ninth European Meeting on Cybernetics and Systems Research* (1988*b*).
20. Rumelhart, D. E., Smolensky, P., McClelland, J. L. & Hinton, G. E. Schemata and sequential thought processes in PDP models. In Rumelhart, D. E. & McClelland, J. L. (eds.) *PDP*, Vol. II, pp. 7–57 (Cambridge Mass: MIT Press, 1986).
21. Sharkey, N. E., Sutcliffe, R. F. E. & Wobcke, W. R. Mixing binary and continuous connection schemes for knowledge access. *Proceedings of the American Association for Artificial Intelligence* (1986).
22. Galambos, J. A. & Rips, L. J. Memory for routines. *Journal of Verbal Learning and Verbal Behaviour* **21**, 260–281 (1982).
23. Bellezza, F. S. & Bower, G. H. Remembering script based text, *Poetics* **11**, 1–23 (1982).
24. Jordan, M. I. Attractor dynamics and parallelism in a connectionist sequential machine. *Eighth Conference of the Cognitive Science Society*, Amherst, Mass., pp. 531–546 (1986).
25. Feldman, J. A. & Ballard, D. H. Connectionist models and their properties. *Cognitive Science* **6**, 205–254 (1982).
26. Sharkey, N. E. & Bower, G. H. The integration of goals and actions in text understanding. *Proceedings of Cognitive Science* **6** (1984).
27. Sharkey, N. E. & Bower, G. H. A model of memory organization for interacting goals. In P. E. Morris (ed.) *Modelling Cognition* (New York: John Wiley, 1987).
28. Sharkey, N. E. & Sutcliffe, R. F. E. Memory attraction: Learning distributed schemata for language understanding. Paper presented to the Edinburgh workshop on Connectionism and Memory.

7 Learning capabilities of Boolean networks

Stefano Patarnello and Paolo Carnevali

IBM ECSEC, Via Giorgione 159, 00147 Rome, Italy

Abstract

Boolean networks can learn to perform specific tasks. Here, some cases are described where a network is trained on a given problem, namely, a sub-set of examples of this task is provided to the system. This procedure results in a final network which is able to perform correctly on instances that differ from those in the examples, thus showing a capability to recover the general rule underlying the task. The training phase amounts to an optimization process which is carried out using simulated annealing, a search strategy derived from statistical physics. Depending on problem complexity, network size, and number of examples used in the training, different learning regimes occur. For small networks an exact analysis of the statistical mechanics of the system shows that learning takes place as a phase transition. Indeed, thermodynamical quantities related to this transition (critical temperature, specific heat) are related to the complexity of the problem. We also show that a problem can be efficiently learned when it can be implemented in many different ways, ie, generalization is an entropy effect. We also discuss a comparison between different learning schemes and optimization algorithms.

1. Introduction

Renewed interest in the study of neural networks has raised a number of interesting questions. On the one hand, people working in the biological framework are addressing problems concerning simplified neural systems or the close modelling of sub-systems (eg, the visual system), in an effort to emulate some basic qualitative features. Therefore in this area the main interest is devoted to quantities such as the storage capacity of the network, the ability to learn temporal sequences, etc.

Computer scientists are more interested in the potential that these paradigms provide to design new machines, which would be possibly more efficient than the state-of-the-art computers in the implementation of 'intelligent' tasks (such as pattern recognition or speech synthesis). In

117

the spirit of this approach, a commonly used strategy consists of specifying a set of examples of the problem (namely, a set of proper input–output associations). The main goal is the design of efficient *learning algorithms*, which can be mostly regarded as search procedures to find a structure of the network that correctly solves the problem. To which extent these algorithms should reproduce a plausible biological scheme to increase efficiency, is an open matter. A natural requirement is that the amount of information provided to the system (ie, the total number of examples) should be minimal, as handling a large set of input data may pose a difficult technical problem (as is often the case in the standard approaches to artificial intelligence). This second item is related to the potential *generalization capability* proper of these systems. The learning process is characterized by two regimes: when a small amount of information is provided to the system, this performs essentially as a memory device, where all the examples of the task are simply stored without recognizing any regularity in the sample set. When enough information is provided, then real learning takes place, and the trained network finally performs well, even when inputs not included in the sample set are presented. When this degree of generality is achieved, one can say that a *rule* has been recognized through the whole process. Unfortunately, the meaning of the transition to this kind of generalization regime is often unclear.

Here some of the items concerning learning networks will be addressed, starting from a specific model that we recently proposed.[1,2] Some of the aspects that will be analysed (generalization, connection with statistical physics, comparison among different training schemes) are quite general, and the conclusions that we draw for our system are likely to be extendible to other machines.

2. Description of the model

Most of the existing software implementations of neural systems are analogue devices. Sometimes the 'formal neurons' which are the information processors of the network are continuous variables within given bounds, and most times the connection strengths ('synapses') are real-valued quantities (for a complete review on the subject, see for example, Lippman 1987). These features provide a richness to the 'space of all possible machines', which is the search space where the learning algorithms act. However, many problems are inherently binary in their formulation, and networks with an integer (or even binary) logic turn out to be very efficient in many cases.

Our system is a kind of binary neural network, as our 'processors' are two-input binary circuits which are connected to the external world through input and output bits. These circuits are the commonly used AND, OR, XOR kind of gates plus other circuits which do not process information (gates which disregard one or both inputs). There are some simple architectural constraints: the gates are numbered (forming a kind of ordered chain) and each gate can take input either from a 'preceding' gate or from an input bit. Therefore no feedback is allowed in the system. On the other hand, each gate can provide input to an arbitrary number of following gates (thus no fan-out problems are considered). The output bits (N_b in total) could in principle be connected to any gate in the network. However, to simplify programming, we decided not to exploit this additional degree of freedom, restricting the output bits to be connected to the N_b gates of the circuit. To each gate are associated some degrees of freedom: two of them specify from which other gates or input bits the gate takes its inputs, and another indicates which Boolean function is performed by this gate. We will symbolically introduce two

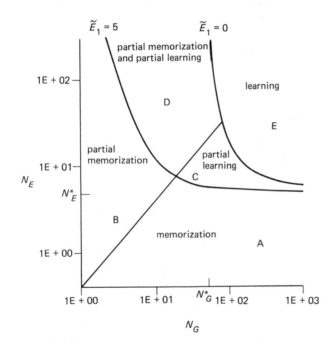

Figure 1   *Phase diagram illustrating the different regions in the plane* (N_G, N_E). *In region* **A** ($E_l = 0, \tilde{E}_l = \frac{1}{2}$) *the system only stores the examples. In region* **B** ($E_l > 0, \tilde{E}_l = \frac{1}{2}$) *memorization is limited by the capacity of the system. In region* **C** ($E_l = 0, \frac{1}{2} > \tilde{E}_l > 0$) *the system is large enough to store all patterns, and generalization starts to take place. Both memorization and learning are partially achieved in region* **D** ($\frac{1}{2} > \tilde{E}_l, E_l > 0$). *In region E* ($E = E = 0$) *the system has been able to generalize fully and is completely error free.*

arrays **X** and **Λ**, the first associated to the pattern of connections among the gates and the second to describe the function performed by each gate.

As far as the learning strategy is concerned, we look at the problem as a global optimization problem, without assigning local rules to backpropagate corrections on some nodes. This procedure is computationally quite expensive but allows a great generality in the search and guarantees that, provided the optimization is done properly, the network so obtained minimizes the average error on the given examples. This training aims to minimize the average error that the network performs on a set of examples of the task. The total number of examples shown, N_E represents the amount of 'experience' provided to the system. The optimization is performed as a Monte Carlo procedure (simulated annealing[4]), where the system under study (the network in our case) is seen as a physical system whose elementary degrees of freedom are the quantities which are varied during the search (the arrays **Λ** and **X**). They key quantity to describe the dynamics of such system is the energy E, which in our specific case is the discrepancy between the correct result of the operation and the one obtained from the circuit, averaged over the number of examples N_E shown to the system (which are chosen randomly at the beginning and kept fixed over the annealing):

$$E\{\Lambda, \mathbf{X}\} \equiv \sum_{l=1}^{N_b} E_l \equiv \sum_{l=1}^{N_b} \frac{1}{N_E} \sum_{k=1}^{N_E} (E_{lk} - A_{lk})^2.$$

Here E_{lk} is the exact result from the lth bit in the kth example, while A_{lk} is the output for the same bit and example as calculated by the circuit. Therefore A_{lk} is a function of $\{\Lambda, \mathbf{X}\}$. Thus, E is the average number of wrong bits for the examples used in the training and for the network described by $\{\Lambda, \mathbf{X}\}$; for a random network $E_l \sim \frac{1}{2}$.

The search for the optimal circuit is done over the space spanned by **Λ** and **X**, while the examples used are chosen at the beginning and kept fixed throughout the training. As the aim of the optimization is to minimize the quantity E, the Monte Carlo simulation must reproduce the physical situation in which the states with low E are most probable, which is the case when the temperature of the system is very low. Therefore a control parameter T is introduced which is slowly decreased toward 0, thus simulating a cooling process.

A step of the optimization procedure simply consists of changing an input connection of a gate or the Boolean function it performs, calculating the resulting energy change ΔE. If $\Delta E < 0$ the change is accepted, otherwise it is accepted with probability $\exp(-\Delta E/T)$. This is the well-known Metropolis algorithm for Monte Carlo simulation, which is guaranteed to converge to the Boltzmann distribution (where a state of energy E is sampled with probability $\exp(-E/T)$) provided that enough simulation steps per temperature are performed. Therefore the simulated annealing procedure will converge to a state of minimum E when the cooling is slow enough.

Our learning procedure is not deterministic in its final results. Two experiments with the same training examples, but with different initial conditions (ie, starting from two different random networks), may produce two different optimal networks. Nevertheless the network which results from a specific training will work in a strictly deterministic way. We stress the point that our learning procedure bears no direct resemblance to the approach used in the so-called Boltzmann machines.[5] In the latter case the learning procedure is based on an information–theoretic point of view and is a kind of steepest descent method. Moreover, the retrieval phase is non-deterministic as a temperature-driven decision rule takes place.

The behaviour of the model has been investigated in two classes of problems:

(1) *Rule-driven tasks*, where a well-defined rule holds, and the generalization capabilities are clearly tested. As an example, we experimented with the self-organization of a network to implement an arithmetic operation (adder or multiplier). Even though this kind of problem appears not to be the most natural for a brain-like architecture, results were strikingly good.[1]

(2) *Recognition or classification problems*, where major benefits are expected from this approach. We have studied the problem of building a network which is able to discriminate a given printed character from all the others, in the presence of noise or small irregularities in the scanning process. These problems are much harder to define in terms of rule extraction, while it is reasonable to expect that a 'neural' approach is able to capture the relevant features in an efficient way. Although our experiments in this framework are at a very preliminary stage, we can state that the learning phase for these problems is relatively shorter, and that there is a definite trend for the system to build some feature analysers which of course depend on the statistical distribution of the input samples.

Coming back to the first class of problems, the definition of a *generalization regime* is straightforward. Consider the problem of building a binary adder with addenda of given length $L = N_b$. As the total number of different additions is $N_O \equiv 2^{2L}$, one can evaluate the average error over all possible additions *after the training*:

$$\tilde{E}\{\Lambda, X\} \equiv \sum_{l=1}^{N_b} \tilde{E}_l \equiv \sum_{l=1}^{N_b} \frac{1}{N_O} \sum_{k=1}^{N_O} (E_{lk} - A_{lk})^2.$$

Here the same quantities E_{lk} and A_{lk} are used as in the previous formula, but the average now refers to all possible input samples. If L is not too large, this average can be performed explicitly with little computational effort (in fact, once the network has been built, the retrieval phase in these machines is extremely fast, involving only very simple logical operations). Only a network which produces zero values for E and $\tilde{E}$ has been able to extract the *rule* underlying the task.

The case which we investigated in close detail is that of an adder with $L = 8$, which implies $N_O = 65\,536$. The overall behaviour of the machine is summarized in Figure 1, where a kind of 'phase diagram' is shown. Each point of this diagram describes the average behaviour of a network with a given number of 'neurons' N_G, trained with N_E examples. The crossover to the generalization regime in this specific case took place at about $N_E = 200$, which is indeed a low percentage over all $65\,536$ possible cases. The training phase for this experiment took roughly one hour CPU on a IBM 3090/VF. It is quite surprising that even an 'unnatural' task of this kind can be efficiently implemented through this approach.

We devote the last part of this section to the analysis of the different computing strategies that the system is able to find during its search. As a gate of the network takes input from another gate or from an input bit, it will be able to process only when its two inputs are available (thus reproducing a kind of dataflow processing model). Therefore it is quite natural to think of our network as structured in subsequent layers. Each layer will take its inputs from previous ones, and a cycle time can be introduced (for analysis purposes only) such that at each new cycle one layer will produce its result. Therefore the speed of the circuit, defined as the number of cycles needed to get the output, can be measured. The typical sequential structure, for which the number of machine cycles required to get an output bit grows linearly with the position of this bit, is the one which is more often found by the training procedure, and corresponds essentially to the algorithm one uses to calculate the sum of two binary numbers by hand. But in some of the experiments the final design is more subtle: instead of performing most of the operations in the first cycle and then one operation per cycle, the system organizes in a circuit which performs more operations simultaneously in most cycles, which results in a faster, parallel algorithm. This was quite surprising to us: even though no attention was paid to the computational speed of the network, the system is sometimes able to find these more efficient algorithms. The fact that these alternative strategies are found rarely sounds reasonable: a less intuitive algorithm is more difficult to find! It is likely that one could obtain even faster adders, approaching the speed of the best-known algorithms,[6] by introducing in the energy a term to penalize circuits with large delays.

3. Some comments on the learning algorithm

The major source of robustness in the use of simulated annealing lies in the introduction of a temperature in the search process. This aims to avoid the system getting stuck in local minima which may be present in the 'energy landscape' of the system. These minima are induced by the topology proper of the optimization process: it may well be the case that any elementary change from a specific configuration (namely, the change of a connection or of the Boolean function performed by one gate in our model) results in a worse network (with larger E). Due to the functional form of the Boltzmann statistical weight, at non-zero temperature there is always a finite probability to 'climb these valleys'.

The relevance of local minima depends of course on the complexity of the task on which the system is trained. A seemingly hard problem such as speech synthesis is implemented with success using backpropagation,[7] which amounts to a kind of steepest descent method. Our experience is that rule-driven problems are strongly affected by the presence of local minima. An attempt to build an adder by rapidly decreasing temperature to zero ('quenching'), thus performing a steepest descent algorithm, results in a network which only memorizes the patterns shown. On the other hand, problems such as pattern recognition tasks, where a proper classification into categories is required, are efficiently learned without the need for special care being paid to the cooling rate. As a matter of fact, even though many problems in computer vision have gained a lot from the introduction of a stochastic component,[8,9] there are also very complex problems such as motion computation[10] which are efficiently solved using a deterministic approach.

One of the main objections concerning most existing algorithms (particularly in the case of supervised learning) is the poor link with any realistic model for biological learning. It is true that the main target is that of building an efficient computer, but it would be desirable to recognize, to some extent, connections with what nature provides. In the next section we will show that, although the microscopic rules for the training are non-biological in their formulation, the kind of hints that one may achieve concerning macroscopic behaviour (in particular the occurrence of generalization) are very general and possibly useful in the biological context.

In this respect we also experimented with the approach of *learning through selection*. Briefly, we select an initial 'population' of networks at random, and evolve it as follows:

- We produce a random mutation on each individual, with the same rules as the elementary modification for simulated annealing.
- We score the mutated individuals, the score being obtained according to the function E.

- We rank the individual according to the score.
- We reproduce them using a 'reproduction probability', which depends on the rank and will ultimately tend to reward the 'best' individuals.

This algorithm is similar to simulated annealing in that a very 'severe' reproduction function corresponds to a fast cooling, as best individuals are rewarded from the very beginning. As a matter of fact, we found that a performance comparable with that of annealing can be achieved when the reproduction function is smoothly modified during the search from an initial flat distribution (all individuals being reproduced with the same ratio) to a final situation where high reproduction ratios are assigned only to the best individuals. Therefore one has to deal again with a kind of 'cooling schedule' and the resulting procedure is neither faster or simpler than simulated annealing. Thus a closer resemblance to a simple evolution model does not imply a gain in efficiency. It might be the case that introducing a kind of 'mating' between different individuals could improve the algorithm.

4. The meaning of generalization

A human being is extremely clever in capturing regularities and abstractions concerning some repetitive task or situation. This is probably the most powerful feature that one would like to include into a neural-like approach to computation. Indeed, this property is hard even to define and the most striking examples of generalization ability in neural networks are far from understood, unless some magic power is attributed to the modellers.[7] Nor can one accept a 'black-box' point of view in which the very fact that the machine works is all that matters, regardless of *why* it works. That is the problem that we faced with our network: how is it possible that the system chose to implement such a complicated process as carrying propagation in addition, rather than some odd pattern matching restricted to the cases it was exposed to?

As the training is a non-deterministic process, the problem of understanding this phase in our model amounts to the computation of some distribution function. In other words, one has to evaluate averages over a statistical ensemble. This is in principle very well prescribed by what we know in statistical physics. Given an ensemble which is sampled with probability $\exp(-E/T)$, the underlying partition function is:

$$Z = \sum_{\text{configurations}} e^{-E/T},$$

where we recall that the configurations are all the possible arrangements of the network, as far as the pattern of connections and the Boolean function performed by each gate are concerned. Given the partition function, all averages can be computed. As an example the average energy (which corresponds to the average error that the network performs on the sample set) is:

$$\bar{E} = \frac{1}{Z} \sum_{\text{configurations}} E\,e^{-E/T} = T^2 \frac{\partial \log Z}{\partial T}.$$

Unfortunately, to clarify the mechanism for generalization by a general thermodynamical analysis of this system, is very difficult and often impossible. From now on we will restrict ourselves to the case of very small networks for which we can afford a complete enumeration of all possible network configurations. Considering $N_1 = 4$, $N_b = 1$, and $N_G = 4$, the total number of network configurations is $N = 46 \times 10^9$.

Since $N_1 = 4$ and $N_b = 1$, each network will implement a Boolean function of four variables or, equivalently, solve one problem consisting of calculating one output bit given four input bits according to some rule. Such a problem can be completely defined by specifying the value of the output bit for each of the $2^4 = 16$ possible configurations of the input bits of the network. Thus, any problem P can be represented by a vector of 16 Boolean-valued components, one for each different input configuration. There are $2^{16} = 65\,536$ such Boolean functions or problems.

Each of the N possible networks will implement a specific input–output mapping, or, in other words, will solve one of these 65 536 problems. It will be clear from what follows that, during the enumeration, we simply need to count how many networks implement each problem P. The result of the enumeration is an histogram $H(P)$ such that $H(P)$ is the number of networks that solve problem P (so that $\sum_P H(P) = N$).

The training of a network to solve problem P would be made by using N_E examples of input configurations for which the correct output would be given. These examples correspond to a sub-set S of the 16 possible input configurations, which can also be represented by a 16-component Boolean vector, with one component for each possible input configuration, a component with the value 1 indicating that the corresponding input configuration is used in the training. There will be N_E components in S with the value 1, or in other words the (L^1) length of S is $|S| = N_E$.

Now, let's imagine that we are actually performing a training procedure for problem P using the set of examples S, and that the training has proceeded down to temperature T. Let P' be the problem solved by the current network. We then have:

$$E = \frac{1}{N_E} S \times (P - P') \quad N_E = |S|; \quad \tilde{E} = \frac{1}{16} |P - P'|,$$

where $|\ldots|$ again denotes the L^1 length, and $\times$ represents the scalar product. The above relations become obvious once one notices that $|P - P'|$ is simply the number of components in which P and P' differ, and that $S \times (P - P')$, similarly, is the number of components of S which are one and for which the corresponding components of P and P' differ.

As explained above, the probability of any network configuration to be sampled will be proportional to $\exp(-E/T)$. On the other hand, since there are $H(P')$ networks which solve P', the probability that, at temperature T, the training procedure produces a network that solves problem P' is proportional to $H(P') \exp(-E/T)$ where E is a function of P' as described above. The coefficient of proportionality is given by the normalization factor $1/Z$, where Z can be more compactly expressed as a sum over problems:

$$Z = \sum_{P'} H(P') \exp\{-E(P')/T\}.$$

Thus computing $H(P)$ allows the *exact* computation of the partition function at all temperatures, and consequently of all interesting average quantities.

We focus the attention on the *probability of learning*. This is the probability that, performing a training on a problem P using a sample set S (of size N_E), a final network is obtained which correctly implements the problem on all possible cases. This quantity can be formally defined as $\langle \delta_{P, P'} \rangle$, and depends explicitly on the specific sample S considered. By averaging over all examples of a given size N_E, one can obtain a quantity which depends on the *amount* of information provided and not on the specific sample chosen.

Let's start by studying the training on a very simple problem, consisting of producing a value of 0 at the output bit regardless of the values of the input bits. In other words, we choose the problem represented by a vector of all zeros. In Fig. 2, curve *a*, we plot the probability of learning at zero temperature as a function of N_E. The curve rises quite fast, and reaches 50% for $N_E = 2$, thus showing that for that N_E the training has 50% probability of resulting in a *perfect* network, ie, one that always produces 0 at its output, even for the $16 - 2 = 14$ input configurations not used in the training (indeed, one can show that there is a *production* of information associated with the training process[2]). This already shows clearly the generalization capabilities of the system we are considering. This fast rise of the learning curve is related to the fact that there are very many circuits that always produce zero at their output. In fact, for this problem, $H(P)/N \sim 14\%$.

Now let's consider a more difficult problem, consisting of reproducing, at the output bit, the value of a specified input bit. The corresponding

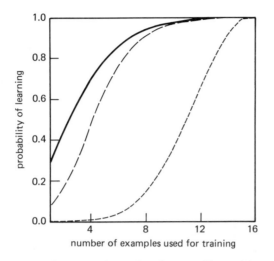

probability of learning

number of examples used for training

Figure 2   *Learning as a function of N_E for three problems: (a)* _____; *(b)*_____;
(c)....

learning probability is plotted in Fig. 2, curve *b*. Generalization still
occurs, but now we need $N_E = 4$ to get 50% chances of finding a perfect
network. Correspondingly $H(P)/N$ has dropped to $\sim 3.4\%$.

We then turn to the even more difficult problem of producing at the
output of the network the AND of three of the four input bits. This
problem is solved by a much smaller number of circuits
$(H(P)/N = 0.047\%)$. From the plot of the corresponding learning
probability (Fig. 2, curve *c*) one can see that generalization almost does
not occur at all, and N_E quite close to 16 (which amounts to giving
complete information describing the problem to be solved) is needed for
the learning probability to be reasonably different from zero ($N_E = 11$ for
50% learning probability).

It is clear at this point that the occurrence of generalization and
learning of a problem is an entropy effect and is directly related to the fact
that that problem is implemented by many different networks. In fact,
with $N_E < 16$, the training procedure will essentially pick one network
randomly for which $E = 0$. If the problem we want to solve, P, is realized
by many different networks, a significant fraction of the networks with
$E = 0$ will actually be solving just problem P, thus yielding $\tilde{E} = 0$ with a
reasonably high probability. The 'complexity' of a given problem is
architecture-dependent and can be measured by how many networks
solve that problem. We note that learning is associated with a degree of
specialization for the architecture considered. In fact to achieve a high
probability of learning for a given problem, this must be solved by many

127

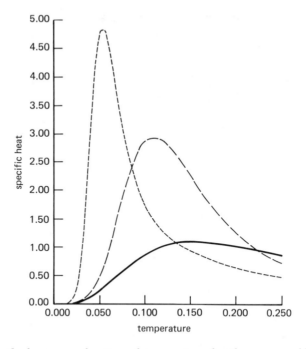

Figure 3   *Specific heat as a function of temperature for the same problems as those illustrated in Figure 2. (a)* _____ ; *(b)* _____ ; *(c)* ....

network configurations. As the number of total configurations is constrained, this abundance must be balanced, and there will be some problems which will be realized in only a few ways or no ways at all. For these problems a training-by-example procedure is of no worth.

The very fact that the annealing schedule has to reach $T \sim 0$ implies that learning takes place as an ordering phenomenon, not much different from what one meets in the theory of phase transitions proper of many-body systems (liquid–solid transition, magnetic ordering, etc.). Knowing Z exactly we have studied the thermodynamics of these small systems and our results agree nicely with this picture. In Fig. 3(a), (b) and (c) we plot the specific heat for three different problems, defined as:

$$C_V = \frac{\partial E}{\partial T}$$

The specific heat is a differential quantity which indicates the amount of heat that the system releases when temperature is infinitesimally lowered, and is a response function of the system. This is a strong indication for the occurrence of a phase transition, as in a wide class of critical systems the resonse functions diverge at the critical temperature. By looking at the plots in Fig. 3, one notices many interesting features:

- For each problem there is a characteristic temperature such that the specific heat has a maximum.
- The harder is the problem, the lower is this characteristic temperature.
- The sharpness of the maximum is related to the difficulty of the problem and in the case of very hard problems this is indeed a peak which reminds one of the singularity in the large critical systems.

To some extent, this result strengthens the link between critical systems and learning in self-organizing networks, but should be investigated in more detail in real-life, larger systems.

References

1. Patarnello, S. & Carnevali, P. *Europhys. Letts.* **4**(4), 503 (1987).
2. Carnevali, P. & Patarnello, S. *Europhys. Letts.* **4**(10), 1199 (1987).
3. Lippman, R. P. *IEEE ASSP Magazine* **4**(2), 4 (1987).
4. Kirkpatrick, S., Gelatt, S. D. & Vecchi, M. P. *Science* **220**, 671 (1983).
5. Sejnowski, T. J., Kienker, P. K. & Hinton, G. E. *Physica* **22D**, 260 (1986).
8. Geman, S. & Geman, D. *IEEE Trans. Pattn. Anal. & Mach. Intell.* **6**, 721 (1984).
9. Carnevali, P., Coletti, L. & Patarnello, S. *IBM Jour. of Res. and Dev.* **29**(6), 569 (1985).
10. Hutchinson, J., Koch, C., Luo, J. & Mead, C. To appear on *IEEE Comp. Magazine.*

PART II
The Logical Perspective

8 The logic of connectionist systems

I. Aleksander

Department of Electrical Engineering, Imperial College of Science and Technology, London, UK

Abstract

A connectionist system is a cellular network of adaptable nodes that has a natural propensity for storing knowledge. This emergent property is a function of a training process and a pattern of connections. Most analyses of such systems first assume an idiosyncratic specification for the nodes (often based on neuron models) and a constrained method of interconnection (reciprocity, no feedback, etc).

In contrast, a general node model is assumed in this paper. It is based on a logic truth table with a probabilistic element. It is argued tthat this includes other definitions and leads to a general analysis of the class of connectionist systems. The analysis includes an explanation of the effect of training and testing techniques that involve the use of noise. Specifically, the paper describes a way of predicting and optimizing noise-based training by the definition of an ideal node logic which ensures the most rapid descent of the resulting probabilistic automaton into the trained stable states.

'Hard' learning is shown to be achievable on the notorious parity-checking problem with a level of performance that is two orders of magnitude better than other well-known error backpropagation techniques demonstrated on the same topology.

It is concluded that there are two main areas of advantage in this approach. The first is the direct probabilistic automaton model that covers and explains connectionist approaches in general, and the second is the potential for high-performance implementations for such systems.

1. Introduction

Connectionism is the study of cellular networks that are in some way like the neural networks of the brain. They possess properties that emerge from the way such nets are connected and trained. The training consists of creating internal states (a state being a 'snapshot' of node outputs at some instant of time) that are models of external events. Such creations

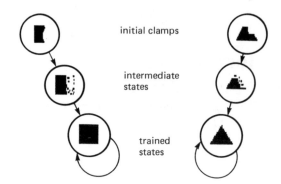

Figure 1   *State transitions after training.*

are effected by adjustments to the input–output function of the net nodes through some 'adaptation strategy'. Typically, a desired state (say an image) is forced on some net outputs (this is called 'clamping'), and the adaptation strategy is deployed so as to associate the node outputs with the node inputs created by the same state.

This means that if the clamping were removed, the net would remain in the selected state. The process is repeated for several states which then represent the system's 'knowledge'. The major mode of computation in such a scheme is that the correct state is entered even if only part of a pattern is clamped into the net. A broad-brush view is shown in Fig. 1. This mode of associative computation can be developed to more sophisticated levels that are well documented in the literature, particularly that compiled by Rumelhart & McClelland.[1] For example, the completion could be the answer to a logical query, or a computation of whether the parts of a pattern are connected or not.

Central to much connectionist work is the function of the node itself. Characteristically this is assumed to be binary and based on a weighted sum of input activity:

$$\sum [w(j)\cdot i(j)] > T, \tag{1}$$

where $w(j)$ is a weighting factor, say $0 \leqslant w(j) \leqslant 1$ ($\leqslant$ reads 'is less than or equal', etc); (j) refers to the jth input to the node; $i(j)$ is the state of firing (1) or not firing (0) of the afferent node connected to the jth input; T is some variable threshold;

If Equation (1) is true, the node is said to fire.

Training schemes are procedures for weight (sometimes, threshold) changing. Although such schemes have been discussed in the context of neural modelling since 1943,[2–8] it is only recently that a better understanding of the way that state structures (ie graphs of states and the transitions between them) may be 'moulded' by training has been gained.

Primarily, Hopfield[9] showed that by assuming reciprocal connections between cells (ie if the output of node A is connected to the input of node B via a weight value **w**, then the output of node B must be connected to the input of node A via the same weight value **w**) the net may be modelled as an energetic system. The trained states form energy wells into which the net eventually settles, particularly if prodded by a partial clamp. Unfortunately, there is no guarantee that the net might not settle in false energy minima. This was Hinton's concern when he defined the Boltzmann machine which uses simulated annealing (reducing amounts of noise) during both the training and recall phases of operation.[10] Rumelhart *et al.* also developed error-correction weight-changing algorithms for nets without feedback (ie no means for signal changes to propagate round physical loops).[11]

This chapter is based on the observation that networks in which the nodes are represented as variable logic devices (which may be described by complete truth tables) may be trained to exhibit emergent properties of pattern completion very similar those obtained with the neural models mentioned above.[12] A consequence of this observation is that it may be possible to provide an explanatory analysis of connectionist systems which is not dependent on the details of the connections (eg the Hopfield reciprocity) and the details of the node function (eg sum-of-weighted-inputs). Also, it is argued that a general, logical framework for training algorithms may be defined.

The thrust of this paper is to illustrate this methodology through the introduction of a node called a PLN (probabilistic logical node), and to argue that not only does it provide a basis for the understanding of connectionist systems, but it also, due to its lookup-table nature (ie implementable as a silicon memory), holds promise for direct implementation similar to that of logic–probabilistic systems for pattern recognition.[13]

2. General definitions

2.1 The connectionist net

A connectionist system may be characterized by a hierarchy of theoretical components. At the top level it is represented by a 4-tuple:

$$C: \langle P, G, Tr, Te \rangle.$$

P is the physical structure which, in turn, is specified by a 2-tuple:

$$P: \langle B, K \rangle,$$

where B is the set of nodes $\{x_1, x_2, \ldots, x_b\}$; K is a specification of the interconnection pattern which states the connectivity (number of inputs per node) of the nodes in a *regular* net or the distribution of connections and connectivity in an *irregular* net.

Before defining the rest of the *C* 4-tuple, it is helpful to illustrate the meaning of some of these elements with an example that will be used later in the paper. This is a toroidally connected two-dimensional $n \times n$ array of nodes where each node is connected to its four nearest neighbours:

$$B: \{xij/i, j = 0, 1, \ldots, n-1\}; b = n \times n.$$

K: connectivity $= 4$; input to xij is from $xi(j-1)$, $xi(j+1)$, $x(i-1)j$, $x(i+1)j$.

Returning now to the definitions:

G is a description of the operation of the node. This, too, needs to be further defined by a 3-tuple:

$$G: \langle A, F, D \rangle$$

where, A is the input–output alphabet of the nodes; $A = \{m_1, m_2, \ldots, m_a\}$, clearly, a is the number of messages that a node can emit; F is the function set from which a node performs one function at any one time; $F = \{f_1, f_2, \ldots, f_v\}$; D is the means for changing the selection from F to advance the process of adaptation. For example, the McCulloch and Pitts model[2] of the neuron is binary making $A = \{0, 1\}$, and F is the set of all linearly separable functions, while there are several models for D that refer to weight-changing, but need not be spelled out here. The nature of G for the general node proposed in this paper will be discussed at some length later.

Tr is a training strategy for a particular net. It generally implies the application of a set K of training examples applied as 'clamps'.

$$K = \{c_1, c_2, \ldots, c_k\}.$$

In Hinton's Boltzmann machine,[10] for example, *Tr* involves the *clamping* of a sub-set from B, say, $U \subseteq B$ ($\subseteq$ reads, 'is a subset of'). Clamping is a process of holding the output of the U nodes to predetermined values from A. The algorithm *Tr* applies some D to all the nodes in the net so that, even if the clamps are removed, the clamped pattern will remain as a stable state of the network. More of this later.

Te is a method of testing the net.

Again,[11] *Te* consists of applying a partial clamp, say $V \subseteq U$, and allowing the net to 'run' according to some constraints (such as annealing). A successful operation leads to the recreation of the appropriate values from A for the whole of U which make up one of the training clamps $c_j \subseteq K$ ($\subseteq$ reads, 'is a subset of').

2.2 The state structure

The behaviour of connectionist systems is usually discussed in terms of some features of its state structure. If S is the set of possible states:

$$S = \{s_1, s_2, \ldots, s_z\}$$

and T is a set of transitions:

$$T = S \times S \, (\times \text{ being the Cartesian product})$$

($t_{jk} \in T$ is the probability of transition from $s_j \in S$ to $sk \in S$, t_{jk} being binary for a deterministic specification and $0 > t_{jk} > 1$ for a probabilistic one), then the state structure SS is defined by the 2-tuple,

$$SS: \langle S, T \rangle.$$

It is assumed that time is discretized: $t = 1, 2, \ldots$, and that state changes as determined by T can only occur at these discrete time values.

It will be seen that since $K \in S$, much of the behaviour of connectionist systems is described in terms of the probability of entering an element of K. Indeed, the energy wells mentioned earlier may be discussed in terms of states or groups of states from K that transit to each other in a cyclic progression.

3. A general probabilistic logic node (PLN)

3.1 The logic of node functions

It is well known that as most neural model nodes are binary, their function may be represented by a lookup table and hence be implemented as a simple silicon random-access memory.[14] Indeed, even if the binary restriction is not assumed, and the model maps real number groups (elements of set A) into real numbers (eg Hinton et al.[11]), this too can be accommodated in a truth table. Formally, this means that a node with j afferent inputs may be represented by a canonical logic expression such as the following:

$$\left. \begin{array}{c} [i(1,1)\&i(2,1)\ldots i(j,1)] \cup [i(1,2)\& \ldots]\ldots \cup [i(1,k)\ldots] \rightarrow m_1 \\ [i(1,1)\&i(2,1)\ldots i(j,1)] \cup [i(1,2)\& \ldots]\ldots \cup [i(1,l)\ldots] \rightarrow m_2 \\ \vdots \qquad\qquad \vdots \qquad\qquad \vdots \qquad\qquad \vdots \\ [i(1,1)\&i(2,1)\ldots i(j,1)] \cup [i(1,2)\& \ldots]\ldots \cup [i(1,p)\ldots] > m_a \end{array} \right\} , \qquad (2)$$

where $i(x, y)$ and $m_z \subseteq A$ for all x, y, z; $\rightarrow$ reads 'implies'; $\cup$ reads 'or' and

& reads 'and'. For a binary system this becomes the familiar sum-of-products Boolean expression, the above being its generalization.

Each term of the form [... & ... & ...] is a *minterm* of the expression. This leads to a more compact and precise notation for the general function.

Let the complete set of minterms for a *j*-input node be

$$M = A \times A \times A \dots (j \text{ times}) \dots \times A.$$

The function of the node is then a partition **P**M of this set:

$$\mathbf{P}M = \{M_1, M_2, \dots, M_a\},$$

where M_p is a block of minterms all of which $> m_p$, for all $p = 1, 2, \dots, a$, recalling that a is the number of elements in A.

A difference between a weighted node and a logical one is that the weighted scheme has a built-in form of generalization. For example, taking a three-input version of inequality (1) in which it is required to map input $i(1), i(2), i(3) = 1\ 1\ 1$ to 1 and input $i(1), i(2), i(3) = 0\ 0\ 0$ to 0 and assuming that some mechanism D has caused the weights to be $w(1)\ w(2)\ w(3) = 1\ 1\ 1$ and the threshold $T = 1.6$, then the truth table for the node is

$i(1)$	$i(2)$	$i(3)$	f
0	0	0	0
0	0	1	0
0	1	0	0
0	1	1	1
1	0	0	0
1	0	1	1
1	1	0	1
1	1	1	1

Not only are the two desired minterms set correctly, but also minterms similar to the desired ones are mapped in the same way. This effect is called node generalization. Should it be that, say, minterm $0, 1, 1$ is incorrectly set, and that D is capable of adjusting this, it might find the solution by reducing $w(2)$ and $w(3)$ to 0.5. This would automatically map minterms $1, 0, 1$, and $1, 1, 0$ to 0 as well. A truth-table representation, on the other hand, has no such effect. It merely assumes that the mapping m_p is set directly by D and affects no other minterms. It will be shown that in such systems the form of generalization described, can be made the responsibility of the training algorithm.

3.2 The probabilistic node

At this point, it seems important to introduce a factor that is missing in most neural models: a 'knowledge' within the node, of whether a particular minterm is set due to the process of training or not and whether the setting is consistent or not. In biological neurons it is widely believed that, before adaptation, the neuron fires or does not fire with roughly equal probability, edging towards certainty as adaptation progresses. The PLN may now be defined so as to include a property.

The general logic Equation (2) above may be rewritten as a collection of sets M_i, where

$$\left.\begin{array}{l} M_1 = \{w_1/w_1 \text{ is a minterm that} \rightarrow m_1\} \\ M_2 = \{w_2/w_2 \text{ is a minterm that} \rightarrow m_2\} \\ \vdots \\ M_a = \{w_a/w_a \text{ is a minterm that} \rightarrow m_a\} \end{array}\right\} . \tag{3}$$

A PLN is defined by:

(a) augmenting $A = \{m_1, m_2, \ldots, m_a\}$ to $A' = \{A, u\}$;

(b) defining u as a node state in which elements of A are emitted with equal probability;

(c) insisting that the node, before the application of algorithm D, has all its minterms $> u$.

3.3 An example

Three logic nodes are connected in a ring:

$P: B = \{x_1, x_2, x_3\}$

$K:$ connectivity $= 2$

x_1 has inputs from x_2 and x_3
x_2 has inputs from x_1 and x_3
x_3 has inputs from x_1 and x_2

$G: A = \{0, 1\}$
   $F:$ logic, as described
   $D:$ direct setting of minterms

$Tr:$ minterms are set to makes states 1 1 1 and 0 0 0 stable (re-entrant)

$Te:$ not used. The discussion concerns the changes that take place in the whole of the state structure SS.

Initially, it is assumed that the nodes are logic truth tables without the probabilistic augmentation. They have randomly chosen minterm mappings, as shown overleaf:

	Node x_1			Node x_2			Node x_3	
x_2	x_3 : x_1		x_1	x_3 : x_2		x_1	x_2 : x_3	
0	0 : 1		0	0 : 0		0	0 : 1	
0	1 : 1		0	1 : 1		0	1 : 0	
1	0 : 0		1	0 : 0		1	0 : 0	
1	1 : 1		1	1 : 0		1	1 : 1	

The resulting state structure is shown in Fig. 2(a). Training consists of clamping the state to 000 and mapping the resulting minterms to 000. This is repeated for 111, resulting in the following truth table.

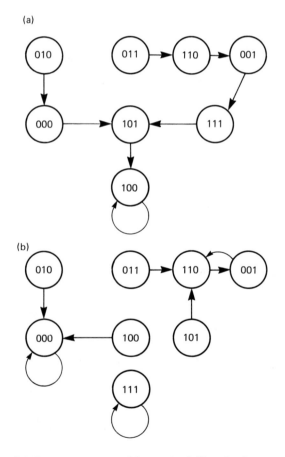

Figure 2   *Deterministic state structures: (a) untrained. (b) trained.*

Node x_1			Node x_2			Node x_3		
x_2	x_3 : x_1		x_1	x_3 : x_2		x_1	x_2 : x_3	
0	0 : 0		0	0 : 0		0	0 : 0	
0	1 : 1		0	1 : 1		0	1 : 0	
1	0 : 0		1	0 : 0		1	0 : 0	
1	1 : 1		1	1 : 1		1	1 : 1	

The corresponding state structure is shown in Fig. 2(b). It is clear that stable re-entrant states have been created by training. However, the presence of unrelated cycles should also be noted. Indeed, if we relate the energy of a cycle to the inverse of the probability of entering that cycle after a burst of noise, then this energy is inversely proportional to the total number of states associated with the cycle. Thus the energies associated with the three cycles created after training are:

Cycle	'Energy'
000	3
111	1
110–001	4

It is the false cycle that is at the lowest energy level. This can act as a trap that defeats the purpose of noise. The probabilistic node avoids this difficulty, as will be seen.

The probabilistic node in the above example has A augmented to

$$A = \{0, 1, u\},$$

where u is the 'unknown' minterm mapping in which the node emits 0 or 1 with equal probability. Initially, all the minterms in each node are mapped into u, but after training (making 000 and 111 re-entrant) each node has the truth table:

in1	in2	out
0	0	0
0	1	u
1	0	u
1	1	1

The resulting overall state transition table for the system is:

Current state			Next state		
0	0	0	0	0	0
0	0	1	*u*	*u*	0
0	1	0	*u*	0	*u*
0	1	1	1	*u*	*u*
1	0	0	0	*u*	*u*
1	0	1	*u*	1	*u*
1	1	0	*u*	*u*	1
1	1	1	1	1	1

This leads to the probabilistic state structure shown in Fig. 3. The transitions are calculated from the state table on the basis that a '*u*' indicates a 50/50 decision to become a 0 or a 1. So, a mapping from, say, 0 1 1 to 1 *u u* is interpreted as a 0.25 probability transition to each of 1 0 0, 1 0 1, 1 1 0 and 1 1 1. The probability of being in state s $(0 \leqslant s \leqslant 7)$ at time t is $p(s, t)$ where this may be calculated by the iteration:

$$p(s, t) = \sum_{j=0}^{7} p(j, t-1) * t_{js},$$

t_{js} being the transition probability from state j to state s.

Assuming an initial probability of 1/8 for every state, it may be seen

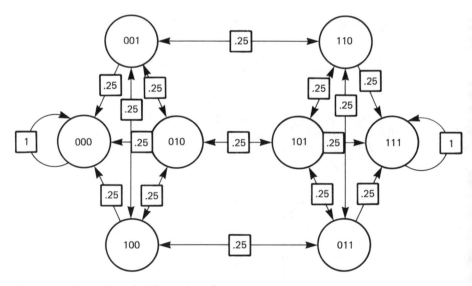

Figure 3   *Trained, probabilistic trained structure.*

that $p(s, t)$ tends to 0.5 with t for $s = 000$ and $s = 111$, and 0 for all the other states. It is possible to conclude that, in this case, training to these two states indeed creates energy wells and that the probabilistic nature of the nodes endows the system with a built-in searching ability that finds the wells.

This explains why the PLN is said to provide a self-annealing feature for connectionist systems. However, the result shows that simple training to create stable states which provides energy wells is not general, and requires the deeper consideration it is given in the next section.

4. Training and noise

4.1 The limitations of stable state creation

Assume that a regular, randomly connected net with a connectivity of n inputs per cell is trained to provide a stable state s and that the nodes are of the PLN kind. Should the state now be changed at just one node output at time $t = 0$, then at $t = 1$, n nodes on average will receive inputs different from s. The probability that one of these n nodes should output an element of s as an arbitrary choice resulting from u is $1/a$. Therefore, on average, the number of nodes outputting incorrectly for s is $n(1-(1/a))$. For $a > 1$ and $n > 1$, both being integers, this number is greater than 1. This means that starting, with a single output disrupted from s, the disruption is greater at $t = 1$, indicating that s is not stable. In fact, a precise statement of this situation is given by the iteration:

$$p(s, t) = (1/a)\{(a-1)p(s, t-1)^n + 1\},$$

where $p(s, t)$ is the probability of emitting an element of s at time t. From this, the change in probability over a single time interval is

$$D = (1-1/a)p(s, t)n - p(s, t) + 1/a \tag{4}$$

and the steady state equilibrium is found by putting $D = 0$. This has two roots: one at 1 which is the trained stable state and another which rapidly tends to $1/a$ with increasing n. Also the latter root is a stable 'attractor' while the former is unstable.

A 256-node, binary ($a = 2$) simulation with $n = 4$ and a regular, arbitrary connection pattern has given $p(s, t)$ tending to an average value of 0.541 (std. dev. $= 0.11$) where the stable root of Equation (4) may be calculated as being 0.543 suggesting that the theoretical argument is accurate.

Another conclusion that can be drawn from this assessment is that Equation (4) has only one root (at 1) for a binary system with $n = 2$ and provides additional explanation for the known stability of 2-connected systems.[15,16]

4.2 An ideal PLN content

For a given set of trained states and a given network, it is possible to define an ideal mapping for the minterms of each node. This is ideal in the sense that the most rapid descent into the trained state is obtained, given that part of the net is clamped uniquely on the state variables of the trained state in question. We start by assuming that the trained states are *orthogonal* in the sense that no PLN sees the same minterm for any two states.

For a randomly connected network, orthogonality can only be assured for a pair of states that are the exact opposite of one another (for example, the all-zero and the all-one states). For a known connection it is possible to construct orthogonal sets of states that are in themselves not opposites of one another. For example, a network of nodes connected in a two-dimensional array, with nodes connected to their four cardinal neighbours, has the following typical set of orthogonal states (shown for a 4×4 array):

0	0	0	0	1	1	1	1	0	0	0	0
0	0	0	0	1	1	1	1	1	1	1	1
0	0	0	0	1	1	1	1	0	0	0	0
0	0	0	0	1	1	1	1	1	1	1	1
1	1	1	1	1	1	0	0	0	0	1	1
0	0	0	0	0	1	1	0	1	0	0	1
1	1	1	1	0	0	1	1	1	1	0	0
0	0	0	0	1	0	0	1	0	1	1	0

The reader may wish to check that no node has four-neighbour patterns shared by any two states. In fact, 16 such states may be found not dependent on the size of the net, but dependent on n (that is, 2^n, to be precise). This leads to a useful assertion:

Assertion 4.2.
The maximum number of independent stable states that may be stored in a net where the state involves all b nodes is a^n, where a is the size of the communication alphabet.

In a randomly connected net, orthogonality between states is approached probabilistically, n being one key parameter and the Hamming distance $h(X, Y)$ for two intended stable states X and Y being another. Writing h for $h(X, Y)$, for b nodes in the net, the probability of orthogonality for any particular node is:

$$1-((b-h)/b)^n.$$

The ideal PLN content may now be defined:

For a pair of desired stable states X and Y, if m_X is a minterm in a PLN related to state X, and m_Y is a minterm related to state Y, then the rest of the minterms should map the same way as m_X if closer in Hamming distance to m_X, and m_Y if closer in Hamming distance to m_Y. If any minterm is equidistant from any pair m_X and m_Y, it should map to the 'unknown' output u.

The effect of an ideal PLN content may be seen from rewriting Equation (4) as:

$$D = (1-1/a)f(p,n)-p+1/a$$

(writing p instead of $p(s,t)$ for brevity), where $f(p,n)$ is the probability of the PLN receiving an input to which it provides the correct response due to the setting of minterms in training.

The ideal PLN content is defined to maximize $f(p,n)$, therefore maximizing the increase of probability of entering the nearest trained state. An example may clarify this issue.

Taking the binary case of $a = 2$, and $n = 4$ with a randomly connected net trained on the all-one and the all-zero state only,

$$f(p,n) = p^4-(1-p)^4$$

(the second term being related to the opposite training state). Considering the case where the state is minimally disturbed by an amount e (ie $p = 1-e$, with $e \leqslant 1$)

$$f(p,n) \simeq 1-4e.$$

Putting this into Equation (4) we obtain:

$$D \simeq e,$$

confirming that the trained state is metastable as the probability of entering it *decreases* by e. Now, for the same system with ideal content,

$$f(p,n) = p^4+4(p^3)(1-p)-4p(1-p)^3-(1-p)^4$$
$$= 1-12e^2-4e^3-e^4.$$

Now, putting this into Equation (4) and retaining significant terms only, we obtain:

$$D \simeq +e,$$

which being positive indicates that the trained state has been made stable.

4.3 Training with noise

Having defined an ideal PLN content, the objective of training becomes the achievement of this ideal. Clearly, this could be done by adding machinery to the node itself which, given the trained minterms, 'spreads' the appropriate mapping to the nearest neighbouring 'Hamming' minterms. The alternative considered here is to disrupt the feedback path in the net with noise to achieve the necessary spread.

So if s_x is a desired stable state, training consists of clamping it to the net outputs, and disrupting the input by an amount of noise q, where $q = h/b$, b being the number of nodes and h the Hamming distance between the noisy version of s_x (say s_x') and s_x itself.

Training consists of mapping the minterms due to s_x and s_x' to deliver the desired clamp s_x. The rule for minterm mapping is that if a minterm state is u it assumes the value from A dictated by the clamp. If the minterm state is a value of A which is different from the clamp, then the minterm reverts to the u value.

The two major parameters for training are therefore q and v, the letter being the number of times that the noisy training step is applied. The analysis which follows, is intended to show the way in which choice of q and v approaches the ideal PLN content.

Let m_x be a minterm in a particular node that is addressed by s_x. Let $m_x d$ be a minterm that differs from m_x by d bits. Then the probability of *any* $m_x d$ minterm being addressed by s_x' is:

$$P(d) = \binom{n}{d} * (1-q)^{(n-d)} * q^d \tag{5}$$

where the first term is the number of ways of taking d from n objects, ie,

$$\binom{n}{d} = \frac{n!}{d! * (n-d)!}.$$

$P(d)$ is also the proportion of the total of $m_x d$ minterms being addressed. The ideal PLN content is such that addressing some (large) values of d constitutes an error, while *not* addressing lower ones also constitutes an error. Also, the total error may be calculated as a function of v using the iterative formula:

$$P(d, v+1) = P(d, v) + (1 - P(d, v)) * P(d, v)$$
$$= 2P(d, v) - P(d, v)^2, \tag{6}$$

where $P(d, v)$ is the probability of addressing $m_x d$ after v training steps. Consider an example.

Let $n = 6$ and let the all-one state be s_x. In anticipation of all-zero being the other desired stable state, the ideal PLN content may be defined as all minterms with zero, one and two zeros mapping into 1, while all others that map into 1 are errors. Putting the noise level at 20% and using Equations (5) and (6), the following trend may be calculated:

v	$d =$	0	1	2	3	4	5	6	Total
				($\% \, mxd = 1$)					error (%)
1		100	39	24	8	2	< 1	< 1	70
2		100	63	43	16	3	< 1	< 1	52
4		100	86	68	29	6	1	< 1	32
8		100	98	90	50	12	1	< 1	22
10		100	100	96	61	17	2	< 1	22

This illustrates the fact that all $m_x d = 1$ probabilities approach 1 asymptotically at rates dependent on the amount of noise. In a case such as that above there is an optimum v for which the error is a minimum found at the crosspoint of error decreasing in the $d = 1$ and $d = 2$ areas and increasing in higher values of d. In the above case this occurs for $v = 9$ and turns out to be 21.5%.

It is of some importance that this points to optimal training strategies where the noise is kept low and v is kept large. For example, in the above case, for 10% noise the minimum error falls to 12% at $v = 28$. Although there may be scope for more analytical work, that would predict optimal error and v, it is not easy to relate this error to eventual performance of the net. One thing is clear, the approach to the ideal PLN is desirable, but its achievement not entirely essential. The following example may serve to illustrate this point.

A net has 256 nodes, each with $n = 4$. It is trained on the all-zero and the all-one states, and tested with a variety of clamps each consisting of 50% ones or 50% zeros. The first test (Fig. 4(a)) illustrates the way in which the content of the PLNs approaches the ideal. In this case, the content simply reaches an optimum and stays there irrespective of the number of steps. The reason for this is that the minterms for $d = 1$ reach their maximum, and the error of untrained $d = 2$ minterms settles at a value determined by noise, as the 'revert back to u' rule comes into play.

Fig. 4(b) shows the effect of training on performance, this being measured as the average transient (for 12 tests, each for a different, randomly selected starting point for the unclamped node outputs). It was noted that for the ideal node content the transient length was three steps.

These results confirm that training is best done with low h and large v, even though departures from this may sometimes be desirable to save

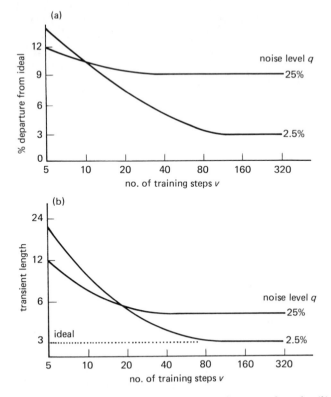

Figure 4 *Experimental results: (a) memory content as a function of v and q; (b) performance as a function of v and q.*

training time. Clearly, the possibility of shaping the training regime in terms of h and v remains open for further work. This is a manoeuvre of the same kind as simulated annealing in Boltzmann machines.[10]

5. Hard learning

5.1 What is hard learning?

The essence of much current work in connectionist systems relates to 'hard learning', which may be described as follows. Certain stable patterns cannot be achieved in a net without the presence of intermediate nodes, which are not clamped, but which provide communication paths between clamped units. These are required because clamping would cause conflicts between the stable states, later clamps modifying the logic set up by earlier ones. Learning is said to be hard because the function for

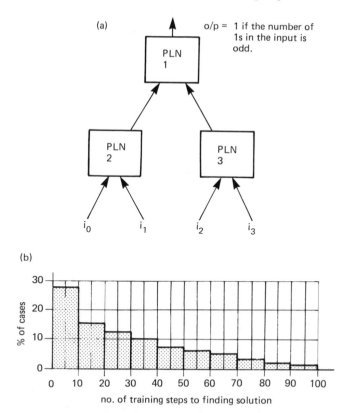

Figure 5   *Hard learning performance: (a) the parity circuit; (b) performance distribution.*

the intermediate units is not explicitly stated by the desired clamp patterns. This function is moulded by some global training algorithm applied to all intermediate nodes, the object of which is to cause changes in the logic that support the clamps.

The well-known perceptron limitation[6] applies to systems that do not allow for this possibility. For this reason 'easy learning' is sometimes called 'perceptron-limited'. The fascination of hard learning is that the intermediate units build up inner representations which make computational sense without the need for such representations to be explicitly stated. A 'benchmark' for hard learning was defined by Rumelhart, Hinton & Williams[11] and relates to a simple parity checker similar to that shown in Fig. 5(*a*). The clamp may only be applied to the inputs *i*0 to *i*3 and the output. All these terminals are assumed to be sensitive to binary information only. There are 16 instances of correct input and output combinations, the input being the 16 possible combinations of four binary digits and the output being 1 there is an odd number of ones in the input pattern.

Rumelhart *et al.*,[11] working with threshold-and-weights nodes have developed an error backpropagation algorithm that gradually adjusts the weights until all errors are removed. It will be seen below that the number of presentations of correct examples required by PLN systems is two orders of magnitude lower than that required by the error backpropagation method.

5.2 A PLN algorithm for hard learning

This algorithm will be discussed in the context of the parity circuit shown in Fig. 5(*a*), although its application is general to all systems with intermediate nodes. It may be stated precisely as follows:

(1) All the minterms in all the nodes are set to the value *u* at the start of the training procedure.

(2) One of the instances of the required function is chosen at random and applied to the net.

(3) The net is allowed to run until
        either (3.1) the output of PLN 1 matches the desired output,
        or (3.2) the output of PLN 1 consistently (16 times, in this case)
        mismatches the desired output.

(4) If 3.1 is true, all the addressed minterms are made to assume their current (0/1) output values and the algorithm returns to step 2.

(5) If 3.2 is true, all the addressed minterms are made to assume the *u* value and the algorithm returns to step 2.

(6) The algorithm halts when the 3.1 loop is entered consistently (32 times in this case).

The key property of this algorithm is that the u minterms provide a search of the function space only in areas that have not been discovered to be correct. This space reduces as correct minterms are found and is reinstated if minterms are set incorrectly.

It may be shown that this algorithm converges on one of the four possible solutions for this structure. Although a rigorous proof of this convergence remains fruitful ground for description elsewhere, it is possible to provide evidence of the soundness of the algorithm both by homing in on some of its major theoretical characteristics, which are described below, and looking at empirical results. The latter are shown in Fig. 5(*b*) where the performance of the algorithm is seen to be truly remarkable. The average number of presentations of instances for an experiment in which 10 000 runs to solution were made, was 32. Fig. 5(*b*) shows the details of the distribution of these results. This can be compared to the results obtained by others for similar topologies. Rumelhart *et al.*[11] in their original discussion of error backpropagation techniques required more than 96 000 presentations of the inputs, while they quote the work of Chauvin who obtained an average of about 4000 presentations. Therefore the result of 32 presentations is additional evidence of the directness of the PLN approach. This performance is due to the theoretical characteristics that are described below.

5.3 Theoretical characteristics of the algorithm

Convergence may be proved from three major characteristics: first, given a set of minterm mappings that are either correct or have the 'don't know' value *u*, a training presentation is more likely to turn the *u* values to correct rather than incorrect 0/1 values; second, incorrect values cannot survive; and third, the solutions are attractors in function space (the space of all possible settings of the minterms).

Say that the function space is represented by the truth table as follows:

		PLN		
		1	2	3
	00	*u*	*u*	*u*
INPUT	01	*u*	*u*	*u*
	10	*u*	*u*	*u*
	11	*u*	*u*	*u*

The above is the initial state.

The first presentation of an arbitrary input will only set up correct values of the minterms. However, which of the four possible solutions is preferred, is determined by this first step. Say that the first presentation is $i0, i1, i2, i3 \rightarrow o/p = 0, 0, 0, 0 \rightarrow 0$ then the function is (showing truth-table contents only):

$$
\begin{array}{ccc}
0 & 0 & 0 \\
u & u & u \\
u & u & u \\
u & u & u
\end{array}
$$

The only solution that fits this setting is:

$$
\begin{array}{ccc}
0 & 0 & 0 \\
1 & 1 & 1 \\
1 & 1 & 1 \\
0 & 0 & 0
\end{array}
$$

which makes it possible to define any departure from this as erroneous. It is now possible to assess the probability of changes caused in the function state assuming an equal probability of occurrence of any presentation. For example the occurrence of $0,0,0,0 \rightarrow 0$ will cause no change while, say, $0,0,0,1 \rightarrow 1$ has only one possible outcome:

$$
\begin{array}{ccc}
0 & 0 & 0 \\
1 & u & 1 \\
u & u & u \\
u & u & u
\end{array}
$$

Therefore, so far, each of the above events may be logged as having a probability of 1/16, the former being neutral and the latter introducing two correct minterms and no error.

But the occurrence of, say, $1,0,0,1 \rightarrow 0$ leads to the following four function states, each with a probability of 1/64:

$$
\begin{array}{ccc|ccc|ccc|ccc}
0 & 0 & 0 & 0 & 0 & 0 & 0 & 0 & 0 & 0 & 0 & 0 \\
u & u & \underline{0} & \underline{0} & u & 1 & u & u & \underline{0} & u & u & 1 \\
u & \underline{0} & u & u & \underline{0} & u & \underline{0} & 1 & u & u & 1 & u \\
u & u & u & u & u & u & u & u & u & \underline{0} & u & u
\end{array}
$$

The erroneous settings have been underlined.

Over the entire set of possible presentations, using the measure:

$$\text{advance} = \text{right minterms} - \text{wrong minterms}$$

it may be calculated that there is an average positive advance of 1.24 minterms for this step. It may also be shown that given an advance in the first step, the advance in the second is even more probable and so on as training progresses.

On the second characteristic, the introduction of an error will, in due course, be corrected in step 5 of the algorithm. This means that the positive bias calculated above is the overall factor that drives the system towards a solution. The errors merely introduce a finite delay, long delays being less likely than short ones, leading to the distribution shape in Fig. 5(*b*). This effect is best seen by examining some of the sequences of the number of *u* minterms as the training progresses (the occurrence of a detected error is underlined):

Example 1
Nine steps to solution (about 28% likelihood).

$$12-9-7-6-4-3-1-1-1-0 \text{ no errors.}$$

Example 2
Forty-one steps to solution (about 8% likelihood)

$\quad$ 12–9–7–4–7–6–6–6–4–7–7–5–8–8–6–4–4–7–4–1–1

$\quad$ –4–3–2–2–2–5–5–4–2–2–2–2–2–2–2–2–1–1–1–1–0

$\quad$ six errors corrected.

The third characteristic (solutions = attractors) is ensured by the fact that once a solution has been found, loop 3.2 of the algorithm cannot be entered, and no further changes will be made through loop 3.1 only. It can also be seen that the presence of slight departures from the solution will re-enter the solution due to the favourable bias described earlier (which, in the vicinity of the solution, is at its maximum).

Clearly, there is additional work to be done not only on the proper modelling of this algorithm (as a probabilistic automaton in function space) but also on the design and analysis of similar, perhaps more efficient, algorithms.

6. Conclusions

Four broad, but central points are made in this paper.

(6.1) Although weight variations as an approach to function variability in the nodes of a connectionist system are close to what is known of neurons, it appears to be idiosyncratic among ways that node adaptability could be expressed. The most general way of expressing this, taken from logic, is adopted in this paper: the definition of a communication alphabet between the nodes, where variability is expressed as an alteration of the mapping of the input minterms of a node into an element of this alphabet at the output.

(6.2) Close neuron models make decisions with greater or lesser confidence, depending on whether the weighted sum of the input is close or far from a threshold (or from zero in the case of the model used for error backpropagation[11]). In this paper this has been generalized in a probabilistic way by defining a 'don't know' mapping for the minterms. In this case the node selects at its output an element of the communication alphabet at random. It is this that gives the net a semblance of 'self-annealing', which removes from retrieval algorithms (such as in Boltzmann machines[10]), the responsibility for selecting optimal annealing rates.

(6.3) In 'easy' learning tasks where the entire net is clamped to the desired state, the logic formulation has been shown to lead to the definition of an optimal minterm mapping for each node. This is optimal as it ensures the most rapid descent into the desired state. It has been

153

shown that training strategies can use noise in a planned way to approach these optimal mappings.

(6.4) A 'hard' learning algorithm has been described in which the hidden nodes search for appropriate representations by virtue of their 'don't know' mappings. It has been argued that the algorithm is convergent on solutions, and empirical results on a parity checker show a marked improvement over the performance of error backpropagation schemes used with closely modelled neurons.

All in all, it is argued that the probabilistic logic node approach brings the advantages of connectionism closer to implementation, and provides the engineer with a predictive theory which leads to informed design. From the perspective of explaining the function of the brain, it is felt that this approach provides insights into a broad class of systems all of which, with the brain as a specific example, follow a set of laws that are clearly expressed through notions of probabilistic automata.

References

1. Rumelhart, D. E. & McClelland, J. L. (eds.) *Parallel Distributed Processing*, Vols. 1 and 2 (Cambridge Mass: MIT Press, 1986).
2. McCulloch, W. S. & Pitts, W. A logical calculus of the ideas imminent in nervous activity, *Bull. Math. Biophys.* **5**, 115–133 (1943).
3. Taylor, W. K. Machines that learn, *Science Journal* **102**(6) (1968).
4. Widrow, B. & Hoff, M. E. Adaptive switching networks, *IRE Wescon Convention Record* (1961).
5. Rosenblatt, F. *Perceptrons: Principles of Neurodynamics* (NY: Spartan Books, 1962).
6. Minsky, M. & Papert, S. *Perceptrons: an Introduction to Computational Geometry* (Cambridge Mass: MIT Press, 1969).
7. Kohonen, T. *Self-organization and Associative Memory* (Berlin: Springer Verlag, 1984).
8. Aleksander, I. Fused adaptive circuit which learns by example, *Electronics Letters* **1**(6) (August 1965).
9. Hopfield, J. J. Neural networks and physical systems with emergent computational abilities, *Proceedings of the National Academy of Sciences, USA*, Vol. 79, pp. 2554–2558 (1982).
10. Hinton, G. E., Sejnowski, T. J. & Ackley, D. H. *Boltzmann Machines: Constraint Satisfaction Networks that Learn* (Tech. Rep., CMU CS 84 119, Carnegie Mellon University. Pittsburgh, 1984).
11. Rumelhart, D. E., Hinton, G. E. & Williams, R. J. Learning internal representations by error propagation. In Rumelhart, D. E. & McClelland, J. L. (eds.) *Parallel Distributed Processing*, Vol. 1 (Cambridge Mass: MIT Press, 1986).
12. Aleksander, I. Adaptive vision systems and Boltzmann machines: a rapprochement, *Pattern Recognition Letters* **6**, 113–120 (1987).
13. Aleksander, I., Thomas, W. V. & Bowden, P. A. WISARD, a radical step forward in image recognition, *Sensor Review* **4**(3), 120–124 (1984).

14. Aleksander, I. Brain cell to microcircuit, *Electronics and Power* **16**, 48–51 (1970).
15. Kauffmann, S. A. Metabolic stability and epigenesis in randomly constructed genetic nets, *J. Theoret. Biol.* **22**, 437–467 (1969).
16. Aleksander, I. & Atlas, P. Cyclic activity in nature: causes of stability, *Int. J. of Neuroscience* **6**, 45–50 (1973).

9 A probabilistic logic neuron network for associative learning

Wing-kay Kan and Igor Aleksander

Imperial College of Science and Technology, University of London, UK

Abstract

There is a developing interest in parallel systems where properties emerge from some aspect of their connections. These are called connectionist systems[1] or parallel distributed processors.[2] Although most of these systems use a cell that is related to the weight-sum-and-threshold neuron model first proposed by McCulloch & Pitts,[3] the element in this paper is based on the random-access memory (RAM) model of the neuron, first proposed by one of the authors.[4] In fact, the element described in this paper is a probabilistic version of the RAM model which responds with a randomly generated output for inputs on which it has not been trained. We call these probabilistic logic neurons (PLN). The multi-layer associative network described here uses PLNs to provide learnt image-to-image transformations with design rules and an algorithm which allow the designer to achieve such transformation with a selected degree of accuracy.

1. Structure

1.1 Probabilistic logic neurons (PLN)

The basic element of the multi-layered associative network is called a PLN neuron (see Fig. 1). The generic form of a PLN neuron consists of

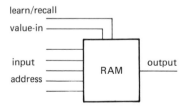

Figure 1 *A PLN in pattern molecules.*

156

(1) a set of input lines; (2) a memory (RAM) which is accessed by being given an 'address' composed of the binary values present on the input lines; (3) an output line which returns a binary value; (4) one or more (or none) internal states indicate the status of the PLN neuron; (5) one or more control lines signify the operation needed to perform, eg read or write operation; and (6) the 'hardware' to perform the operations.

Like other neuron models, a PLN neuron performs a logical function by returning a value for a given input. Both input and output values are assumed to be binary, namely, 0 or 1. Training of a network system of neurons is to adjust the 'modifiable' part of the neurons to give desired values for given inputs. The modifiable parts of a McCulloch–Pitts neuron are the weights and the threshold.[3] The modifiable parts of a PLN neuron are the contents of the memory and the states. A PLN neuron performs logical functions on inputs by saving the desired values into the locations 'addressed' by the given inputs. The memory of a PLN neuron is always made large enough to save all of the possible logical functions for the inputs. Therefore, unlike a McCulloch–Pitts formal neuron which is unable to perform some of the logical functions, a PLN neuron is capable of performing all of the possible logical functions.

The primitive form of a PLN neuron is exactly like a random access memory chip, which has only one control line for read/write operation and uses no internal states. This form was first used in the WISARD vision system[5] and then in other WISARD-like systems.[6] The PLN neuron used in the multi-layered associative network is more complex than the primitive form. Firstly, it has an internal state. The value of the state decides what should be written into the memory of a node during the training. Secondly, unlike the primitive form which stores only binary values, the PLN neurons used in the multi-layered associative network has an initial value of 'undefined' before training. This initial value signifies a guess to the correct answer is required. The introduction of the special value of 'undefined' also enhances the performance and the generalization of the network. More will be said about this special value in the section where the learning algorithms of the network are presented.

1.2 Memory modules

A layer of PLN neurons is called a memory module. The output of a memory module is the output values of the PLN neurons. The input terminals of a memory module receives a set of binary values from another memory module. The input lines of each PLN neuron connect randomly to the input terminals of the memory module. The random connections are fixed when the memory module is built and no connections can be changed thereafter. A PLN neuron of a memory module is also called a node of a memory module.

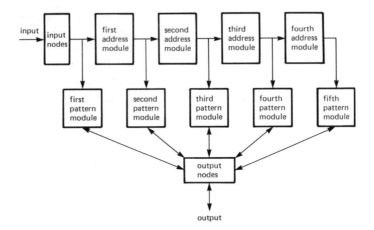

Figure 2   *A multi-layered associative network of four layers.*

1.3 Multi-layered associative network

There are two kinds of memory modules: address modules and pattern modules, classified by the type of functions they perform within the network. A layer of modules in the multi-layered associative network consists of exactly one address module and one pattern module. An address module of each layer accepts inputs from another address module and connects its output to both a pattern module and the address module of the next layer. The framework of the multi-layered associative network is formed by a number of such pairs of memory modules (see Fig. 2). The first layer consists of one pattern module and a memory buffer called input nodes. Pattern modules of all layers are connected to a memory buffer called output nodes. Input nodes and output nodes are buffers for external devices (eg a frame store containing an image). Both the input and output nodes are called 'clamped' nodes and are accessible to a user. The nodes of all memory modules are called 'hidden' nodes and are accessible only internally by the nodes of other memory modules.

1.4 Multi-layered associative network with feedback

If the values of the output nodes go back to the input nodes, the result from the previous operations may help the next operation of the network. The structure of the multi-layered associative network with feedback (see Fig. 3) is same as the network in Fig. 2, except that the outputs from the pattern modules go back to the input nodes through the 'clamps'. The clamps are where the users supply information for learning and recalling patterns. It is expected that the network with feedback has emergent

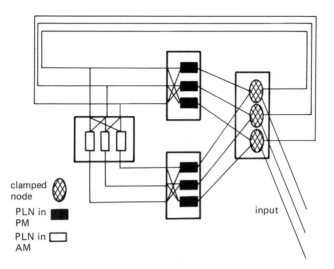

Figure 3   *A two-layer PLN network with feedback.*

characteristics such as pattern completion and auto-association, as will be discussed.

2. Operations

2.1 Associative learning

Multi-layered associative network is designed to perform associative learning in the sense that it learns to produce a particular pattern on the output nodes whenever another particular patterns occurs on the input nodes. In general the learning algorithms should allow arbitrary patterns on both the input and output nodes.

There are two types of associative learning[2]—pattern association and auto-association. A pattern association is to build up an association between a set of patterns with another set of patterns. During training, selected patterns are presented to both input and output nodes. The contents of the memory of the PLN neurons are modified so that whenever a particular pattern reappears on the input nodes, the associated pattern will appear on the output nodes. There is usually a teacher input indicating the desired pattern association during the training. An auto-association is the case in which a pattern is associated with itself. The multi-layered associative network with feedback is of that type. The goal in auto-association is pattern completion. Whenever a part of the input pattern is given, the rest of the pattern is to be filled in.

Simple pattern association is a special case of auto-association. Auto-association also allows more sophisticated operations on patterns, such as recalling a pattern by being given different parts of the pattern.

2.2 Distributed representation

The success of a massively parallel system relies on three conditions: a good parallel search technique (recalling procedure); an appropriate internal representation; and an efficient learning algorithm to build up the internal representations. These conditions are, of course, not independent of each other. An appropriate internal representation scheme should allow the network to be used efficiently for encoding the patterns being searched.

Given a network of nodes to represent patterns, it is easy to think of using one node for each pattern. This is called local representation. The neural network of the human brain, however, seems to rely on a different way of storing knowledge. Much information is stored in many different places, not just one piece of information in each place. The multi-layered associative network mimics this way of representing patterns. This representation scheme is called 'distributed representation'.[7]

The distributed representation of knowledge in the multi-layered associative network is determined by the way the network stores the patterns into the memory of the PLN neurons. Each pattern is stored by distributing it over many nodes, and each node is involved in representing many different patterns. The systems using the distributed representation are able to generalize and provide the best solution for given constraints. One of the other advantages of this representation scheme is its reliability against damages to the network. Destruction of one or more nodes of the network loses a small fraction rather than the whole of the knowledge entities.

2.3 Learning algorithms

A pattern on the input nodes of the network with feedback represents a network state of the network. From one network state, every node determines its next state completely by the contents of its memory. The operation of the network is assumed to be synchronous. A network state has only one exit and the network states form a set of 'confluents' of states (see Fig. 4). Starting from one state, the network will eventually reach a cycle of states (or one state).

The set of all possible network states is called the state space of the network. There are four kinds of network states: (1) the precursor states which have no predecessor states; (2) the transient states which have both successor and predecessor states, and are traversed once only; (3) the cyclic states which are traversed repeatedly once the network enters into

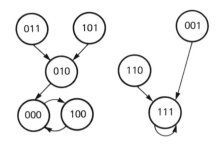

Figure 4 *State diagram for three nodes.*

any of the states in the cycle; and (4) the invariant states which are cycles containing only one state. The network will not change its state once it reaches an invariant state.

A successful learning algorithm is a set of procedures which results in the 'trained' states becoming invariant states. A 'trained' state is the patterns to be associated. The learning algorithms are also required to change the structures of the state space such that the states similar to the trained state will eventually reach the trained state. When the network starts with a state similar to a trained state, after a few operations the network should reach the trained state. For example, when a pattern is given on input nodes, the network is able to complete the associated pattern on the output nodes after a few operations of the network.

2.3.1 Problem of pre-existing structures in a state space

The difficulties of many learning algorithms are mainly due to the pre-existing structures of the state space before training. Depending on the initial value of the memory of the nodes before training, arbitrary confluents of states exist. The learning algorithms not only have to create an invariant state for the trained pattern, but are also required to disrupt the pre-existing structures and move the similar states such that any one of them eventually reaches the invariant state via a path of network states. However, the state space of the network is usually so large that most learning algorithms are incapable of moving the similar states so that they might reach the invariant state. The network is easily trapped into another confluent of states during a recall and is unable to reach the correct trained state starting from a similar state. Some networks[8,9] employ an 'annealing' process which requires repeatedly training with the same pattern a large number of times in order to remove most of the incorrect stable points in the state space.

The multi-layered associative network solves the problem by filling the memory of the nodes with a special value of 'undefined' before training. When an addressed location has the value of 'undefined', a random binary value is put on the output of the node. A different value may appear, even if the same location is addressed next time. Unless no nodes address the locations with the value of 'undefined', a state does not have a fixed next state. Therefore the structures of the state space keep changing all the time. The learning algorithms cause the trained states to become the invariant states by writing binary values into the appropriate locations of the memory. The rest of the state space are 'untrained' states of which part or all of the addressed locations have the value of 'undefined'. During a recall operation, the network moves from one state to another until it reaches an invariant state and stays there. The initialization of the memory with undefined values may be thought as a way to separate the trained states from the untrained states. This has the effect that after the separation, the learning algorithms no longer need to handle the huge number of untrained states and are able to be both faster and simpler.

Fig. 5 shows an example of how the use of 'undefined' value solves the

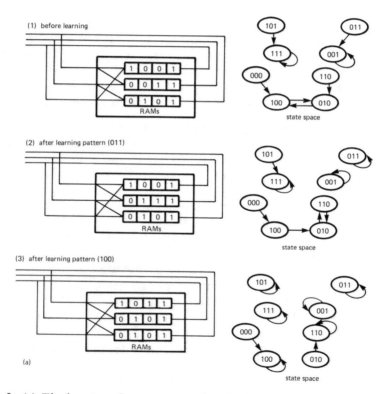

Figure 5 (a) *The learning of two patterns when RAMs are filled with random binary values before learning.*

problem of pre-existing structures in a state space. The feedback network consists of one memory module with three nodes and two input lines per node. A simple learning algorithm, the stable-state creation algorithm, is used. During learning, a selected pattern is applied to the clamps. Each node writes the value of the corresponding clamped value into the location addressed by the given pattern. Fig. 5(*a*) shows the learning process when the RAMs are filled with random binary values before learning. After more patterns are learned, there are more stable points in the state space and the network is hardly stable to either of the learned patterns. Fig. 5(*b*) is the learning process when the RAMs are filled with the undefined values before training. Every state has the same probability of going to the other states before learning. The diagram here shows only the relevant state transitions. We can observe the increase of the probabilities of the states similar to the learned states going to the learned pattern after learning. The learned state also goes back to itself and there is only one stable point in the state space. After learning both patterns, the state space nearly separates itself into two confluents of states. The states similar to the learned states are of greater probability

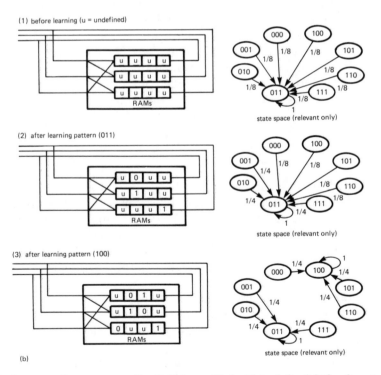

(b)

(*b*) *The learning of two patterns when RAMs are filled with 'undefined' before learning.*

leading into the learned states, and have no transition probability going the other learned state. There are only two stable points in the state space and the network is expected to settle itself into either one of the learned states after a number of iterations. Moreover, the network is likely to stabilise into the learned state to which the initial state of the network is similar.

2.3.2 The problem of the disruption of stored information during training

When a new item is learned, the modifications made to the network should not wipe out the existing items. To perform a write operation during learning, a node may address the memory location which has already been written during the previous training. If the new value needed to be written differs from the stored value in the location, the old value will be lost. For a system using distributed representation for storing knowledge, every change made to a node causes many network states to change their next network states at the same time. Newly created state transitions may cause changes of the 'trained' structures of the state space and are very likely to disrupt the stored information in the network.

It is possible to prevent the disruption by giving the guarantee that all new write operations to the nodes are made only to those locations which have never been addressed before. Consider a memory module of K_0 nodes, K_i input terminals and N input lines per node. Let H_m be the smallest Hamming distance between the trained patterns. The condition of Equation (1) should be satisfied if such a guarantee can be provided.[10] For a network with given size of the input and output nodes, we may choose to increase N or H_m to satisfy the condition.

$$K_0\left(1 - \frac{H_m}{K_i}\right)^N < 1. \tag{1}$$

2.3.3 Generalization vs. precision

We may increase the number of input lines per node (N) to prevent the disruption of the stored information. However, this reduces one of the most desirable capabilities of the networks: they automatically give rise to generalization which allows the network to deal effectively with the patterns that are similar but not identical to the previously trained patterns.

Every node in the network receives only part of the information from the inputs since the number of input lines per node is usually less than the number of input terminals per memory module. If the given input is similar to one of the previously trained patterns, most of the nodes still obtain the set of identical values on their input lines and hence provide the same output. The number of nodes which give either 'undefined' values or incorrect values for a given input increases exponentially with the Hamming distance between the given input and the trained pattern most similar to it.[10] If they are similar enough, the network is able to produce the trained pattern if even part of the given input is incorrect or missing. The larger the number of input lines a node has, the larger the part of a given input must be correct in order to produce the same output. Details of this kind of behaviour are well-known.[11]

However, a network with a small N also shows poor performance. When N is very small, most patterns look alike to each node. The network easily gives a wrong answer. The network may not give a 'don't know' result given an input that is different from any trained patterns. Therefore the network with a small N has better generalization but poorer precision on the results of the association. This trade-off is at its most severe for single-layer nets. The multi-layered approach has the property that overcomes this problem.

The multi-layered associative network is an example of a way that we can have both better generalization and higher precision at the same time. We recall that we can change the Hamming distance (H_m) between the trained patterns to satisfy the requirement of the Equation (1). In the multi-layered associative network, N is kept small to obtain better generalization, while the precision is improved by increasing the value of H_m internally. As the trained patterns may not have the necessary differences, we use an algorithm to amplify the Hamming distances at the intermediate levels until they become the required values. The address modules are used to store the patterns of enlarged difference for the trained patterns. The differences of the trained patterns are amplified from layer to layer until the internal patterns differ at least H_m bits from other internal patterns in the same address module. A memory module with the internal pattern as input will entirely address the locations which have never been written before. The pattern modules are the memory modules which store the trained patterns using the internal patterns as inputs.

Let H_0 be the Hamming distance of two input patterns P_1 and P_2 of an address module, and let H_1 be the Hamming distance of their corresponding output patterns. The output of a node in the address module gives a different value for P_1 and P_2 only when the node addresses a different location of the memory and the location has a different value. The Equation (2) shows how much the differences between input patterns and output patterns are amplified in a memory module:

$$H_1 = I\left[1 - \left(\frac{K - H_0}{K}\right)^N\right]. \tag{2}$$

The internal Hamming distance I, is the required average Hamming distance of the internal patterns in the address modules. For a network of four layers with an address module having 256 input terminals, eight input lines per node and 128 bits of internal Hamming distance, the following table (Table 1) illustrates how Hamming distances are amplified in the network.

Table 1. *Amplification of Hamming distance in a network of four layers*

Layer	1	2	3	4
H_0	2	8	29	79
H_1	8	29	79	121

2.4 Learning phase

An associative operation in the multi-layered associative network has two phases: a learning phase and a recalling phase. During a learning phase, both associated patterns are clamped on the input and output nodes. (Only one pattern is clamped on the input nodes for the network with feedback.) A teacher automaton sends a teach input (the read/write control in the Fig. 3) to all nodes of the memory modules. A sequence of write operations is then performed successively from the first layer to the last layer of the memory modules. An address module accepts inputs from the address module of the previous layer, excepting the first layer which accepts inputs from the input nodes. A new internal pattern is created and stored into the memory using the internal pattern creation algorithm described in the next section. The newly created internal pattern is the input to the address module of the next layer. The pattern module of the same layer also uses the internal pattern to store the pattern of the output nodes into its memory. The learning phase is terminated when the pattern module of the last layer completes its operations.

2.4.1 Internal pattern creation algorithm

An internal pattern should have the Hamming distance larger than a specified value from other internal patterns in the same address module. The algorithm described in the next paragraph allows each node to decide independently its value for the creation of a pattern with a specified difference which is half of the number of the nodes in an address module. The algorithm is highly parallel, since each node needs only the local information obtained from its memory and its state. The algorithm is also designed for machines like the network of PLN neurons which only have simple computation power. To obtain the simplicity and parallelism, the algorithm does not guarantee to give the internal patterns the specified Hamming distance but has a likelihood of improving the Hamming distance. In fact, the simulations reveal that few patterns actually have differences less than the specified value.

When a pattern is given to the input terminals of an address module, each node of the address module writes a binary value into the addressed location if the addressed location has an 'undefined' value. The value to be written is determined by the state of the node. After the write operation, the state of the node will also change its value. A state of a node has one of three possible values, namely, one, zero and 'undefined'. The value of a state of a node indicates which binary value will give the largest difference from the binary values in the memory of the node. It eliminates the counting of the number of binary values in the RAM for every learning phase. If a state of a node has the value of either one or zero, the value of the state will be written into the addressed location and the state of the node changes its value to 'undefined'. If a state has a value of 'undefined', a random binary value is written into the addressed location and the state of the node has the complement value of the random value. The states of all nodes have the value of 'undefined' before training. If the addressed location has a binary value, that value will not be changed. The state of the node changes its value to 'undefined' if both the value of the state and the value of the addressed location are the same.

train pattern	addressed location	created pat. (name)	states after learning
101000	uuuuuu	101101 (P1)	010010
101011	uuuuuu	010010 (P2)	uuuuuu
101101	0u11uu	011100 (P3)	100011
101110	1u00uu	100011 (P4)	u1uu00

(a)

	P1	P2	P3
P2	6		
P3	3	3	
P4	3	3	6

(b)

Figure 6   *An example of the internal pattern creation algorithm:* (a) *creation of four internal patterns;* (b) *Hamming distances of the created patterns.*

167

Otherwise, the value of the state is the complement value of the value of the addressed location. Fig. 6 gives an example of how the internal patterns are created in an address module of six nodes and each node has three input lines. The input patterns all differ in two bits. The example shows that the patterns created all have the Hamming differences greater than that of the input patterns.

2.5 Recalling phase

The multi-layered associative network is content addressable. We can recall an entire pattern by giving just part of it, or something similar to it. Recalling a pattern in the network does not rely on a high degree of accuracy because it acquires information through a trial-and-error process. The value of 'undefined' indicates where a guess is needed to be made during a recall. The intermediate result which contains both the guesses and correct responses is produced from each layer. The results are then combined using a special technique discussed below in order to produce the best-matched answer into the output nodes. The recall operation can also be repeated many times in the network with feedback.

During a recalling phase, a pattern is applied to the input nodes. (Part of a pattern is given for the network with feedback and the rest of the clamped nodes, which is called the unclamped area, is filled with undefined values). A sequence of read operations is then performed from the first layer to the last layer of the memory modules. An address module accepts an input from the address module of the previous layer and uses the input to read its memory and produce a pattern on its output lines. If a node in the address module addresses a location having a value of 'undefined', a random binary value is put on the output line, the node. It is analogous to a 'guess' procedure of filling up the incomplete information. Otherwise, the value of the addressed location is put on the output line. The pattern module uses the output from the address module of the related layer to address its memory and pass the result to the output nodes. The output nodes combine the output from the first layer to the last layer such that the output with binary values from the later layer overwrites the values on the output nodes. Not every value of the output nodes will be written over because the values on the output nodes are not changed if the corresponding locations of the pattern module have undefined values. The 'undefined' values from the pattern modules represent the 'don't know' situation. The combination technique requires that the information provided on the memory modules of the later layers should be more accurate than that of the preceding layers. In fact, this assurance has been made during the learning phases when the Hamming distances of the internal patterns in the address modules are made larger than those of the preceding layers.

3. Simulations

A number of simulations for the multi-layered associative networks have been done to demonstrate their capabilities. Two of them are shown here. The results of other simulations and the mathematical analysis of the learning algorithms are given in another report.[10]

The first simulation is for the multi-layered associative network without feedback. The pairs of the associated patterns are patterns of 26 alphabets of 16 by 8 bits and the patterns with 5 bars of 16 bits representing the corresponding 5-bit ASCII codes. The associated patterns are trained into the network during a number of learning phases. After learning all patterns, a number of recalls are performed. For each recall, a pattern of the alphabets are clamped on the input nodes. To emulate the noisy environment, some of the input nodes are randomly chosen and the values of the nodes are changed to their complements. The network then operates in a recalling phase and produces a pattern in the output nodes. The recalled pattern is compared with the pattern associated with the alphabet during training. The percentage of the matched bits are recorded for each recall. The same operations are repeated a number of times for the same pattern. The process continues for each alphabet and then for different noise levels. The results are summarized in Table 2, from which we observe the outstanding performance of the recognition, even with a fair amount of noise.

Table 2. *The results of alphabet recognition*

Noise (%)	Matched-bits (%)
0	100
1.6	98
2.6	95
6.3	86

The second simulation is for the network with feedback. A trained pattern consists of 16 bars of 16 bits width. Each pattern is the same Hamming distance from all other trained patterns. Ten patterns are trained into the network during a number of learning phases. After the training, one of the trained patterns is clamped on the input nodes and then part of the input nodes (unclamped area) is filled with the value of 'undefined'. After a recalling phase, part or all of the unclamped area will be filled with binary values. The network repeats the recall operation using the given inputs and the values kept on the unclamped area. The network performs the feedback operations a specified number of times

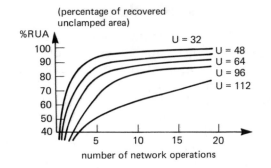

Figure 7   *Results of pattern completion in a feedback network with varying size of the unclamped area U.*

and the pattern of the unclamped area is compared with the corresponding part of the pattern trained into the network. The percentage of the matched bits, which is called the percentage of the recovered unclamped area (%RUA), is recorded. The same procedure is repeated for the same pattern a number of times. The whole process continues for all of the trained patterns and then with a different size of unclamped area. Fig. 7 gives the results of the pattern completions. Each point is the average of 20 simulations. From the diagram, we can confirm that the feedback operations of the network are stable and convergent. It is also interesting to note that the network also reaches a high percentage of the recovered unclamped area if the unclamped area is smaller than one-quarter of the input size.

4. Conclusion

This paper has introduced the probabilistic logic neuron which in itself has interesting properties. Its main feature is that the 'undefined' state and its generation provide a network of such devices, a random search facility which reduces with training. Compared with other connectionist approaches that use annealing principles, such as Boltzmann machines[8], this gives RAM-like networks a property of self-annealing. This requires further analysis in general networks and opens the way for the design of effective training algorithms in such nets.

While the implementability of the PLN is a major feature of the system proposed here, the nature of the analysis also merits close attention. It is based on a direct application of probability theory to finite state machine models, and in that sense makes fewer demands on network restrictions than either Hopefield models, which require reciprocal connections, or error propagation models,[12] which require a very large number of presentations of training examples.

The multi-layered associative network presented here is an example of the latter point in the sense that training does not involve error propagation, but relies instead on the faster method of local adjustment based on the Hamming distance amplification. Clearly, more work could be done on exact comparisons between these two methods. But, for the time being, common sense tells us that local, parallel adjustments are more effective than error propagations.

References

1. Feldman, J. A. & Ballard, D. H. Connectionist models and their properties, *Cognitive Science* 6, 205–254 (1982).
2. Rumelhart, D. E. & McClelland, J. L. *Parallel Distributed Processing*, Vol. 1: *Foundations* (Cambridge Mass: MIT Press, 1986).
3. McCulloch, W. S. & Pitts, W. A logical calculus of the ideas immanent in nervous activity, *Bulletin of Mathematical Biophysics* 5, 115–133 (1943).
4. Aleksander, I. *Microcircuit Learning Computers* (London: Mills and Boon, 1971).
5. Aleksander, I., Thomas, W. V. & Bowden, P. A. Wisard: a radical step forward in image recognition, *Sensor Review*, 120–124 (July 1984).
6. Aleksander, I. Emergent intelligent properties of progressively structured pattern recognition nets, *Pattern Recognition Letters* 1, 375–384 (1983).
7. Hinton, G. E. *Distributed Representation*, Technical Report CMU-CS-84-157 (Department of Computer Science, Carnegie-Mellon University, October 1984).
8. Hinton, G. E., Sejnowski, D. H. & Ackley, D. H. *Boltzmann Machines: Constraint Satisfaction Networks that Learn* (Technical Report CMU-CS-84-119, Carnegie-Mellon University, 1984).
9. Milligan, D. K. Annealing in RAM-based learning networks, obtained from author (March 1986).
10. Kan, W. K. A probabilistic neural network for associative learnings, PhD Dissertation, Imperial College, London (in preparation) (1989).
11. Aleksander, I. & Wilson, M. Adaptive windows for image processing, *IEE Procs.*, Vol. 132, Pt. E, No. 5 (September 1985).
12. Rumelhart, D. E., Hinton, G. E. & Williams, R. J. Learning internal representations by error propagation. In *Parallel Distributed Processing*, Volume 1: *Foundations*, Rumelhart, D. E. & McClelland, J. L. (eds) (Cambridge Mass: MIT Press, 1986).

10 Applications of *N*-tuple sampling and genetic algorithms to speech recognition

A. Badii
Schlumberger Technologies, Central Research Department, Farnborough, UK

M. J. Binstead
17 Myddleton Road, Uxbridge, Middlesex, UK

Antonia J. Jones
Department of Computing, Imperial College of Science and Technology, University of London, London, UK

T. J. Stonham
Department of Electrical Engineering, Brunel University, Uxbridge, Middlesex, UK

Christine L. Valenzuela
Department of Computer Science, Teesside Polytechnic, Middlesbrough, Cleveland, UK

Abstract

N-tuple nets are conceptually a highly parallel architecture for pattern recognition, implemented in hardware as a device called WISARD. However, high-speed serial emulations of *N*-tuple nets offer considerable advantages of flexibility and cost efficiency in applications, such as speech recognition, requiring only moderate bandwidth.

In this chapter we first describe a software technique for designing dynamically evolved *N*-tuple nets and illustrate the process whereby the designed structure can be progressively mapped into hardware to a level determined by the application requirements.

Next, we summarize some simulation studies which apply *N*-tuple nets to isolated word recognition and vowel detection.

For isolated word recognition it is shown that with raw data (non-pre-emphasized, noisy speech), *N*-tuple recognition yields improvement over dynamic time warping, while providing substantial savings in processing time.

For vowel detection, two distinct, single-speaker studies are described.

In the first experiment we attempt to accommodate to variation in the length of articulation of a vowel by training six distinct discriminators for each class of vowel, each of the six being trained over a different timescale.

In the second experiment on vowel detection, results are presented for a task specific optimization of a single mapping WISARD pattern recognizer using Holland's genetic algorithm.

1. Introduction

In this chapter we provide a synopsis of work, carried out by the authors under the auspices of the Pattern Recognition Laboratory, Brunel University, on the application of the N-tuple sampling paradigm of Bledsoe & Browning[1] to speech recognition.*

Networks of the type under consideration are simulations of extremely stylized models of biological neural networks. Such systems are usually characterized by some very simple algorithm, frequently little more than an inner product, replicated a large number of times as parallel, sometimes loosely coupled, processes. Examples of such systems in the literature include perceptrons,[3] WISARD nets,[4] Kohonen's topologizing nets,[5] the goal seeking components of Barto & Sutton[6] and, more recently, the conformon nets of Fish.[7] In this chapter we will concentrate on the implementation of WISARD nets, described below, applied to speech recognition.

The advantages of the WISARD model for pattern recognition are:

- Implementation as a parallel, or serial, system in currently available hardware is inexpensive and simple.
- Given labelled samples of each recognition class, training times are very short.
- The time required by a trained system to classify an unknown pattern is very small and, in a parallel implementation, is independent of the number of classes.

The requirement for labelled samples of each class poses particular problems in speech recognition when dealing with units smaller than whole words; the extraction of samples by acoustic and visual inspection is a labour intensive and time consuming activity. It is here that paradigms such as Kohonen's topologizing network, as applied to speech by Tattershall, show particular promise. Of course, in such approaches there are other compensating problems; principally, after the network has been trained and produced a dimensionally reduced and feature-

---

* Section 2 is based on [2], and more detailed reports on the work described in Sections 3 and 4 will appear elsewhere.

clustered map of the pattern space, it is necessary to interpret this map in terms of output symbols useful to higher levels. One approach to this problem is to train an associative memory on the net output together with the associated symbol.

Applications of N-tuple sampling in hardware have been rather sparse, the commercial version of WISARD as a visual pattern recognition device able to operate at TV frame rates, being one of the few to date— another is the optical character recognizer developed by Binstead & Stonham. However, one can envisage a multitude of applications for such pattern recognition systems as their operation and advantages become more widely understood.

Typically the real-time system is preceded by a software simulation in which various parameters of the theoretical model are optimized for the particular application. We begin by describing a software framework which is sufficiently general to cope with a large class of such net-systems, while at the same time preserving a high degree of computational efficiency. In addition, the structure produced has the property that it is easily mapped into hardware to a level determined by the application requirements.

The rationale for believing that N-tuple techniques might be successfully applied to speech recognizers is briefly outlined by Tattershall & Johnson,[8] who demonstrated that N-tuple recognizers can be designed so that in training they derive an implicit map of the class conditional probabilities. Since the N-tuple scheme requires almost no computation it appears to be an attractive way of implementing a Bayesian classifier. In a real-time speech recognition system the pre-processed input data can be slid across the retina and the system tuned to respond to significant peaking of a class discriminator response, see Fig. 4.

Two types of application to speech recognition are discussed. First, comparative results for *isolated word, single-speaker speech recognition* are presented for a variety of N-tuple recognizers. These results are then contrasted with the observed performance for the same data using a standard dynamic time warping algorithm used as a control in this context.

Next, preliminary investigations in vowel detection are reported; two distinct experiments are described. These experiments were restricted to *vowel detection for a single speaker*. Both experiments used the same data. In the first experiment we attempt to accommodate to variation in the length of articulation of a vowel by training six distinct discriminators for each class of vowel, each of the six being trained over a different timescale. In the second experiment one mapping is used for all vowels, each vowel having a single discriminator, and Holland's genetic

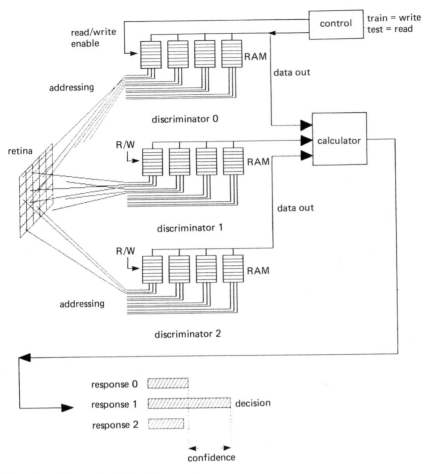

Figure 1   *Schematic of N-tuple recognizer.*

algorithm is used in an attempt to optimize this map for the specific task of vowel detection.

2. A simulation system

2.1 The WISARD model

WISARD (WIlkie, Stonham, Aleksander Recognition Device) is an implementation in hardware of the *N*-tuple sampling technique first described by Bledsoe & Browning.[1] The scheme outlined in Fig. 1 was first proposed by Aleksander & Stonham.[4]

The sample data to be recognized is stored as a two-dimensional array (the 'retina') of binary elements with successive samples in time stored in successive columns and the value of the sample represented by a coding of the binary elements in each column. The particular coding used will generally depend on the application. One of several possible codings is to represent a sample feature value by a 'bar' of binary 1s, the length of the bar being proportional to the value of the sample feature.

Random connections are made onto the elements of the array, N such connections being grouped together to form an N-tuple which is used to address one random access memory (RAM) per discriminator. In this way a large number of RAMs are grouped together to form a class discriminator whose output or score is the sum of all its RAM's outputs. This configuration is repeated to give one discriminator for each class of pattern to be recognized. The RAM's implement logic functions which are set up during training; thus the method does not involve any direct storage of pattern data.

A random map from array elements to N-tuples is preferable in theory, since a systematic mapping is more likely to render the recognizer blind to distinct patterns having a systematic difference. Hard-wiring a random map in a totally parallel system makes fabrication infeasible at high resolutions. In many applications, systematic differences in input patterns of the type liable to pose problems with a non-random mapping are unlikely to occur since real data tends to be 'fuzzy' at the pixel level. However, the issue of randomly hard-wiring individual RAMs is somewhat academic since in most contexts a totally parallel system is not needed as its speed (independent of the number of classes and of the order of the access time of a memory element) would far exceed data input rates. At 512×512 resolution a semi-parallel structure is used where the mapping is 'soft' (ie achieved by pseudo-random addressing with parallel shift registers) and the processing within discriminators is serial but the discriminators themselves are operating in parallel. Using memory elements with an access time of 10^{-7} s, this gives a minimum operating time of around 70 ms, which once again is independent of the number of classes.

The system is trained using samples of patterns from each class. A pattern is fed into the retina array and a logical 1 is written into the RAMs of the discriminator associated with the class of this training pattern at the locations addressed by the N-tuples. This is repeated many times, typically 25–50 times, for each class.

In recognition mode, the unknown pattern is stored in the array and the RAMs of every discriminator put into READ mode. The input pattern then stimulates the logic functions in the discriminator network and an overall response is obtained by summing all the logical outputs. The pattern is then assigned to the class of the discriminator producing the highest score.

Where very high resolution image data is presented, as in visual imaging, this design lends itself to easy implementation in massively parallel hardware. However, even with visual images, experience tends to suggest that a very good recognition performance can often be obtained on relatively low resolution data. Hence in many applications, massively parallel hardware can be replaced by a fast serial processor and associated RAM, emulating the design in micro-coded software. This was the approach used by Binstead & Stonham in optical character recognition, with notable success. Such a system has the advantage of being able to make optimal use of available memory in applications where the N-tuple size, or the number of discriminators, may be required to vary.

2.2 The development of N-tuple systems

Practical N-tuple pattern recognition systems have developed from the original implementation of the hardware WISARD, which used regularly sized blocks of RAM that store only the discriminator states. As memory has become cheaper and processors faster, such heavily constrained systems are no longer appropriate for many applications. Algorithms can be implemented as serial emulations of parallel hardware and RAM can also be used to describe a more flexible structure.

In such a system we might require a dynamically variable number of classes, RAMs per class or mappings. N-tuple mappings need no longer map each retinal pixel uniquely and might be varied during training and across classes according to some heuristic supplied by the programmer—for example, Holland's genetic algorithm.[9] Having different mappings for each class does require that each class be given a separate opportunity to respond, but in some applications this may well be worth the extra overhead in time or hardware.

One might easily imagine that the price to be paid for this enhanced flexibility would be excessive complexity and slow performance. However, this turns out not to be the case and we will briefly outline why this is so.

2.3 Software system for dynamic reallocation of N-tuples

Conceptually it is helpful to think of the entire experimental design process of an N-tuple classifier as the growing and filling of a dynamic tree.

Initially this tree will have a root from which all else will grow. In practice 'root' is a pointer (down) to the first of the next level nodes, which for now we may choose to think of as class zero. (However, first-level nodes could equally be 'machine types' so that decomposition at the first level would then be into a series of parallel machines.) At the class level, each class has a pointer (across) to the next class and a pointer (down) to the first RAM associated with that class.

We can iterate this process to create a tree–machine (ie data structure) which consists of:

(1) Classes—which in turn form collections of RAMs;

(2) RAMs—which form collections of input pointers (mappings) and pointers to the block of memory used to store the RAM state.

Fig. 2 illustrates the general structure of the tree. It is important to note that the nodes can hold extra information, for example statistics of their usage, a unique identifier and other pointers which can be used for memory control. This last feature is an essential part of a dynamically re-allocatable system.

Ultimately, memory will contain two types of information: the nodes which are joined by pointers to create the tree structure, and the memory which actually holds the taught information (the *N*-tuple storage). The memory requirement is strongly dependent on the *N*-tuple address size— adding an extra input to every RAM (although one could add an extra

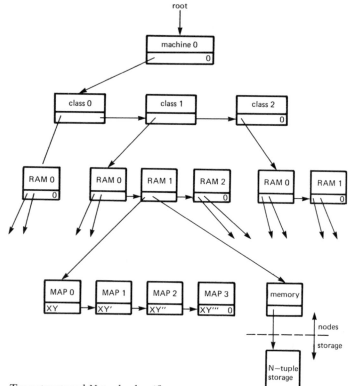

Figure 2   *Tree structured N-tuple classifier.*

input to just one RAM if desired) will linearly increase the number of nodes used but double the amount of N-tuple storage.

To access the memory it is necessary to traverse the tree to reach the requisite point. For example, suppose it was required to add an extra class. It becomes necessary to traverse the tree down to the class level and then along to the last-used class node, where a new node may be reclaimed from the 'node pool' maintained by memory control and added to form a new class by manipulating the necessary pointers. The same process may be repeated in order to add RAMs to the newly formed class.

In virtually every operation involving the tree a single very simple recursive algorithm, the *traverser*, is used. When calling the traverser, two parameters are passed: one is the base of the sub-tree to be traversed and the other is a pointer to a table of actions to be performed at each node visited. The table itself contains lists of actions for each possible node type. At present only two actions are used; the first is called when the node is entered and the other when the node is exited for the last time in the current traversal. For example, if one wanted to perform a classification: the first action on entering the node of type class would be to clear that class's response; upon leaving, the score (number of addressed RAMs in the discriminator which contain a logic '1') will have been updated by the lower levels so that the second action might be to print its value and to check if it is larger than the largest class score so far encountered.

Depending on the network being modelled the node types and actions can be chosen appropriately. For instance, if Kohonen's topologizing network were being modelled, one node type would be a *node*, in Kohonen's sense, which stores a state vector of the dimensionality of the data—his network is essentially an array of such nodes, and one action would be to modify the states of 'nearby' nodes according to the response of the current node to the data being presented.

A C-code listing of the traverser algorithm is given in Appendix I.[2] In most cases it will not be necessary to visit all nodes of the tree. So the traverser algorithm has extra switches that allow branches to be bypassed or the traversal aborted. In this way, for example, the search can be confined to a single level of the tree and aborted when a specific condition or node is attained.

Thus a flexible and simple experimental system, having all the proposed properties, has been created. It is now relatively straightforward for the experimenter to implement his chosen heuristics to control the evolution of the final system design. Moreover, since the structure consists largely of threaded pointers, very little calculation is required during the training and testing phases. Consequently, simulation times are considerably reduced.

Comparisons with earlier simulation systems, such as JAN, give an improvement of a factor between 2 and 4. Direct comparison is difficult since the earlier systems were so slow that they were modified to look only at input data which had changed, and they only dealt with regular sized discriminators, etc. If systems such as JAN had to deal with variable-sized discriminators then accessing a multi-dimensional array, say (class, RAM, element), could no longer be done using tables and would involve two multiplications and one addition, whereas in the present system access is via a pointer and involves no calculation.

When the fully trained system is complete the network of pointers will have become rather tangled. However, this poses no real problem since the structure of memory can be rationalized into appropriate blocks to facilitate implementation into hardware. This process is easily accomplished by a software module which reorders the pointers.

For historical reasons the final system has been named NEWJAM. It promises to be the vehicle for much of the net-systems research work of the adaptive systems and pattern recognition group at Brunel over the next few years.

2.4 Mapping the real time system into hardware

An important advantage conferred by NEWJAM is that since the data structure produced is tree-like it naturally decomposes into hardware at several alternative levels. Thus the actual decomposition can be chosen depending upon the bandwidth and response time required for the real-time system.

In Fig. 3 we sketch one possible approach for implementing the real-time recognition system (envisaged as a co-processor connected to a micro-computer host). The principal components of this system are:

68000/68020 CPU
This performs input–output functions and, initially, all actions called for via the action table memory. Every action is intrinsically a very simple process and consequently the most frequently called actions can be progressively replaced by special purpose hardware (Node type A processor, Node type B processor, etc., in Fig. 3).

Memory controller
This is the hardware which performs the traverser algorithm recursively. It could easily be implemented as a gate array and requires a small stack and access to a small number of status registers. In principle the traverser accesses the system memory via a separate bus (the tree bus) and can disable–enable the 68000 bus. In practice the traverser and the 68000 may share a common bus transparently, with the traverser able to control priority and refresh.

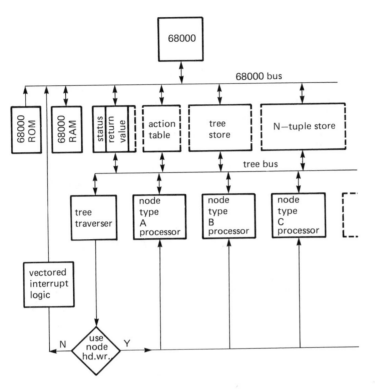

Figure 3   *Tree traverser—block diagram.*

Tree memory
The traverser locates a particular node of the tree by consulting a
particular base address in tree memory. The block of memory starting at
this address contains information describing the node (type, etc.). This
memory is not particularly large and could be implemented in fast RAM.

Action table memory
Having located a particular node and recovered the address of the
associated action type from tree memory the traverser consults this
address in the action table memory which acts essentially as a function
lookup table. As the number of action types is small this memory could
be implemented in fast RAM.

N-tuple storage memory
This is the largest block of memory and can be implemented in slower,
cheaper RAM.

When an action request is initiated, the corresponding module, or the
68000, must place an acknowledgement in the traverser status register.

Upon completion of the action a return value is placed in the status register.

Having decided upon the action type currently required the traverser places the request onto the action bus where it is either vectored to the 68000, if no special purpose hardware exists to perform the action, or passed to the appropriate action module. Initially there would be no action modules and the 68000 would perform all these actions. As action modules are slotted into the system they take over the corresponding role from the 68000.

An additional advantage conferred by this design is that if an action module fails, the 68000 can resume performance of the action until the module can be replaced.

3. Isolated word recognition

3.1 Introduction

In this section comparative results for *isolated word, single-speaker speech recognition* are presented for ten different N-tuple recognizers. These results are then contrasted with the observed performance for the same data using a standard dynamic time warping algorithm used as a control in this context.

Samples of 16 words from a diagnostic rhyming test list were collected from a single speaker on a carefully standardized data acquisition system (Shure SM12A microphone, flat pre-emphasis profile and a Sony model 701ES tape recorder) for subsequent automatic retrieval and digital processing using sample labelling and a modular A–D, D–A system with 16-bit resolution. This data was then stored on a VAX 11–750 to enable precise comparison of different recognition algorithms.

The speech data bank for the speech research includes the rhyming set, the alpha-numerics, simple command words and their synonyms, and the phonotactically permissible CVC–VCV constructs from a large speaker population under both controlled and noisy environments.

However, for the preliminary stages of the investigation it was decided to test N-tuple recognition systems under unfavourable signal conditions and using the minimum of pre-processing (ie non-pre-emphasized, non-normalized input speech). Thus if the performance of a simple system, operating on minimally pre-processed data from the rhyming set, was acceptable, then it could reasonably be expected that for a given corpus the early results would improve with a more advanced N-tuple recognizer using optimally tuned pre-processing and normalization techniques.

Accordingly, the experiments described here were run on data from the noisy environment samples, allowing recognition to take place on sample data having no pre-emphasis or time normalization. Pre-processing was limited to a 19-channel vocoder bank,[10] simulated by fast Fourier transform (FFT), and scaling the result as input to the *N*-tuple recognizers.

The diagnostic test set was chosen so that the acoustic dissimilarity within rhyming sets (eg one/run—short) is minimal and the range of perceived phonological length did not markedly vary among the confusable rhyming sets (eg one/run/want—short; wonder/rudder—long). The 16-word diagnostic corpus was as follows:

Word set			
0	one	8	shoe
1	run	9	toot
2	want	10	tattoo
3	begun	11	toothache
4	wonder	12	cooler
5	rudder	13	tee
6	win	14	three
7	two	15	see

Two important dimensions of assessment for a speech recognition algorithm are: robustness in the face of a large speaker population and the rolloff in recognition accuracy as the vocabulary size increases. These aspects are *not* investigated in the present study, primarily because of resource constraints. However, this work represents a necessary first step in the evaluation of *N*-tuple sampling applied to speech recognition.

3.2 Experimental procedure for speech recognition

The strategy adopted for the present experiments was chosen to provide flexibility and repeatability with the same data, thus enabling comparison of differing recognition and pre-processing techniques. For this reason, simulations of the training and recognition process for eight different designs of *N*-tuple recognizer were performed on previously stored data using a VAX 11–750 system. Real-time performance was not a factor since it is known that the systems under consideration can be implemented with a satisfactory real time response when a suitable design has been proven.

3.3 Pre-processing algorithm

The raw-time domain files were subjected to a 10-ms wide FFT producing 19 8-bit samples of each filter channel every 5 ms. In the first six experiments the 8-bit value was reduced to a 4-bit value using one of three encoding methods discussed below (encoding of data). The 4-bit intensity can be considered as a weighting of each pixel on the retina and the 19 samples as a single slice in time encoded as a vertical column on the WISARD retina. In this way each word was reduced to a 120×19 array of 4-bit elements. The total duration being 0.6 s.

After the first six experiments the 4-bit intensity of each filter channel was replaced by a single bit which was set if a pre-determined threshold (determined experimentally) was exceeded, thus reducing the word data to a 120×19 array of single bits for the final four experiments.

3.4 The WISARD retina

The WISARD retina was sized at 100 (horizontal) by 19 (vertical), each component consisting of four bits initially and one bit subsequently.

In the recognition stage of a real system the sample data can be visualized as stepping across the retina in steps of one horizontal unit (5 ms). Precise alignment in comparison with the training data would therefore not be a problem—as the data slid across, the system would be looking for a sharp peaking of one discriminator, see Fig. 4. Of course, one discriminator could be trained on the ambient noise. Thus segmentation of speech from background becomes an implicit property of this paradigm.

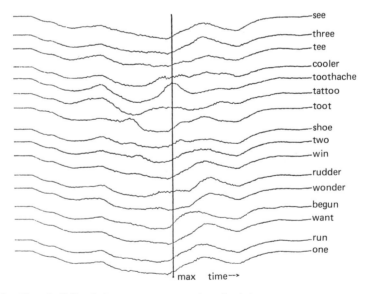

Figure 4   *Plot of all discriminator responses to 'toothache'.*

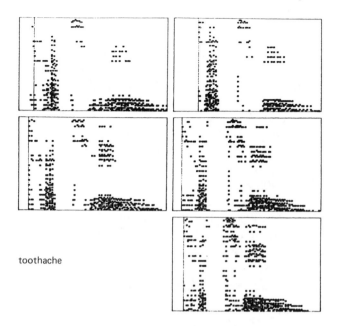

Figure 5   *FFT images of the word 'toothache'.*

Because the computational cost of scanning the image across the retina in 5-ms steps is too high in a simulation of this type, the start of a word in the sample frame was arbitrarily decided to occur when a 10% increase in the ambient energy level (summed across all filter channels) was observed. In training, each such sample was presented three times, representing a 'jitter' of ± 5 ms about the determined start point.

Fig. 5 shows FFT samples for the word 'toothache'. The vertical line indicates the time at which the threshold was exceeded; the subsequent 100 columns (500 ms) are taken as the retinal image.

3.5 Encoding and mapping

Four different kinds of encoding of the 8-bit samples produced by the FFT were employed. In the first six experiments each encoding reduced the 8-bit data to four bits. In the remaining two experiments the 8-bit sample was reduced to a single bit (binary encoding).

(1) *Linear-encoding*: here the top four bits of the 8-bit sample were selected and their binary image slotted into the retinal column in the position determined by which filter the output originated.

(2) *Thermometer-encoding*: for this encoding the interval [0, 255] was partitioned into five equal sub-intervals and integers in each sub-interval were mapped into a 4-bit value.

(3) *Gray-scale-encoding*: here the interval [0, 255] was divided into 16 equal sub-intervals. Each sub-interval is indexed by a 4-bit value in such a way that the Hamming distance between the indices of adjacent intervals is always 1. This form of indexing amounts to traversing all the vertices of a hypercube. The idea being that a small change in the value of the signal being encoded will produce a small change of Hamming distance in the encoded image.

(4) *Binary encoding*: finally the 8-bit sample was reduced to a single bit by thresholding at an experimentally determined level.

In the initial six experiments $N = 4$ and so $19 \times 100 \times 4/4$ N-tuples are chosen from the 1900×4 bits of the retina to define the mapping. Two types of mapping were used, namely *linear*, where N-tuple addresses are taken from consecutive pixels in a column, and *random*, where the addresses are composed from bits sampled randomly across the entire retina.

3.6 Results and conclusions for the 4-bit–4-tuple recognizers

Single-speaker recognition results with the 16-word repertoire. 4-tuple, 40-μs sampling rate (25 kHz, BW 0–8 kHz):

In the 4-bit encoding, 4-tuple experiments the best overall performance was obtained with linear encoding and a linear map or, equivalently, with Gray-scale encoding and a linear map. Initially we found this result rather unexpected in that the linear map employed took 4-tuple addresses from a single time slice, whereas the random map also looked across time. However, further comparison with the 1-bit encoding, 4-tuple experiments suggests that 4-bit encoding may have been presenting the system with excessive, relatively unrepeatable, detail.

It would appear that most learning occurs during the first five training instances of any given class, at which point the system gives around 85% accuracy. Subsequent training tends initially to reduce recognition performance and recovery is thereafter progressive but slow until saturation becomes a significant effect. We will return to the question of how the progress of the system towards saturation can be effectively monitored. However, our results suggest that with these system configurations, training on more than 25 instances from each class causes overall recognition performance to degrade.

With 4-bit encoding, a linear mapping and a 25-word teach set, the average performance of 90% looks quite promising as an initial result under the unfavourable conditions of the experiment. But the accuracy per word over the entire training sequence of 5, 10, 15, 20 and 25 patterns respectively was as shown in Table 1. Each discriminator consisted of 100×19 16-bit RAMs, ie a 3.8 (8-bit) Kbytes per word. Since there were

Table 1. *4-tuple–linear map–4 × 19 × 100–linear encoding*

			Training		
Class	5	10	15 % Accuracy	20	25
one	60	36	40	44	52
run	80	76	80	76	88
want	48	72	96	100	96
begun	100	96	96	96	96
wonder	92	92	88	92	92
rudder	100	92	92	96	100
win	80	84	80	76	76
two	88	84	84	84	84
shoe	92	100	100	100	100
toot	92	88	92	92	92
tattoo	100	100	100	100	100
toothache	96	96	96	100	96
cooler	100	100	100	80	100
tee	80	84	80	100	80
three	92	96	100	76	96
see	60	44	60	88	92
Average	85.00	83.75	86.50	88.00	90.00

16 class discriminators this comprised a total of 60.8 Kbytes of RAM used by the 4-bit–4-tuple recognizers.

Table 1 shows that the performance on the word 'one' (the worst case) was plainly unsatisfactory. A graphical confusion matrix for this experiment is given in Fig. 6. The confusion between the first three utterances, which uttered with no context would be particularly confusable even to the human listener, can mainly be ascribed to the fact that both the phonological duration as well as word-final and word-initial qualities are almost identical.

In an attempt to gauge the efficiency with which the discriminator RAMs were being used, two sets of statistics were produced for the case of 4-bit–4-tuple linear mapping with linear encoding. The first concerned the number of bits set in each 16-bit RAM versus class. The second gave the number of identical RAMs for all classes and the number of identical RAMs in pairs of classes. We briefly summarize this information.

Almost all zero-addressed locations were set, indicating that virtually every 4-tuple had seen $(0, 0, 0, 0)$, ie a complete absence of activity in the retinal cells sampled, during training.

Typically, each discriminator had around 1000 ± 400 RAMs, from a possible 1900, with exactly one bit set. The previous observation suggests that in most of these it will be the zero-addressed bit which is set. So that

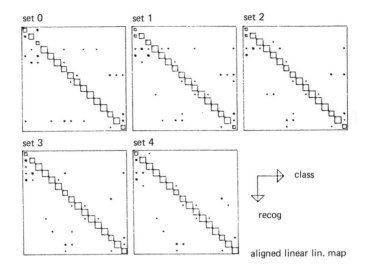

Figure 6   *Confusion matrices with 5/10/15/20/25 training examples.*

anywhere between 31 and 73% of the RAMs was each merely affirming the *absence* of some 16 particular activity features as a basis upon which to classify.

The number of RAMs per discriminator with more than one bit set was typically around 500. One might say that approximately 25% of RAMs were providing a contribution to classification based on between one and 15 observed activity features.

There were 91 RAMs which were identical for all classes. Thus most RAMs contributing on the basis of an observed activity feature were providing useful classification information.

Typically the number of identical RAMs in pairs of classes was in the range 500–1000, ie in any pairwise decision 50–75% of all relevant RAMs made a useful contribution, even if most of these were reporting absences of activity features.

Of the $28\,500 = 1900 \times 15$ non-zero-addressed bits per discriminator around 3000 were normally set (about 10%) as compared to a total number of bits set in the range 5000–7000 (max. possible 30 400). One can interpret this in one of two ways: one can argue that 10% RAM utilization is inefficient (in a 2-class system with ideal preprocessing the probability of any discriminator bit being set after training should be 0.5, with no commonality between discriminator contests); or one can say that this state of affairs reflects our ignorance of precisely what constitutes the critically significant features of the speech signal. (Such debates have a certain air of circularity.)

3.7 Results and conclusions for the 1-bit–*N*-tuple recognizers

A WISARD net is saturated when all discriminators give maximal response to sample data. This could occur, for example, as a result of over-training. In practice one trains the system almost to the point where the dynamic range of discriminator responses becomes insufficient to give an adequate margin upon which to base a classification decision.

To monitor the effectiveness of training in the last four experiments we define the following parameters of the system response with respect to any particular test sample:

Response = $\begin{cases} \text{the discriminator score expressed as a percentage of} \\ \text{maximum possible.} \end{cases}$

Min-response = the minimum response from any class.
Ave-response = the average response of all classes.

Let $D(i)$ be the response of the ith discriminator. For any particular class j let

$$d(j) = \max \{D(i): \text{all } i \text{ not equal to } j\}.$$

Thus $d(j)$ is the best response from all discriminators excluding the jth. Suppose now the data sample belonged to the jth class. Then $D(j) - d(j)$ is a measure of the margin by which the classification was made. If $D(j) - d(j)$ is negative then the sample was incorrectly classified.

Table 2. *4-tuple–linear-map–19 × 100–binary encoding*

Class	5	10	15 % Accuracy	20	25
one	96	72	52	76	64
run	56	64	64	76	76
want	88	92	96	96	96
begun	100	100	100	92	92
wonder	100	96	96	96	96
rudder	96	84	88	88	88
win	88	88	84	88	88
two	92	92	92	92	96
shoe	64	96	100	100	96
toot	92	100	100	100	100
tattoo	84	96	96	100	100
toothache	100	96	96	100	100
cooler	100	100	96	100	100
tee	76	72	80	84	84
three	92	96	100	96	96
see	92	92	96	96	100
Average	88.25	89.75	89.75	92.50	92.00

Table 3. *4-tuple–linear-map–19 × 100–binary encoding*

Class	5	10	15	20	25	
			Statistics			
one	89.6	92.8	94.4	95.8	96.6	Response
	56.4	67.2	71.2	74.5	75.8	Min-response
	74.4	80.6	83.9	87.4	88.7	Ave-response
	2.3	0.7	−0.2	0.3	0.4	Margin
cooler	85.6	90.4	92.3	94.9	96.3	Response
	49.7	58.4	66.0	68.9	70.2	Min-response
	68.8	75.7	79.0	81.5	82.9	Ave-response
	7.9	6.8	6.2	6.0	6.1	Margin

As training and testing progresses, the quantity $D(j)-d(j)$ can be averaged over the test samples to provide a progressive picture of how training gradually reduces the margin of decision. Over a test set T of samples we can define for each class j:

$$Margin = \text{the average of } D(j)-d(j) \text{ over } T.$$

In the last four N-tuple experiments these statistics were collected to provide a running picture of the extent to which each class could benefit from further training.

Table 4. *4-tuple–random-map–19 × 100–binary encoding*

Class	5	10	15	20	25
			% Accuracy		
one	88	88	64	72	68
run	52	72	56	72	76
want	96	96	96	96	96
begun	100	100	100	96	96
wonder	100	96	96	96	100
rudder	96	84	84	84	88
win	92	92	88	92	88
two	92	92	92	92	96
shoe	60	96	96	96	96
toot	92	92	92	92	92
tattoo	64	88	100	100	100
toothache	100	96	92	92	92
cooler	100	84	88	96	100
tee	76	56	48	72	68
three	84	92	92	96	96
see	92	92	100	100	100
Average	86.50	88.50	86.50	90.25	90.75

Table 5. *4-tuple–random-map–19 × 100–binary encoding*

Class	5	10	15	20	25	
			Statistics			
one	90.4	93.8	95.3	96.3	96.9	Response
	31.4	40.6	48.2	59.4	61.9	Min-response
	63.2	70.6	75.0	80.9	82.9	Ave-response
	3.5	1.8	0.4	0.3	0.3	Margin
cooler	84.2	89.0	91.1	94.8	96.8	Response
	32.2	40.4	49.4	52.1	53.7	Min-response
	58.9	68.1	71.9	75.4	77.0	Ave-response
	10.4	7.0	6.2	5.7	6.5	Margin

The experiments were conducted for both 4-tuple and 8-tuple mappings over a wide range of threshold values (10- to 50-channel intensity). It was found that the systems were relatively insensitive to the threshold for the binary encoding over this range, there being almost no detectable difference in performance. We will present the results for a threshold of 20 as being typical in Table 2.

For the 1-bit–4-tuple recognizers the RAM cost is 950 bytes per discriminator, giving a total of 14.84 Kbytes for all 16 classes. However the margin of decision decreases very rapidly as training progresses. We give the worst and best case figures in Table 3.

Table 6. *8-tuple–linear-map–19 × 100–binary encoding*

Class	5	10	15	20	25
			% Accuracy		
one	92	88	80	84	72
run	64	76	84	88	84
want	88	96	96	92	92
begun	96	96	100	96	96
wonder	92	96	92	92	92
rudder	96	88	88	88	88
win	84	92	92	96	96
two	100	100	96	92	92
shoe	68	88	92	96	96
toot	92	92	100	100	100
tattoo	80	96	100	100	100
toothache	100	100	100	100	100
cooler	100	96	100	100	100
tee	76	60	76	84	84
three	92	96	100	100	100
see	72	76	88	96	96
Average	87.00	89.75	92.75	94.00	93.00

Table 7. *8-tuple–linear-map–19 × 100–binary encoding*

Class	5	10	15 Statistics	20	25	
one	77.1	82.6	85.0	87.8	89.6	Response
	30.8	40.7	46.6	52.9	55.4	Min-response
	54.8	62.3	66.4	71.2	72.9	Ave-response
	3.8	3.2	1.9	2.4	2.6	Margin
cooler	67.0	74.5	78.5	82.7	86.3	Response
	25.3	32.1	38.3	40.3	41.3	Min-response
	45.9	52.6	56.3	59.4	61.2	Ave-response
	10.9	11.1	12.1	13.7	15.8	Margin

The result given in Table 3 is significantly better than the corresponding results for the 4-bit encoding experiments, at a fraction of the RAM cost. It provides evidence that the 4-bit systems were being presented with excessive detail. We next compare the corresponding performance with a random map (Tables 4 and 5).

Once again the linear map provides consistently better results. Turning now to the 1-bit-8-tuple results we have (Tables 6 and 7).

For the 1-bit–8-tuple recognizers the RAM cost is 7.42 Kbytes per discriminator, giving a total of 118.75 Kbytes for all 16 classes. The

Table 8. *8-tuple–random-map–19 × 100–binary encoding*

Class	5	10	15 % Accuracy	20	25
one	88	92	92	88	84
run	56	76	84	84	88
want	80	96	96	96	96
begun	100	100	100	100	96
wonder	96	96	96	96	96
rudder	96	88	88	88	88
win	92	96	96	96	96
two	92	96	92	96	96
shoe	52	76	92	96	96
toot	92	92	92	92	92
tattoo	56	88	96	100	100
toothache	100	100	100	100	100
cooler	100	88	88	92	100
tee	76	48	52	80	80
three	60	100	100	100	100
see	72	92	100	100	100
Average	81.75	89.00	91.50	94.00	94.25

Table 9. *8-tuple–random-map–19 × 100–binary encoding*

Class	5	10	15 Statistics	20	25	
one	71.1	80.1	84.6	87.3	89.0	Response
	3.7	5.8	8.2	19.2	22.0	Min-response
	31.8	39.0	44.9	50.8	53.5	Ave-response
	7.5	7.1	4.3	4.1	3.3	Margin
cooler	55.3	66.1	70.4	76.2	82.4	Response
	4.4	7.1	11.0	12.0	12.9	Min-response
	23.8	31.6	35.5	38.7	40.7	Ave-response
	18.0	16.9	16.0	18.6	22.1	Margin

results are somewhat better and, as one might expect, the margin of decision decreases less rapidly as training progresses (Tables 8 and 9).

These final results are marginally better for the random map. This suggests that ability to perceive the logical conjunction of several formant features (in this instance an 8-tuple recognizer) is required before the expected advantage results from attempting to extract features across the time domain of a sliding FFT.

3.8 Comparative results using conventional time-warping

We next describe the results obtained with the original 16-word set but using conventional time-warping–template-matching recognition. Comparison of these results with those of the N-tuple recognition system shows that, on the same data, 8-tuple sampling provided significantly improved recognition accuracy.

3.8.1 DTW algorithm description

Assume, for the moment, that words are not finite temporally ordered sequences of spectra but continuously time-varying, vector valued functions. Suppose $\mathbf{a}(t)$, $\mathbf{b}(t)$ $(0 \leqslant t \leqslant T)$ are two words which we wish to compare. We may define a metric at the level of primitive patterns as

$$D(\mathbf{a}, \mathbf{b}) = \int_0^T d(\mathbf{a}(t), \mathbf{b}(t)) \mathrm{d}t,$$

where d is some suitable metric of spectral difference.

We know that very large local variations in the rate of articulation of a word can be tolerated without compromising its intelligibility. This suggests that a better metric should be largely invariant to changes of timescale. One way to accomplish this is to define a function $q(t)$ which maps the timescale of $\mathbf{b}(t)$ onto that of $\mathbf{a}(t)$. Modifying the previous equation accordingly we obtain

$$D^*(\mathbf{a}, \mathbf{b}) = \min_q \int_0^T d(\mathbf{a}(t), \mathbf{b}(q(t))) dt.$$

Essentially this is an instance of a classical variational problem whose solution is found by solving the corresponding Euler–Lagrange equation. However, D^* must not be calculated with respect to an arbitrary change of timescale; we must place some constraints on q and these complicate the problem so as to make it, in general, analytically intractable. Fortunately, as Bellman has shown,[11] a numerical solution can be efficiently obtained by means of dynamic programming. It was this line of reasoning which first led Vintsyuk[12] to apply dynamic programming to speech recognition, often called dynamic time warping. The DTW algorithm described below is based on the work of Sakoe & Chiba.[13]

Let $\mathbf{a}_i$ $(1 \leqslant i \leqslant u)$, $\mathbf{b}_j$ $(1 \leqslant j \leqslant r)$ be sequences of spectral vectors. If $d(\mathbf{a}_i, \mathbf{b}_j)$ is a suitable measure of distance between $\mathbf{a}_i$ and $\mathbf{b}_j$ the DTW algorithm finds a path connecting $(1, 1)$ and (u, r) such that the cumulative distance is minimal, the guiding principle being that if a locally correct decision is made at every point then a globally correct path will be found (this is often obscured by specific implementations). If the current point is (i, j), then we choose the next point (i', j') by examining the three possible paths as illustrated below:

$$
\begin{array}{ll}
(i, j+1) & \longrightarrow (i+1, j+1) \\
\uparrow & \\
(i, j) \longrightarrow & \longrightarrow (i+1, j)
\end{array}
$$

and choosing a path corresponding to the minimum value of

$$d(\mathbf{a}_i, \mathbf{b}_{j+1}), d(\mathbf{a}_{i+1}, \mathbf{b}_{j+1}), d(\mathbf{a}_{i+1}, \mathbf{b}_j),$$

where any point outside the rectangular region is omitted. The cumulative distance $D^*(i, j)$ is then updated:

$$D^*(i', j') = D^*(i, j) + d(\mathbf{a}_{i'}, \mathbf{b}_{j'}), \quad D^*(1, 1) = d(\mathbf{a}_1, \mathbf{b}_1).$$

The final value $D^*(u, r)$ provides a time normalized measure of distance between $\mathbf{a}$ and $\mathbf{b}$. When performing recognition the unknown $\mathbf{a}$ is compared against every $\mathbf{b}$ in the vocabulary and assigned the class for which D^* is minimal.

3.8.2 Results using conventional DTW
The DTW algorithm compares two arrays *ref* (the template—vertical axis) and *unknown* (the test sample—horizontal axis). Figs. 7 and 8 show complete cumulative distance contours and an optimal path for two runs

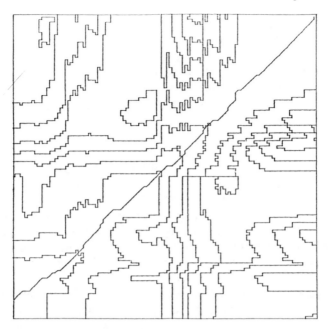

Figure 7   *DTW for two different sample of 'toothache'.*

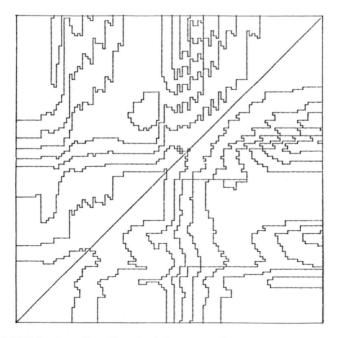

Figure 8   *DTW for time-aligned 'toothache' against reference.*

of the program. In Fig. 7 the word 'toothache' is compared with a different sample of the same word. As a test of these routines a sample of 'toothache' was compared with the reference 'toothache' and the resulting path used to warp the sample to conform to the reference. In Fig. 8 a second DTW is then performed, comparing the time-aligned sample against the reference; the resulting optimal path is, as expected, a straight line; this acts as a good test of the code.

In applying the algorithm, only one template is used for each reference word, but that reference is based on 5, 10, 15, 20 or 25 words taken from the teach sample. For example, in the first experiment five samples of the same word were selected. The first was taken as the basic reference and the remaining four were time normalized against the first in the usual way. In the sample vs. sample distance array so produced, each diagonal path was used as a time-distorting function to normalize the sample against the basic reference. Having eliminated as much time variation as possible all five samples were then averaged to produce the single reference.

It seems likely that one would get better results for DTW if each word in the teach set were used as a separate reference rather than by combining them as described above. However, the computational overhead in recognition would be so high that it is difficult to imagine a real-time system performing in this way.

Table 10. *DTW results*

Class	5	10	Training → 15 % Accuracy	20	25
one	76	80	84	84	84
run	80	88	88	88	88
want	92	92	92	92	92
begun	100	100	100	100	100
wonder	76	20	76	76	76
rudder	100	100	100	100	100
win	88	92	88	88	88
two	76	76	84	80	80
shoe	80	92	92	92	96
toot	80	80	80	80	80
tattoo	60	64	64	64	68
toothache	92	80	88	88	92
cooler	100	100	100	100	100
tee	92	92	92	92	92
three	92	92	92	92	92
see	100	100	100	100	100
Average	86.5	84.2	88.7	88.5	89.2

It would appear that the technique of averaging (time normalized) templates does provide some progressive improvement in accuracy as the number of templates increases—at least within the framework of this experiment—but that this improvement is not great (Table 10).

These are good results, admittedly at enormous computational cost, and emphasize the value of time normalization. Nevertheless, comparison with Table 8 shows that an 8-tuple WISARD recognizer (having no time normalization and, in principle, virtually zero computational overhead) obtained significantly better results on the same data. The inference would seem to be that if it were possible to provide a WISARD recognizer with time normalized data, at reasonable computational cost, the resulting system should have a remarkably good performance. This was confirmed by a later set of experiments.

3.9 Summary of results and conclusions

In this initial series of experiments in the application of *N*-tuple sampling to the problem of speech recognition some interesting lessons were learnt (Table 11).

These experiments demonstrate that under the most unfavourable conditions (noisy rhyming test utterances from a naive speaker, no pre-emphasis, no signal conditioning, no time or amplitude normalization) *N*-tuple sampling, applied to single-speaker isolated-word recognition with a 16-word diagnostic vocabulary, yields an improvement in accuracy of around 5% (in the range 90–100%) over conventional DTW using the same data.

Table 11. *Summary of results*

Tuple	Encoding	Data bits per channel	Mapping	RAM per word (bytes)	% Accuracy
4	Linear	4	Linear	3.8 K	90*
4	Linear	4	Random	3.8 K	88
4	Thermometer	4	Linear	3.8 K	79.75
4	Thermometer	4	Random	3.8 K	80.50
4	Gray	4	Linear	3.8 K	90*
4	Gray	4	Random	3.8 K	87.25
4	Binary	1	Linear	950	92
4	Binary	1	Random	950	90.75
8	Binary	1	Linear	7.42 K	93
8	Binary	1	Random	7.42 K	94.25
8-bit per channel — 19 channel DTW					89.20

* identical.

With amplitude normalization and active range encoding of the pattern vectors a further improvement can be expected to result.

Moreover, a WISARD implementation of N-tuple sampling has virtually no computational overhead (as compared to the high computational cost of DTW, or other recognition paradigms), and can, in principle, be built so that the response time is independent of the number of classes.

A further advantage of this paradigm is that for a real system discriminator responses monitored continuously can provide whole word recognition of connected speech without the necessity for segmentation.

4. Vowel detectors

4.1 Introduction

A desirable goal for a speech recognition system would be to identify phonemic segments of continuous speech accurately. Phonemic recognition need not be exceedingly accurate; accuracies around 80% might well suffice, since relatively simple linguistic knowledge based systems can detect something approaching 60% of randomly induced errors in a phonemic stream of English utterances (Badii, Hui & Jones— in preparation). Phonemic rule based error detection can also be enhanced to provide some degree of error correction. Higher levels of syntactic, semantic and contextual knowledge might then be used in a similar fashion to process the phonemic stream into text. Such a system could in principle cope with an unlimited vocabulary, in contrast to the limited vocabulary word recognition systems currently in use.

Certainly the goal of speech recognition must be beyond isolated word recognition towards the effective recognition of continuous speech. Systems such as COHORT and TRACE (see [14], Chapter 15, for example) point the way but do not promise cheap implementation in the medium run.

Despite the fact that some authors[15] report correct segmentation of continuous speech into phonemes with up to 97% accuracy, Rumelhart objects to segmentation before recognition:

> Because of the overlap of successive phonemes, it is difficult, and we believe counterproductive, to try to divide the speech stream up into separate phonemes in advance of identifying the units. A number of other researchers (eg Fowler, 1984; Klatt, 1980) have made much the same point. ([14], pp. 60–61)

Rumelhart prefers the approach of allowing the phoneme identification process to examine the speech stream for characteristic patterns, without first segmenting the stream into separate units.

It is interesting that either approach is practical using a WISARD-type device. The advantage of prior segmentation is that it permits some degree of time normalization before presentation to the recognizer, and work at the Pattern Recognition Laboratory at Brunel University has shown that a very considerable improvement in recognition occurs if WISARD is presented with time-normalized data.

We may define a *static* pattern recognition system to be one which stores its training experiences in memory and refers to memory in seeking to classify unknown patterns. This contrasts with a *dynamic* system which continually undergoes state transitions and whose output depends on the current (and possibly previous) state(s) and the input rather than the input alone. While, dynamic pattern recognition systems are of considerable interest, the current theoretical situation is largely speculative and it seems likely that it will be some time before any practical system for vision or speech will be realized along these lines.

In a static pattern recognition system the goal is to optimize the map between input patterns and memory while preserving the real-time performance and keeping training to a minimum. In applications such as speech, the situation is rendered more difficult by the fact that the significant features of the signal are not really well understood. Without feedback, WISARD is a static model which makes no *a priori* assumptions about the input patterns and is easily implemented to give a suitable real-time performance.

As we have observed, WISARD is very simple and fast to train, provided one has suitably labelled samples of each class.

This last requirement creates serious logistical problems in applying static pattern recognition models to speech at a level below whole words. The speech signal must be examined visually and acoustically by a human operator who defines the boundaries of a segment which hopefully represents an example of the particular class. This sample can then be used for training or testing. Since many such samples are required for each class the construction of a suitable database is a very time consuming process. However, once such a database has been prepared it can be used for many different experiments and can enable direct comparison of different algorithms on identical data.

The experiments reported here were restricted to *vowel detection* for a *single speaker*.

4.2 Vowel detection using multiple discriminators per vowel

The words were pronounced in word pairs which instantiated the same vowel in an attempt to obtain the coarticulative effects which would normally be present in continuous speech.

The sample speech was collected and passed through a 16-channel filter bank to produce frequency domain data. The frequency information was in 5-ms steps.

For both the training and test phases it was necessary to create a parallel file containing an indication at each step as to which class the 5 ms sample corresponded (or to no class). This second file was hand crafted and identification was accomplished by traversing the time domain data in small steps while playing back progressively nested samples through the D-to-A. Consequently, there is an element of subjectivity inherent in this identification process. One variant of each vowel was selected, these were:

A as in fAte
E as in mEt
I as in bIt
O as in gOat
U as in dUe

The *Concise Oxford English Dictionary* was used as a guide in defining which vowels were to be expected in the pronunciation of each word. It should be noted that various dictionaries are by no means in agreement as to the precise quality of each vowel that occurs in a given word and, of course, there is considerable variation between speakers.

In an attempt to deal with the fact that samples of a given class are liable to considerable variation of duration, each vowel segment in the training frequency data (once identified as above) was, in this initial experiment, linearly scaled to a uniform duration in order to fit a standard 16×16 8-tuple WISARD retina with one thresholded bit per pixel.

The variation in the vowel lengths was typically from 45 to 250 ms. Although we actually know how long the vowel samples are in the test phase, we cannot use this information during recognition, since the ability to cope with such variation is intrinsically part of the recognition process.

To deal with this we used six different scale factors. The incoming sound was placed in a buffer long enough to accommodate at least 250 ms (the longest observed vowel length). Every 5 ms this buffer was updated and six snapshots of differing lengths were presented to the WISARD recognizer. The classifiers with their different scale factors were treated as though they were separate classes so that during testing the highest responses would hopefully detect both the correct vowel and its duration.

Table 12. *Six discriminators for duration per class*

| Vowel | Percentage recognition accuracy | |
	Duration and class	Class only
A	23.1	61.5
E	29.2	54.2
I	37.0	59.3
O	4.2	54.2
U	31.8	81.8
Average	25.2	61.8

4.2.1 Results and conclusions

As Table 12 might suggest, a confusion matrix for response against class and duration shows that correct classification of class was more reliable than correct classification of duration within the class. This is probably explained by the fact that estimating the vowel duration while preparing both the training and test data-classification file is a difficult and rather imprecise affair.

A second confusion matrix looking only at response against correct class is probably more significant and is given in Table 13. In general terms the idea is to present a sliding window of the frequency domain data from the test utterance to the WISARD net and determine whether the vowel discriminator responses are detecting the embedded vowels. Fig. 9 summarizes the result of one such simulation and consists of four traces. The top two traces indicate the strength of response and the confidence (the difference between the best and second-best classifications) for all window positions. The next trace details which vowel was producing the largest response as the words slid past the window. The bottom trace indicates where the vowel was found by the experimenter.

From these results it can be seen that single-speaker vowel detection from within continuous speech can be performed by a WISARD net using spectral energy data with a reasonable degree of accuracy.

Table 13. *Confusion matrix for class response*

| | | Classified as → | | | | |
		A	E	I	O	U
	A	23	4	6	1	6
	E	3	14	7	2	—
Actual class	I	1	1	16	—	12
	O	20	—	1	15	1
	U	1	4	7	—	30

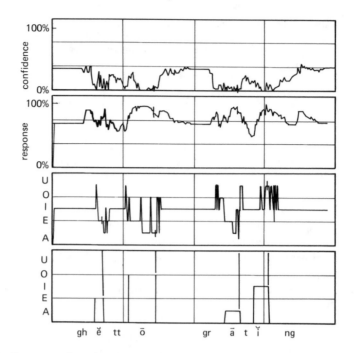

Figure 9   *Summary of continuous response.*

However, it should be emphasized that we are only attempting to recognize one particular type of each vowel quality.

It is possible to envisage a number of improvements in the experiment described above. For example, most of the energy in vowels is concentrated in the lower frequencies. Therefore a suitable pre-emphasis profile would no doubt improve the reliability of such a system.

The significance of these preliminary vowel detection results is to demonstrate the feasibility of using WISARD nets to recognize significant speech fragments within words of connected speech, but the results would be more interesting if generalized to a comprehensive set of building blocks such as phonemes or phoneme-like fragments.

4.3 Breeding vowel detectors using Holland's genetic algorithm

Given that the initial mapping from the retina to memory, that is, the assignment of N-tuple bits across the retina is random, the question arises as to whether the mapping can be improved for a particular type of application. For example, if the task were face recognition, then a better performance might be expected if the N-tuples were sampling more densely in that area of the retina where significant features such as the eyes, hairline, and mouth are presented.

202

As a vowel detector, a relatively difficult task, WISARD gives a reasonably creditable performance considering the lack of time normalization. Across the five classes, as we saw in the preceding section, typical recognition accuracies exceed 50%, and in particular classes are as high as 80%, as against the expected 20% of pure chance. Of course, carefully crafted vowel detectors can do much better than this, Jassem[16] reports accuracies of 92–97% in his review of speech recognition work in Poland. However, WISARD is a very simple recognition paradigm and the question addressed by the present experiment is: *by how much the*

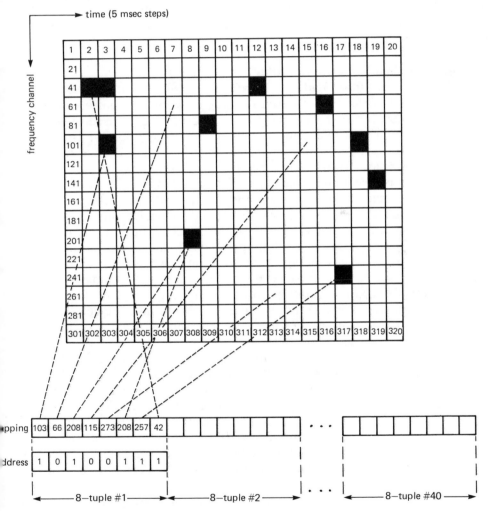

Figure 10   *Representing mappings as strings.*

performance can be improved using Holland's genetic algorithm to 'breed' better mappings?

Holland's algorithm[9] was chosen because it is a very powerful adaptive search technique and because the mapping from retina to N-tuples is easily described as a string: each position on the retina is numbered and each block of N such numbers in the string describes the mapping for a particular N-tuple, see Fig. 10. This is a particularly pleasant situation, because the usual difficulty with genetic algorithms is representing the objects being optimized as strings in such a way that after using a genetic operator, eg mutation to alter an element, the resulting string still represents a valid object. In the present case this is not a problem since any string of integers in the correct range (in this case $[1, 320]$) represents a valid mapping.

4.3.1 Holland's genetic algorithm

Simulated evolution had been tried before Holland with extremely poor results. All of these were based on the 'mutation and natural selection' model of evolution. Holland's genetic algorithms are based on a 'sexual reproduction and selection' model: his principal operator is crossing-over, that is, the creating of a new object for the next generation by combining parts from *two* independent objects in the current generation. Mutation plays a minor role in genetic algorithms.

Many experiments have been done with genetic algorithms, and they have proved to be remarkably effective and robust learning systems. For the most part they have been tested as function optimizers, where the objects in a generation are 'numbers' and their survival–reproductive value is given by the function whose maximum we wish to find.

One of the most interesting aspects of genetic algorithms is that they not only find the optimum object, but in doing so they discover properties that are common to many near-optimal objects (so-called higher-order schemata). In some instances, this information is at least as valuable as the optimum itself.

As the name 'genetic algorithm' suggests, the inspiration for Holland's work is taken from an analogy with biological systems. The mathematics of genetic evolution is now a very sophisticated tool which has changed our perception of how the evolutionary process works. For example, it is now known that simple mutation alone is insufficient to explain the rate of biological adaptation. Instead, mutation plays the role of background 'noise' which, by occasional random perturbation, prevents a specie from becoming frozen at a local optimum. Other factors explain the rapid rate of adaptation.

Holland constructs adaptive plan programs based on the following basic ideas. We are given a set, A, of 'structures' which we can think of in the first instance as being a set of strings of fixed length, l say. The object of the adaptive search is to find a structure which performs well in terms of a measure of performance:

$$v: A \rightarrow \text{real numbers} \geqslant 0.$$

We have so far a knowledge base of competing structures and measure v of the observed performance of generated structures. For example, if the problem were one of function optimization the structures, or strings, could be the binary expansion of a real number to some fixed number of places, and the function v could be the function to be maximized. Then v evaluated at the real number represented by a string would be a measure of the string's fitness to survive.

Representing strings as

$$a(1)a(2)a(3)\ldots a(l) \quad (a(i) = 1 \text{ or } 0),$$

we can designate sub-sets of A which have attributes in common, these are called schemata, by using '$*$' for 'don't care' in one or more positions. For example,

$$a(1)*a(3)**\ldots*$$

represents the schemata of all strings with first element $a(1)$ and third element $a(3)$, all other elements being arbitrary. Thus any particular string of length l is an instance of 2^l schemata. If l is only about 20 this is still over a million schemata. An evaluation of just one string therefore yields information about a large number of schemata.

The next ingredients of Holland's model are the operators by which strings are combined to produce new strings. It is the choice of these operators which produces a search strategy that exploits co-adapted sets of structural components already discovered. The three principal operators used by Holland are crossover, inversion, and mutation.

Crossover
Proceeds in three steps:

(1) Two structures $a(1)\ldots a(l)$ and $b(1)\ldots b(l)$ are selected at random from the current population.

(2) A crossover point x, in the range 1 to $l-1$ is selected, again at random.

(3) Two new structures:

$$a(1)a(2)\ldots a(x)b(x+1)b(x+2)\ldots b(l)$$
$$b(1)b(2)\ldots b(x)a(x+1)a(x+2)\ldots a(l)$$

are formed.

In modifying the pool of schemata, crossing over continually introduces new schemata for trial whilst testing extant schemata in new contexts. It can be shown that each crossing over affects a great number of schemata.

Inversion
For some randomly selected positions $x < y$ in the string we perform the transformation:

$$a(1)a(2)\ldots a(l) \rightarrow a(1)\ldots a(x)a(y-1)a(y-2)\ldots a(x+1)a(y)\ldots a(l).$$

Inversion increases the effectiveness of crossover by promoting close linkage between successful alleles (instantiations of string components). Linkage occurs when co-adapted alleles are close together in the genotype, thus reducing the probability that the group will be separated by crossover. This requires an order free string representation and a mechanism for making strings homologous before crossover (see [9] p. 109). The effects of inversion are only apparent over a relatively long time scale, ie a large number of generations. For the purposes of the present discussion inversion may be ignored; our inversion was merely a rather brutal mutation.

Mutation
Each structure $a(1)a(2)\ldots a(l)$ in the population is operated upon as follows. Position x is modified, with probability p independent of the other positions, so that the string is replaced by

$$a(1)a(2)\ldots a(x-1)za(x+1)\ldots a(l),$$

where z is drawn at random from the possible values. If p is the probability of mutation at a single position, then the probability of h mutations in a given string is determined by a Poisson distribution with parameter p. Mutation is a 'background' operator, assuring that the crossover operator has a full range of alleles so that the adaptive plan is not trapped on local optima.

The basic paradigm of a program of this type is as follows:

(1) Randomly generate a population of M strings

$$S(0) = \{s(1,0),\ldots,s(M,0)\}.$$

(2) For each $s(i,t)$ in $S(t)$, compute and save its measure of utility $v(s(i,t))$.

(3) For each $s(i,t)$ in $S(t)$ compute the selection probability defined by

$$p(i,t) = v(s(i,t))/(\text{sum over } i \text{ of } v(s(i,t))).$$

(4) Select a string $s(j,t)$ in $S(t)$ according to the selection probabilities:
- apply crossover with probability P_c to $s(j,t)$ and $s(j',t)$, where $s(j',t)$ is

again selected from $S(t)$ according to the selection probabilities; select one of the two resultants (equally likely) and designate it $s(k, t)$;
- apply simple inversion with probability P_i to $s(k, t)$. Designate the result $s(k, t)$;
- with probability P_m (small) apply mutation to each element of $s(k, t)$. Designate the result $s(k, t)$.

(5) randomly select a string in $S(t)$, where each string is equally likely to be selected (probability $1/M$), and replace the selected string by $s(k, t)$.

(6) Compute $v(s(k, t))$ and replace the corresponding element in the saved array of values of v.

(5) Goto 3.

The main advantages of this adaptive strategy are:

(a) It concentrates strings increasingly towards schemata that contain structures of above average utility.

(b) Since it works over a knowledge base (i.e. the population of structures) that is distributed over the search space, it is all but immune to getting trapped on local optima.

4.3.2 Optimizing the WISARD mapping

Cavicchio[17] first suggested that genetic algorithms might be used for the selection of suitable detector sets for pattern recognizers. However, Holland's theoretical work[9] was based on representations of solutions as strings, where each component of the string has a precise, position-dependent meaning. WISARD mappings as solution strings (in common with many other pattern detectors) substantially lack these semantics of position. Brindle discusses the problem of set representation for the application of genetic algorithms.[18]

The patterns used in training and testing the WISARD simulation consisted of 100 ms of speech data arranged on the retina as 20 columns, each representing successive 5-ms segments, by 16 rows corresponding to a 16-channel filter bank. The imaged data therefore represented a 100-ms sample of speech in the frequency domain.

A WISARD model with $N = 8$ was used. Strings representing mappings therefore consist of 40×8-tuple $= 320$ elements, integers in the range 1–320, see Fig. 10. Unlike many WISARD experiments the random maps used were not 1–1, ie were not necessarily permutations of the integers $1, 2, \ldots, 320$.

To provide a population 50 random strings were generated at the start of an experimental run. The mapping defined by each string was used to train and then test WISARD. The results of testing provide the necessary information from which a measure of fitness can be calculated for each string. By far the most computation time is spent on training and testing in order to calculate the fitness.

Each new string generated by the algorithm therefore requires a complete train and test sequence, typically 40 or 50 training examples per class and around 25 testing samples. It was decided to set the maximum number of iterations to 2000. Even so, each experimental run took around one week on a SUN workstation. With present levels of readily available technology, processing speed and memory, limit the scope of such experiments considerably.

In this context it is instructive to reflect upon the size of the search space. There are 320^{320} possible strings, ie around 10^{801}. Although there are a number of equivalence relations between strings, eg it does not matter in which order the different 8-tuples are placed in the string, or in which order the individual elements of the 8-tuples are placed (these two together effect a reduction by at most a factor of 10^{52}), these do not substantially affect this figure. Generously, assuming a computer capable of testing 10^{10} strings per second it would take approximately 10^{732} years, a time vastly exceeding the estimated age of the universe (a generally accepted upper bound for which is 1.2 times 10^{11} years) to search the entire space exhaustively.

4.3.3 Experimental procedure

The sample speech was collected in the time domain as word pairs, in an attempt to produce some co-articulation effects, and passed through a 16-channel filter bank to produce frequency domain data which was also saved. The frequency information was in 5-ms steps and stored on a VAX 11–750 as a file of unsigned bytes.

For both the training and test phases it was necessary to create a parallel file containing an indication at each step as to which class the 5 ms sample corresponded (A, E, I, O, U or 'no class'). This second file was hand crafted and identification was accomplished by traversing the time domain data in small steps and inspecting a defined area of the file both visually and acoustically.

Variation in vowel length was typically from 45–250 ms, but most vowels tended to be around the 100-ms mark—hence the choice of 100 ms for the retina. No attempt was made to time normalize the data. Other experiments, mentioned earlier, using time normalized training and test data suggest that time variation is the principal limitation on accuracy for this type of task, and we were interested to see to what extent the techniques discussed here could accommodate to this problem. Yet another reason for this decision was that if the initial recognition performance were too good it would not be possible to observe the improvements, if any, effected by the genetic algorithm.

Below is a summary of the vowel sounds used in the word set (in British 'English' as opposed to N. American 'English').

Vowel	Number in training	Number in testing
A as in fAte	47	26
E as in mEt	46	24
I as in bIt	53	27
O as in gOat	52	24
U as in dUe	40	22

Total storage of the speech data in the frequency domain occupies about 10 Mbytes.

As a final stage in pre-processing the data, the 16 unsigned bytes (0–255) at each 5-ms step, each byte representing the intensity of activity in a frequency channel, were converted to a single thresholded bit. Obviously in doing this, much of the original information is lost, but speech recognition involves selective data reduction on a massive scale and generally we have found that it is the presence or absence of activity, rather than the intensity, which is significant in a particular frequency channel.

To determine appropriate thresholds we calculated arithmetic means for each class at each of the 16 frequencies over all the samples in the training data. The processing of sample data in the experiment proceeded by replacing a particular unsigned byte by 0 if its value was lower than the corresponding threshold and by 1 if the value was greater than the threshold.

Given the size of the retina, 320 pixels, the 8-tuple system requires one set of 40 256-bit (eight address lines) RAMs for each of the five classes; a mere 1280 bytes per recognizer or 6400 bytes altogether. One could improve the performance of such a system by increasing the retinal coverage, which is not in any event 1–1, and using more RAM. However, in the context of the present experiment this would increase the length of the string required to describe the mapping, exponentially increase the size of the search space and significantly reduce the rate of convergence. Since 50 WISARD systems are used (recall the population consists of 50 strings) in the experiment the total memory required for RAM is 312.5 Kbytes.

Twenty time slices of data from the frequency file were written onto the retina and moved up one column at each stage. Training and testing were done when the first column of the retina was positioned at the start of a vowel as indicated by the parallel file.

The genetic algorithm, as sketched above, was applied to a population of 50 strings with operator probabilities of

$$P_c = 0.06, P_i = 0.06, P_m = 0.005.$$

Two different measures of utility were tried:

(i) The first measure was chosen to select for 'orthogonality' of discriminator responses, ie two conflicting requirements on each discriminator, a high score on samples from the correct class and a low score on samples from other classes, were combined into one global measure of utility across all discriminators. We do this as follows.

For a given mapping $\mathbf{M}$ if $r(i, j) \geqslant 0$ is the score of discriminator i, on a sample from class j, $1 \leqslant i, j \leqslant 5$, normalized to the range $[0, 1]$, then

$$\cos A = r(j,j)/\sqrt{(r(1, j)^2 + r(2, j)^2 + \ldots + r(5, j)^2)}$$

is a measure of how far from ideal ($\cos A = 1$) is the response of the whole system to the sample from class j; it measures the angle A between the vector of discriminator responses and the ideal vector. Let the average of $\cos A$ for a single class j over the test samples be $C(j)$. Then we define

$$U(\mathbf{M}) = (C(1) + C(2) + \ldots + C(5))/5.$$

This is taken as the measure of utility of the mapping $\mathbf{M}$; $\mathbf{M}$ would be an ideal mapping if $U(\mathbf{M}) = 1$. We note that any positive monotonic transformation $Q(U)$ of this function will also correctly measure the utility of $\mathbf{M}$.

(ii) The second measure of utility was less subtle. In this case the strings were bred simply to maximize the average accuracy of discriminator responses across all classes. Thus for any particular mapping $\mathbf{M}$ the response to the test samples in class j can be taken as

$$N_c/T_j,$$

where N_c is the number of correct classifications and T_j is the total number of test samples in class j. This figure averaged over all classes j gives a measure of utility $V(\mathbf{M})$ for the mapping $\mathbf{M}$. Once more, $\mathbf{M}$ is ideal if $V(\mathbf{M}) = 1$.

We found the adaptive search procedure worked more efficiently if a positive monotonic transformation was carried out on the utility measure in order to increase the probability of a superior string contributing to the next generation and decrease the probability of an inferior string contributing to the next generation. To do this we based the probability of selection on utility raised to the power 16.

4.3.4 Summary of results
Orthogonality
Fig. 11 shows the measure of orthogonality across 2000 generations (iterations). Breeding for orthogonality is a more difficult task than merely breeding for accuracy. However it can be argued that this might be more important in a real system which is scanning continuously rather

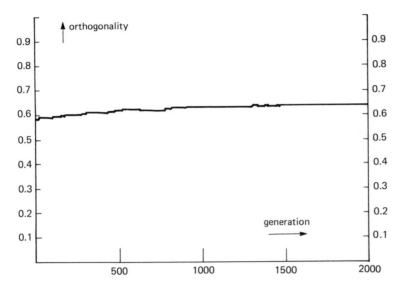

Figure 11   *Breeding for orthogonality.*

than just looking at test vowels, since it may help to suppress spurious discriminator response to features that do not discriminate vowels, ie increase selectively. In fact we found that, although there was measurable improvement in orthogonality, from 0.583 51 to 0.638 75, this did not correlate well with accuracy (which decreased).

Accuracy
In Fig. 12 the average percentage accuracy across all classes, for the best string, is plotted against the current generation. The improvement is significant but not startling—an improvement from 58.7–65.3% across 2000 generations. Broken down across classes the results were as shown in Table 14. Examination of the best string of the search showed that the

Table 14. *Effect of Holland's genetic algorithm*

| | Percentage recognition accuracy | |
Vowel	Initial best string	Final best string
A	61.5	65.4
E	37.5	45.8
I	59.3	63.0
O	62.5	75.0
U	72.7	77.3
Average	58.7	65.3

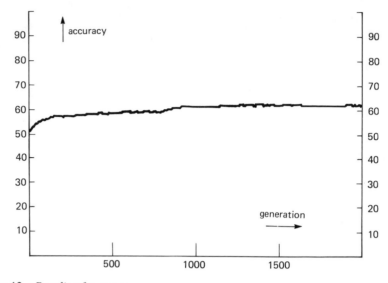

Figure 12   *Breeding for accuracy.*

pixels selected for the 8-tuples were evenly scattered over the retina. No specific frequencies or time slots seemed to be particularly favoured.

The overall effect across the entire population, rather than individual best strings, can be observed in the histograms of Fig. 13. The top row represents the initial performance, on each vowel, of the entire

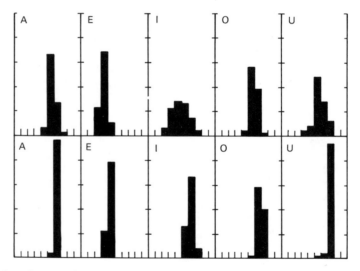

Figure 13   *The overall effect on the entire population.*

population. Horizontal divisions are percentage accuracies in the ranges 0–10, 10–20, ..., 90–100. The vertical scale represents frequency (total — 50 strings in each case). Note there was one initial string giving a recognition in the range 70–80% for *A* (presumably a worse performance on other vowels) but in the final population no such string existed. This results from breeding for *average* accuracy across recognition classes. How significant is this improvement in accuracy compared with that which might be expected from a random search through 2050 strings?

Assuming that the distribution of average accuracy across the population of random strings is normal (an assumption reasonably in accordance with the observed facts) we can approximately gauge the efficiency of the search as follows. We first calculate the mean, *M*, and standard deviation, *S*, for the initial population of average accuracies and then compute

$$(B-M)/S,$$

where *B* is the average accuracy for the best final string. The figure obtained was 3.92 standard deviations.

The probability that at least one string is as good, or better, than the best string found after a random search through 2050 strings is

$$1-(\text{Area to left of 3.92 on normal distribution})^{2050},$$

ie approximately 0.1. By this measure the genetic algorithm was about ten times more efficient than an exhaustive search.

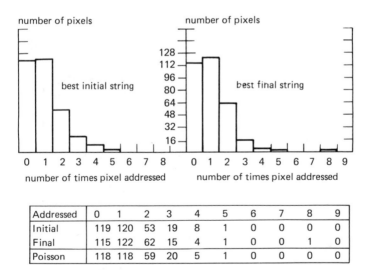

Addressed	0	1	2	3	4	5	6	7	8	9
Initial	119	120	53	19	8	1	0	0	0	0
Final	115	122	62	15	4	1	0	0	1	0
Poisson	118	118	59	20	5	1	0	0	0	0

Figure 14   *Initial and final distributions of pixel addressing.*

We were interested to see if there was a significant change in the distribution of frequency with which individual retinal pixels are sampled. Given an initially random selection of pixels one might expect the frequency with which an individual pixel is addressed to be Poisson with mean 1. In Fig. 14 the initial and final distributions for the best strings are given and compared with the expected Poisson distribution. From this it can be seen that no significant shift occurred after 2000 generations.

If there were a performance advantage to be gained from a 1–1 mapping one would expect the number of pixels addressed zero times to decrease with the number of generations, whereas Fig. 14 shows that this effect did not occur in any significant way.

4.4 Conclusions

If we compare the results of the multiple discriminator per vowel experiment with the genetic algorithm experiment, some interesting points emerge.

Vowel	A	E	I	O	U
MDV	61.5	54.2	59.3	54.2	81.8
IGA	61.5	37.5	59.3	62.5	72.7
FGA	65.4	45.8	63.0	75.0	77.3

MDV = multiple discriminators per vowel.
IGA = initial performance in genetic algorithm experiment.
FGA = final performance in genetic algorithm experiment.

The 'most difficult' vowel E and the 'easiest' vowel U have plainly benefited in the first vowel experiment from having discriminators trained over a variation of timescales. On the other hand, the genetic algorithm was able to tailor a *single* mapping to compensate to a significant degree for variations in rate of articulation of these vowels.

However, while some improvement in average accuracy of recognition across classes can be effected using genetic algorithms, the bunching of the population in the histograms of Fig. 13 demonstrates that for each vowel there is a definite limit beyond which no improvement can be expected using a single mapping for all classes. Indeed, from Fig. 13, we can roughly estimate the upper bound for average accuracy for this system as lying in the range 72–82%.

The evidence seems to suggest that the principal reason for this upper limit in performance is the time variation in the samples used. By using a *separate mapping for each class* the results using genetic algorithms may well improve to the point where it would not be necessary to have multiple discriminators per class. However, once the extra overhead of a separate mapping for each class is accepted, then other, simpler, possibilities exist for optimizing mappings which should be explored first, possibly keeping the genetic algorithm in reserve for fine tuning at the final stage.

Certainly genetic algorithms offer considerable gains in efficiency over exhaustive search in tailoring pattern recognition systems operating on real data. The improved mappings produced by the genetic algorithm showed no tendency to become 1–1. We found this an interesting observation but hesitate to draw a general conclusion.

Acknowledgement

The authors gratefully acknowledge the support of British Telecom Research Laboratories R 18.3.2, Martlesham, under contract number MSP3231A/25 Control 318028, for major parts of the work described in this chapter. We are also indebted to IEE Proceedings for kind permission to reproduce much of [2].

References

1. Bledsoe, W. W. & Browning, I. Pattern recognition and reading by machine, *Proc. Eastern Joint Computer Conf.* (Boston, Mass: 1959).
2. Binstead, M. J. & Jones, A. J. A design technique for dynamically evolving N-tuple nets, *IEE Proceedings*, Vol. 134, Part E, No. 6, pp. 265–269 (November, 1987).
3. Minsky, M. & Papert, S. *Perceptrons—An Introduction to Computational Geometry* (Cambridge Mass: MIT Press, 1969).
4. Aleksander, I. & Stonham, T. J. A guide to pattern recognition using random-access memories, *IEEE Journal Computers and Digital Techniques* 2(1), 29–40 (1979).
5. Kohonen, T. *Self-Organisation and Associative Memory* (Berlin Springer Verlag, 1984).
6. Barto, A. G. & Sutton, R. S. *Goal Seeking Components for Adaptive Intelligence: An Initial Assessment* (University for Massachusetts, Amhurst: Technical Report no. AFWAL-TR-81-1070, 1981).
7. Fish, A. N. The conformon: a synaptic model of learning (Ph.D. thesis, University of Manchester, Department of Psychology, 1981).
8. Tattershall, G. D. & Johnson, R. D. Speech recognition based on N-tuple sampling, *Proc. Spring. Conf. Inst. Acoustics Swansea*, Vol. 9, No. 2 (April, 1984).
9. Holland, J. H. *Adaptation in Natural and Artificial Systems* (University of Michigan Press, 1975).
10. Holmes, J. N. The JSRU channel vocoder, *IEE Proceedings*, Vol. 127, Part F, No. 1, pp. 53–60 (February, 1980).
11. Bellman, R. E. *Dynamic Programming* (Princeton University Press, 1957).
12. Vintsyuk, T. K. Element by element recognition of continuous speech composed of the words of a given vocabulary, *Kibernetica* 2, 133–143 (1971).
13. Sakoe, H. & Chiba, S. A dynamic programming approach to continuous speech recognition, *Proc. of Int. Cong. of Acoust.*, Budapest, Hungary, pp. 200–213 (1971).
14. McClelland, J. L. & Rumelhart, D. E. (eds) *Parallel Distributed Processing*, Vol. 2 (Cambridge Mass: MIT Press, 1986).

15. Leszek, Kot. A syntax-controlled segmentation of speech on the basis of dynamic spectra, *Int. Conf. on Acoustics, Speech and Signal Processing*, pp. 2015–2017 (1982).
16. Jassem, W. Speech recognition work in Poland, Chapter 23 of *Trends in Speech Recognition* (Prentice-Hall, pp. 499–511, 1980).
17. Cavicchio, D. J. Adaptive search using simulated evolution (PhD thesis, University of Michigan, 1970).
18. Brindle, A. Genetic algorithms for function optimization (PhD thesis, University of Alberta, 1980).

11 Dynamic behaviour of Boolean networks

D. Martland

Department of Computer Science, Brunel University, Uxbridge, Middlesex, UK

Abstract

Boolean networks have been the subject of study by several workers, including Kauffman[1] Walker[2] and Martland.[3,4] Practical recognition systems which are based on Boolean function units have been developed by Aleksander.[5]

This chapter introduces the concept of Boolean networks, and presents some of the properties of this class of network. A treatment of the activity levels within certain types of Boolean networks is presented in easily understood mathematical terms.

1. Boolean networks—what are they?

A Boolean network is a system composed of interconnected units, each having a number of inputs, and a single output. The output may fan-out to several other units, as shown in the example in Fig. 1.

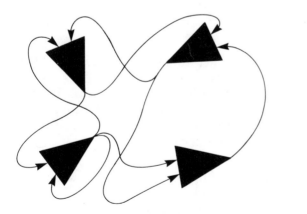

Figure 1

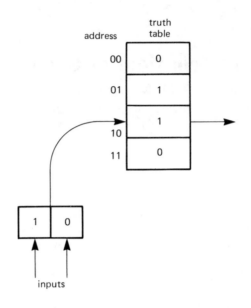

Figure 2

Each unit within the network evaluates its inputs, which are taken to lie in the domain $B = \{0, 1\}$, and produces an output also in the domain $\{0, 1\}$. Thus each unit i in the network evaluates a function $f_i : B \times B \times B \times \ldots \times B \to B$ or just $f_i : B^n \to B$, where n is the number of inputs to each unit. There are no constraints on the functions which can be used within the network, and they can be conveniently represented by a truth table within each unit, as shown in Fig. 2. Each unit may perform a different Boolean logic function within the network.

1.2 Operational modes

There are several possible modes of operation of these networks. Most of the studies of this type of network have been on rigid networks, for which the network connections do not alter with time. Interesting results can be obtained by varying the Boolean functions with time, and using networks which have external inputs,[4] but in this chapter networks will be assumed to be autonomous, with fixed functions in each unit.

Possible operational modes are:

(a) parallel update (synchronous), in which all units perform their evaluation at the same instant, or clock pulse;
(b) deterministic serial update, in which each unit updates independently of all the others, and in a pre-determined order;

(c) non-deterministic serial update, in which each unit updates independently of all the others, but in a randomly determined order;
(d) asynchronous, partially parallel update, in which a fraction of the units update at each time step.

The networks which have been studied extensively are those using parallel update, but results will be presented which also apply to other modes.

2. How do the networks behave?

There are several characteristics which can be examined for each type of Boolean network. Particular characteristics of interest include cyclic behaviour, stability, and network activity. These will be discussed in the following sections.

2.1 Cycles

Each net has states, represented by values within B^m, where m is the number of units in the network. Each net has a behaviour, which is characterized by the transitions from one state to the next state.

For networks which operate synchronously, the system behaves deterministically as a finite state machine, and for any starting state S_0, must have the characteristic behaviour shown in Fig. 3, where some states $(S_0 \ldots S_{i-1})$ belong to the transient (or run-in) state sequence, and some states $(S_i \ldots S_k)$ belong to a state cycle. The length of the transient sequence is i, and the length of the cycle is $k-i+1$. Some cycles are of length 1, and correspond to stable states.

The concepts of cycles and transient sequences are not meaningful for networks which operate non-deterministically.

2.1 Activity

The number of units which change on each time step is a measure of activity within the network. Additionally, it is useful to consider the

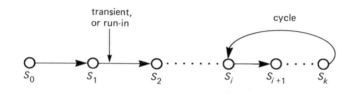

Figure 3

number of units which are outputting a 1 at each time interval, and to consider the density of such units, defined by:

$$\rho = \frac{\text{number of firing units}}{\text{net size}}.$$

These concepts apply both to deterministic and non-deterministic networks.

2.2 Stability

For any two network states S_i, S_k, the Hamming distance $|S_i - S_k|$ between the states is just the number of units which differ in output in the two-state representations. States for which their Hamming distance is small are said to be close, and states for which their Hamming distance is large are said to be distant. It is interesting to study the behaviour of states which are close. For deterministic nets, each state cycle defines an equivalence class, containing all the states in the cycle, or within any transient leading into it. Notice that for any equivalence class for a network with more than one cycle, there is always at least one state not contained within the class, which is a unit Hamming distance away from some state within the class. Also notice that within any cyclic equivalence class there could be two states with Hamming distance m, where m is the size of the network.

The first observation shows that if a unit Hamming distance disturbance is made to a state in the transient sequence, it is possible that the disturbed state will belong to a different cyclic equivalence class, and the network would run into a different cycle from that state.

Network stability can be determined by allowing the network to run into a cycle, and then applying a disturbance to states within the cycle. If the disturbed state runs back to the cycle from which it was displaced, the network shows stability, whereas if it runs into a different cycle it is considered to be less stable.

The concept of stability depends on cycles, and does not apply without modification to non-deterministic networks. Extensive work on the stability of Boolean networks has been undertaken by Walker.[2, 6]

3. State structure of random networks

Kauffman gives results for randomly connected networks with different numbers of inputs per unit.[1] In particular, Kauffman considered fully connected networks, and networks with one, two and three inputs per unit. Fully connected networks can be shown, using results from Rubin & Sitgreave[7] and Harris[8] to have cycle and transient lengths of order $m^{1/2}$

where m is the number of possible network states, which is 2^n where n is the number of units in the network. Even for modest-sized networks, the cycles and transient sequences will be very long, and approximately $\frac{1}{2}(2\pi\sqrt{m})$ with a variance of $m[(2/3)-(2\pi/16)]$.

Much of Kauffman's work concerned networks with two input units. Using networks with random connections, and random Boolean functions, Kauffman found empirically that the average cycle and transient length for a network of size n is $O(\sqrt{n})$. Even very large networks with 1 000 000 units would only have cycle lengths of the order of 1000. This is very much smaller than the corresponding expected cycle length for fully connected nets. The cycle lengths observed by Kauffman were around 8 for a network with 1000 units.

Kauffman also noted that the number of cycles in a net was small, and conjectured that this also was $O(\sqrt{n})$. Again, the empirical observation is that the number of net cycles is approximately $\frac{1}{2}\sqrt{n}$. As an example of this, consider a network with 1000 units. This would have about 16 cycles, with around eight states per cycle. Thus approximately 100 states would belong to cycles, and $2^{1000}-100$ would belong to transient sequences. As a result of Kauffman's work, it is possible to surmise that the state structure for a network of two input units looks like that given in Fig. 4. Most of the states belong to the confluent tree structures, with a few states belonging to one of a few cycles. Kauffman found slightly longer cycles with networks of three-input units, but the tendency to have relatively short cycles was maintained.

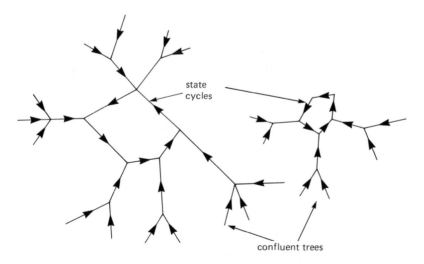

Figure 4

221

Kauffman considered randomly connected networks with random Boolean functions. Martland,[3] considered networks in which the output of each unit had some probability other than 0.5 of being a 1. It appears that if the average truth table density of ones is ρ, this will correspond to the average output density of ones. This observation, although intuitively obvious, prompted investigation of networks in which each unit in the network performed the same Boolean function. Networks corresponding to each of the two input Boolean functions were simulated, and results of the typical cycle and transient lengths noted, and also the density of ones in the output during the run-in and cycle. The experimental data provided useful clues to the behaviour of this type of network with respect to the output density, which resulted in a simple mathematical modelling of this network type.

4. Theoretical model

Many mathematical treatments of network behaviour have been developed for networks of threshold units, and much work has been undertaken on methods of training and adapting such networks, and providing mathematical justification for their behaviour. In particular, Amari,[9–12] who has studied the properties of networks as associative memories, and Little,[13] who has applied the mathematics of Ising spin-glass systems to networks, have enhanced our knowledge of threshold unit networks. There has been little work done on Boolean network systems. This section presents a simple method for determining the behaviour of randomly connected, synchronous, Boolean networks. The model applies to networks with any number of inputs per unit, but is simplest to understand for two-input networks.

Consider a network made up of two-input Boolean units. Select one unit for attention. Denote its truth table elements by T_{00}, T_{01}, T_{10} and T_{11}. Now, replace the unit by a similar probabilistic unit, with truth table probabilities P_{00}, P_{01}, P_{10} and P_{11}. Thus P_{00} is the probability that the unit outputs a 1 if the inputs to the unit are both 0. Note that replacing the Ts by Ps just generalizes the behaviour of the unit, and is consistent with the behaviour of the unit which was replaced.

The probability that the unit outputs a 1 is now easily seen to be

$$\rho' = P_{00}(1-\rho)^2 + P_{01}\rho(1-\rho) + P_{10}\rho(1-\rho) + P_{11}\rho^2 \qquad (1)$$

where ρ' is the density of outputs which are 1 on the next time step, and ρ is the current output density.

This function can be evaluated for each of the 16 two-input Boolean functions, and used to plot a graph for each one. Examination of the graph associated with each function allows the dynamics of the network behaviour to be predicted with accuracy depending on the size of the network. It should be clear that the method also applies to networks of three-input units, and generalizes to networks containing units with an arbitrary number of inputs.

The estimation of the next output density as a function of the current density can also be extended to asynchronous networks, if some appropriate meaning is given to the notion of firing. In the case of Boolean networks, the output of each unit is determined by its truth table, and firing the unit corresponds to determining a new output value consistent with the currently applied inputs. If each unit fires with probability f on each time step, the expression for ρ becomes

$$\rho' = f \times (P_{00}(1-\rho)^2 + P_{01}\rho(1-\rho) + P_{10}\rho(1-\rho) + P_{11}\rho^2) + (1-f)\rho \tag{2}$$

For small values of f, the expression reduces to $\rho' \sim \rho$.

5. Classification of network behaviour

In this section a number of different types of network behaviour will be considered. These correspond to the graphs for ρ' plotted against ρ shown in Fig. 5. (a) shows a parabolic curve, with a maximum value of 0.675. Note that a network with this characteristic has a stable point at density $\rho = 0$, and also another stable region where the curve crosses the line $\rho' = \rho$. The arrowed line shows how the network density will

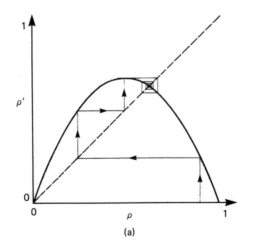

(a)

Figure 5(a) $\rho' = 2.7\rho(1-\rho)$

223

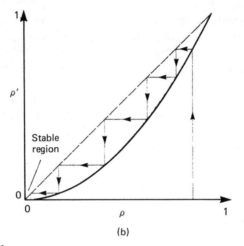

Figure 5(*b*) $\rho' = \rho^2$

progress at each time step up to the stable region. In (*b*) the stable region is close to $\rho = 0$, with network density steadily decreasing on each step. (*c*) is similar to 5(*b*), except that the network density increases, rather than decreases. (*d*) shows a situation in which every value of ρ is potentially stable. There is no tendency for the network density to move in any particular direction, up or down. (*e*) shows the curve $\rho' = 1 - \rho$. If the network is started with $\rho = \rho_0$, it will tend to oscillate about states with densities ρ_0 and $1 - \rho_0$. It follows that such a network is likely to fall into

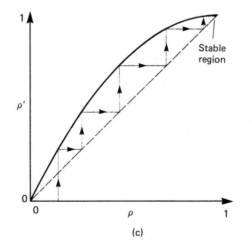

Figure 5(*c*) $\rho' = \rho(2 - \rho)$

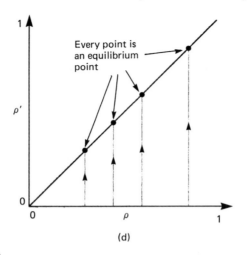

(d)

Figure 5(d) $\rho' = \rho$

a cycle with an even length. (f) shows a converging oscillation towards $\rho = 0.5$. (g) shows a diverging oscillation. The network will fall into an even cycle in which alternate states are very far apart in Hamming distance. (h) shows another curve which has a stable region around $\rho = 1$. (i) illustrates a similar curve, which has a stable region around $\rho = 0.5$. (j) shows a curve which has several stable equilibrium regions. Note that, although any point of intersection of the curve with the line $\rho' = \rho$ can represent a point of stability, only those points of intersection where the slope of the curve is less than 1 represent stable regions in the sense that they are immune to small disturbances. Other points of intersection represent unstable equilibrium points.

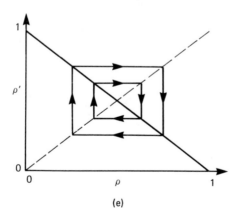

(e)

Figure 5(e) $\rho' = 1 - \rho$

225

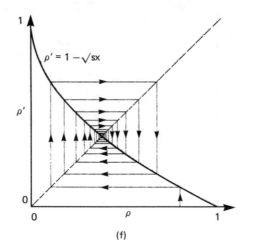

(f)

Figure 5(f) $\rho' = 1 - \sqrt{\rho}$

Fig. 6(a) shows a curve that should give rise to periodic behaviour, with periodicity 2. This curve is parabolic, with a maximum at 0.75, and corresponds to a periodic attractor.[14] This curve corresponds to the ρ' against ρ curve for a network of three-input units, where $P_{000} = P_{111} = 0$, and all other Ps are 1. If the curve of (a) is altered, so that the

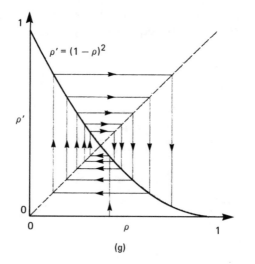

(g)

Figure 5(g) $\rho' = (1 - \rho)^2$

226

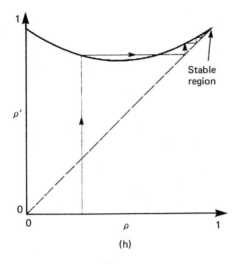

(h)

Figure 5(*h*)

height of the curve increases towards 0.89, the number of attractive regions should increase, by ascending powers of 2, to form periodic attractors of periodicity, 4, 8, 16 and so on. (*b*) shows a curve with a peak just below 0.89, which represents a periodic attractor of periodicity 4. Note that as the periodicity increases, the periodicity becomes difficult to

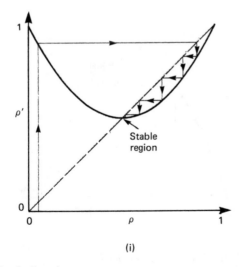

(i)

Figure 5(*i*) $\rho' = 1 - 2\rho(1 - \rho)$

227

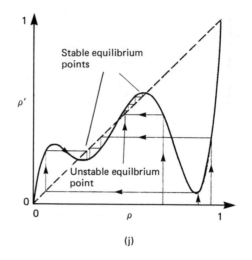

(j)

Figure 5(j) $\rho' = 100(\rho - 0.24)(\rho - 0.45)(\rho - 0.6)(\rho - 1) + \rho$

detect by examining diagrams. (c) shows a parabolic curve with a peak value greater than 0.9. This curve generates chaotic behaviour, which is aperiodic.

6. Experimental results

The model developed here has been tested by simulation, and shown to

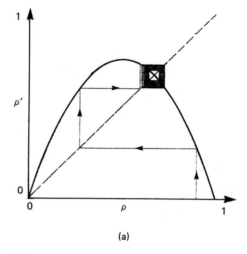

(a)

Figure 6   *Periodic and chaotic network dynamics for specified $\rho' - \rho$ curves*
(a) $\rho' = 3\rho(1 - \rho)$, giving periodicity 2

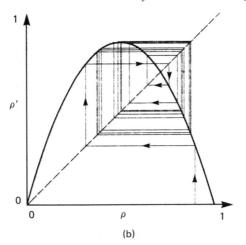

(b)

Figure 6   (b) $\rho' = 3.51\rho(1-\rho)$, *giving periodicity 4*

be approximately valid even for quite small networks. The results for larger networks tend towards the predicted curves quite well. Fig. 7 shows the results for networks with 50 and 200 units, for three of the Boolean functions. The results were gathered by running typical networks, and finding the output density at each time step. Using this data, adjacent pairs were plotted to produce the figures.

Note that the results should apply to networks with mixtures of different Boolean functions within the network. The only requirement for the network analysis is that the mixture of functions is homogeneous, and

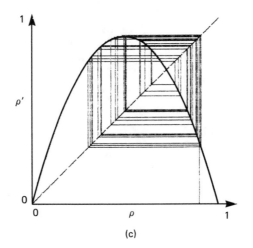

(c)

Figure 6(c) $\rho' = 3.63\rho(1-\rho)$, *giving chaotic behaviour*

229

D. Martland

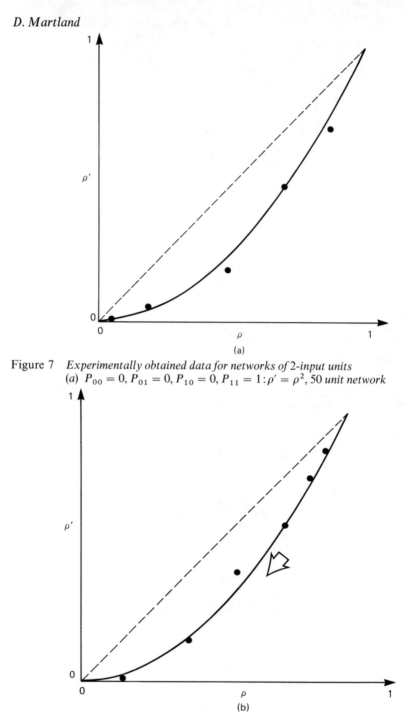

(a)

Figure 7   *Experimentally obtained data for networks of 2-input units*
(a) $P_{00} = 0, P_{01} = 0, P_{10} = 0, P_{11} = 1 : \rho' = \rho^2$, 50 *unit network*

(b)

Figure 7   (b) $P_{00} = 0, P_{01} = 0, P_{10} = 0, P_{11} = 1 : \rho' = \rho^2$, 200 *unit network*

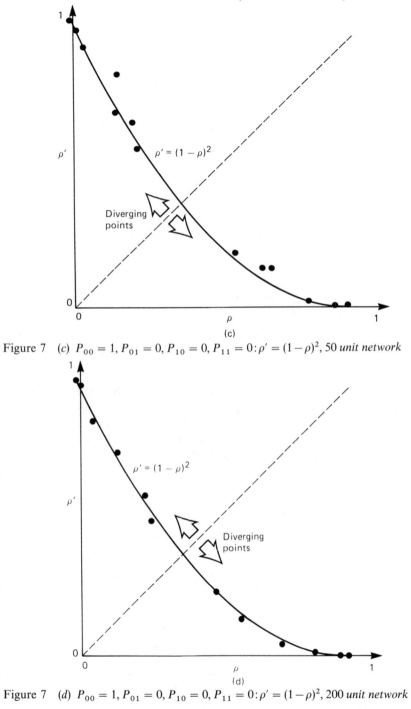

Figure 7   (c) $P_{00} = 1, P_{01} = 0, P_{10} = 0, P_{11} = 0 : \rho' = (1 - \rho)^2$, 50 *unit network*

Figure 7   (d) $P_{00} = 1, P_{01} = 0, P_{10} = 0, P_{11} = 0 : \rho' = (1 - \rho)^2$, 200 *unit network*

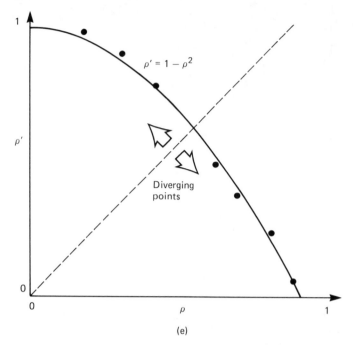

(e)

Figure 7   (e) $P_{00} = 1, P_{01} = 1, P_{10} = 1, P_{11} = 0: \rho' = 1 - \rho^2$, 50 unit network

that it is possible to calculate the values for the *P*s. The values for the *P*s which have to be used are averaged out over small regions of the network. Thus, the curve for a randomly connected network of two-input functions containing a balanced mixture of XOR and EQ gates, should have probabilities $P_{00} = 0.5, P_{01} = 0.5, P_{10} = 0.5$, and $P_{11} = 0.5$.

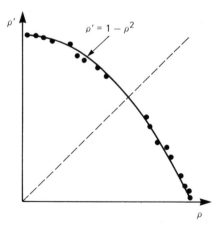

Figure 7(*f*)

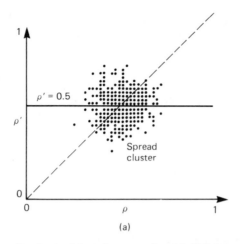

Figure 8   *Experimentally obtained data for networks with 50 2-input units*
           (*a*) *Balanced mixture of XOR and EQ units*

Fig. 8(*a*) shows how such a network satisfies the prediction. In fact, although the output density does behave according to the theory, for networks with a large number of units, it can be seen that for a balanced mixture of XOR and EQ gates, settling down into cycles takes a considerable time, and that there is a considerable spread of values around those predicted. Fig. 8(*b*) shows the comparable behaviour for a random mixture of two-input Boolean functions, showing that shorter

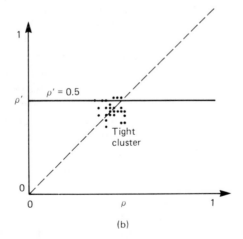

Figure 8   (*b*) *Randomly assigned truth table values* ($P_{00} = P_{01} = P_{10} = P_{11} = 0.5$)

233

cycle lengths are more likely for this class of network. Thus it can be seen that the theory does not give any guidance about transient and cycle lengths, even for networks which should have similar behaviour with respect to output density.

Notice also, that it was earlier stated that in a network with randomly assigned Ps, the output activity appeared to depend on the number of 1s in the truth table for the whole network. It is easily seen that, if $P_{00} = P, P_{01} = P, P_{10} = P$ and $P_{11} = P$ where P is a constant in the range 0 to 1, that

$$\rho' = P(1-\rho)^2 + 2P(1-\rho)\rho + P\rho^2$$

which reduces to

$$\rho' = P,$$

which is the expected result.

Lastly, note that if a Boolean network operates asynchronously, with firing probability f less than 1, tendencies of the network to oscillate will be reduced, in accordance with Equation (2).

7. Applications of the theory to Boolean network machines

Systems based on Boolean units have been used to construct hardware for pattern recognition applications,[5] and have been shown by Martland to have potential applications for pattern sequence acceptors.[4]

The application of theoretical results to Boolean networks is still in its infancy. The results given here are useful in the sense that they provide repeatable patterns of behaviour of any reasonably large network based on random connections of Boolean units, and these behaviour modes could be used to detect hardware and software failures in systems which could be configured to model any of the network types discussed. Systematic failures, for example of a common address line, could be detected and diagnosed by observing the characteristic curve for the modelled network and comparing it with the expected. By comparing the characteristic behaviour curve with a set of expected curves corresponding to different network parameters, it may be possible to identify the failure precisely.

Failures in a few units in the network will be hard to detect by this method, as they will merely contribute small amounts of noise. Whether this will be detected will depend on the effect of such noise on the network behaviour, and how easily the effects can be observed.

234

8. Conclusion

It would be useful if the results obtained could be used for designing network based systems, or for proving theorems concerning the behaviour of useful networks. The systems studied in this chapter are very simple, and have understandable behaviour. It has not so far been possible to analyse mathematically the behaviour of more complex networks which have potentially more practical applications. This is partly because of the different structure of the systems, and partly because the patterns presented to practical systems for processing do not have the characteristics of random noise patterns described in this chapter. The hope for the future is that useful networks constructed out of Boolean units will be constructed, and that they will become much more easily understandable as more research into their applications and operation is carried out.

References

1. Kauffman, S. A. Metabolic stability and epigenesis in randomly connected genetic nets, *Journal of Theoretical Biology* **22**, 437–467 (1969).
2. Walker, C. C. Stability of equilibrial states and limit cycles in sparsely connected, structurally complex Boolean nets, *Submitted for publication* (1987).
3. Martland, D. Behaviour of autonomous (synchronous), Boolean networks, *Proceedings of the first IEEE Conference on Neural Networks, San Diego* **II**, 243–250 (1987).
4. Martland, D. Auto-associative pattern storage using synchronous Boolean networks, *Proceedings of the first IEEE Conference on Neural Networks, San Diego* **III**, 355–366 (1987).
5. Aleksander, I., Thomas, W. V. & Bowden, P. A. WISARD, a radical step forward in image recognition, *Sensor Review* **4**, 120–124 (1984).
6. Walker, C. C. Behavior of a class of complex systems: the effect of system size on properties of terminal cycles, *Journal of Cybernetics* **1**, 55–67 (1971).
7. Rubin, H. & Sitgreave, R. Probability distributions related to random transformations on a finite set, *Tech. Report No. 19A* (Appl. Maths. and Stats. Lab., Stanford University, 1954).
8. Harris, B. Probability distributions related to random mappings, *Ann. Math. Stat.* **31**, 1045–1062 (1960).
9. Amari, S. I. A theory of adaptive pattern classifiers, *IEEE Trans. Electronic Computing* Vol. EC-16, pp. 299–302 (1967).
10. Amari, S. I. Characteristics of randomly connected threshold elements and network systems, *Proc. IEEE* Vol. 39, pp. 33–47 (1971).
11. Amari, S. I. Learning patterns and pattern sequences by self-organizing nets of threshold elements, *IEEE Trans. Comput.* Vol. C21, pp. 1197–1206 (1972).
12. Amari, S. I. Field theory of self-organising neural nets, *IEEE Trans. Systems, Man and Cybernetics* pp. 741–748 (1983).
13. Little, W. A. The existence of persistant states in the brain, *Mathematics Bioscience* **19**, 101–120 (1974).
14. Feigenbaum, M. J. Universal behavior in nonlinear systems, *Los Alamos Science* **1**, 4–27 (1980).

PART III
Analysis and Implementations

12 Statistical mechanics and neural networks

C. Campbell

Department of Applied Physics, Kingston Polytechnic, Kingston-upon-Thames, UK

and

D. Sherrington & K. Y. M. Wong

Department of Physics, Imperial College, University of London, London, UK

Abstract

This review discusses the application of analytical methods from statistical mechanics to various neural network models of associative memory. The relevance of statistical mechanics stems from the discovery that some neural network models have a direct analogy with spin glass models of theoretical solid state physics. By using this analogy, one is able to study many of the properties of neural networks such as storage capacity, quality of retrieval and the effects of noise.

1. Introduction

The human brain is superior to contemporary computers in a wide range of computational tasks, particularly in areas such as pattern recognition or non-algorithmic problem solving. Remarkably, the brain excels in these tasks through the use of neural components which are slow, inaccurate and limited compared with electronic counterparts. The brain achieves speed and error tolerance in the processing of information by distributing the operation over a very large number of neural processors. At the same time the brain apparently achieves speed in the storage and retrieval of information by distributing that information in the (synaptic) connections between the processors.

It is believed that neural activity is governed by a non-linear neuronal dynamics with competing synaptic interactions. This type of dynamics can typically be described by a phase space in which the motion

239

converges towards fixed, cyclic or chaotic attractors. Furthermore, neural systems, such as the brain, have very large numbers of simple and operationally identical elements. These points indicate that statistical mechanics can be usefully applied to neural network theory.

A great advantage of relating neural network theory to statistical mechanics is that a rigorous analytical approach can be developed. As a result, it is now possible to obtain definite and precise predictions about the properties of neural network models. At the same time the conceptual basis of neural network theory can be strengthened.

In 1982 Hopfield[1] proposed a neural network model which had a strong affinity with statistical mechanics. This model is very similar to several models studied in solid state physics. In particular, it is related to models used in the theoretical analysis of certain materials called spin glasses. These are magnetic materials which have a random orientational ordering (glass) of magnetic moments (spins). The spin sites are randomly interconnected by positive and negative competing interactions. Like the Hopfield and other neural network models, the spin glass dynamics is governed by a phase space with a large number of attractors.

It was the Hopfield model which stimulated the current surge of interest in the relationship between neural networks and statistical mechanics. The purpose of this article is to examine this relationship by reviewing recent developments in the study of the statistical properties of neural network models.

The outline of the article is as follows. In Section 2, we present the dynamical equation for a class of neural network models. For symmetrical interactions, it can be shown that the system evolves towards the minimum of an energy function, while biological noise can be imitated by temperature. In this way, concepts in neural network theory are directly related to analogues in statistical mechanics.

Having considered the relationship between the two, we proceed to elucidate the properties of the Hopfield model in Section 3, by studying the free energy of the system, which can be expressed as a function of the overlaps. Roughly speaking, the overlaps determine the closeness between the configuration of the network and the stored patterns during retrieval. The overlaps satisfy a set of self-consistency equations, from which statistical properties of the network are easily derived.

Having demonstrated the power of statistical mechanics for the particular case of the Hopfield model, we consider various extensions to the model in Section 4. In Section 5 we examine attempts to increase the storage capacity beyond that dictated by the Hebbian learning rule (eg Equation (4)). In particular, the calculation of the optimal storage capacity in the space of connection strengths is another success of statistical mechanics. Section 6 contains our conclusion.

240

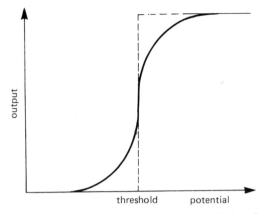

Figure 1 *Sigmoid output function of a neuron (continuous line) and the sgn (x) function idealization (dashed line). In equation (1) the potential has a sharply defined threshold at $\phi = 0$.*

2. The dynamics of neural networks

2.1

The Hopfield and other models consist of networks of N nodes (representing neurons) with each node connected to the other nodes through a (synaptic) connection strength matrix $\mathbf{T}_{ij}$. Following the McCulloch–Pitts model[2] of the neuron, the nodes are taken to be simple processing elements with two possible outputs $+1$ and -1 (see Fig. 1). Biologically, the $+1$ and -1 represent respectively, the firing and non-firing states of the neurons. At a given time, the state of the network consists of a pattern of $+1$ or -1 values. Consequently, the configuration of the system can be represented by a vector $\mathbf{h}_i$ of length N with components ± 1.

Suppose we want to store a number of random pattern in the network, the **g**th pattern being a vector $\mathbf{g}_i^{(s)}$ of length N with components ± 1. Starting from some initial configuration, the network recalls one of these patterns by evolving iteratively towards it according to some dynamical rules. Typical dynamical rules in neural networks belong to a general class of rules of the form:

$$\mathbf{h}_i(t+1) = \text{sgn}\left(\sum_{j=1}^{N} \mathbf{T}_{ij}\mathbf{h}_j(t) \right), \tag{1}$$

where $\text{sgn}(x) = 1$ if $x > 0$ and $\text{sgn}(x) = -1$ if $x < 0$. The quantity:

$$\phi_i = \sum_{j=1}^{N} \mathbf{T}_{ij}\mathbf{h}_j \tag{2}$$

corresponds to the biological membrane potential. Consequently, the effect of the dynamical rule is to cause alignment between this potential vector and the next state vector (ie $\mathbf{h}_i(t+1)\phi_i(t) \geqslant 0$).

As the system evolves according to the dynamical rule, Equation (1), it typically settles down to a long-term recurring pattern. Motions from neighbouring states will tend towards such stable persisting states, which therefore act as attractors. Plainly a stable long-term persisting pattern would satisfy:

$$\mathbf{h}_i(t = \infty) = \text{sgn}\left(\sum_{j=1}^{N} \mathbf{T}_{ij}\mathbf{h}_j(t = \infty) \right). \tag{3}$$

If the nodes update asynchronously and the connection strengths are symmetric then only fixed point attractors occur (in the absence of noise). The Hopfield model is an example of such a system. If the updating in Equation (1) is performed synchronously on all the nodes, then cyclic attractors can also occur. In the synchronous model proposed by Little[3]

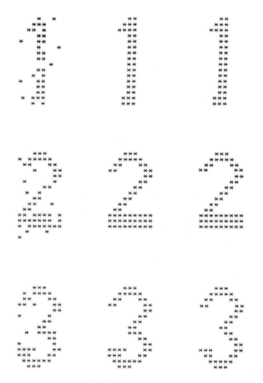

Figure 2   *Recall of numeric patterns (for a 144-node network with five stored memories.*

and Little & Shaw,[4] cyclic states exist (at least for finite N), though it can be shown that the only persisting cyclic states are those of cycle length two (consisting of two conjugate patterns).[5] Finally, if we model the biological situation and use asymmetric connection strengths, then all three types of attractor seem to appear, namely point, cyclic and chaotic states.

A neural network model of associative memory can now be constructed by specifying the $\mathbf{T}_{ij}$ so that the stored patterns are attractors. That is, the $\mathbf{T}_{ij}$ are constructed so that a noisy or incomplete initial pattern will settle onto an attractor which is similar to, or identical with, a previously stored pattern. This process is illustrated in Fig. 2 where attracting states consisting of numeric patterns are reached from noisy initial numeric patterns.

One of the simplest ways of constructing a suitable $\mathbf{T}_{ij}$ matrix is given by the Hebbian learning rule. In terms of the stored patterns, $\mathbf{g}_i^{(s)}$, the connection strength matrix is given by:

$$\left. \begin{aligned} \mathbf{T}_{ij} &= \frac{1}{N} \sum_{s=1}^{p} \mathbf{g}_i^{(s)} \mathbf{g}_j^{(s)} \quad (i \neq j) \\ \mathbf{T}_{ii} &= 0 \end{aligned} \right\}, \tag{4}$$

with the sum on s taken over all the stored memory patterns. Mirroring the effect of synaptic efficacy, the connection strength matrix can be 'excitatory' or 'inhibitory', depending on the sign of $\mathbf{T}_{ij}$.

Substituting the matrix, Equation (4), into the potential, Equation (2), we obtain:

$$\phi_i(\mathbf{g}_i^{(s)}) = \frac{(N-1)}{N} \mathbf{g}_i^{(s)} + \frac{1}{N} \sum_{j \neq i} \sum_{t \neq s} \mathbf{g}_i^{(t)} \mathbf{g}_j^{(t)} \mathbf{g}_j^{(s)}. \tag{5}$$

Consequently it is possible to see that the patterns $\mathbf{g}_i^{(s)}$ can be fixed points of the dynamical rule Equation (1). The first term in Equation (5) causes alignment with the vector $\mathbf{g}_i^{(s)}$, while the second term acts as a noisy background. Since the first term has a magnitude $(N-1)/N$ while the second term has mean 0 and variance $(N-1)(p-1)/N^2$, the former dominates provided that the number of patterns is not too large, and the pattern $\mathbf{g}_i^{(s)}$ will be a fixed point of (1). Furthermore, we can see that if $p \sim N$, the interference of the noise term cannot be neglected, and the quality of retrieval will deteriorate.

In summary, neural network models such as Hopfield's consist of two parts: (a) a learning rule for storing information; and (b) a dynamical rule for retrieving information. In Hopfield's model, the learning rule is specified as in Equation (4) and the dynamical rule is that given in Equation (1).

2.2 The energy function

Hopfield[1] noted that if one chooses a symmetric connection strength matrix, such as Equation (4), it is possible to define an energy function for each configuration of the network:

$$E = -\frac{1}{2}\sum_{ij} T_{ij}h_i h_j. \tag{6}$$

With each iteration this energy function will either decrease or remain constant. In fact, it is straightforward to prove this for arbitrary symmetric T_{ij} with $T_{ii} = 0$. For each iteration:

$$\Delta E = -\sum_{\substack{ij \\ i \neq j}} T_{ij}(\Delta h_i)h_j. \tag{7}$$

Cross-terms $T_{ij}\Delta h_i \Delta h_j$ are absent because of the asynchronicity and the condition $T_{ii} = 0$. From the dynamical rule (1) it can be readily seen that:

$$\Delta h_i \left(\sum_j T_{ij}h_j \right) \geq 0. \tag{8}$$

Consequently the result $\Delta E \leq 0$ is immediate.

We may regard the energy function as defining a complicated energy surface in the phase space of the system, with the dynamics constituting iterative movement towards local or global minima of E. These minima are therefore identified with the attractors, the fixed points of the dynamics which lie at the bottom of the 'valleys' or 'basins' in this energy landscape.

2.3 Thermodynamics of the Hopfield model

Biological synapses are sources of noise, and further randomness is introduced in the input integration process at the neural soma.[6,7] In fact, noise may play an important role in neural networks by enabling the system to escape from spurious attractors.

Noisy activity can be simulated and quantified by the introduction of a 'temperature' T. In the generalized Hopfield model, thermal noise is incorporated by replacing the deterministic dynamics above with a probabilistic thermodynamics. Thus when each node is updated, it is given the new value at i with a probability $p(h_i)$:

$$p(h_i(t+1)) = [1 + \exp[-\beta\phi_i(t)h_i(t+1)]]^{-1} \tag{9}$$

where $\beta = 1/T$ (in units with Boltzmann's constant $k_B = 1$) and $\phi_i = \sum_j T_{ij}h_j$ is the local potential (sum of the inputs to node i). Consequently, as the temperature is increased, the output function at a node deforms from an initial step function shape (Fig. 1) towards a less and less steeply inclined sigmoid shape.

For non-zero temperature, the attractors of the dynamics are minima of the corresponding free energy function rather than Equation (6). The free energy is defined by:

$$F = -\beta^{-1} \ln Tr_{\{\mathbf{h}_i\}} \exp(-\beta E(\mathbf{h}_i)), \qquad (10)$$

with the trace taken over the set of states $\{\mathbf{h}_i\}$. The free energy in (10) is identical in form to the free energy used in several Ising spin glass models. The two-valued spin orientations per site in the Ising spin glass correspond to the two-valued components of the network vectors $\mathbf{h}_i$, and the exchange interactions between spins correspond to the connection strengths $\mathbf{T}_{ij}$. However, in the spin glass model the exchange interactions are randomly distributed, whereas in the generalized Hopfield model the $\mathbf{T}_{ij}$s are constructed to store specific patterns using a learning rule such as Equation (4). Nevertheless, for randomly constructed and uncorrelated patterns $\mathbf{g}_i$, the generalized Hopfield model and these spin glass models will have similar self-consistent attractor solutions.

3. The Hopfield model and statistical mechanics

3.1

When we consider systems with a large or infinite number of nodes the methods of statistical mechanics become applicable. For the large N limit there are two cases, depending on whether the number of patterns does or does not scale extensively with N.

For a network of N nodes and p stored patterns we may define the ratio $\alpha = p/N$, which behaves as a storage ratio, quantifying the number of patterns stored per node. Therefore the number of patterns, p, can remain finite, so that $\alpha \to 0$ as $N \to \infty$. Alternatively, the ratio α can remain finite as $p \to \infty$ and $N \to \infty$. For both these limits there exist corresponding spin glass models. For finite p, the appropriate spin glass models have been proposed by Mattis,[8] Luttinger,[9] van Hemmen[10] and Provost & Vallee.[11] In the Mattis model (a special case of the Luttinger model[9]) $p = 1$ in Equation (4) and consequently there are only two minima ($\pm \mathbf{g}_i$) of the free energy. Van Hemmen[10] and Provost & Vallee[11] have generalized the Mattis and Luttinger models to the intermediate situation of $p > 1$ but with p remaining finite. For finite α, the corresponding spin glass model is the Sherrington–Kirkpatrick (SK) model.[12,13] For this model the random distribution of the interaction strengths results in a complex energy surface with an infinitely large number of metastable solutions of the SK free energy function (in the limit of an infinite number of spin sites). In the following we will consider the finite p and finite α cases separately.

3.2 Finite p

To investigate the attractor structure at finite p it is necessary to find the local and global minima of the averaged free energy per node:[14]

$$F = \lim_{N \to \infty} [\beta^{-1} N^{-1} \langle \ln Z \rangle], \tag{11}$$

where $\langle \ldots \rangle$ denotes an average over the set of stored patterns $\{\mathbf{g}_i^{(s)}\}$, and Z is the partition function defined by:

$$Z = Tr_{\{\mathbf{h}_i\}} \exp(-\beta E). \tag{12}$$

From the energy function stated in Equation (6) we see that:

$$Z = \exp\left(-\frac{\beta p}{2}\right) Tr_{\{\mathbf{h}_i\}} \exp\left[\frac{\beta}{ZN} \sum_s \left(\sum_i \mathbf{h}_i \mathbf{g}_i^{(s)}\right)^2\right]. \tag{13}$$

The sums over nodes (i) and the sums over patterns (s) may be decoupled by using the standard identity:

$$\exp\left(\tfrac{1}{2} \lambda a^2\right) = \int_{-\infty}^{\infty} \frac{dm}{\sqrt{2\pi}} \exp\left(-\tfrac{1}{2} m^2 + ma\sqrt{\lambda}\right) \tag{14}$$

which implicitly defines a new parameter $\mathbf{m}$. Rescaling $\mathbf{m}_s \to \mathbf{m}_s \sqrt{(N\beta)}$ and taking the trace on $\{\mathbf{h}_i\}$ we obtain:

$$Z = \left(\frac{N\beta}{2\pi}\right)^{p/2} \exp\left(-\frac{\beta p}{2}\right) \int_{-\infty}^{\infty} \prod_{s=1}^{p} dm_s$$

$$\exp\left[-\frac{N\beta m_s^2}{2} + \sum_i \ln\left[2\cosh\left(\beta m^2 \mathbf{g}_i^{(s)}\right)\right]\right]. \tag{15}$$

For finite p, this integral may be straightforwardly evaluated using the saddle point method:

$$-N^{-1}\beta^{-1} \ln Z = \frac{1}{2}\sum_s \mathbf{m}_s^2 - N^{-1}\beta^{-1} \sum_i \ln\left[2\cosh\left(\beta \sum_s \mathbf{m}^s \mathbf{g}_i^{(s)}\right)\right], \tag{16}$$

with the corresponding saddle point equation:

$$\mathbf{m}^s = N^{-1} \sum_i \mathbf{g}_i^{(s)} \tanh\left(\beta \sum_t \mathbf{m}^t \mathbf{g}_i^{(t)}\right). \tag{17}$$

For finite N, $\ln Z$ and $\mathbf{m}$ would depend on the given set of $\{\mathbf{g}_i^{(s)}\}$ vectors. However, in the infinite node limit random fluctuations about the mean values tend to zero, so the sums $(1/N \sum$ can be replaced by averages over the $\{\mathbf{g}_i^{(s)}\}$. That is, $\ln Z$ and $\mathbf{m}$ are self-averaged quantities.[11] As a result we obtain the free energy as a function of the $\mathbf{m}^s$:

$$F(\beta) = \tfrac{1}{2}\mathbf{m}^2 - \beta^{-1} \langle \ln [2 \cosh (\beta \mathbf{m} \cdot \mathbf{g})] \rangle \qquad (18)$$

with the $\mathbf{m}^s$ satisfying the self-consistency equation:

$$\mathbf{m} = \langle \mathbf{g} \tanh (\beta \mathbf{m} \cdot \mathbf{g}) \rangle, \qquad (19)$$

where $\mathbf{m} = (m_1, \ldots, m_p)$, $\mathbf{g} = (g_1^1, \ldots, g_N^p)$ and $\langle \ldots \rangle$ denotes averages over the set $\{\mathbf{g}_i^{(s)}\}$. Equations (18) and (19) are the central results[14] from which the statistical properties of the network are easily derived.

The $\mathbf{m}$ can be interpreted as the average overlap between a stored pattern $\mathbf{g}_i^{(s)}$ and the thermal average of the state vectors $\mathbf{h}_i$ (denoted $\bar{\mathbf{h}}_i$):

$$\mathbf{m}^s = \langle \mathbf{g}_i^{(s)} \bar{\mathbf{h}}_i \rangle \qquad (20)$$

Above the temperature $T = 1$, there is no stable solution of Equations (18) and (19) with a non-zero overlap $\mathbf{m}$ between $\bar{\mathbf{h}}_i$ and a stored pattern.[14] However, below this temperature there appear solutions, each of which have a non-zero overlap with a single stored pattern but zero overlap with the rest. Furthermore, if we take the second derivatives of the free-energy in Equation (18) we find that these states are always minima (below $T = 1$) and hence they are stable solutions.[14] These solutions are the analogues of the Mattis states found in the Mattis model.

Below $T = 1$ there also exist solutions of Equations (18) and (19) which have non-zero overlaps between $\bar{\mathbf{h}}_i$ and several stored patterns. Near $T = 1$, the second derivatives of the free-energy indicate that these solutions correspond to saddle points of Equation (18) and hence they are not stable. However, as the temperature is reduced, some of these solutions become local minima of the free energy and thus stable solutions. For example, symmetric mixture states with equal non-zero overlaps on three patterns become metastable attractors below a transition temperature $T_3 = 0.461$. The instability of mixture states at higher temperatures suggests that synaptic noise may be necessary for controlling or avoiding spurious mixture states in biological neural networks.[14]

Though we have considered infinite-node models ($N \to \infty$) in the above, there are some differences between networks with finite N and those at the $N \to \infty$ limit. The overlap between pairs of random patterns is of order $O(1/\sqrt{N})$. In the infinite node limit the overlap between patterns is therefore negligible and the patterns are stored orthogonally.

However, for finite N, the overlap between patterns is significant, contributing a noisy background which can completely destroy the stability of stored patterns (the second term in Equation (5) provides the noise contribution). Using arguments from probability theory, several authors[15-17] have shown that exactly stored states are stable against such noise provided that:

$$p < \frac{N}{2 \ln N}. \tag{21}$$

3.3 Finite α

For finite α, the number of stored patterns scales extensively with N, so that $\alpha = p/N$ remains finite as $p \to \infty$ and $N \to \infty$. Consequently, the $O(1/\sqrt{N})$ random overlaps between patterns have a significant effect in the infinite N limit. As a result, memory patterns can be retrieved but the quality of recall is not perfect. Amit et al.[18-20] have called these states *retrieval attractors* to distinguish them from the Mattis-like states mentioned above.

When we consider finite α, the self-averaging used in Equations (18) and (19) does not hold. Consequently, in order to derive the free energy and corresponding saddle point equations, it is necessary to use a more complex argument (involving the replica method[21]). The resulting free

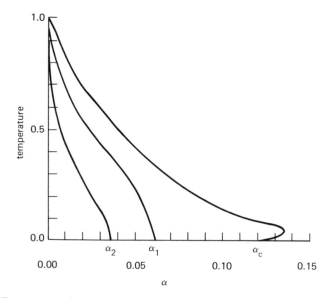

Figure 3 *Temperature dependence of the transition points $(\alpha_c, \alpha_1, \alpha_2)$. The retrieval states are global minima below α_1.*

energy has an infinitely large number of minima (at $N \to \infty$), though most of these are spurious metastable states.

An analysis with finite α discloses a complex pattern of transitions as α and the temperature of the network are varied (Fig. 3). These transitions result from variations in the distribution of the minima, and appear as changes in the properties and existence of retrieval and other states.[18-20]

For α less than $\alpha_2 \simeq 0.03$, spurious mixture states exist with non-zero overlaps with several stored patterns. For all values of α at low temperatures there also exist further spurious attractors called spin glass states. These spin glass states have a vanishingly small overlap (of order $O[1/\sqrt{(\alpha N)}]$ with all the stored memories, and in terms of network behaviour they correspond to non-retrieval.

For all values of α up to $\alpha_c \simeq 0.145$ there exist retrieval states with a high overlap with a single stored pattern. In fact at α_c the average overlap **m** is as high as 0.967, while below α_c the average retrieval overlap asymptotically approaches 1 as $\alpha \to 0$:

$$\mathbf{m} = 1 - \sqrt{\frac{2\alpha}{\pi}} \exp\left(-\frac{1}{2\alpha}\right) \tag{22}$$

These retrieval states are global minima of the free energy up to a value $\alpha_1 \simeq 0.05$ (for small T). Above this point the spin glass solutions become the global minima and the retrieval states become metastable.

Beyond $\alpha_c \simeq 0.145$ (for small T) the spurious spin glass states are the only attractors, so that the network is devoid of meaningful recall ability. The value of the critical storage ratio α_c has been estimated from computer simulations[18-20] to be $\alpha_c = 0.145 \pm 0.009$. On the other hand, theoretical calculations[20] based on the free energy suggest a critical value of $\alpha_c = 0.144$, in remarkable agreement with the simulation result.

4. Extensions of the Hopfield model

4.1

Though the Hopfield model is not intended as a precise neurobiological model, it is worth examining modifications which would bring the model closer to known neurobiological findings. All the nodes in the Hopfield model are fully connected. In contrast, for the cortex, a typical neuron is only connected to about $O(10^4)$ of the $O(10^{10})$ neurons present. Consequently, it is worthwhile looking at the effects of limited connectivity. In addition, the Hebbian rule, Equation (4), leads to symmetric T_{ij} connection strength matrices, so that node i influences node j in exactly the same way that j influences i. In contrast, the connections between biological neurons are asymmetric pathways.

Finally, learning rules such as Equation (4) are inadequate models of synaptic processes, since the matrix $\mathbf{T}_{ij}$ is unbounded and can have arbitrarily large values. It is known that only a restricted number of vesicles of neurotransmitter molecules are discharged at synaptic junctions, indicating that the synaptic efficacy cannot have a very broad spectrum of values. We will now consider extensions of the Hopfield model incorporating some of these features.

4.2 Models with limited connectivity

Limited connectivity can be simulated by randomly breaking a percentage of the connections in a Hopfield network. To achieve this, Sompolinsky[22] changed Equation (4) to:

$$\mathbf{T}_{ij} = \frac{1}{N} \mathbf{A}_{ij} \sum_s \mathbf{g}_i^{(s)} \mathbf{g}_j^{(s)}, \tag{23}$$

where the weight $\mathbf{A}_{ij}$ has a value c^{-1} with a probability c, and a value zero with a probability $(1-c)$. The effect of reducing connectivity is very similar to the introduction of a random noise with a typical variance:

$$\sigma^2 = \alpha[\overline{\mathbf{A}_{ij}^2} - \overline{\mathbf{A}_{ij}^2}] = \alpha\left(\frac{1-c}{c}\right). \tag{24}$$

This noise supplements any noise generated by random overlaps between patterns, so that reducing the connectivity leads to a gradual decline in the critical storage parameter α_c. Despite this, the retrieval overlap $\mathbf{m}_c$ at α_c remains good even for values of $(1-c)$ approaching 1.

The performance of a Hopfield network is only gradually affected by reduced connectivity, a fact which highlights an important property of both neural network models and their biological counterparts: they are very fault or error tolerant. If some connections are broken or some nodes fail, recall performance is not significantly affected.

4.3 Asymmetric models

The learning rule in (23) can also be used to simulate asymmetry. This time the $\mathbf{A}_{ij}$ weights are not symmetric so that the (ij) and (ji) components can have different values. To achieve asymmetric dilution, synapses are selected at random and in each case one of the $\mathbf{A}_{ij}$ or $\mathbf{A}_{ji}$ is set to zero. This is repeated until the required level of dilution is obtained. 50% dilution would mean that half the connections are unidirectional, while 100% dilution means completely unidirectional connectivity.

Simulations[23-24] appear to suggest that spurious spin glass attractors are suppressed by increased asymmetry. However, retrieval does not seem to be improved, since there is a corresponding increase in the number of cyclic attractors and chaotic states (the latter may only be genuinely chaotic in the $N \to \infty$ limit). For 50% dilution, the network can effect retrieval with overlaps greater than 0.98 for values of α up to about 0.1. For 100% dilution, retrieval is possible up to a value of about $\alpha = 0.06$, at which point chaotic attractors begin to dominate.

Parisi[25] has stressed the importance of asymmetry in other respects. Hopfield networks will always 'recognize' an input, iterating down on the nearest attractor. That is, there is no mechanism which switches the network from recognition to learning when the pattern presented is too distant from all the stored memories, and there is no means of distinguishing retrieval states from spurious states. Asymmetry might offer a resolution of these problems. Asymmetric networks have good retrieval-attractors, while outside the basins of attraction of the retrieval states the attractors are generally cyclic or chaotic. After a number of processing steps, retrieval would result in a static configuration, while cyclic or chaotic behaviour would be signalled by continuing activity. Persisting activity would therefore indicate non-recognition and learning would occur.

4.4 Bounded connection strengths and non-linear learning rules

In biological neural networks the synaptic efficacies do not appear to have an unlimited range of values and this fact should be considered in the construction of neural network models. The simplest way of bounding the connection strengths is to alter the learning rule, Equation (4), so that each time a new pattern is stored the connection strength matrix $\mathbf{T}_{ij}$ is replaced by $\mathbf{T}'_{ij}$ where:[26, 27]

$$\mathbf{T}'_{ij} = f\left(\mathbf{T}_{ij} + \frac{1}{N}\mathbf{g}_i\mathbf{g}_j\right). \tag{25}$$

The bounds on $\mathbf{T}_{ij}$ are then implemented by introducing limiting values for the function $f(x)$:

$$\left.\begin{aligned} f(x) &= -A/\sqrt{N} & x &< -A/\sqrt{N} \\ f(x) &= x & -A/\sqrt{N} &< x < A/\sqrt{N} \\ f(x) &= A/\sqrt{N} & x &> A/\sqrt{N} \end{aligned}\right\}. \tag{26}$$

As a result of these bounds the system overwrites previously stored patterns. As several authors[26–28] have pointed out, this process is similar to 'forgetting' and could have a counterpart in human short-term memory.[26] Interestingly, bounded connection strengths enable a Hopfield network to avoid recall loss through saturation, since the number of stored patterns can be kept within the saturation limit

$p < 0.145N$ by using this mechanism to 'forget' older patterns when storing new ones.

For the Hebbian rule, the connection strength matrices are distributed as an approximate Gaussian function with variance α. Since loss of recall will occur at $\alpha \simeq 0.14$, the limit A must be less than the standard deviation $\sqrt{(0.14)} \simeq 0.37$. The network has a high retrieval probability when recalling the most recent memory, and the retrieval probability decreases after further memory-inputs up to a limit.[25,26] The above method is not a unique way for avoiding memory saturation, and in fact several other 'forgetting' mechanisms have been proposed.[26-28]

Apart from bounding the connection strengths, there are other ways of restricting the range of T_{ij} values. Instead of the Hebbian rule, Equation (4), we could use a non-linear learning rule of the form:

$$T_{ij} = f\left(\sum_s g_i^{(s)} g_j^{(s)}\right),\qquad(27)$$

where $f(x)$ would have a restricted range. An example would be the 'clipped' model[22] where T_{ij} is restricted to two values by the functional relation $f(x) = \text{sgn}(x)$. The general class of non-linear learning rules has been investigated both for finite α and p.[29-31] For finite α, the sub-class of models satisfying Equation (27) is reducible to the linear Hopfield model, but with the addition of a noise term.[29-31] Consequently these models have a critical storage ratio α_c and this critical α_c will never exceed the critical ratio for the Hopfield model α_c (Hopfield) $= 0.145N$.

5. Learning rules with optimal storage properties

5.1

The Hopfield model, with the Hebbian rule, is relatively inefficient in terms of its storage capacity. It will only store a maximum of about $p = 0.145N$ uncorrelated patterns on an N-node network. On the other hand it has been shown that the optimal storage capacity for an N-node network is $2N$ for uncorrelated patterns,[32-34] and more if the patterns are correlated.[35]

The storage capacity of the Hopfield model is limited by the noise generated by random overlaps between patterns. If we store correlated patterns instead of uncorrelated states, then the overlap between patterns is increased, leading to a further decline in the maximal storage capacity and quality of recall. One way of evading this problem is to use a learning rule which can store the memory states orthogonally without overlaps between patterns. Personnaz *et al.*[36] and Kanter & Sompolinsky[37] have investigated general learning rules capable of storing linearly independent patterns orthogonally. In the model of Personnaz *et al.* the learning rule is based on a connection strength matrix defined as follows:

$$\mathbf{T}_{ij} = \frac{1}{N} \sum_{s,t}^{p} (\mathbf{M}^{-1})_{st} \mathbf{g}_i^{(s)} \mathbf{g}_j^{(s)}, \tag{28}$$

where $\mathbf{M}^{-1}$ is the inverse of a $(p \times p)$ mutual overlap matrix:

$$\mathbf{M}^{st} = \frac{1}{N} \sum_{i=1}^{N} \mathbf{g}_i^{(s)} \mathbf{g}_i^{(t)}. \tag{29}$$

The maximum number of patterns that can be stored is in fact $p = N$ (ie $\alpha_c = 1$). Furthermore, the memories can be retrieved without error and are stable against a moderate amount of thermal noise. However, though this model gives better results than the Hopfield model, its storage capacity and basins of attraction are not optimal.

So far we have considered learning rules in which each pattern is memorized and 'embedded' in the connection strengths through a single-step learning process. With the $\mathbf{T}_{ij}$ set by such learning rules, the problem has been one of finding the resulting storage capacity and quality of recall. However, to find models with maximal storage capacities or optimal basins of attraction we need to solve the opposite problem. That is, instead of fixing the connection strengths $\{\mathbf{T}_{ij}\}$ according to certain learning rules, we now fix the stored patterns $\{\mathbf{g}_i^{(s)}\}$ and look for solutions in the space of the connection strengths $\{\mathbf{T}_{ij}\}$ which optimize the storage properties.

Recently several authors[38-44] have looked at iterative improvement algorithms which progressively alter the $\mathbf{T}_{ij}$ until the optimal storage properties of the network are achieved. Thus in place of a single-step learning rule there is an iterative modification sequence $(\mathbf{T}_{ij} \rightarrow (\mathbf{T}_{ij} + \delta \mathbf{T}_{ij}))$ with a finite number of steps. Basically this process involves 'sculpturing' of the energy landscape so as to deepen and broaden the basins of attraction of retrieval states as well as eliminating those basins corresponding to spurious attractors.

A sub-class of these iterative improvement methods[41-44] consist of algorithms which enforce the embedding condition:

$$\mathbf{g}_i^{(s)} \left(\sum_j \mathbf{T}_{ij} \mathbf{g}_j^{(s)} \right) \geq K. \tag{30}$$

When the network settles onto a stable state of the dynamical rule, Equation (1), the states $(\mathbf{h}_i)$ of each node may be correctly aligned with the local (membrane) potential $\varphi_i = \sum \mathbf{T}_{ij} \mathbf{h}_j$, but most will not be strongly aligned. That is, $\mathbf{h}_i \varphi_i$ will be positive but can be small. Weak alignment indicates small basins of attraction,[42] consequently enforcing the stability condition, Equation (30), enhances the local alignment of the stored patterns and therefore increases the sizes of the basins.

For the space of connection strengths $\{\mathbf{T}_{ij}\}$ satisfying the normalization:

$$\sum_{j \neq i} \mathbf{T}_{ij}^2 = N. \tag{31}$$

Gardner[35,44] has shown that the maximum value of α_c is a solution of:

$$\frac{1}{\alpha_c} = \int_{-K}^{\infty} \frac{dt}{\sqrt{2\pi}} \exp\left(-\tfrac{1}{2}t^2\right)(t+K)^2 \tag{32}$$

For $K = 0$ the maximal storage capacity is 2 in agreement with known results.[34,45] As the stability K of the patterns is increased, the basins of attraction are enlarged but the maximum value of α decreases. Several authors[41-44] have proposed iterative improvement algorithms which can enforce the embedding condition, Equation (30), after a finite number of steps (at least for finite N).

5.2 Multi-node interactions

In the dynamical rule, Equation (1), the connection strengths $\mathbf{T}_{ij}$ describe two-node interactions. An obvious generalization is to consider q-node interactions with a corresponding dynamical rule:

$$\left.\begin{array}{l} \mathbf{h}_i(t+1) = \mathrm{sgn}\,(\phi_i(t)) \\[2mm] \phi_i = \displaystyle\sum_{i_2 < i_3 \ldots < i_q} \mathbf{T}_{ii_2 \ldots i_q} \mathbf{h}_{i_2} \ldots \mathbf{h}_{i_q} \end{array}\right\}. \tag{33}$$

Thus, for example, the q-node generalization of the Hebbian rule is:

$$\mathbf{T}_{i_1 \ldots i_q} = \frac{q!}{N^{q-1}} \sum_s \mathbf{g}_{i_1}^{(s)} \ldots \mathbf{g}_{i_q}^{(s)}. \tag{34}$$

Multi-node models have been considered by a number of authors.[46-50] The storage properties of these models are a natural extension of those for two-node interactions. The maximal value of α_c increases with q though there is a corresponding decrease in the size of basins of attraction for $\alpha \leqslant \alpha_c$.

6. Conclusion

Neural network theory has gained a rigorous quantitative basis by its association with statistical mechanics. Analysis has revealed a rich structure of attractors for comparatively simple network models. It is now possible to explore the properties of these models using precise analytical techniques. Exact predictions can be compared with computer simulations.

However, the benefit has not been entirely one-way. Neural network theory has raised new and interesting problems for statistical mechanics and spin glass theory. It has stimulated an interest in asymmetric models and models with diluted connectivity. The issue of optimal storage has inverted the usual spin glass problem: during learning the T_{ij} interaction strengths become dynamical variables, while the g_i state vectors become quenched variables in the dynamical process.

Of course, there are many other interesting avenues for research in neural network theory. Instead of single-layered networks with feedback, one could consider multi-layered models with intervening layers of hidden nodes between the input and output layers. The Hopfield–Little model has a straightforward multi-layered generalization. However, the class of multi-layered models is much wider since there is a considerable measure of freedom in specifying the connection weights between layers and in the number of nodes per layer.[51]

Undoubtedly many more neurobiological features could be successfully incorporated into neural network models. For example, it would be worthwhile examining in more detail the effects of nodes which are solely excitatory or inhibitory[52] or (veto) nodes which gate the action of other nodes or synapses. Hierarchical systems and models with modular organization are another essential area for the future development of the subject. So far only a few hierarchical models have been proposed.[53–55] Further interesting topics include learning rules which can store sequences of patterns[56] and models which use analogue neurons.[57]

Contemporary neural network models are only capable of mirroring a few of the most elementary functions of the brain. More sophisticated models will have to possess increasingly complex pattern forming and recognition qualities such as the ability to form prototypes or categories, or the ability to order information hierarchically. It seems clear that methods from statistical mechanics will continue to play a major role in the development of such models.

Acknowledgement

One of the authors (CC) is grateful to Dr Elizabeth Gardner for helpful comments on his contribution to this article.

References

1. Hopfield, J. *Proc. Natl. Acad. Sci. USA* **79**, 2554 (1982). Ibid **81**, 3088 (1984).
2. McCulloch, W. & Pitts, W. *Bull. Math. Biophys.* **5**, 115 (1943).

3. Little, W. *Math. Biosci.* **19**, 101 (1974).
4. Little, W. & Shaw, G. Ibid **39**, 281 (1978).
5. Frumkin, A. & Moses, E. *Phys. Rev.* **A34**, 714 (1986).
6. Perretto, P. *Biol. Cybern.* **50**, 51 (1984).
7. Kienker, P. K., Sejnowski, T. J., Hinton, G. E. & Schumacher, L. E. *Perception* **15**, 197 (1986).
8. Mattis, D. C. *Phys. Lett.* **56A**, 421 (1976).
9. Luttinger, J. M., *Phys. Rev. Lett.* **37**, 778 (1976).
10. Van Hemmen, J. L. *Rev. Lett.* **49**, 409 (1982).
11. Provost, J. P. & Vallee, G. *Phys. Rev. Lett.* **50**, 598 (1983).
12. Kirkpatrick, S. & Sherrington, D. *Phys. Rev.* **B17**, 4384 (1978).
13. Sherrington, D. & Kirkpatrick, S. *Phys. Rev. Lett.* **35**, 1792 (1975).
14. Amit, D. J., Gutfreund, H. & Sompolinsky, H. *Phys. Rev.* **A32**, 1007 (1985).
15. Weisbuch, G. & Fogelman-Soulié, F. *J. Phys. Lett.* **46**, L623 (1985).
16. Bruce, A. D., Gardner, E. & Wallace, D. J. *J. Phys.* **A20**, 2909 (1987).
17. McEliece, R. J., Posner, E. C., Rodemich, E. R. & Ventatesh, S. S. *The Capacity of the Hopfield Associative Memory*, Caltech preprint, submitted to *IEEE Trans.* in IT.
18. Amit, D. J. In *Proceedings of the Heidelberg Colloquium in Glassy Dynamics and Optimization* (Springer Verlag, 1987).
19. Amit, D. J., Gutfreund, H. & Sompolinsky, H. *Ann. Phys.* **173**, 30 (1987), *Phys. Rev. Lett.* **55**, 1530 (1985).
20. Crisanti, A., Amit, D. J. & Gutfreund, H. *Europhysics Lett.* **2**, 337 (1986).
21. Edwards, S. F. & Anderson, P. W. *J. Phys.* **F5**, 965 (1975).
22. Sompolinsky, H. *Phys. Rev.* **A34**, 2571 (1986).
23. Hertz, J. A., Grinstein, G. & Solla, S. A. In *Proceedings of the Heidelberg Symposium on Glassy Dynamics* (1986; NORDITA preprint—86/18).
24. Gutfreund, H. & Stein, Y. (to be published), reported in ref. 23.
25. Parisi, J. *J. Phys.* **A19**, L675 (1986).
26. Parisi, G. *J. Phys.* **A19**, L617 (1986).
27. Nadal, J. P., Toulouse, G., Changeux, J. P. & Dehaene, S. *Europhysics Lett.* **1**, 535 (1986).
28. Mézard, M., Nadal, J. P. & Toulouse, G. *J. Physique* **47**, 1457 (1986).
29. Sompolinsky, H. In *Proceedings of the Heidelberg Colloquium on Glassy Dynamics and Optimization* (June, 1986), (Springer Verlag, 1987).
30. Van Hemmen, J. L. & Kühn, R. *Phys. Rev.* **57**, 913 (1986).
31. Van Hemmen, J. L. *Phys. Rev.* **A36**, 1959 (1987).
32. Baldi, P. & Venkatesh, S. *Phys. Rev. Lett.* **58**, 913 (1987).
33. Gardner, E. & Derrida, B. *Optimal Storage Properties of Neural Network Models. J. Phys.* **A21**, 271 (1988).
34. Cover, T. M. *IEEE Transactions EC* **14**, 326 (1965).
35. Gardner, E. *Maximum Storage Capacity of Neural Networks. Europhys. Lett.* **4**, 481 (1987).
36. Personnaz, L., Guyan, I. & Dreyfus, G. *J. Physique Lett.* **46**, L359 (1985).
37. Kanter, I. & Sompolinsky, H. *Phys. Rev.* **A35**, 380 (1987).
38. Gardner, E., Stroud, N. & Wallace, D. J. *Training with Noise, and the Storage of Correlated Patterns in a Neural Network Model* (Edinburgh Preprint 87/394).
39. Bruce, A. D., Canning, A., Forrest, B., Gardner, E. & Wallace, D. J. In Neural networks for computing, J. S. Denker (ed.) *AIP Conference Proceedings, Snowbird, Utah.* Vol. 151 (*Am. Inst. of Phys.*) 1987.
40. Pöppel, G. & Krey, U. *Europhysics Lett.* **4**, 979 (1987).
41. Diederich, S. & Opper, M. *Phys. Rev. Lett.* **58**, 949 (1987).
42. Krauth, W. & Mezard, M. *J. Phys.* **20**, L745 (1987).

43. Forrest, B. *Content-Addressibility and Learning in Neural Networks* (Edinburgh Preprint 87/413, 1987).
44. Gardner, E. *The Phase Space of Interactions in Neural Network Models* (Edinburgh Preprint 87/396, 1987).
45. Venkatesh, S. In *Proceedings of the Conference on Neural Networks for Computing, Snowbird, Utah* (1986).
46. Gardner, E. *J. Phys.* **A20**, 3453 (1987).
47. Lee, Y. C. *et al. Physica* **22D**, 276 (1986).
48. Abbot, L. F. & Arian, Y., *Phys. Rev.* **A36**, 5091 (1987).
49. Horn, D. & Usher, M. *Capacities of Associative Memory Models. J. Physique* **49**, 389 (1988).
50. Perretto, P. & Niez, J. J. *Biol. Cybern.* **54**, 53 (1986).
51. Rumelhart, D. E. & McClelland, J. L. (eds) *Parallel Distributed Processing* (Cambridge Mass: MIT Press, 1986).
52. Shinomoto, S. *Biol. Cybern.* **57**, 197 (1987).
53. Parga, N. & Virasoro, M. A. *J. Physique* (*Paris*) **47**, 1857 (1986).
54. Cortes, C., Krogh, A. & Hertz, J. A. *Hierarchical Associative Networks. J. Phys.* **A20**, 4449 (1987).
55. Dotsenko, V. S. *J. Phys.* **C18**, L1017 (1985).
56. Sompolinsky, H. & Kanter, I. *Phys. Rev. Lett.* **57**, 2861 (1986).
57. Hopfield, J. J. & Tank, D. W. *Biol. Cybern.* **52**, 141 (1985).

13 Digital neural networks, matched filters and optical implementations

J. E. Midwinter & D. R. Selviah

University College London, Torrington Place, London, UK

Abstract

There has been much interest in the possibility of implementing associative memories using optical techniques, much of it centred recently around implementations of the Hopfield model of a neural network. In this chapter, we show how this model can be recast in terms of 'matched filters' whose properties have been well studied in electrical engineering. From this observation, we are then able to present the Hopfield neural network as a bank of filters and a thresholding stage. This formalism allows one to analyse the operation of the filter bank and its associated threshold without resort to digital simulation. A prime purpose of this approach has been to set the foundations in place for a detailed analysis of the scale-ability of an optical implementation and to allow some specification to be placed upon the requirements of the thresholding elements to be used since the signal-to-noise performance and memory size requirements to meet any reasonably complex network requirement remain uncertain. To our knowledge, this latter work remains incomplete, so that here we outline the problem and indicate why optical elements offer some new opportunities over and above electronic implementations.

1. Introduction

The use of a matched filter model, whilst being formally equivalent to the Hopfield model in the mathematical sense, has a particular interest when questions of information coding and noise performance arise, both vital to any serious optical implementation. Holographic elements are frequently proposed as a possible basis for implementing the complex wiring (synapse) patterns inherent in neural networks, since they are potentially capable of combining in a single optical element both the interconnections and their associated weights. The use of two-dimensional arrays of optical input and output devices may then open up the use of complex networks with very fast cycle times. Our discussion is presented entirely in terms of the use of the Hopfield model as a pattern recognition memory. However, we note that many of the concepts can be expected to carry over into other optical implementations of computing networks involving vector-matrix processing.

2. The Hopfield neural network

Before introducing our particular model of the Hopfield neural network in Section 3, we will first examine the general properties of the Hopfield pattern recognition neural net. Its aim is to recognize a partial or distorted input pattern, or code state vector, as being one of its previously memorized state vectors and to output the perfect and complete memorized version. Two isomorphic forms of net have been described. In the first, an asynchronous model which most closely resembles the living brain, a series of neurons are highly interconnected by synapses having various interconnection strengths. Each neuron examines the signals at its input from the other neuron nodes via the weighted synapses at a random time, and changes its state according to some probabilistic response algorithm and the sum of its inputs. The input state vector is the series of initial potentials on the neuron nodes and the output state vector is the final stable series of neuron potentials into which the network settles after the asynchronous random updating. Thus, the neurons at any particular time have a certain probability of changing their state depending on their inputs.

Although such a model may resemble the living brain, which is remarkably good at pattern recognition, the stochastic neural behaviour is not convenient to implement using optoelectronic components. Thus, deterministic thresholds are often preferred whereby the output depends on the input according to some direct non-linear relationship. If, in addition, all the interconnections have identical delays and if all bits of the input vector are entered in parallel, then all neurons will update their states at the same time. This is known as synchronous operation and seems more appropriate to an optical implementation. Hopfield has shown that the synchronous deterministic net behaves similarly to the original asynchronous stochastic network.[1]

The second isomorphic form is essentially a vector–matrix multiplier followed by a non-linear threshold and feedback. In effect, all the thresholds are drawn into one place while all the weighted interconnections are drawn together into another, the vector–matrix multiplier. The matrix elements are given by

$$T_{dt} = \sum_{i=1}^{M} s_{id} s_{it} \quad (d \neq t), \tag{1}$$

$$T_{tt} = 0 \qquad (2)$$

where s_{it} is the tth bit of the ith memorized state vector. The second condition (Equation (2)) implies neurons are not connected to themselves. The state vectors are assumed to have N bits, each of which can take any analogue value. The output of the vector–matrix multiplier is given for an input vector $\mathbf{r}$ by

$$\mathbf{r}'_t = 1/N \sum_{d=1}^{N} \mathbf{r}_d T_{dt}, \qquad (3)$$

where the $1/N$ factor provides the correct normalization, eg if only one vector is stored, that vector will reform itself correctly on passage through the interconnection network. Memorized vectors are assumed to be bipolar $(+1, -1)$. After the vector–matrix multiplication the intermediate vector passes through the threshold array in parallel. The thresholds can be either stochastic or deterministic and the operation can be asynchronous or synchronous.

3. Matched filter model of the Hopfield neural network

In this section we introduce the matched filter formalism and apply it to model the interconnections (in the first Hopfield neural net isomorphism) ie the vector–matrix multiplication in the second isomorphism. It is well known that an optimum recognition strategy for an input pattern obscured by noise is the technique of maximum entropy.[2] For random noise this reduces to performing the correlation of the input $\mathbf{r}(t)$ with each of the memorized patterns in turn, $s_i(t)$. The correlations give the closeness of match between the input and each memorized pattern. The memorized pattern having the largest correlation with the input is thus the best match and so is the best choice of recognized pattern to be output. No better choice of recognized pattern can be made for input signals in random noise than by maximum entropy arguments. To relate this to a Hopfield network we proceed as follows.

This optimum pattern recognition strategy can be implemented as shown in the first part of Fig. 1 which shows a matched filter model of the Little–Hopfield neural network.[3,4] The input signal $\mathbf{r}(t)$ is divided between the M channels (one for each of the M memorized bipolar patterns, $s_i(t)$) so the signal in each channel is reduced to $\mathbf{r}(t)/M\mathbf{r}(t)/M^{1/2}$ to conserve power. For convenience the diagram is drawn in the time domain (like an electrical circuit) so the input code consists of a time sequence of bits, each having an analogue value. Nevertheless, all the following arguments hold directly for spatially pixelated input patterns (such as in an optical implementation) with a corresponding change of

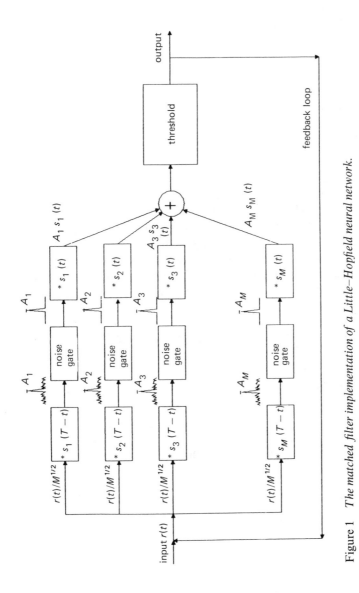

Figure 1   *The matched filter implementation of a Little–Hopfield neural network.*

dependent variable from time to space. Each channel consists of a matched filter with an impulse response of $s_i(T-t)$ where T is the memorized signal duration. The output of the matched filter when the two signals are coincident is, using conventional normalization,

$$A_i = \frac{1}{T}\int_0^T \mathbf{r}(t) \cdot \mathbf{s}_i(t)dt, \tag{4}$$

or in digital form

$$A_i = \frac{1}{(M^{1/2}N)}\sum_{d=1}^N \mathbf{r}_d \mathbf{s}_{id} \tag{5}$$

where the number of bits in the code sequence is N and the subscripts d indicate which bit of the code is being considered. After this first bank of correlating matched filters an effective spectrum is created by the correlation peak magnitudes in each channel. The aim of the remainder of the network is to select the channel having the strongest correlation peak and to output the memorized code corresponding to that channel.

In our matched filter model of a Hopfield neural network (Fig. 1), the correlating matched filter is followed by a noise gate which generates an ideal delta function scaled by the correlation peak amplitude, A_i. This passes into a convolving filter which has an impulse response of s_i and which gives an output when excited by the scaled delta function of

$$A_i \mathbf{s}_i(t), \tag{6}$$

or in digital form:

$$A_i \mathbf{s}_{it} = \frac{1}{(M^{1/2}N)}\sum_{d=1}^N \mathbf{r}_d \mathbf{s}_{id} \mathbf{s}_{it}. \tag{7}$$

All of the M channel outputs are then summed to yield

$$\sum_{i=1}^M A_i \mathbf{s}_i(t) \tag{8}$$

or, for digital codes:

$$\sum_{i=1}^M A_i \mathbf{s}_{it} \tag{9}$$

$$= \frac{1}{(M^{1/2}N)}\sum_{i=1}^M \sum_{d=1}^N \mathbf{r}_d \mathbf{s}_{id} \mathbf{s}_{it}, \tag{10}$$

$$\mathbf{r}'_t = \frac{1}{(M^{1/2}N)}\sum_{d=1}^N \mathbf{r}_d \sum_{i=1}^M \mathbf{s}_{id} \mathbf{s}_{it}, \tag{11}$$

$$\mathbf{r'}_t = \frac{1}{(M^{1/2}N)} \sum_{d=1}^{N} \mathbf{r}_d T_{dt} \tag{12}$$

$$T_{dt} = \sum_{i=1}^{M} s_{id} s_{it}. \tag{13}$$

The final two equations are identical to those of the Hopfield interconnection network except that the memory matrix diagonal elements are equal to M, ie, all the neurons are connected to themselves and there is an extra $1/M^{1/2}$ factor due to the M-way division of the input between the M channels. In fact the matrix equation is identical to the definition of the autocorrelation matrix given by Kohonen[5] for use in a vector–matrix pattern recognition memory. Since our equations are derived from the optimum pattern recognition strategy we can conclude that we have derived a third isomorphic form of the basic Hopfield neural network and have shown mathematically that for optimum pattern recognition properties, the interconnection memory matrix must have diagonal elements with a magnitude of M rather than zero as proposed by Hopfield. This optimization of the diagonal elements is confirmed by the numerical work of Bayley & Fiddy[6] and Selviah & Midwinter[7] who show that for deterministic synchronous behaviour which is most convenient for hardware implementation, far fewer spurious states result when diagonal elements of M rather than zero are used.

4. Orthogonal bipolar codes

Having introduced the matched filter formalism in the previous section, we now use it to find the optimum choice of memorized code in the case when the input signal-to-noise-ratio is poor. Consider an input signal consisting of one of the memorized codes plus noise. If the noise is random and white, it will generate noisy outputs from each of the matched filters of similar magnitude. Only those components of the input noise having high correlations with the memorized digital codes will be passed; all other noise is suppressed. In order to recognize the correct code the auto-correlation peak magnitude in the correct channel must differ from the cross-correlation peak magnitude in any other channel by at least twice the noise peak magnitude after the first filter bank. For a given noise magnitude input, the weakest input signal will be detected when the cross-correlation peaks are minimized. This will occur if the memorized codes are chosen to be members of an orthogonal set in which case the cross-correlations are zero. Hence, the orthogonal code set is optimum as far as the detection sensitivity is concerned in the first set of correlating matched filters. This is another way of expressing Kohonen's results[5] that the correlation matrix, when used with orthogonal codes, reduces to the linear associative matrix operator having the optimal error correcting properties for pattern recognition. A separate question is whether the second set of convolving matched filters, the summation of the codes and the threshold are able to select the code corresponding to the channel having the highest correlation peak. This is addressed in a later section.

An orthogonal bipolar code set contains N codes each of N-bits length which form a mathematically complete set due to the N degrees of freedom. Thus any N-bit digital code with bits taking any analogue value can be expanded as the sum of a set of N, N-bit orthogonal bipolar codes with various coefficients. If a complete set of N, N-bit orthogonal bipolar codes is memorized in a neural net, then the correlation peak magnitudes for any input code give these coefficients in the form of a true spectrum generated by the digital code transform. In such a net the second convolving set of filters and code summation effectively reconstitutes the original input code by the inverse digital code transform. Hence an upper limit on the number M of orthogonal N-bit codes that may be stored in a neural net is N. This is the same result as found by Abu-Mustafa and St Jacques for arbitrary N-bit code sequences.[8]

This result leads to an important conceptual understanding of the function of the weighted interconnections. If the weighted interconnections are to perform a useful function other than the trivial one of being a parallel highway, fewer than N, N-bit orthogonal bipolar codes must be stored. The network then acts as a digital code filter suppressing those orthogonal codes in the complete input code expansion which are not memorized. The output of the interconnection network consists of a sum with the various coefficients of the memorized codes only. It now remains for the non-linear threshold to select, in some way, the strongest memorized orthogonal code. For an input consisting of a memorized code plus noise, it is clear that an interconnection network storing M, N-bit orthogonal codes has the effect of suppressing the noise that would otherwise have been passed by the $(N-M)$ orthogonal channels which are absent.

5. Non-linear threshold and neural network behaviour

In this section we outline the results obtained when the matched filter formalism is used to tackle important questions concerning the threshold behaviour. Detailed derivations and arguments may be found in Selviah & Midwinter.[9] In a neural net the output of the weighted interconnection net, which is also the input to the non-linear threshold,

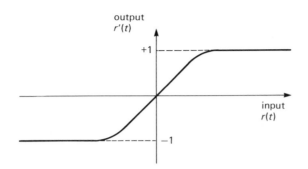

Figure 2   *A typical soft threshold characteristic.*

consists of a sum of several of the *M* memorized bipolar arbitrary codes with various amplitudes.

5.1 Weakly distorted input codes or input memorized codes with good signal to noise ratio

If the absolute amplitude of one of the codes is larger than the combined sum of all the other absolute code amplitudes, then it is clear that the polarity of the bits will always be the same as that of the strongest code. As a result, the strongest code can be recognized and formed by amplifying the filtered code sufficiently and limiting it to regain the bipolar memorized code characteristics. This can be done in a limiting or saturating amplifier which preserves polarity. Such a threshold characteristic might look like Fig. 2.

If the amplifier gain is sufficiently large only one pass through the threshold is required, corresponding to a 'hard threshold' (Fig. 3). When the gain is reduced, as in a 'soft threshold' (Fig. 2), more iterations are required before convergence. Note that in this case, if the input distorted

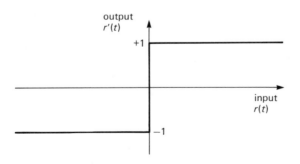

Figure 3   *The related hard threshold.*

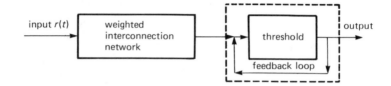

Figure 4   *An alternative implementation allowing single-pass recognition.*

pattern is only presented to the neural network for an instant, then after the first pass through the interconnection network the code sum circulating only consists of memorized codes. This sum always passes through the interconnection (or matched filter) net unaltered. Since the interconnection net only plays a filtering role on the first pass, an alternative net with the same behaviour is given in Fig. 4. It is made of two modules, the weighted interconnection net and a threshold with integral feedback in order to raise the gain. This configuration avoids repeated passes through the interconnection net which is expected to be lossy (see Section 8) and so reduces the system induced noise.

5.2 Seriously distorted input codes or input memorized codes having poor signal-to-noise ratio

If the absolute amplitude of the strongest code is less than the combined amplitudes of the other absolute code amplitudes, several types of behaviour can occur depending on the nature of the codes, the form of the threshold and the relative amplitudes. We saw earlier how orthogonal memorized codes offered the greatest discrimination after the first set of correlating filters so we consider these first.

5.2.1 Orthogonal bipolar memorized codes with hard threshold

If the input to the threshold consists of the sum of two equal magnitude memorized codes, then if the threshold allows a zero level to be output this sum circulates in the loop and is output as reported by Bayley & Fiddy[6] as a result of their numerical simulations for arbitrary codes. If, however, the zero level is not allowed but is a symmetrically unstable equilibrium position, the neural net converges on one or other of the two equal magnitude codes, directed by noise.

   If the input to the threshold consists of the sum of three memorized codes where the strongest is weaker than the sum of the absolute magnitudes of the other two, an interesting phenomenon occurs. The hard threshold non-linearly multiples the three codes s_1, s_2 and s_3 together and generates a new code, $s_4 = -(s_1 s_2 s_3)$. All four are then output with identical amplitudes. It can be shown that any code generated in this way from three orthogonal codes must also be a member of the same orthogonal set and that the sum of four such codes is truly bipolar. Whether the fourth code, s_4, is memorized or not, the four-code sum is a stable spurious bipolar state of the system. This is obvious if s_4 is memorized. If it is not, then it will be filtered out by the interconnection net and regenerated again by the hard threshold on each iteration.

In a similar way, spurious bipolar stable output states exist for the sum of higher numbers of codes with various coefficients. A neural net storing orthogonal codes converges after only one pass through the neural net onto the correct memorized state or onto a spurious code state but it cannot converge onto an incorrect memorized state.

5.2.2 Orthogonal bipolar memorized codes with soft threshold

Use of the matched filter formalism has revealed a remarkable property of soft thresholds when all the input memorized codes are weak (amplitudes a little less than $0.7/b$) where b is the threshold gain at the origin. As a hard threshold is made softer by reducing the gain, the number of code sum spurious stable states reduces at the expense of an increased number of iterations before convergence. If the loop gain is too low (less than unity if the rest of the loop is lossless), then the net converges onto the trivial all-zeros null vector for all inputs as also found by Hopfield[1] and Sompolinsky & Kanter.[10] A gain of $1 < b < 1.2$ results in convergence to the sum of all the non-zero orthogonal memorized codes in the input code expansion. They all have equal magnitudes in the final convergent code which is not, in general, bipolar. A compromise loop gain of about 10 appears to give convergence to a single bipolar output code with the minimum false alarm rate (ie number of spurious states) and a reasonable convergence time.

5.2.3 Arbitrary bipolar memorized codes with hard threshold

In this situation, it can be shown that spurious stable states exist which consist of the sum of four equal magnitude codes whose mutual product is $s_1 s_2 s_3 s_4 = -E$ (where E is the identity or all-ones state), whether or not the codes are orthogonal. This arises from the binary bipolar nature of the codes. Similarly, spurious codes consisting of sums of higher numbers of codes also exist. In addition, the neural network can converge onto an incorrect memorized state which may even have a very low degree of match with the input. This is a serious drawback of arbitrary binary codes since there is no way of knowing whether the result is right or wrong just by examining the output. This behaviour can be minimized by ensuring that the stored codes lie similar, and as large as possible, distances apart in the Hamming sense. Furthermore, the neural net may not converge but may remain cycling around a loop of two or more codes, all of which lie similar distances from a stable state.

5.2.4 Arbitrary bipolar memorized codes with soft threshold
Hopfield has shown that the number of stables states of the neural network is reduced by employing a soft threshold with arbitrary bipolar codes.

6. Optical implementations

In 1985, Psaltis & Farhat[11] reported a simple model of a Hopfield neural network that demonstrated the use of optical techniques to realize the essential features of such systems. Their experiment is illustrated in Fig. 5. It consists of a linear array of N light emitting diode (LED) sources that enter into the processor an N bit binary digital vector. An optical lens system images each LED onto a single row of an N^2 transmission matrix. This can be formed from photographic film for demonstration purposes but, in a more realistic case, a liquid crystal spatial light modulator array re-programmed under electrical control may be used. Each 'pixel' of the matrix has a pre-set transmission value T_{ij}, formed for the purposes of initial experiment by exposing photographic film. At the output end of the optical processor, is placed a linear array of N photodiodes, each arranged to scan the output of a single column of the transmission matrix. Thus, every input data line is connected to every output data line, with the mask providing N^2 individually adjustable weighting functions. It is the ability of optics to provide this type of complex wiring pattern with the associated individual weights that constitutes one reason for considering its use in this context. Since the Hopfield model implies the use of thresholding and feedback, this must be provided between the

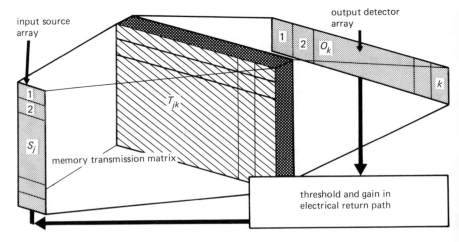

Figure 5   *The Psaltis & Farhat implementation of a neural network in optics.*

photodiode array and the source array. In the demonstration system reported, this was done electrically. The Hopfield model assumes in its mathematical description that positive and negative values can be handled, both for the input data (assumed $+1$ or -1) and for the stored weights. In the optical implementation, signal level is associated with optical intensity which can only be positive. One solution to this problem may be to use two-channel operation, with one channel for positive integers and the other for negative. This would imply twice as many sources and photodetectors (N becomes $2N$) with a consequent fourfold increase in the number of weights needing to be stored, even if half will always be inoperative. An alternative approach may be to bias the optical system to operate about a mean level of unity, and is particularly appropriate in the case modelled above using orthogonal codes with zero disparity.

7. Storage capacity and coding

The wiring pattern associated with the T_{ij} matrix corresponds to a particularly complex one if it is to be implemented electrically, since it is most naturally set out in three dimensions. The fact that optical implementation allows many discrete beams of light to travel either in parallel or on intersecting paths through space without interacting constitutes one reason for considering its use. The T_{ij} matrix description highlights the fact that it is also necessary to be able to individually adjust the weights at each of the N^2 data points. A closely analogous situation is that of the volume hologram where it is well known that a complex three-dimensional input pattern can be used to generate a different but equally complex three-dimensional output pattern or image. In the terminology given above, we can consider a single hologram as connecting a particular input pattern or digital word to a similar but different output pattern via a fully interconnected pixel-to-pixel wiring comparable to that of the T_{ij} type matrix.

To quantify the upper limit to the complexity of interconnection possible in this manner, consider a plane source area of A cm^2. If the wavelength of light is L cm, then the number of resolvable points within the area is of the order A/L^2. Using light of 1 µm wavelength (10^{-4} cm), then in 1 cm^2, this corresponds to 10^8 resolvable points although 10^6 is probably a more practical value if they are to be separately addressed. Thus, as an extreme case, it might appear that a holographic element connecting such an input plane to a similar output plane necessarily provides 10^{16} (10^{12}) truly independent connections. However, a simple consideration of scaling shows that this is likely to be false.

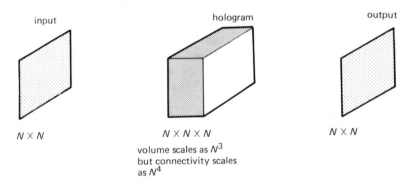

input

hologram

output

$N \times N$

$N \times N \times N$

volume scales as N^3
but connectivity scales
as N^4

$N \times N$

Figure 6   *The effects of scaling the optical interconnection network.*

Consider increasing the linear dimensions of all the elements in Fig. 6 by a factor F. Then the stored interconnection data at best can only scale as F^3, in proportion to the volume of holographic material available. Since the area of the input and output planes scales as F^2, for full connectivity, the number of possible connections thus scales as $F^2 \times F^2 = F^4$. It follows that the linear packing density of source points that can be allowed if truly free interconnection is to be possible must at best scale as $F^{3/4}$. The number of I/O data points is then restricted to scale as $F^{3/4} \times F^{3/4} = F^{3/2}$ and the total number of interconnections scales as F^3 as required. Note that for small values of the parameter F, it is not really necessary to scale all linear dimensions equally, but for large F the system will rapidly become un-implementable in optics if this is not done.

To estimate the actual number of interconnections appropriate to this model on basic information capacity criteria, we consider the use of a photo-refractive material for the holographic medium. Possible crystals include barium titanate or lithium niobate, while materials such as dichromated gelatin offer greater index change but are less mechanically stable. We further consider an arbitrary holographic volume of 1 cm^3 for purposes of discussion. Later we will consider the same connection element in terms of power scattering efficiency. The maximum index change typically achieved in such materials using optical writing gives a value for $dn/n = 10^{-2}$. Thus, for a sample of thickness 1 cm, we might reasonably expect to be able to change its phase thickness by approximately 100 wavelength units so that it could be sliced into 100 layers, each of which could hold a 0° or 180° phase thickness state. Each might thus be considered as a discrete written data point whose state might be tested optically. In the input plane, we could have of the order of A/L^2 resolvable units, corresponding to approximately 10^8. Hence, a photo-refractive hologram $1\,cm^3$ thick might in principle store some 10^{10} digital (0 or 1) states or resolvable connections implying the potential for 10^5 input points interconnected to 10^5 output points. (Allowing for a more practical 10^8 stored data points, we would have 10^4 pixels in each input and output plane and could allow some weighting of the connections.) Spreading these uniformly over the $1 \times 1\,cm$ input and output planes implies packing them on about 30-μm centres (or 100 μm using the practical figures). Such packing densities for discretely addressable optoelectronic elements are plausible and compatible with modern lithographic based device fabrication techniques.

The above arguments have been presented on a purely information content basis without giving any indication as to how the data should be coded. Consideration of the physics involved in interconnecting two discrete points via a volume hologram points to further constraints. If we consider a single point in each of the input and output planes and place the thick hologram in the far field region between them, then the holographic pattern needed to interconnect them is a three-dimensional plane grating tilted at such an angle as to act as a mirror, Bragg-reflecting light from one to the other. Because we have postulated a thick hologram, this mirror only reflects the chosen wavelength at the chosen angle to the normal. Evidently, if cross-talk is to be avoided, we require there to be a unique set of mirror planes for each input–output point connection. The nature of the Bragg grating is such that if we represent its action on a stereogram plot, see Fig. 7, then the direction normal to the

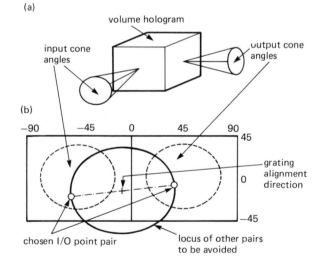

Figure 7 (a) *The physical coupling regions for the thick holographic interconnect with* (b) *its sterographic representation showing the degenerate coupling points for each grating.*

271

grating planes lies at an angle midway between the input and output beam angles. Light at the same wavelength and angle to the grating normal will be reflected regardless of azimuthal direction. Hence, drawing a circle centred around the direction normal and passing through the input and output angle points will connect all possible pairs of points, located at opposite ends of every diameter, for which the grating is equally reflective. It thus becomes apparent that having established one pair of input–output points on a given circle, no other pair must be allowed to lie on another diameter of the same circle. One might also require that no other points lie on the circle. This would minimize stray reflections but is probably not necessary when the scattering efficiency for each grating is low. Thus, in placing the input and output data points, we must both meet the conditions associated with the nature of holographic wiring and simultaneously approach as closely as possible the limits set by information storage considerations. Some pointers as to how this might be done have been given already, although much work remains. Given a solution to this problem, then independent interconnection becomes possible between each input point and each output point. Since each is then connected by a discrete grating, varying its strength varies the weighting of the individual connection.

8. Programming an optical network

The association that we have drawn with holograms points clearly to a direct approach to setting the weights, T_{ij}, of the interconnection matrix. The act of forming a hologram by photographically recording the interference pattern between the 'signal' and 'reference' beams establishes a connection network that, given the 'signal', reconstructs the 'reference' and vice-versa. In electronic implementations of neural networks, much attention is focussed on algorithms for setting the individual weights. Translating this to the optical domain seems to imply that individual pixel pairs in the input and output planes should be illuminated at the appropriate intensity levels and the associated weight, T_{ij}, recorded. For an N^2 input pixel to N^2 output pixel pattern-resolution, this implies N^4 exposures. Noting that the total index change than can be optically written into the holographic medium is strictly limited, say to dn, then the clear implication is that for any one writing operation (pixel pair), the maximum allowed index change would be dn/N^4. Simple analysis of the scattering efficiency of holograms rapidly leads to the conclusion that this approach leads to a vanishingly small scattering or coupling efficiency for any one input pattern to its associated output pattern. However, we believe this view to be fundamentally misleading, since it is falsely based upon a rigid attempt to implement an 'electronic' implementation.

To find a more realistic approach, we return to the problem in hand and ask how best to implement it. The objective is to associate one 'image' with another, not 'pixel' with 'pixel'. The description in terms of T_{ij} matrix elements is given for mathematically convenient purposes. Starting from this viewpoint, we note that for N^2 input pixels, the number of pattern pairs that are to be associated is likely to be less than N^2 and possibly much less. Thus, if we build up our memory bank by relating whole patterns at each exposure, the number of exposures is less than N^2 and the available index excursion per recorded pattern varies as dn/N^2. Mathematically, this involves doing nothing different in the establishment of the T_{ij} matrix, other than setting a group of N^4 partial weights at a single time and then building up the full weightings in N^2 separate exposures.

We will now attempt to quantify this result in terms of a photo-refractive hologram material. If we assume, as before, that a path length of 1 cm is used (in a 1-cm cube of material) to set the value of M, the number of Bragg grating planes, then for scattering the beam through 90°, we have approximately $M = n/L$ where L is the wavelength in cm and n is the refractive index. For a 1 μm wavelength and $n = 2$, this is 2.10^4. In the earlier analysis we suggested that it might be feasible to handle input data words of 10^4 bit complexity. This would imply storing of order 10^4 holograms and require a power scattering efficiency of -50 dB per filter or hologram to remain firmly in the low total scatter-power regime ($10^4 \times -50$ dB scatter $= -10$ dB). Hence, for a single grating giving 10^{-5} power scattering efficiency, this implies a value of peak index excursion of about 3.10^{-7} per grating. To store 10^4 such gratings and always remain firmly in the linear index regime requires an allowed refractive index peak change of 3.10^{-3} which is inside the typical value for such materials of 10^{-2}. Thus, we conclude that it may be possible to store 10^4 words in a 1 cm^3 crystal, with a power scattering efficiency per word (or filter) of -50 dB.

This result has led to the conclusion that the scattering efficiency per recorded pattern now varies as $1/N^2$. Apart from falling off much less rapidly with N than the earlier result, and resulting in much higher scattering efficiency for large values of N, it also agrees with one's expectations from the matched filter model. There it was apparent that the memory store was equivalent to a bank of order (less than) N^2 filters. Accessing them optically implied splitting the input optical power N^2 ways in equal amounts to each filter. It followed that the insertion loss of the filter bank for any single stored pattern must be N^2, in turn implying a minimum gain in the threshold feedback circuit of N^2. Noting that the sigmoid threshold analysis discussed above identified a loop gain of 10 for small signals as being near to ideal, it appears that our threshold stage must provide a power gain of less than $10 \times N^2$.

Other implications seem to follow from this analysis of scaling the optical system to large N. The fact that we have spoken of writing a complete stored image pair at a time in holographic form implies that both 'signal' and 'reference' beams are mutually coherent. This cannot be achieved using independent pixel sources (discrete lasers or LEDs) but, rather, implies the use of a single laser source generating both patterns via some array of modulators. Typical candidates are liquid crystal based spatial light modulators and the OELD circuit described below, both of which are potentially capable of fabrication in large arrays. It also follows that to achieve the sought coupling efficiency in operation, coherent 'image' patterns must be generated, again requiring the use of arrays of modulators illuminated by a single source. The need to provide high gain in each threshold element feedback path seems to rule out the use of discrete detector–amplifier–source pairs simply on the basis that fabricating massive arrays of amplifiers presents a forbidding challenge. Coupled with the coherence requirement suggested above, it appears to be fundamentally ruled out. The general form of optical implementation that seems to emerge from this discussion is illustrated in Fig. 8 which, indicates both the 'matched filter–threshold element loop' but also data input and output channels as well as an input channel for 'teaching' the hologram what is to be recognized.

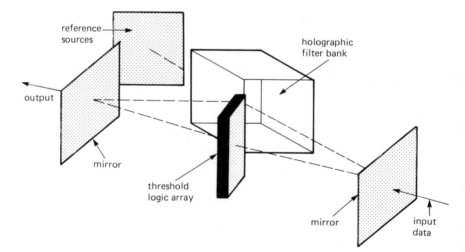

Figure 8 *Suggested layout for an optical implementation of the Hopfield model with two-dimensional input, output and holographic interconnect.*

9. Optical threshold elements with high gain

The combination of a photodetector, limiting amplifier and electrically driven light source such as a laser or LED can be fabricated to match a wide range of arbitrary threshold functions and gains, with power gains of 60 dB or greater. However, as noted above, fabricating such sub-systems in closely packed two-dimensional arrays presents more of a challenge and strongly favours the use of simpler optoelectronic elements, which, even if they have less than ideal responses, may be readily fabricated.

One class of optically activated spatial light modulators relies upon the use of a photoconductive detector–liquid-crystal modulator sandwich to provide the required function, as shown in Fig. 9.[12] In a recent review paper, projected performances for such devices encompassed resolutions of 1000×1000 pixels, response times of less than 1 ms and input sensitivities below $1\,\mu\mathrm{J\,cm}^{-2}$ to give greater than 90% of the maximum output modulation. Assuming also a resolution of $50\,\mathrm{lp\,mm}^{-1}$, this would imply a device of about 5-cm diameter. Noting that the use of 10^6 input pixels would imply a loop gain of order 10^7, this then implies an output optical power from the device of order 40 W. While this is undeniably large, it is at least possible to generate the required input power levels from powerful lasers and SLM devices already handle these power levels in projection display applications. Thus, the use of the SLM device perhaps suggests an ability to handle data vectors of 10^6 bit complexity and to operate at kHz cycle rates. Other devices are being studied that offer faster response times but often at some penalty in resolution or sensitivity. To obtain a feel for the range of device performances, the reader is referred to the review paper.

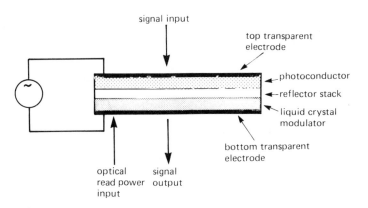

Figure 9 *Diagrammatic representation of a liquid crystal light valve or spatial light modulator in cross-section.*

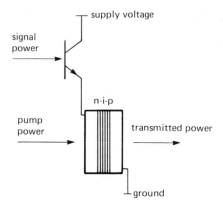

Figure 10   *The hybrid opto-electronic device potentially offering faster response with good gain and a suitable response curve.*

A completely independent approach to solving the problem might rely exclusively on semi-conductor technology using a photo-transistor– multiple-quantum-well modulator 'sandwich' shown in Fig. 10.[13] The response function is shown in Fig. 11. It is expected that power gains in the range 20–25 dB will be readily achievable in its existing form. Higher gains might be achieved using an additional electronic gain stage. The device is expected to be fabricated with dimensions of order $10 \times 30\,\mu m$ so that packing 10^3–10^4 devices per cm^2 is far from inconceivable. However, the available gain values rather point to the desirability of

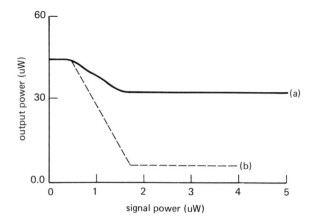

Figure 11   *The response I/O characteristics for the device in Fig. 10: (a) first experimental result; (b) projected with improved device fabrication.*

partitioning the network into sub-networks of typical size 10^2–10^3 'neurons' for ease of fabrication, with each doing a sub-classification in a tree-like information processing system. Such an approach to partitioning the network may also increase the total storage capacity for a given error rate.

10. Speed and power

So far we have said little about speed of operation. The optics of such a system is, by nature, parallel. The speed of light is about $30 \, \text{ps cm}^{-1}$ so that on a 10-cm optical path length, the transit time would be well under 1 ns. The liquid crystal devices proposed above have response times of many microseconds or milliseconds whilst the III–V devices seem likely to operate at speeds well into the nanosecond region. Thus one could conceive of recognition times measured in nanoseconds for a suitably configured processor of the form outlined above using the latter devices.

To achieve a reasonable signal-to-noise-ratio at the input to each element, we might reasonably expect to see a signal of 10^3–10^4 photons per cycle per pixel. Taking the photon energy at $1 \, \mu\text{m}$ wavelength to be $2.10^{-19} \, \text{J}$, and using 10^4 parallel channels with a network insertion loss of 40 dB, the total number of photons per cycle entering the filter bank is 10^{11}–10^{12}. Thus one watt of optical power is notionally capable of driving the system at a cycle rate of 10–100 MHz. Since lasers delivering CW powers in the range 1–100 W are available commercially, this is at least compatible with our other assumptions.

11. Conclusions

To aid the implementation of neural network type processors in pseudo-analogue electronic or optical form, we have developed the matched filter model since it allows one to draw directly upon much well-established engineering thinking and leads to analytical conclusions, removing the need to rely upon digital simulation of special cases. Using it, we are actively pursuing the implications for the optical implementation of such networks. The clear motivation for such an approach is to exploit the innate ability of light to carry information in parallel through space, so avoiding the bottlenecks implicit in planar electronic implementations. These scaling studies seem to suggest that the potential exists for large and fast recognition machines in optics. The challenge is to implement such concepts and to develop more subtle ways of configuring them to allow them to go beyond direct learned pattern association operations towards the drawing of inferences.

References

1. Hopfield, J. J. Neurons with graded response have collective computational properties like those of two state neurons, *Proc. Natl. Acad. Sci. USA* **81**, 3088–3092 (1984).
2. Chambers, W. G. *Basics of Communication and Coding*, pp. 101–103 (Clarendon Press, 1985).
3. Little, W. A. Existence of persistent states in the brain, *Math. Biosci.* **19**, 101–120 (1974).
4. Hopfield, J. J. Neural networks and physical systems with emergent collective computational abilities, *Proc. Natl. Acad. Sci. USA* **79**, 2554–2558 (1982).
5. Kohonen, T. *Self Organisation and Associative Memory* (Berlin: Springer Verlag, 1988).
6. Bayley, J. S. & Fiddy, M. A. On the use of the Hopfield model for optical pattern recognition, *Optics Comm.* **64**, 105–110 (1987).
7. Selviah, D. R. & Midwinter, J. E. unpublished results.
8. Abu Mustafa, Y. & St Jacques, J. M. Information capacity of the Hopfield model, *IEEE Transactions on Information Theory*, Vol. IT-31, pp. 461–464 (1985).
9. Selviah, D. R. & Midwinter, J. E. Correlating matched filter model for analysis and optimisation of neural networks, to be published in IEE Proceedings Part F.
10. Sompolinsky, H. & Kanter, I. Temporal association in asymmetric neural networks, *Phys. Rev. Letters* **57**, 2861–2864 (1986).
11. Psaltis, D. &. Farhat, N. H. Optical information processing based upon an associative memory model of neural nets with thresholding and feedback, *Opt. Letters* **10**, 98 (1985).
12. See, for example, Tanguay, A. R. Materials requirements for optical processing and computing devices, *Optical Engineering* **24**, 2 (1985).
13. Wheatley, P. *et al.* A novel non-resonant optoelectronic logic device, *Electronic Letters* **23**, 92–93 (1987).

14 Hetero-associative networks using link-enabling vs. link-disabling local modification rules

Vernon G. Dobson

Department of Experimental Psychology, University of Oxford, Oxford, UK

Alan Johnston

Department of Psychology, University College London, UK

and

Michael J. Wright

Department of Human Science, Brunel University, Uxbridge, Middlesex, UK

Abstract

Hetero-associative networks[1,2] usually consist of an input and an output array, with each input cell projecting one link to each output cell (Figs. 1 and 2). The function of these networks is to associate pairs of activity patterns, or vectors, in the input and output arrays, so that subsequent representation of a 'key' input vector leads to the reproduction of the associated output vector. Networks can be distinguished by the local link modification rules used to associate patterns in the net, and by the local output cell activity state rules used to retrieve output patterns. This paper is concerned with a class of hetero-associative networks called 'binary' networks, and the objective is to distinguish the alternative kinds of binary hetero-associative network in terms of computational theory, structure and performance.

1. Overview

In the simplest binary associative networks, all network parameters are constrained to two states only. Links are either enabled or disabled. Link modifications are either 'incrementing' or 'decrementing', and can be triggered by either active or inactive output cell states, so that there are four alternative link modification rules in all. As each network is

279

restricted to using only one of these modification rules, there are four basic kinds of binary network, each of which generates a different circuit structure in the process of associating the same set of pattern vectors.

The local output cell activity state rules giving optimal output pattern retrieval in different nets can be determined by exhaustive testing of alternatives.[3] In this paper we show that the simplest retrieval rules are provided by output cells emulating Boolean disjunctive and conjunctive logic-gates. When these are applied to the circuits generated by the alternative link modification rules, it becomes clear that disjunctive logics have a wider range of application than conjunctive logics. Moreover, when the binary input vectors 'overlap', and share common active elements, networks using incrementing modification rules make errors of retrieval which cannot occur in those using decrementing rules.

Networks using disjunctive retrieval rules will be called 'disjunctive networks'. For each disjunctive network there is an equivalent 'single-sign' network, in which all link signals are either positive or negative, and which uses a threshold logic function to determine output cell states. For each single-sign network there is an equivalent 'opponent-sign' network in which each node is filled by a parallel pair of links of opposite sign. One of these links is modifiable, and the other is unmodifiable. In opponent-sign networks, output cells implement threshold logics rather than disjunctive logics. More sophisticated opponent-sign nets can be constructed in which the unmodifiable links are combined into threshold-control circuits monitoring global activity over cells in the input or output arrays.

Both incrementing and decrementing single-sign networks can be translated into equivalent opponent-sign networks with the same performances. However, opponent-sign networks are not restricted to emulating either the incrementing or the decrementing single-sign network alone. By varying the ratio of the gains of their excitatory and inhibitory links, the opponent-sign nets can implement algorithms providing any level of performance intermediate between the two kinds of net.

This flexibility has a significant cost, in terms of the complexity and quality of the circuits required to implement opponent-sign networks which match the optimal performances of the equivalent single-sign networks. In opponent-sign networks, parallel links of opposite sign must be precisely matched for number, gain and temporal summation of signals, and output cells must sum signals of opposite sign linearly, while there are no corresponding implementational requirements in single-sign networks. When the performances of equivalent networks are compared in randomly generated connectivities, it becomes apparent that the opponent-sign networks can make errors that cannot occur in the equivalent single-sign networks, and that these errors are more expensive to prevent and correct.

2. Pattern association and recall in disjunctive networks

2.1 Enumeration of the simplest local link modification rules

To facilitate general discussion of link modification rules some special terminology will be introduced. The local pattern of activity which triggers link modification will be called the 'trigger' pattern. In binary networks, only trigger patterns modifying links from active input cells can be used to associate input and output vectors. The state of the output cell in the trigger pattern will be generally referred to as the 'target' state, and its complementary state as the 'ground' state. Link modifications can either enable or disable links, but links will generally be referred to as being in their 'modified' or 'unmodified' states. As cells have only two activity states, each array can represent binary vectors or patterns, with active cells standing for 'ones', and inactive cells representing 'zeros'.

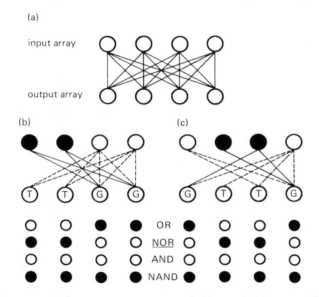

Figure 1   *Decrementing hetero-associative network: (a) initial connectivity; (b) connectivity after associating one pattern-pair; (c) connectivity after associating two pattern pairs.*

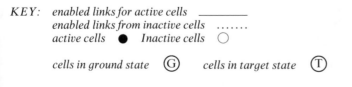

KEY: *enabled links for active cells* _____
    enabled links from inactive cells ....
    active cells ● *Inactive cells* ○

    cells in ground state Ⓖ   *cells in target state* Ⓣ

2.2 Pattern association in networks using incrementing and decrementing link

2.2.1 Modification rules

Figs. 1 and 2 represent the development of circuits in small hetero-associative networks using decrementing and incrementing link modification rules respectively. Each network is shown in its initial state (Figs. 1(*a*) and 2(*a*)), with no patterns established, and then just after the association of first one pattern-pair (Figs. 1(*b*) and 2(*b*)), and then a second pattern-pair (Figs. 1(*c*) and 2(*c*)).

In these diagrams, active input cells are represented by filled circles, and inactive input cells by empty circles. To simplify the diagrams, only enabled links are shown. Solid links represent enabled links from active

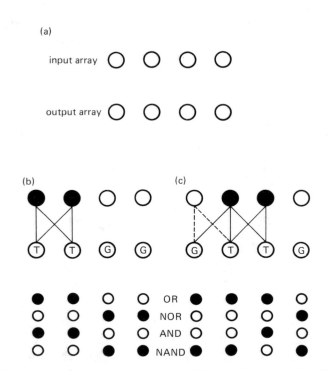

Figure 2   *Incrementing hetero-associative network: (a) initial connectivity; (b) connectivity after associating one pattern-pair; (c) connectivity after associating two pattern pairs.*

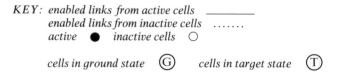

KEY: enabled links from active cells _____
         enabled links from inactive cells ....
         active ● *inactive cells* ○

         cells in ground state Ⓖ   *cells in target state* Ⓣ

input cells, and dashed lines indicate enabled links from inactive cells. Output array cells are represented by T for cells in their target state, and G for cells in their ground state. The target state is always either active or inactive, in any given network, and the ground state is its complement.

During pattern association, links from active input cells to output cells in their target state are modified. In Figs. 1 and 2 this modification process is assumed to have just been completed. The networks in Fig. 1 use decrementing modification rules, so that their output cells receive operative links from all the input cells with which their target states have never been associated. The use of incrementing rules in the networks in Fig. 2 means that their output cells receive operative links from all the input cells with which their target states have been associated.

The first pattern pairing (Figs. 1(*b*) and 2(*b*)) is between input vector 1,1,0,0 and output vector T,T,G,G where T,T,G,G represents 1,1,0,0 in networks where the target state T = 1, and 0,0,1,1 in networks where T = 0. The second pattern pairing (Figs. 1(*c*) and 2(*c*)) is between input vector 0,1,1,0 and output vector G,T,T,G. Note that there is an overlap between input vectors in the first and second pattern-pairs, each sharing elements in target and ground states.

2.3 Pattern recall using Boolean conjunctive and disjunctive logic gates

During pattern retrieval an input vector is re-established. Each output cell must apply some contingency rule to its input signals so as to assign itself to its target state only if this state has been associated with all the active cells in the input vector. The simplest set of rules which an output cell can apply to the binary signals from its active operative links are the Boolean disjunctive and conjunctive logical operators NOR, OR, NAND and AND. The outcome of applying these operators to the signals received by the output cells in Figs. 1 and 2 is represented under the corresponding cell. Filled circles represent active output cells, empty circles represent inactive cells. Output patterns which are recalled correctly are underlined with their operators.

The disjunctive primitives OR and NOR prove to be most useful for retrieving output patterns in binary nets. The default state of OR gates is inactive, but they are activated by any signal, while NOR gates are normally active, but they are inactivated by any signal. In decrementing networks (Figs. 1(*b*) and (*c*)), NOR-gates give optimal performance where the target state is active (T = 1), and OR-gates give best performance if the target state is inactive (T = 0). Note that they give reliable pattern recall with overlapping input vectors (Fig. 1(*c*)). In incrementing networks, disjunctive logic gates can recall patterns reliably only if there is no overlap between input vectors, and each cell is involved in only one pattern-pair association (Fig. 2(b)). NOR-gates give optimal performance where the target state is inactive (T = 0), and OR-gates give best performance if the target state is active (T = 1). However, they do not give reliable pattern recall with overlapping input vectors (Fig. 2(c)).

The conjunctive primitives AND and NAND can distinguish between the cases where output cells are, or are not, receiving signals from all their operative links. In decrementing networks this distinction is not relevant to pattern recall (Fig. 1). In incrementing networks, conjunctive logic gates can only provide optimal recall if there is no overlap between output vectors (Figs. 2(b) and 2(c)). However, it is also unclear how conjunctive logic gates should assign the states of output cells with no modified links, so networks using conjunctive retrieval rules will not be considered further.

The conclusion to be drawn here is that the retrieval of overlapping pattern vectors in decrementing nets is a simple task, involving the detection of the mere presence or absence of enabled link signals, and can be performed reliably by Boolean disjunctive logic gates. However, the corresponding task in incrementing networks is relatively complicated, requiring output cells to determine whether they are receiving signals from all the active input cells. This is not equivalent to determining whether they are receiving signals from any or all of their operative links, and so cannot be performed by either disjunctive or conjunctive Boolean logic gates.

3. Pattern recall using threshold logic units and signed link signals

3.1 'Single-step' networks

McCulloch & Pitts proved that the logical operations of each Boolean primitive can be emulated by an equivalent threshold logic.[4] Consequently, for each of the disjunctive networks which can retrieve patterns using disjunctive logic gates (Figs. 1(b), 1(c) and 2(b)), there is an equivalent single-sign network using threshold logic units (TLUs), and link signals which are all either positive (excitatory) or negative (inhibitory).

Disjunctive networks using NOR-gates, can be translated into single-sign networks in which all link signals are negative, or inhibitory, and the output cells are 'NOR–TLUs' which are active as long if the sum of signals they receive is zero or more (threshold = 0). NOR–TLUs are inactivated by inhibitory signals, but are unaffected by excitatory signals. Similarly, networks using OR-gates can be translated into networks in which all link signals are positive, or excitatory, and the output cells are

'OR-TLUs' which are active only if the sum of signals they receive is greater than zero (threshold > 0). The performance of a single-sign TLU network is exactly the same as that of the corresponding disjunctive logic gate network. For example, only single-sign networks using decrementing modification rules can operate reliably with overlapping input patterns, like the network in Fig. 1(c).

Decrementing single-sign networks using inhibitory signals have been studied by Dobson[5-7] and Albus[8,9] has studied related networks using excitatory signals.

3.2 'Opponent-sign' networks

Each of the four possible single-sign networks can be transformed into an equivalent opponent-sign network, by replacing each link with a parallel pair of links of opposite sign. These parallel link-pairs emit signals which sum to the same value as the signals from the corresponding link in the single-sign network. For example, the inhibitory decrementing single-sign network represented in Fig. 1 can be transformed into an excitatory incrementing opponent-sign network in which each input cell makes one permanently enabled inhibitory link, and one incrementing excitatory link, to each output cell. This network is shown in Fig. 3, with solid lines representing inhibitory circuits and dashed lines representing excitatory links.

If the gains of the parallel links are precisely equal, when enabled, then the total net signal from each parallel link pair is exactly the same as that from corresponding links in an inhibitory decrementing single-sign network. Before modification, only the unmodifiable inhibitory link emits signals, but, after modification, the incremented excitatory link signals exactly cancel or mask the signals from their parallel inhibitory links, to produce a net modified link signal of zero. Thus incrementing opponent-sign nets can precisely mimic the signals generated in the equivalent decrementing single-sign networks, and they can operate

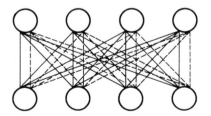

Figure 3   *Excitatory incrementing opponent-sign network.*

KEY: inhibitory links (unmodifiable) ─────────
    excitatory links (incrementing)   . . . .

reliably with overlapping input pattern vectors by using NOR-TLUs to determine output cell activity states.

However, if the gains of the unmodifiable inhibitory circuits are progressively reduced, relative to those of the enabled excitatory links, then reliability with overlapping input vectors declines until, when the gains of the inhibitory links are zero, performance is the same as that of the excitatory incrementing single-sign network—i.e. only non-overlapping vectors can be stored. Thus, by varying the gains of their unmodifiable inhibitory circuits, opponent-sign networks can match the performances of excitatory incrementing and inhibitory decrementing single-sign networks, and the range of intermediate performance.

3.3 Opponent-sign networks using circuits monitoring global activity in neural arrays: threshold-modulated and most-support networks

For each of the four possible opponent-sign networks, there is an equivalent 'threshold-modulated' network in which the local unmodifiable circuits are replaced by global circuits summing activity over the input array as a whole. For example, the opponent-sign network in Fig. 3 can be transformed into the 'threshold-modulated' network shown in Fig. 4, by replacing all the local unmodifiable inhibitory links by a single inhibitory feedforward threshold-modulating circuit. This circuit sums excitation from all active input cells and projects this to all output cells as an inhibitory threshold signal.

As described for opponent-sign networks, the performance of the threshold-modulated network can also be varied to emulate that of the

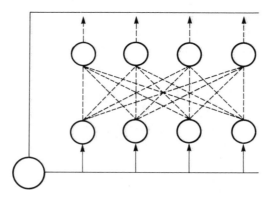

Figure 4   *Excitatory incrementing threshold-modulated network.*

KEY: feedforward inhibitory threshold modulating links _____
      modifiable excitatory links (incrementing) ....

excitatory incrementing and inhibitory decrementing single-sign networks, and the intermediate range, by varying the gain of the inhibitory threshold circuit.

Excitatory incrementing networks using threshold logics for pattern recall have been studied by Steinbuch,[10] Marr, Willshaw, Buneman & Longuet-Higgins,[12] and Palm.[2]

3.4 'Most-support' networks

An alternative arithmetical rule for assigning output cells to their target states in networks using incrementing synaptic rules is to select the output cells receiving 'most support', in terms of the number of modified excitatory link signals they receive from the input vector. However, in order to determine whether or not they are receiving most support, output cells must be able to compare their own support with that of all the other cells on the basis of local signals. This global information can be provided by feedback inhibitory circuits measuring the global support being received by the output array as a whole. The local support to individual output cells can be progressively reduced by a function of this global support until only the cells receiving most support remain active. Most-support networks with feedback inhibitory circuits are represented in Fig. 5. As described for the other opponent-sign networks, if the gain of the inhibitory circuits is zero, the performance of a most-support network is the same as that of the single-sign incrementing network, and as the gain of the inhibitory circuits is increased, so the capacity to deal with overlapping input vectors improves. Most-support networks have been studied by Feldman & Ballard,[34] and McClelland.[17]

3.5 'Tandem' single-sign networks

Single-sign networks using links with opposite signs and modification rules can be combined to form 'tandem' networks, in which signals from

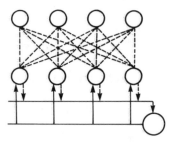

Figure 5   *Excitatory incrementing most-support network.*

KEY: feedback inhibitory threshold modulating links _____
      modifiable excitatory links (incrementing) ....

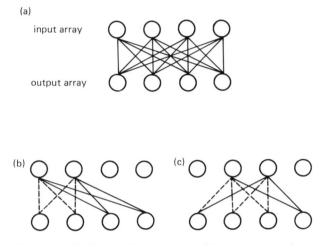

Figure 6   *Tandem network: (a) initial connectivity; (b) connectivity after associating one pattern-pair; (c) connectivity after associating two pattern pairs.*

KEY: active cells ●   inactive cells ○
enabling inhibitory decrementing links _____
enables excitatory incrementing links   ....

different networks are analysed separately, and conflicts between the outputs from the two networks are resolved in favour of the decrementing network.

Fig. 6(*a–c*) represents a tandem network consisting of two single-sign networks, the inhibitory decrementing network and the excitatory incrementing network, associating the same patterns as in Figs. 1 and 2. The target state of the output cells in both these networks is active, so active cells can be represented by filled circles and inactive cells by empty circles. Enabled inhibitory links are indicated by solid lines and enabled excitatory links by dashed lines. Initially, only the inhibitory links are enabled (Fig. 6(*a*)). During link modification (Fig. 6(*b, c*)), inhibitory links are disabled and the parallel excitatory links are enabled. In order to simplify the diagrams, only enabled links from active cells are represented in Fig. 6, enabled links from inactive cells, and disabled links, are not shown.

The output cells are divided into two compartments, or segments (not shown separately in Fig. 6). The first segment receives all the excitatory link signals and applies an OR rule, so that the output cell is activated by any excitatory signal. The second segment receives all the inhibitory link signals and applies a NOR rule, so that the output cell is inhibited by any inhibitory signal. The second segment gates the signal from the first segment so that it can only be transmitted to the output line in the absence of inhibitory signals. Thus, in this tandem network, the output cells adopt their active (target) state if they receive any excitatory signals and no inhibitory signals, and they adopt their inactive (ground) state if they receive no excitatory signals, or any inhibitory signals. In Fig. 6(*c*) the leftmost output cell receives both an excitatory and an inhibitory signal from the key input pattern, and the inhibitory signal over-rules the excitatory signal.

The tandem network in Fig. 6 gives better performance than the decrementing network in Fig. 1, in that all output cells do not spuriously become active if all input cells are inactive. In tandem networks, the output cells as a whole emulate OR–NOT gates. Koch & Poggio[13] have proposed a related model in which segments of neural dendritic trees act as AND–NOT gates in mediating direction and orientation selectivity in the visual cortex.

4. Performance of single-sign and threshold-modulated networks in ideal and non-ideal circuits

While opponent-sign and threshold-modulated networks are more flexible than single-sign networks, they are also more complicated. To match the performance of decrementing single-sign networks with overlapping input vectors, they require parallel circuits of equal gain but opposite sign between each input and output cell, and should deliver exactly the same net total signals to their output cells as the equivalent single-sign network. This additional complexity does not cause problems in 'ideal' circuits, which are assumed to have been specified to the level of precision required for optimal performance. However, it becomes disadvantageous in 'non-ideal' circuits produced by random growth processes, or which are subject to random damage during manufacture or use.

Appendix I describes mathematical models of the performance of single-sign and threshold-modulated networks associating randomly generated patterns in ideal circuits. Both of these networks can only make errors in which output cells spuriously adopt their target state, and both networks make exactly the same errors when recalling the same pattern set.

Appendix II describes mathematical models of the performance of these networks operating in circuits which have been generated by profuse random growth processes, and in sparse circuits produced by random ablation of ideal circuits. In non-ideal circuits, single-sign networks can still only make errors in which output cells spuriously adopt their target state, while, in threshold-modulated networks, cells can spuriously adopt either ground or target states. Measures which reduce errors of one type in threshold-modulated networks lead to an increase in errors of the other type. Consequently, however well the various network parameters are tuned, the performance of threshold-modulated networks in non-ideal circuits is always significantly less accurate than that of the corresponding single-sign network in recalling the same set of patterns. However, threshold-modulated networks can give reasonably reliable performance if the average gain of the threshold circuits and the load of patterns to be associated are both significantly reduced.

Mathematical models of the performance of binary networks in random connectivities have also been studied by Longuet-Higgins, Willshaw & Buneman,[14] Gardner-Medwin,[15] Palm,[2] Lansner & Ekeberg[16] and McClelland.[17]

Most-support networks operating in randomly generated connectivities suffer from the same kind of problem as threshold-modulated networks. If the gain on the feedback inhibition is too weak, some output cells will be spuriously active and, if it is too strong, some will be spuriously inactive. Mutual inhibition between active cells in the output vector also tends to amplify random differences in the support they receive, until only one or a few of these cells remain active. This source of error can be eliminated if all output vectors are base vectors containing only one active cell, and the most-support net is used to classify input vectors in terms of these base vectors in the output array. The performance of most-support networks can also be improved if feedforward inhibitory circuits like those shown in Fig. 4 are used to reduce the total number of cells initially contributing to the feedback inhibition between the output array cells.

4.1 Error prevention in non-ideal neural circuits

Not only are threshold-modulated networks more prone to error than single-sign networks in non-ideal circuits, but these errors are also significantly more difficult to prevent, detect and correct. In single-sign and tandem networks, errors can occur if links fail to form initially, or if link gains are so small that the signals received by an output cell are too weak to be distinguished from the background. Errors due to the failure of links to form can be prevented by increasing the density of links initially produced. Errors due to weak link signals can be corrected in the short-term simply by allowing them to summate over time until they are detectable. The failure of an active link to change its output cell activity state within a minimum period can also serve as a reliable local error signal triggering corrective gain increments which cease when the link is performing effectively.[7]

In threshold-modulated networks, errors can be caused by the formation of too few or too many links, and by link signals which are too weak or too strong. After associating sufficient numbers of overlapping vectors, the range of total signals received by the target state cells is likely to overlap with that received by the ground state cells, so that they cannot be separated by varying the relative numbers, gains or temporal summation rates of links of differing sign. Moreover, in these nets, link signals do not invariably produce a particular output cell state, so they produce no distinctive local error signals which can be used to initiate gain corrections in the appropriate direction.

5. Discussion: computational strategies in incrementing and decrementing networks

The differences in performance between incrementing and decrementing networks can be explained in terms of differences in computational theory.[18-20] A computational theory for the task of an output cell in a binary hetero-associative network is that the cell should adopt its target state if ALL its links from the active key input cell have been modified, and should adopt its ground state if ANY of these links are unmodified. In the simplest binary networks, output cells can only receive signals from either modified or unmodified links, but not both. In incrementing networks, only modified links are enabled, and in decrementing networks, only unmodified links are enabled. However, after the association of pattern-pairs with overlapping input vectors, signals from modified and unmodified links convey qualitatively different messages to their output cells.

The difference between the information represented in modified and unmodified links is analogous to the difference between the value of observations in testing a universal hypothesis such as 'all swans are white'. Observations of many white swans cannot, by themselves, conclusively confirm this hypothesis, but the observation of a single coloured swan conclusively falsifies it. Similarly, signals from any unmodified links clearly indicate that the output cell's target state has not been associated with all the active cells in the key pattern, and that the output cell should adopt its ground state. However, signals from one or more modified links, by themselves, only indicate that the output cell's target state has been associated with SOME of the active key pattern cells, and so give no clear indication as to which state the output cell should adopt.

Single-sign decrementing networks thus use a 'falsificationist' computational strategy,[21] by which each output cell uses the unambiguous information in signals from its unmodified links to falsify the hypothesis that its target state has been associated with all active cells in the key input vector, and that it should adopt its target state. During pattern association, modified links are selectively disabled, so that the output cell's task is simply to detect unmodified link signals and to emulate a disjunctive logic gate.

Incrementing networks use the alternative 'confirmationist' computational strategy by which each output cell uses the signals from its modified links to confirm the hypothesis that its target state has been associated with all active cells in the key input vector. This hypothesis is 'confirmed', and the output cell adopts its target state, if the number of modified link signals reaches a threshold. For optimal performance, a second set of threshold-modulating links is required to vary this threshold with the number of active input cells. Threshold-modulating circuits monitor input array activity and deliver a threshold signal of opposite sign to that of the modified links, so that these cancel out by algebraic summation of opposites, and any surplus of modified link signals indicates that the hypothesis has been confirmed.

In logical terms, the output cells in confirmationist networks should not adopt their target state unless they can confirm that the set of input cells from which they are receiving modified link signals is identical to the set of active input cells in the key pattern. Incrementing opponent-sign networks can perform this task using threshold arithmetic, assuming that their circuitry has been pre-specified according to the correct arithmetical ratios. Any disturbance of these ideal numerical ratios impairs performance relative to that of the corresponding single-sign decrementing networks, which do not depend on arithmetically pre-specified circuits. However, performance degrades gracefully, so that, even in random connectivities, incrementing opponent-sign nets can deliver quite reliable performance with small pattern sets and low thresholds.[14]

Clearly, the computational strategies of incrementing and decrementing network algorithms have differing requirements at the level of implementation. The degree of randomness in these circuits exerts powerful bottom-up constraints on the efficiency of incrementing networks, but is of minor consequence to decrementing networks.

While the simplest binary networks are restricted to using either modified or unmodified link signals, more complex networks can use both kinds of signals, and both kinds of computational strategies, in parallel. Conflicts arising between these parallel networks in non-ideal circuits can be resolved by allowing the unambiguous signals from the decrementing network to over-rule those from the incrementing network. In the tandem networks described in Fig. 6, inhibitory unmodified link signals over-rule signals from excitatory modified links.

5.1 Binary associative networks in integrated circuit devices and biological systems

In this paper, binary associative networks have been described at four levels of increasing complexity. In the disjunctive networks, signals are unsigned, and simply represent binary logic values. In single-sign networks signals are signed, positively or negatively, but all signals in a given network are of the same sign. In opponent-sign networks signals of both signs are used in parallel, but only one of these are modifiable. In tandem networks, links of both signs are modifiable, and there is the possibility of threshold-modulated tandem circuits. Arguments from parsimony suggest that the simplest networks would tend to be selected for during the evolution of both technological and biological implementations of associative networks.[7] As simpler networks are likely to be less expensive to implement, and therefore more cost-effective, they are more likely to be selected for.[22] These arguments appear to hold true for integrated circuit networks, where design precedes existence. However, the evolutionary process is essentially unplanned, and involves progressive refinements and opportunistic adaptations of preceding functional structures. This can lead to compromise solutions, incorporating features from several networks which can be combined economically in the physiology available, but without implementing any of these systematically, or in their theoretically optimal form.

5.2 Binary associative networks in integrated circuit devices

PROMs (programmable read-only memories), and EPROMs (erasable programmable read-only memories) are integrated circuit memory devices which can modify their own circuits during training on the basis of local binary activity rules.[23] Significantly, both PROMs and EPROMs always use disjunctive logic gates for pattern recall. Moreover, in PROMs, where information is stored by physically altering circuit structure, all links are initially intact and modified links are selectively fused or disabled according to decrementing rules. This is because it is much easier to design the networks to disable their own pre-existing links, in response to local signals, than to build new ones. In EPROMs, the links themselves remain physically intact, and links are reversibly enabled or disabled by trapped electrical charges. This allows both incrementing and decrementing binary link modifications to be used.

However, in both PROMs and EPROMs, input vectors are pre-processed by an exhaustive encoder which allocates a unique input array cell, or 'word-line' to each vector. For example, input vectors with three components would address one of eight (2^3) word-lines. As only one word-line can be active at a time, there is no need to recall output vectors which have been associated with overlapping input array vectors, and errors from this source are prevented.

5.3 Binary associative networks in brain systems

As binary associative networks are the simplest associative networks, computationally, they are likely to have been implemented, in some form, in real brain circuits, probably in addition to more complex associative networks.[20, 24] As all neural signals are signed, excitatory or inhibitory, and all brain cells receive inputs of both signs, it is unlikely that single-sign networks will be found in their simple form. However, the Albus[8] model of the cerebellar parallel-fibre circuits is a version of a powerful single-sign excitatory decrementing network operating in tandem with a less powerful single-sign inhibitory incrementing network, and this model has gained significant empirical support.[25, 26]

There are good reasons for predicting that at least some regions of the cerebrum use excitatory incrementing opponent-sign networks, and several models of cerebral circuitry are based upon this assumption.[2, 27, 28] As the precursor networks from which cerebral associative networks evolved were likely to have been mainly excitatory and randomly grown, it is quite conceivable that these may have evolved into excitatory incrementing opponent-sign networks. Initially, these networks may have served learning tasks such as imprinting, or target lock-on, which only require the storage of one or a few pattern associations. However, some opponent-sign networks may have evolved further in response to selection pressures to associate increasing numbers of overlapping pattern vectors reliably.

The simplest way to increase the power and reliability of opponent-sign networks in non-ideal circuits is to progressively improve the accuracy of the match between the gains of parallel excitatory and inhibitory circuits. This is evolutionarily plausible, because it is conservative and involves making a series of small changes. However, progressively more precisely pre-specified neural circuits are likely to become expensive, physiologically, and, at some point, it may become more economical to interpolate an inhibitory decrementing network between the input and output arrays, to produce a tandem threshold-modulated network. The advantage of this combination of networks is that the inhibitory decrementing circuits can be self-correcting, and can operate reliably in random connectivities, but would not need to be very powerful when operating in conjunction with parallel threshold-modulating circuits.

Once inhibitory decrementing networks have been installed, further evolution could take the form of progressively simplifying and economizing the circuitry to approximate that of a single-sign inhibitory decrementing network. This might occur, for example, if it was necessary to associate large numbers of overlapping input vectors in random, predominantly inhibitory connectivities.

A third way to improve the performance of excitatory incrementing networks with overlapping input vectors is to encode the input vectors so that they do not overlap. In EPROMs, for example, where input vectors are exhaustively encoded to prevent any overlap, disjunctive networks using incrementing and decrementing link modifications are equally reliable. It follows that, by developing efficient encoders, brain circuits could avoid the need to equip their excitatory incrementing networks with the threshold modulating circuits and ancillary inhibitory decrementing networks described above. However, encoding is also expensive in terms of circuits; for example, binary input vectors with 20 components, or input lines requires 2^{20} word lines for exhaustive encoding. While significant improvements in performance can be derived from simple, but incomplete, encoding strategies the benefits derived from exhaustive encoding in brain circuits are outweighed by the costs.[5, 29]

From an evolutionary perspective, the advantages to be gained from developing progressively closer approximations to exhaustive encoding follow the law of diminishing returns. Similarly, the process of increasing the standardization of physiological components in threshold-modulated networks becomes progressively less profitable. Consequently, evolutionary processes may produce circuits combining principles from several different associative networks, but only exploiting those features which can be most readily and cost-effectively incorporated into the pre-existing physiology. These 'opportunistic conservative compromises' are also most likely to be produced when the evolutionary process commences at inconvenient starting points such as the excitatory incrementing network (Fig. 2).

One consequence of these arguments is that brain regions using incrementing associative networks would be under greater pressure to evolve efficient encoders than regions using decrementing networks. The brain regions where decrementing networks are most likely to be found are the cerebellum,[8] and the basal ganglia, which contain a predominance of inhibitory circuits,[30] and so could emulate the simple and efficient single-sign inhibitory decrementing networks (P. Somogyi personal communication, 1986). Neither of these regions appear to use sophisticated encoding strategies. In the hippocampus, the proportion of inhibitory cells is so low that they are unlikely to perform more than general threshold control functions,[27] leaving information storage to the excitatory circuits. In the cerebral cortex, however, up to one-third of cells are inhibitory,[31,32] suggesting that, if inhibitory decrementing networks are used in the cortex, they may be used in conjunction with excitatory incrementing threshold-modulated networks. In the cerebral cortex, of course, the various primary sensory cortices perform sophisticated encoding functions upon their inputs, and recent theories of hippocampal function suggest that it may act as an adaptive encodor for higher cortical regions.[33]

It is interesting to speculate that the more sophisticated encoding strategies used in the cerebral cortex may have evolved partly to compensate for the relatively poor performance of its incrementing networks with overlapping input vectors. As the higher cognitive capacities depend on the development of efficient codes, the cortex may have turned a short-term misfortune to its long-term advantage.

Appendix I

1. Performance of binary associative nets in ideal connectivities

The performance of single-sign inhibitory decrementing networks and opponent-sign excitatory incrementing networks in ideal connectivities can be described by the same mathematical model. Fig. A1 illustrates the performance of both networks in 'ideal' connectivities, where each node is initially filled by precisely one modifiable link. Both input and output arrays consist of A cells, and both input and output patterns contain C active cells, the remainder being inactive or inhibited.

In ideal connectivities, both nets can only make errors of commission in recall, and they do this by failing to inhibit output cells in the background pattern. The error rate per pattern retrieved E varies with p

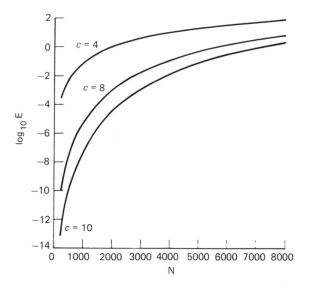

Figure A1. *Performance of binary hetero-associative networks in ideal circuits with complete and incomplete 'key' patterns. Increase in error rate ($\log_{10} E$) with number of pattern pairs associated (N) using 'key' input patterns of $c = 4$, 8 and 10 active cells. Each array consists of $A = 1000$ cells and patterns contain $C = 10$ active cells per array.*

the proportion of links modified by learning, and c the number of active cells in the key pattern, and p depends on A, C, and N, the number of patterns associated.

$$p = 1 - ((A^2 - C^2)/A^2)^N, \tag{1}$$

$$E = p^c * (A - C). \tag{2}$$

Fig. A1 shows how the error rate ($\log_{10} E$) varies with N for key patterns containing $c = 4, 8$ and 10 active cells.

Appendix II

1. Performance of decrementing nets in randomly generated circuits

In 'randomly grown' circuits each input cell randomly donates an average of L links to each output cell. This means that, at some nodes, no links form at all: q, the proportion of empty nodes in which no links form is given by the first term of the Poisson distribution:

$$q = e^{-L}. \tag{3}$$

In decrementing nets, the probability of error increases with q; however, the errors caused by empty nodes are errors of commission, like those caused by empty nodes due to decrementing link modification. The total error rate due to links cut by learning and links which fail to form during random growth is

$$E = A*(p+q-p*q)^c. \tag{4}$$

This equation also applies to 'randomly ablated' circuits which are produced by randomly cutting q of the links in an ideal network.

2. Performance of incrementing nets in randomly generated circuits

Incrementing nets operating in randomly generated circuits can make both errors of commission, where background pattern cells spuriously receive threshold levels of excitation, and errors of omission, where target pattern cells spuriously receive sub-threshold levels of excitation. The total error rate $E = E^- + E^+$, where E^- is the rate of errors of omission, and E^+ is the rate of errors of commission per output pattern retrieved. While E^- can be reduced by reducing the gain on the threshold circuits, E^+ can only be reduced by increasing thresholds. For optimal performance in random connectivities, the threshold must be set to minimize both values. However, this optimal threshold setting is a function of L, N, and c, instead of being a simple linear function of c, as in ideal connectivities. The rate of errors of omission, E^-, is equal to the product of the number of active cells in each output pattern C, and the proportion of output cells receiving subthreshold numbers of links from the active input cells, P_S. For any threshold value T, P_S is equal to the sum of the first $T-1$ terms of the Poisson expansion with a mean of $x = C*L$:

$$P_S = e^{-x} + x \times e^{-x} + x^2 \times e^{-x}/2! \ldots + x^{(T-2)} \times e^{-x}/(T-2)! \qquad (5)$$

The rate of errors of commission, E^+, can be calculated for each value of T as follows:

$$E^+ = (A-C)*P_T. \qquad (6)$$

The proportion of cells receiving the threshold level of excitatory signals from operative firing links, P_T, for any threshold value T, is equal to $1-$ the sum of the first $(T-1)$ terms of the Poisson distribution with a mean of $p*c*L$, the average number of operative links received by each output cell from the active cells in each input pattern (p is given by Equation (1)).

The validity of Equations (1–6) has been confirmed with computer simulations with arrays of 31–64 cells.[6]

Figs. A2 and A3 show the error rates of decrementing and incrementing nets in randomly grown versions of the net in Fig. A1, with

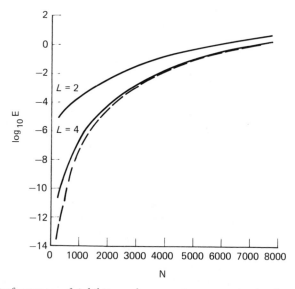

Figure A2 *Performance of inhibitory decrementing networks in dense random connectivities. Increase in error rate ($\log_{10} E$) with number of pattern pairs associated (N) in 'ideal' circuits (dashed line) and in 'randomly grown' circuits with 'dense' connectivity ratios of $L = 2$ and 4. Each array consists of $A = 1000$ cells and patterns contain $C = 10$ active cells per array.*

300

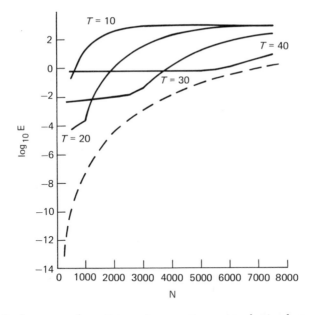

Figure A3 *Performance of excitatory incrementing networks in dense random con-nectivities. Increase in log error rate* (log$_{10}$ E) *with N, the number of patterns associated, and T, the threshold setting, in a randomly connected excitatory incrementing net with a connectivity ratio of L = 5. Solid lines show performance with threshold settings of T = 10, T = 20, T = 30 and T = 40. Broken line indicates performance in ideal circuits and that of the corresponding inhibitory decrementing net. Each array consists of A = 1000 cells and patterns contain C = 10 active cells per array.*

$A = 1000$ cells per array and $c = C = 10$ active cells per pattern. The corresponding performance of both nets in ideal connectivities is represented by the dashed curves for comparison.

The solid lines in Fig. A2 show how the decrementing net error rate (log$_{10}$ E) varies with N, the number of patterns associated, in randomly grown nets with an average of $L = 2$ to $L = 4$ links per node. When $L = 4$, $q < 0.05$ and log$_{10}$ E approaches that of a net with ideal connectivity.

Fig. A3 shows how log$_{10}$ E varies with N for an incrementing net operating in randomly grown circuits with a link density of $L = 5$. The solid lines represent performance at fixed threshold settings of $T = 10$, 20, 30 and 40.

Whereas Fig. A2 shows that the error rate of decrementing nets in dense randomly grown circuits $(L > 4)$ approximates optimal performance in an ideal net, Fig. A3 shows that the error rate of the corresponding fixed threshold incrementing net exceeds the optimal

301

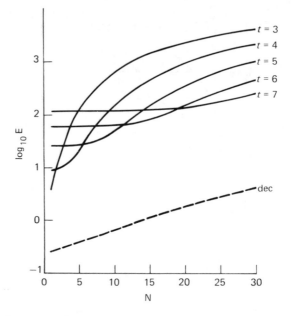

Figure A4   *Performance of excitatory incrementing networks in sparse random connectivities. Solid lines show increase in log error rate* ($\log_{10} E$) *with N, the number of
patterns associated, in a randomly connected excitatory incrementing network with threshold
settings of* $t = 3$ *to* $t = 7$. *This network consists of* $A = 10\,000$ *cells with a sparse
connectivity ratio of* $L = 0.1$, *the network associated patterns containing* $C = 1000$ *active
cells, and retrieved them from key patterns consisting of* $c = 100$ *active cells. Broken line
indicates performance of the corresponding inhibitory decrementing network.*

value by a factor of between 10 and 10^8. The optimal performance of a
threshold modulated incrementing net is also worse by a factor of from
10 and 10^3.

Fig. A4 illustrates the performance of both nets in sparse randomly
grown connectivities with the same parameter values as those in the
network analysed by Gardner-Medwin.[15] There are $A = 10\,000$ cells per
array, and the average number of links per node is $L = 0.1$. This net
was assumed to have learned $N = 1$–30 patterns containing $C = 1000$
active cells, and to have been tested with key patterns consisting of
$c = 100$ active cells. The dashed line in Fig. A4 shows the error rate of a
decrementing net predicted by (Equations (1–4)). The solid lines in Fig.
A4 represent the error rates predicted by Equations (5 and 6) for
incrementing nets with fixed thresholds of from 3–7. These suggest a
slightly better performance than the Gardner-Medwin model which
predicts about 10% more errors in incrementing nets at thresholds lower
than 6.

However, even if the threshold T of the threshold modulated incrementing net is varied optimally with N, L, and c, its error rate is worse than that of the decrementing net by a factor of 10–10^2 over the whole range. The relative superiority of the decrementing net increases significantly with increasing numbers of active cells in the key patterns. For example, after $N = 10$ patterns have been learned, key patterns of $c = 500$ cells produce error rates of $E = 3*10^{-17}$ in the decrementing net (Equations (1–4)), and error rates of $E = 2*10^{-3}$ at the optimal threshold setting of 21, in the incrementing net (Equations (5 and 6)).

Acknowledgements

We would like to thank Edmund Rolls, David Rose and Andrew Ray for constructive criticism and encouragement. This work was partly supported by the MoD and the MRC.

References

1. Kohonen, T. *Self Organisation and Associative Memory* (Berlin: Springer Verlag 1984).
2. Palm, G. *Neural Assemblies* (Berlin: Springer Verlag 1982).
3. Rose, D. & Dobson, V. G. Methodological solutions for neuroscience. In: D. Rose & V. G. Dobson (eds). *Models of Visual Cortex* 533–46 (Chichester: J. Wiley 1985).
4. McCulloch, W. S. & Pitts, W. A logical calculus of the ideas immanent in nervous activity *Bulletin of Mathematical Biophysics* **5** 115 (1943).
5. Dobson, V. G. Pattern learning and the control of behaviour in all inhibitory neural network hierarchies *Perception* **4** 35–50 (1975).
6. Dobson, V. G. *Towards a Model of the Development of Adaptive Behaviour in All-Inhibitory Neural Network Hierarchies* Unpublished M. Phil. Thesis (Brunel University 1980).
7. Dobson, V. G. Superior accuracy of decrementing over incrementing associative networks in initially random connectivities *Journal of Intelligent Systems* **1**, 43–78 (1987).
8. Albus, J. S. A theory of cerebellar function *Math. Biosci.* **10**, 15–61 (1971).
9. Albus, J. S. *Brains Behaviour and Robotics* Peterborough N.H.: Byte (1981).
10. Steinbuch, K. Die Lernmatrix *Kybernetica* **1**, 36–35 (1961).
11. Marr, D. A theory of cerebellar function. *Journal of Physiology* **202**, 437–470 (1969).
12. Willshaw, D. J., Buneman, O. P. & Longuet-Higgins, H. C. Non-holographic associative memory *Nature (London)* **222**, 960–962 (1969).
13. Koch, C. & Poggio, T. The synaptic veto mechanism: does it underlie direction and orientation selectivity in the visual cortex? In: D. Rose & V. G. Dobson (eds). *Models of Visual Cortex* (Chichester: J. Wiley, 1985).
14. Longuet-Higgins, C. H., Willshaw, D. J. & Buneman, O. P. Theories of associative recall. *Quarterly Reviews of Biophysics* **3**(2) 223–244 (1970).
15. Gardner-Medwin, A. R. The recall of events through learning associations between their parts *Proceedings of the Royal Society (London)* B **194** 375–402 (1976).
16. Lansner, A. and Ekeberg, O. Reliability and speed of recall in an associative network *IEEE Pattern Recognition and Machine Intelligence* −7 **4**, 490–499 (1985).
17. McClelland, J. L. Resource requirements of standard and programmable nets.

In Rumelhart, D. E. & McClelland, J. L. (eds). *Parallel Distributed Processing, I* 460–486 (Cambridge Mass: MIT Press, 1986).

18. Marr, D. *Vision* (San Francisco: Freeman 1982).
19. Broadbent, D. A question of levels: comment on McClelland and Rumelhart. *Journal of Experimental Psychology* **114**, General, 189–192 (1985).
20. Rumelhart, D. E. & McClelland, J. L. PDP models and general issues in cognitive science. In Rumelhart, D. E. & McClelland, J. L. (eds). *Parallel Distributed Processing,* I 110–146 (Cambridge Mass: MIT Press 1986).
21. Maxwell, N. Methodological problems of neuroscience. In: D. Rose & V. G. Dobson (eds). *Models of Visual Cortex* 11–22 (Chichester: J. Wiley, 1985).
22. Orgel, L. E. & Crick, F. H. C. Selfish DND the ultimate parasite. *Nature* **284**, 604–607 (1980).
23. Clark, W. A. Aspects of integrated circuit hardware. In: D. Aspinal (ed). *The Microprocessor and its Applications* 1–39 (1978).
24. Singer, W. Activity-dependent self-organization in the mammalian visual cortex. In: D. Rose & V. G. Dobson (eds). *Models of Visual Cortex* 123–136 (Chichester: J. Wiley 1985).
25. Gilbert, P. F. C. & Thach, W. T. Purkinje cell activity during motor learning *Brain Research* **128** 309–328 (1977).
26. Ito, M., Miller, N. & Tongroach, P. Action of cerebellar climbing fibres during learning *Journal of Physiology* (London) **324** 113–134 (1982).
27. McNaughton, B. L. & Morris, R. G. M. Hippocampal synaptic reinforcement and information storage. *Trends in Neuroscience* **10** 408–415 (1987).
28. Lynch, G. & Baudry, M. The biochemistry of memory: a new and specific hypothesis *Science* **224** 1057–1063 (1984).
29. Hinton, G. E., Rumelhart, D. E. & McClelland, J. L. Distributed representations. In: Rumelhart, D. E. & McClelland, J. L. (eds). *Parallel Distributed Processing, I* 45–74, 77–109 (Cambridge Mass: MIT Press, 1986).
30. Groves, P. M. A theory of the functional organization of the neostiatum *Brain Research Reviews* **5**, 109–132 (1983).
31. Jones, E. G. & Hendry, S. H. C. Co-localization of GABA and neuropeptides in neocortical neurones *Trends in Neuroscience* **9** 71–76 (1986).
32. Somogyi, P. & Martin, K. A. C. Cortical circuitry underlying inhibitory processes in cat area 17. In: D. Rose & V. G. Dobson (eds). *Models of Visual Cortex* 504–513 (Chichester: J. Wiley, 1985).
33. Rolls, E. T. Functions of neuronal networks in hippocampal cortex. In: J. H. Byrne & W. O. Berry (eds). *Neural Models of Plasticity* (New York: Academic Press 1988).
34. Feldman, J. A. & Ballard, D. H. Connectionist models and their properties *Cognitive Science* **6** 205–254 (1982).

15 Generation of movement trajectories in primates and robots

Rolf Eckmiller

University of Düsseldorf, Düsseldorf, Federal Republic of Germany

Abstract

The design of brainlike machines for robot motor control ultimately requires a radical departure from the current robotics approach of implementing kinematics and internal space representation by means of software in synchronous, digital, and sequential 'general purpose' computers. Instead, neural net motor control of intelligent robots aims at hardware implementation of kinematics and internal space representation by means of self-organizing neural nets, which operate asynchronously, as fully parallel 'special purpose' analogue computers. On the basis of our present knowledge of the neural control of movements in the primate brain, recent concepts and models of artificial neural net motor control are being presented.

1. Introduction

The most prominent output of the various information processing events in the brain is represented by continuous signal time functions to control the various motor systems (eg eye, speech or arm movements). Thereby the brain continuously generates movement trajectories, namely spatio-temporal events. Each muscle is continuously being controlled by the neural impulse trains of thousands of neurons to participate (together with the other muscles controlling the same component) not only in moving but also in holding a given position.

Biological motor systems are typically redundant (with more degrees of freedom than necessary for the desired types of movement), non-linear, and non-orthogonal systems. Moreover, the neural impulse trains of individual motoneurons (controlling the dynamic contractions of a small portion of one muscle) consist of an asynchronous sequence of discrete analogue signals (impulse intervals). In case of the vertebrate oculomotor system, a given position of the eye ball (in head coordinates) is determined by six muscles. The six eye muscles in humans are controlled by about 20 000 neurons each carrying its own signal time course.

Obviously nature can (or even wants to) deal with such parallel, asynchronous, redundant, and non-linear motor systems. Novel technologies for implementing networks with many thousands of processing elements (neurons), distributed memory elements (synapses), and flexible network topology offer the opportunity to overcome some major obstacles towards building brainlike (of course at a very primitive level) machines for motor control. It is assumed that this new approach allows one to:

(a) drop the requirement for a complete mathematical description of the system (including kinematics); and

(b) replace the current software solutions using general purpose computers by self-organizing special purpose hardware solutions.

This chapter begins with a brief review of a well-studied sensorimotor system in primates: the pursuit eye movement system, in order to indicate the organization and function of biological neural motor control systems. Against this background several recent concepts and models for the development of intelligent robots are presented. It will become obvious that the design of brainlike machines for robot motor control (as for any other special purpose function) ultimately requires a radical departure from current approaches. Instead of implementing kinematics and internal space representation by means of software in synchronous, digital, and sequential computers, hardware implementations on asynchronous, analogue, and fully parallel neural computers will be required. For an interim phase, of course, most neural nets will be simulated on the available software-controlled general purpose computers.

2. Neural control of pursuit eye movements in primates

Biological motor control systems for rhythmic time functions such as controlling heartbeat, locomotion, and respiration are assumed to be based on a small number of neurons.[1,2] In these cases the time parameter is represented by oscillations and time constants of neural activity within a small neural net that is capable of internally generating the required time functions, even without sensory feedback from muscles or joints.

For quasiballistic goal-directed movements (eg reaching, pointing, saccadic eye movements) various mathematical and neural models have been proposed to explain the typical correlation between amplitude, velocity profile, and duration of the movement.[3–8]

A quite different kind of neural motor program generator is required for non-rhythmic and non-ballistic smooth movements such as speech movements, voluntary limb movements (dancing, drawing, or gesticulating), or pursuit eye movements. Biological data on neural networks that act as function generators for such smooth movement trajectories are scarce.[9-12] The neural motor program generator for such smooth movements has to meet the following requirements:

(a) continuous adjustment of the movement trajectory in order to minimize the retinal position error of the target projection relative to the fovea centralis in the central retina;
(b) learning of a desired movement trajectory;
(c) prediction of the immediate future of the trajectory;
(d) retrieval of a previously learned trajectory.

Pursuit eye movements (PEM) in primates, which will be described in more detail, serve continuous maintenance of vision of a moving target as occurs during fixation (for review see Eckmiller (1987a). It has proven useful to distinguish betweem initiation and maintenance of PEM. Since the visual system typically recognizes a new target within the first few seconds of fixation, maintenance of PEM over a longer time span is employed mainly to provide information about where the target is rather than what it is.

Retinal events during PEM
It is assumed that for initiation of PEM the neural network within the retina and the afferent visual system monitors the trajectory of the target movement on the stationary retina. Retinal position error and slip velocity relative to the centre of the fovea (functional centre of the retina with highest visual acuity) are evaluated in a still largely unknown fashion, to generate the time course of pursuit initiation, which consists of a foveating saccade (rapid, quasiballistic eye movement) superimposed on the initial portion of the smooth PEM time course. Once PEM has been initiated within 400–500 ms after target movement onset, the target projection moves in an irregular fashion on the central retina. It is interesting to note that position errors larger than 10–20 min of arc typically lead to correctional saccades during fixation, whereas position errors up to several degrees relative to the foveal centre can be tolerated during PEM. For theoretical reasons, slip velocity has to be minimal and of varying direction during maintenance of PEM because both target and eye must move with approximately the same velocity or the target projection would slip outside the fovea. Furthermore, the position error has to be continuously minimized.

PEM requires light adaptation (adaptation luminance above $5 \, \mathrm{cd \, m^{-2}}$) since the central retina including the fovea is functionally blind for small targets during dark adaptation.

A vast body of neurophysiological and anatomical data on the various

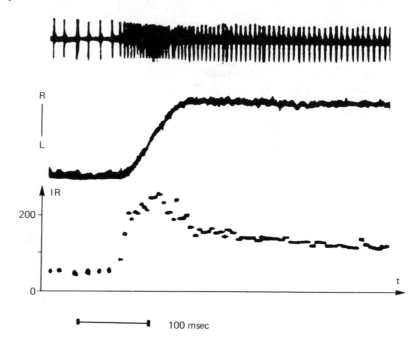

Figure 1 *Impulse train, horizontal eye position (R = right), and instantaneous impulse rate IR (imp s⁻¹) of an ocular motoneuron during a rapid eye movement in an alert monkey.*

brain regions participating in the neural control of PEM has been accumulated. Only a few points can be made here in order to indicate essential features of biological neural nets for motor control.

Fig. 1 gives a set of recording traces of the oculomotor system in an alert macaque monkey. The top trace shows the impulse sequence of a single motoneuron that participates (in parallel with about 4000 other motoneurons) in the control of the contraction time course of one eye muscle (here: the lateral rectus muscle for rightward movements of the right eye) for a rapid eye movement to the right. The horizontal eye position is indicated by the middle trace. The sequence of single dots at the bottom of Fig. 1 corresponds to the instantaneous impulse rate IR (Imp s⁻¹), namely the inverse of the impulse interval values, of the impulse train above. This example illustrates several points:

(1) Single neurons typically communicate with each other via a sequence of brief impulses of about 1 (ms) duration and encode the transmitted information as a sequence of discrete analogue values (impulse intervals).

(2) Since the propagation velocity of these impulses along the nerve fibre (axon) varies for individual neurons, synchrony of a given parallel

impulse pattern at the source (eg a nucleus or cortical region) is not
assured at the receiving structure (in our case one whole eye muscle).

(3) A single muscle typically receives several thousand individual
control signals from different motoneurons in parallel.

(4) The neural activity of these motoneurons can be considered as a
superposition of two separate control signals for eye position and eye
velocity.

Fig. 2 gives a typical recording episode during maintenance of PEM in
another, trained macaque monkey. The instantaneous impulse rate IR
(middle trace) of this motoneuron increased with eye movements to the
right since this motoneuron (as did the one in Fig. 1) participated in the
control of the right lateral rectus muscle. Top and bottom traces indicate
horizontal movements of a small visual target and the pursuing right eye
respectively. Please note the machine-like smooth time course of the
neural impulse rate, which exhibits a slight phase lead representing the
superposition of an eye position and an eye velocity signal.

Primates are capable of pursuing maneouverable targets with high
perfection and seemingly employ a neural predictor mechanism to

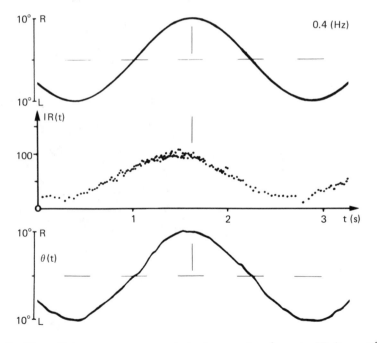

Figure 2 *Sinusoidal target movement, instantaneous impulse rate IR (imp s⁻¹) of an
ocular motoneuron, and corresponding horizontal pursuit eye movement in a trained
monkey.*

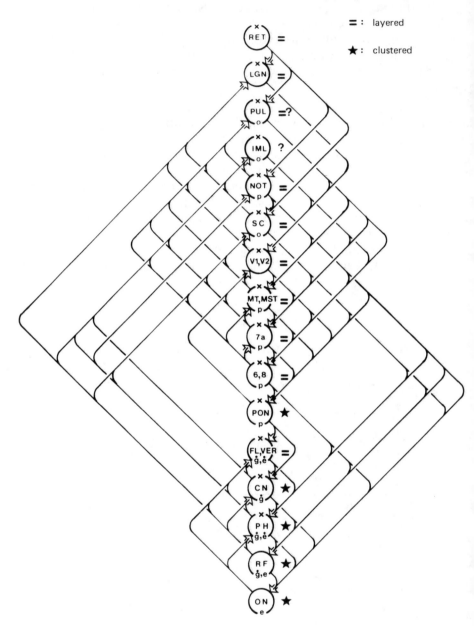

Figure 3 *Circuit diagram of the brain regions in the monkey, which contributes to the neural control of pursuit eye movements. See text for symbols.*

compensate for the time delay between retinal events and eye muscle contraction (about 150 ms) and to continue pursuit even during temporary target disappearance.

A detailed circuit diagram of those regions of the macaque's brain which participate in the neural control of pursuit eye movements is given in Fig. 3 and incorporates data from more than 400 recent publications on the structure and function of the primate pursuit system.

The different types of neural activity that were recorded in the corresponding brain regions in alert macaques are indicated by symbols, with x for afferent visual activity, o for oculomotor activity without a specific correlation during PEM, p for pursuit related oculomotor activity without specific correlation with gaze- or eye velocity, $\dot{g}$ for pursuit related activity in phase with gaze velocity, $\dot{e}$ for pursuit related activity in phase with eye velocity and, finally, e for eye position coded activity during all kinds of eye movements.

The layout of this circuit diagram, Fig. 3, indicates anatomically and neurophysiologically confirmed connections between any two brain regions, always in clockwise direction to distinguish 'down-stream' connections on the right from 'up-stream' connections on the left. Bidirectional connections between any two brain regions should not be interpreted as simple feedback, particularly since the output neurons at a given brain region are different from the input neurons and typically belong to different neural layers (in brain regions with layered architecture) or sub-clusters (in brain regions with clustered neural net architecture). The brain regions in this diagram between the retina (RET) at the sensory input and the various oculomotor nuclei (ON) as clusters of motoneurons for the six eye muscles at the motor output include the following structures (for details, see Eckmiller (1987a).

- thalamus with lateral geniculate nucleus (LGN), pulvinar (PUL), and internal medullary lamina (IML);
- pretectum with nucleus of the optic tract (NOT);
- superior colliculus (SC);
- occipital and temporal cortex with predominantly sensory areas V1, V2, MT, and MST;
- parietal cortex with area 7a;
- precentral cortex with predominantly motor areas 8, and 6aβ;
- pontine nuclei (PON);
- cerebellar cortex with flocculus (FL) and vermis (VER);
- cerebellar nuclei (CN);
- prepositus hypoglossi nucleus (PH);
- reticular formation (RF).

Please note that those brain regions indicated as having a clustered neural net architecture do not exhibit a random connectivity pattern but, rather, a complex three-dimensional network topology.

One can hypothesize that the 'first draft' of the required pursuit motor program, which may be represented by pursuit-related activity, p, is being generated within the neocortex (areas 8 and 6aß) due to its unique location within this circuit plan. The available data do not allow definite statements to be made about the specific contributions of the pathways from neocortex to cerebellum via PON versus the non-cerebellar pathways to RF and PH. However, the neurophysiological findings suggest a certain signal processing sequence:

(a) generation of a pursuit-related signal in the desired direction;

(b) generation of a gaze velocity signal;

(c) superposition of the gaze velocity signal and a head velocity signal to generate the required pursuit eye velocity signal; and finally

(d) neural integration of the eye velocity signal to generate the required eye position signal for the motoneurons.

For the purpose of comparing biological neural networks with technical neural net designs, several aspects need to be emphasized:

(1) A typical sensory-motor task such as visually guided pursuit eye movements (desirable for intelligent robots), involves a large number of brain regions that also participate in various other brain functions.

(2) Each brain region has its specific neural network architecture rather than consisting of large numbers of neurons with random connections.

(3) The specific signal processing power of the various brain regions is still largely unknown with the partial exception of the retina, the primary visual cortex (V1), and the cerebellar cortex.

(4) There is increasing evidence for the assumption that the functional neural net topology, for example of a given layered cortical structure, is not fixed as might appear from anatomical studies, but that the functional topology can be rapidly modulated by special neural subsystems.

A more descriptive model of the primate pursuit system[5,13] is given in Fig. 4. A pursuit area (PA) about the foveal centre with a radius of several degrees is indicated at the top and again at the bottom as part of the whole retina. The projection of a small target is depicted as a block (at the retinal eccentricity r). The position error signal r in the spatial domain is detected by a class of neural eccentricity detectors, the ST neurons, the output of which is interpreted as eye acceleration signal $\ddot{\Theta}$ (to change the currently generated eye velocity signal) in the temporal domain. This spatio-temporal translation (STT) signal is fed into the centre neuron C of the motor program generator (MPG) with neural lattice architecture

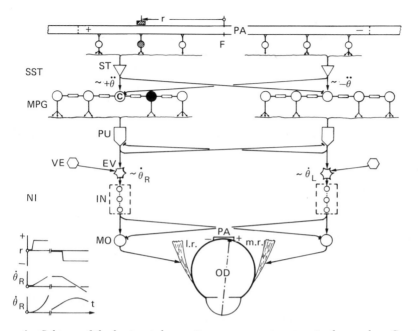

Figure 4   *Schema of the horizontal pursuit eye movement system in the monkey. See text
for abbreviations.*

(see Section 4). The MPG output is assumed to be represented by pursuit
neurons (PU), which serve as eccentricity detectors of the travelling
activity peak on the neural lattice of MPG. The neural activity of PU
neurons in alert monkeys was found to be modulated proportional to
gaze velocity $\dot{g}$ during PEM. The outputs of PU neurons and vestibular
VE neurons (encoding head velocity) converge onto eye velocity neurons
(EV), which were found to generate pursuit eye velocity signals ($\dot{e} = \dot{\Theta}$) to
the right ($\dot{\Theta}_R$) or to the left ($\dot{\Theta}_L$).

The subsequent stage for neural integration (NI) is represented in Fig.
4 by a cascade of intermediate phase neurons (IN), which feed into
motoneurons (MO), thus controlling the lateral rectus (l.r.) and the
medial rectus muscle (m.r.) for horizontal eye movements.

The inset in the bottom left of Fig. 4 indicates the relationship between
retinal position error step r being interpreted as the eye acceleration step
signal by the ST neuron, the eye velocity ramp signal $\dot{\Theta}_R$ of the EV
neuron, and the corresponding parabolic eye position signal Θ_R of the
MO neuron.

Pursuit eye movements in primates are, like most other types of
movements in vertebrates, controlled by internally generated motor
programs, which do not necessarily require (but can be guided and

313

modified by) sensory (eg visual or vestibular) information. The proposed arrangement of the pursuit system into a sequence of STT, MPG, and NI in Fig. 4 forms a valid framework. However, neurophysiological data on the function of an MPG, which also incorporates neural prediction, are presently not available.

3. Intelligent robots as federations of special purpose modules

The vertebrate central nervous system with its many distinct brain regions can be considered to be a federation of 'special purpose' neural nets (eg visual cortex, cerebellum). The hierarchy and communication lines within this federation, as well as the special purpose functions of its members, evolve during early stages of ontogeny on the basis of pre-set initial neural net architectures, learning rules for self-organization, and learning opportunities.

One could argue that it is impossible to decode (and copy) an information processing mechanism which required many millions of years to evolve. However, the rapidly growing research in the field of neural computers[14, 15] is based on the optimistic assumptions that:

(1) It is possible to technically implement various initial neural net architectures with the capability of self-organization;

(2) It is possible to find and subsequently 'imprint' learning rules that lead to robust and rapidly converging self-organization of a neural net with initial architecture or even to changes in a previously established self-organization.

(3) It is possible to generate and possibly even predict a desired information processing function by exposing an initial neural net architecture with its imprinted learning rule to a set of learning opportunities, including experience of imperfect performance in the learning phase.

(4) Following a certain amount of learning experience a given neural net is able to generalize from a limited set of correctly learned functions to an entire class of special purpose functions (eg robot pointing to any visually marked point within the entire pointing space independent of the initial robot position).

Intelligent robots are currently being conceived and designed that consist of various neural net modules with special purpose functions, such as: (a) pattern recognition; (b) associative memory; (c) internal representation of patterns and trajectories; (d) generation of motor programs; and (e) sensory as well as motor coordinate transformation.[16] Let's consider two typical tasks for intelligent robots:

(1) 'Speak what you hear' is the ability to generate sound vocalizations that closely match a newly presented unknown word.

(2) 'Draw what you see' is the ability to draw (or write) visually induced trajectories without seeing the drawing arm.

The modules eye and ear in Fig. 5 represent modules for visual and auditory trajectory detection (not necessarily including pattern recognition). Both sensory input modules receive signal time courses, which occur as spatio-temporal trajectories at the level of the corresponding sensory receptor array (retina or basilar membrane in vertebrates). For example, the vision module (eye) monitors the event of a letter 'b' being written by a teacher on the $x-y$ plane, whereas the hearing module (ear) is thought to monitor the acoustic event of a spoken 'b'.

It is assumed here that each sensory module is connected with the internal representation module via a specific sensory coordinate transformation module (depicted as a three-layered structure). The function of these coordinate transformation modules is to generate a normalized spatio-temporal trajectory to be stored in the internal representation module. For the sake of simplicity we might think of these internally stored trajectories as paths in the three-dimensional space of a neural net, along which a particle, neural activity peak, or soliton can travel with constant or varying speed. The internal representation module can store very many different trajectories, which could share neural elements in this three-dimensional network.

The subsequent generation of a corresponding movement trajectory for drawing a letter 'b' or speaking a 'b' is assumed here to require the

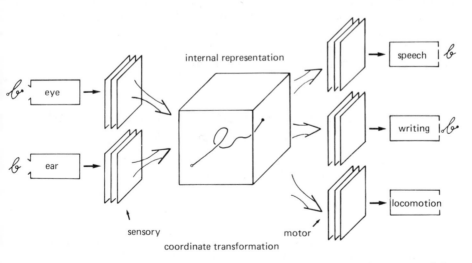

Figure 5   *Schema of an intelligent robot as a federation of various special purpose modules.*

315

activation of the appropriate stored trajectory. Please note that pattern recognition is not required for these two sensorimotor tasks. In fact, the pattern recognition process might operate on the basis of the internally stored trajectories, which are available for iterative recognition procedures after the end of the sensory event. For the purpose of motor program generation (see Section 4) an activity peak travels along the stored path on the neural net of the internal representation module with a pre-defined velocity, thus generating various time courses for the spatial components of the desired trajectory.

The desired trajectory can be thought of as the three-dimensional trajectory of the fingertips while drawing the 'b' or as the virtual centre of contraction of all speech muscles while vocalizing as 'b'.

In such typically redundant motor systems, specific motor coordinate transformation modules serve to transform the internally generated desired trajectory into a set of simultaneous control signals for the individual actuators (motors, muscles).

The schema of an intelligent robot shown in Fig. 5 emphasizes the notion that large portions of information processing in both primates and robots with neural net control involve *handling of spatio-temporal trajectories* for the purpose of detection, recognition, storage, generation, and transformation. The time parameter in these 'trajectory handling neural nets' is not defined by a central clock but is implicitly represented by the propagation velocity of neural activity within the neural net.

Obviously the general purpose digital computers presently available are not particularly well suited for trajectory handling, whereas special purpose neural nets are particularly ill-equipped for most mathematical, logical operations. This principle difference between self-organizing neural computers and software-controlled digital computers should, however, not be interpreted as a problem but rather as an indication of two application areas with minimal overlap.

4. Generation of two-dimensional trajectories with a neural triangular lattice

The generation of non-rhythmic and non-ballistic smooth velocity time courses (see Section 2) requires a flexible neural net acting as a function generator. A neural net model for internal representation and generation of two-dimensional movement trajectories including PEM, is described below.[13] This model accounts for sensory updating, prediction, and storage, and it is biologically (at least in principle) plausible, though it is not based on experimental data. The key features of this neural function generator can be summarized as follows:

(1) The velocity time course in one movement direction is represented by the trajectory of a neural activity peak (AP) that travels with constant velocity from neuron to neuron.

(2) The neural net is arranged as a neural triangular lattice (NTL) on a circular surface.

(3) The NTL output signal is proportional to the eccentricity of AP relative to the NTL centre (see Section 2 for the special case of PEM).

NTL topology
Consider a large number of identical processing elements (neurons) with analogue features. These neurons are arranged in a neural triangular lattice (NTL), in which they are connected only to their six immediate neighbours.

Such a NTL with a radius of 50 neurons from the NTL centre to its periphery would consist of about 8000 neurons. The connectivity strength c_T of tangential synaptic connections between neurons located along concentric circles about the NTL centre is slightly larger than c_R for radial synapses. Each neuron has a sub-threshold potential, P, similar to the membrane potential of biological neurons; P is always assumed to represent the average of the potential values of all immediate neighbouring neurons due to continuous equilibration of possible potential gradients via neural connections. External potential changes can only be applied to the NTL centre, thus yielding a centre symmetrical potential field. Such an input-dependent potential field can be thought of as an elastic circular membrane whose centre is being pushed up or down.

NTL dynamics
A supra-threshold activity peak (AP) can be initiated (or extinguished) only at the NTL centre, and becomes superimposed on the potential field. For the sake of simplicity AP can be thought of as a neural action potential[17] or a soliton,[18] which travels away from the NTL centre (following the potential field gradient during a positive potential input) in the same angular direction (3 o'clock).

AP travels with constant propagation velocity from one neuron to one of its neighbours, and its activity does not otherwise spread. Every time AP arrives at a neuron, a decision has to be made concerning its next destination. Due to certain transient constraints imposed on the adjacent synapses by the travelling AP, only those three of the six neighbouring neurons can be selected that are located in forward (straight, right, or left) continuation of the trajectory. The decision as to which of the three possible target neurons is selected, is based on a combined evaluation of the connectivity strength c and the potential gradient dP/dR between the neighbouring neurons. If the potential field P is flat throughout the NTL,

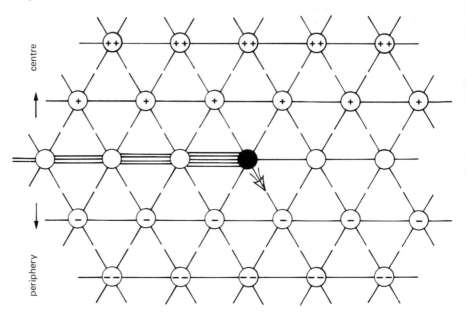

Figure 6   *Portion of a neural triangular lattice (NTL) with a travelling activity peak (AP).*

AP will select the tangentially adjacent neuron, since c_T is slightly larger than c_R for radial connections. In case of a positive potential input at the NTL centre, however, the potential field exhibits a radial gradient towards the periphery, which in effect pulls AP towards the NTL periphery (equivalent to higher velocities at the NTL output). Similarly, a negative input attracts AP towards the centre.

A portion of the NTL together with AP (filled circle) and the last portion of the memory trace of its trajectory is shown in Fig. 6. Horizontal connections in Fig. 6 are assumed to follow circles about the NTL centre. AP had travelled from the left and is about to move towards the NTL periphery due to an assumed sudden positive step input at the NTL centre.

A memory trace of the most recently traversed portion of the trajectory is created by means of a temporary increase of the connectivity strength as indicated by the number of connecting lines in Fig. 6. It is assumed that the memory trace, which gradually fades with a time constant of about 1 s, serves as a trajectory guide for subsequent movements, for example during post-pursuit eye movements after sudden target disappearance and for neural prediction during pursuit of a periodically moving target. Once a memory trace exists, it can be used to reduce the amount of time necessary for updating during periodical movements in one dimension

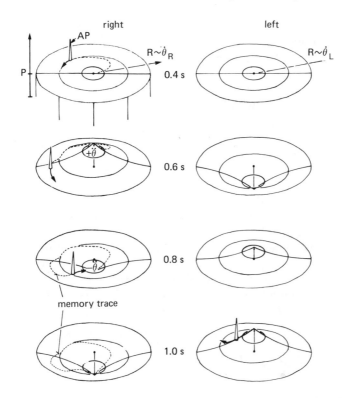

Figure 7   *Development of a trajectory of a travelling AP on a pair of NTLs encoding velocity to the right or to the left at four subsequent times. The membrane-like NTL surfaces indicate the potential fields P.*

(eg horizontal), which are generated by repeated creation of the same alternating velocity trajectories on the two velocity NTLs (Fig. 7).

The potential fields on the two velocity NTLs including the location of AP and the gradually increasing memory trace are shown in Fig. 7 at four successive times. AP trajectories always start and end in the NTL centre, which corresponds to zero velocity. When the NTL input signal changes from zero to a positive or negative value, the topology of the two NTLs changes by equal amounts in opposite directions. It is assumed here that AP had been initiated in the centre of the NTL for velocities to the right (left-half of Fig. 7) at time zero and was travelling towards the periphery (starting in the 3 o'clock direction) due to a positive input. The memory trace is indicated as a dotted line. At 0.4 s AP is travelling on a circle due to the flat potential field (zero input). At 0.6 s AP travels towards the periphery in response to a positive input and at 0.8 s towards the centre due to a negative input. Please note that the potential field of the other

319

NTL is always identical except for the sign and the absence of an AP. At 1.0 s AP had already reached the centre of the NTL and became extinguished there. Simultaneously, AP became initiated at the opposite NTL for velocities to the left (right-half of Fig. 7) and is now travelling towards the periphery. The radial location of AP is continuously being monitored by neurons, which serve as eccentricity detectors (see Fig. 4).

The correlation between two typical velocity time courses $\dot{\Theta}(t)$ and the corresponding trajectories on an NTL are depicted in Fig. 8. The following assumptions have been made for this example: the velocity function generator should be able to generate any smooth velocity time course for velocities up to $50° \, s^{-1}$ and accelerations up to $200° \, s^{-2}$.

The constant time it takes for AP to travel from one neuron to the selected neighbour is $T = 5$ ms, which corresponds to a velocity $v = 200$ neurons per second. The direct radial distance between the centre and the circular NTL periphery border shall be covered by 50 neurons.

Under these assumptions, $\dot{\Theta}_1(t)$ in Fig. 8 with constant acceleration yields a logarithmic spiral as an NTL trajectory, whereas the sinusoidal half-cycle $\dot{\Theta}_2(t)$ corresponds to a circular trajectory. The equations for these two trajectories are:

$$\dot{\Theta}_1(t) = 100 \times t + 1; \quad \phi_1(t) = 1.73 \times \ln \dot{\Theta}_1,$$
$$\dot{\Theta}_2(t) = 50 \times \sin 4t; \quad \phi_2(t) = 4t.$$

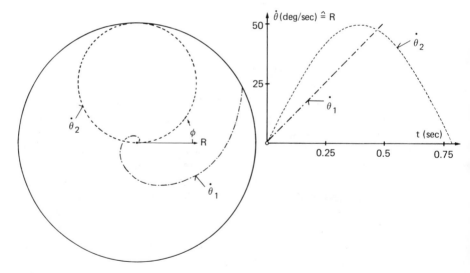

Figure 8   *Two examples for the representation of two velocity time functions* Θ *(right diagram) as trajectories NTL (left).*

The general relation between the polar coordinates $R(t)$, $\phi(t)$ of a trajectory and propagation velocity v of AP is given by the equation:

$$(R\,d\phi)^2 + (dR)^2 = (v \times dt)^2.$$

Mechanism for learning and retrieval of trajectories

The detailed synaptic connectivity pattern of three adjacent NTL neurons is shown in Fig. 9 to describe the architecture of an element of this triangular lattice. NTL neurons (large open circles with axon-like projections and synapses) are reciprocally connected via synapses. Two additional neurons with pre-synaptic synapses (synapse on another synapse), a pattern retrieval neuron (PR) and a velocity modulation neuron (VM) have contacts with the NTL. The PR neuron belongs to a large population of identical PR neurons for storage and retrieval of entire trajectories that always begin and end in the NTL centre. It is assumed that each PR neuron has excitatory synapses (small circles) on each of the NTL synapses. In contrast, the VM neuron has inibitory synapses (depicted as open blocks) on each of the NTL synapses in order to control the propagation velocity v of AP on the NTL.

When a given trajectory has to be learned (stored), while being

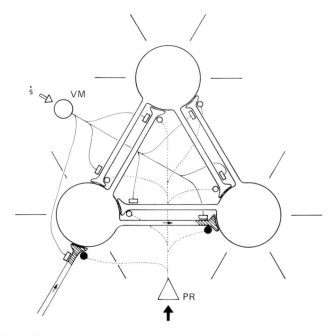

Figure 9   *Neural net architecture of three adjacent NTL neurons, together with a pattern retrieval (PR) neuron and a velocity modulation (VM) neuron.*

generated by means of input modulation of the potential field, one of the PR neurons (that had not been used before) is first selected for this task, as indicated by the big arrow.

In the present example it is assumed that AP travels along a given trajectory (from bottom left to right) including the two hatched NTL synapses in Fig. 9. The connectivity strength of those few synapses, which belong to the selected PR neuron and have a pre-synaptic connection with the NTL synapses along the AP trajectory (here, the two hatched synapses) becomes permanently increased. This process is assumed here to represent learning (memory) and is indicated by an enlargement of the two corresponding PR synapses (filled circles). The synapse connectivity of the other synapses as well as of all synapses of the non-selected PR neurons remains low (except for those synapses that were involved in storing other trajectories). In this way a single PR neuron stores one trajectory during the process of its first generation on the NTL. The later retrieval of this permanently stored trajectory is implemented by a brief activation pulse for the corresponding PR neuron. This activation pulse is assumed to yield a strong temporary enhancement of those NTL synapses that compose the desired trajectory, thus creating a memory trace. Immediately afterwards, AP becomes initiated in the NTL centre. AP travels (although the potential input to the NTL centre is zero) along this temporarily existing memory trace, as in the groove of a record. Again the NTL output monitors the radial AP distance during the constant propagation velocity of AP and thereby generates the previously stored velocity time function $R(t) \sim \dot{\Theta}(t)$.

The concept of a motor program generator with NTL topology and a travelling AP incorporates elements of soliton theory[18] and of cellular automata theory.[19]

5. Learning to draw visually monitored 2-dimensional trajectories

The NTL function generator (Figs. 6–9) is equipped with mechanisms for storage and retrieval of numerous smooth velocity time courses. A pair of NTLs is required to generate one-dimensional movements in both directions plus subsequent neural integrators (see Fig. 4) to generate various movement trajectories. However, the NTL concept can be further optimized to allow for the generation of two-dimensional trajectories. Let's consider an intelligent robot with neural net modules (Fig. 5), which has to learn how to draw visually monitored patterns. The proposed process is schematically demonstrated in Fig. 10 by means of four diagrams.[20] The upper left diagram gives a typical writing trajectory

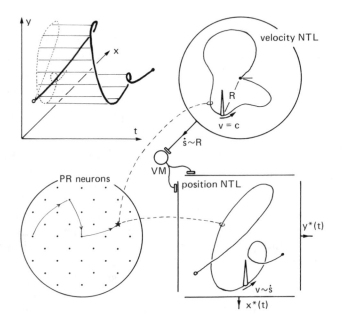

Figure 10   *Schema for generation of a drawing movement trajectory for a letter 'b' by means of a velocity NTL and a position NTL.*

for letter 'b' in the $x-y$ plane with start at the open circle and stop at the filled circle. It is assumed that the intelligent robot has the following modules available:

(1) Vision module with retinotopic internal representation and with neural detectors of target eccentricity relative to the fovea (position error), as well as of target slip velocity and target slip acceleration. The target is the tip of a writing element, which the teacher uses to write (draw) on the $x-y$ plane.

(2) Velocity NTL with potential input at the NTL centre as shown in the upper right of Fig. 10. AP travels with constant velocity $v = c$.

(3) Position NTL (lower right in Fig. 10) with a velocity modulation (VM) neuron at the input to modulate the travel velocity of AP. In this case the AP position on the NTL is not monitored as radial distance from the NTL centre but as horizontal (x^*) and vertical (y^*) eccentricity. The VM neuron has a tonic activity, which normally inhibits AP movement on the position NTL. However, the output of the velocity NTL inhibits the VM neuron activity, thus yielding a propagation velocity of AP on the position NTL proportional to the output signal of the velocity NTL.

323

Learning and subsequent drawing or writing of a two-dimensional trajectory such as letter 'b' consist of the following functions:

(1) Teacher draws letter 'b' with the writing element in x–y plane.

(2) Vision module detects acceleration $\ddot{s}$ of writing element in the direction of drawing trajectory $s(t)$ and uses $\ddot{s}(t)$ to modulate the potential input of the velocity NTL. This operation yields a velocity $\dot{s}(t)$, which trajectory is immediately stored by a selected PR neuron (depicted as star in group of PR neurons; lower left in Fig. 10).

(3) Upon completion of the teacher's drawing task, the vision module projects the entire pattern of letter 'b' onto the position NTL, where the same selected PR neuron (having synapses on both NTLs) stores the pattern.

(4) If the robot has to draw the newly stored letter 'b' sometime later, the corresponding PR neuron (star) becomes briefly activated, thus generating the memory traces on both NTLs. The start location of AP on the position NTL is not the centre but the start position (open circle) of the trajectory for letter 'b'. The simultaneously travelling APs on both NTLs generate the appropriate horizontal and vertical components of the desired trajectory to drive a two-dimensional drawing device (eg x–y plotter).

Please note that this arrangement does not require a neural integrator and that the spatial parameters of the trajectory are stored on the position NTL, whereas the temporal aspects are stored separately on the velocity NTL. This important concept can be compared with the situation of a car on a race track, in which the driver is only told how to change his speed with time, but not how the track is formed. Only when he actually drives along the race track (equivalent to a two-dimensional path), the spatio-temporal trajectory unfolds and can be monitored by two orthogonally placed eccentricity detectors.

6. Future research on neural net motor control of intelligent robots

The following considerations are based on the assumption that the schema in Fig. 5 is realistic for biological sensorimotor systems and is also feasible for robots with neural net modules. The relevant modules for motor control are:

(a) internal representation of external space and of desired movement trajectories in real time (abbreviated as: neural space net); and

(b) kinematics representation and transformation of desired movement trajectories into a set of simultaneous control signals for the corresponding actuators in real time (abbreviated as: neural kinematics net).

The research goal for the next decade is the development of neural space nets and neural kinematics nets for the control of redundant, nonlinear, and non-orthogonal motor systems. Such future systems should have the following main features:

(a) acquisition of the required knowledge regarding external space and kinematics by means of self-organization during a learning phase;

(b) ability to consider obstacles within the grasping space for trajectory planning;

(c) adaptation to partial functional errors and defects or environment changes (eg load, friction, etc).

Progress in these developments will depend on our detailed knowledge of the corresponding modules in the vertebrate brain as well as on the availability of powerful simulation tools either as software for self-organizing virtual neural nets with programmable architecture (eg neural net workstation), or as hardware for large numbers of neurons and adaptive synapses with computer-controlled network topology.

Various research groups have recently begun to consider self-organization for knowledge acquisition in functionally flexible neural nets by using a combination of initial net topology, learning rules and learning opportunities.[20,21,16,22-26] It can be expected that this approach will soon expand and yield important advances not only in the area of industrial robots but also in the field of prosthetics.

References

1. Grillner, S. & Wallen, P. Central pattern generators for locomotion, with special reference to vertebrates, *Ann. Rev. Neurosci.* **8**, 233–261 (1985).
2. Selvertson, A. I., (ed.) *Model Neural Networks and Behaviour* (NY: Plenum Press, 1985).
3. Arbib, M. A. Perceptual structures and distributed motor control. In Brookhart, J. M., Mountcastle, V. B. & Brooks, V. B. (eds.), *Handbook of Physiology*, Section 1: The nervous system, Vol. II, Motor control, part 2, pp. 1449–1480 (Baltimore, MD: Williams & Wilkins, 1981).
4. Berkinblit, M. B., Feldman, A. G. & Fukson, O. I. Adaptability of innate motor patterns and motor control mechanisms, *Behav. and Brain Sci.* **9**, 585–638 (1986).
5. Eckmiller, R. Neural control of foveal pursuit versus saccadic eye movements in primates—single-unit data and models, *IEEE Trans. on Systems, Man and Cybern.* **SMC-13**, 980–989 (1983).
6. Haken, H., Kelso, J. A. S. & Bunz, H. A theoretical model of phase transitions in human hand movements, *Biol. Cybern.* **51**, 347–356 (1985).
7. Hogan, N. An organizing principle for a class of voluntary movements, *J. Neurosci.* **4**, 2745–2754 (1984).
8. Miles, F. A. & Evarts, E. V. Concepts of motor organization, *Ann. Rev. Psychol.* **30**, 327–362 (1979).

9. Baron, R. J. The high-level control of movements. In Baron, R. J. (ed.) *The Cerebral Computer—An Introduction to the Computational Structure of the Human Brain* pp. 402–452 (Hillsdale, NJ: Lawrence Erlbaum Publ., 1987).

10. Eckmiller, R. Neural control of pursuit eye movements, *Physiol. Rev.* **67**, 797–857 (1987*a*).

11. Morasso, P. & Mussa Ivaldi, F. A. Trajectory formation and handwriting: a computational model, *Biol. Cybern.* **45**, 131–142 (1982).

12. Soechting, J. F., Lacquaniti, F. & Terzuolo, C. A. Coordination of arm movements in three-dimensional space. Sensorimotor mapping during drawing movement, *Neurosci.* **17**, 295–311 (1986).

13. Eckmiller, R. Computational model of the motor program generator for pursuit, *J. Neurosci. Meth.* **21**, 127–138 (1987*b*).

14. Eckmiller, R. & v. d. Malsburg, C. (eds.) *Neural Computers* (Heidelberg: Springer Verlag, 1988).

15. Feldman, J. A. & Ballard, D. H. Connectionist models and their properties, *Cognitive Sci.* **6**, 205–254 (1982).

16. Eckmiller, R. Neural networks for motor program generation. In Eckmiller, R. & Malsburg, C. v. d. (eds.), *Neural Computers* pp. 359–370 (Heidelberg: Springer Verlag, 1988).

17. Rall, W. Core conductor theory and cable properties of neurons. In Kandel, E. (ed.), *Handbook of Physiology, The Nervous System I* Vol. 1, part 1, pp. 39–97 (Baltimore, MD: Williams & Wilkins, 1977).

18. Lamb, G. L. jr. *Elements of Soliton Theory*. (NY: John Wiley & Sons, 1980).

19. Toffoli, T. & Margolus, N. *Cellular Automata Machines—A New Environment for Modeling* (Cambridge Mass: MIT Press, 1987).

20. Albus, J. S. Mechanisms of planning and problem solving in the brain, *Math. Biosci.* **45**, 247–293 (1979).

21. Barhen, J., Dress, W. B. & Jorgensen, C. C. Applications of concurrent neuromorphic algorithms for autonomous robots. In Eckmiller, R. & Malsburg, C. v. d. (eds.), *Neural Computers* pp. 321–333 (Heidelberg: Springer Verlag, 1988).

22. Kawato, M., Furukawa, K. & Suzuki, R. A hierarchical neural-network model for control and learning of voluntary movement, *Biol. Cybern.* **56**, 1–17 (1987).

23. Kuperstein, M. Adaptive visual-motor coordination in multijoint robots using parallel architecture. In *IEEE Int. Conf. on Robotics and Automation*, Vol. 3, pp. 1595–1602 (San Diego: SOS Publ., 1987).

24. Pellionisz, A. & Llinas, R. Tensor network theory of the metaorganization of functional geometries in the central nervous system, *Neurosci.* **16**, 245–273 (1985).

25. Ritter, H. & Schulten, K. Extending Kohonen's self-organizing mapping algorithm to learn ballistic movements. In Eckmiller, R. & Malsburg, C. v. d. (eds.), *Neural Computers* pp. 393–403 (Heidelberg: Springer Verlag, 1988).

26. Eckmiller, R. Neural network mechanisms for generation and learning of motor programs. In *Proc. IEEE First Int. Conf. on Neural Networks*, Vol. IV, pp. 545–550 (San Diego: SOS Publ., 1987*c*).

Part IV
The PDP Perspective

16 A review of parallel distributed processing

I. Aleksander

Department of Electrical Engineering, Imperial College, London, UK

Abstract

Undoubtedly the most influential text in neural computing (or connectionism) has been that partly written by and edited by David Rumelhart and Jay McClelland on behalf of the 'Parallel Distributing Processing' Group in the USA. In contrast with the ring of engineering in the title, the sub-title 'Explorations in the Microstructures of Cognition', reveals the common interest of the 16 members of this group. I have set out to review in detail what is said in the 26 or so chapters of these two volumes. There are several reasons for this, but my intention is not to prevent anyone reading the volumes themselves. The main reason is diametrically opposite: I have had great pleasure in reading these books, particularly as they have made clear many issues that have occupied my mind over the last 20 years or so. So I hope that the short reviews will act as appetizers which direct the reader to the detailed ideas contained in the books. Furthermore, the authors of this present book make copious references to PDP chapters, and it is for completeness that it is necessary to make some of this material available.

But the review is not a passive paraphrase. It is mostly my own understanding of the subject matter, which comes from a background of design and engineering of neural systems for application rather than brain modelling. I have also added personal comments not expressed in PDP books, in square brackets, where I felt it necessary.

PART I. The PDP perspective

1. The appeal of parallel distributed processing (McClelland, Rumelhart & Hinton)

The question asked here is 'why is PDP an alternative mode of artificial intelligence and why is it attractive'? The answer has a two-pronged nature. First, when we compare human problem solving with problem solving by conventional AI methodology, we are struck by the inherent parallelism of the human way and the serial nature of the AI way. But it is more than just parallelism, it is the ability of the human brain to handle a group of constraints simultaneously. Parallel distributed processing gives physical life to this notion by allowing a computational unit for each constraint (in the first instance).

Several examples are given, but perhaps the most dramatic one is the way in which a typist, on thinking of a particular word, adjusts the fingers and hand into an optimal configuration before activating the fingers. The PDP computational model is one that contains a computational unit for each letter of the alphabet, groups of which form stable activation patterns with units that represent words. The former units drive the fingers. A given word activates a word unit which is rapidly formed into a pattern of stable activity with the appropriate letter units which, in turn, activate the fingers. Other examples drawn from the literature include the constraint-propagation method of Marr & Poggio which computes depth in random-dot stereoscopic images.[1]

The second part of the two-pronged appeal is the emergent behaviour of neural nets: neurons 'come to some consensus' by exercising inhibitory and excitatory influences on each other and arriving at some stable firing state or repeated sequence of firing states. The argument here is that PDP is not only more like human information processing from an introspective stance, but also from an anatomical one.

[It may be an error to relate these two aspects too readily by imagining that there is a single neuron for each concept that the brain can handle. The implication of PDP is that one-neuron-per-concept may well be an upper bound in the thinking capacity of the brain. However (and this is pointed out in the chapter) a concept could always involve the firing patterns of a *group* of neurons.] Much of this sounds like associative memory. But we are warned by the authors that the PDP model has much more interesting emerging properties than a purposely designed hardware associative store: the main one is that it can create concepts within a given database without these being explicitly stated.

Learning is highlighted as the main mode of knowledge acquisition in such systems and examples are given of the way in which a set of input nodes can be made to influence a pattern of a set of output nodes. This uses the familiar sum-of ((inputs) × (weights)) formulation. The authors draw attention to the fact that algorithm design for weight alteration, given examples of the given task, is a fruitful area for research.

The chapter ends with a list of authors who have mostly influenced the PDP group and rightly draws attention to the fact that PDP has been of interest for an indefinite period of time.

2. A general framework for parallel distributed processing (Rumelhart, Hinton & McClelland)

This definitional chapter largely lays down terms which are either used or abused in the remainder of the two volumes. The authors extol the virtues of having a general framework into which the many variants of neural net research can be placed. [The same objective was sought by the present author in Chapter 8 of this book. The reader may find it interesting to compare the differences in the generality: Rumelhart's stemming from linear algebra and Aleksander's stemming from logic.] The definitions given in Rumelhart's framework are summarized here.

A set of processing units, N

This is the starting point which defines a network: N processing units. No assumption is made about the concepts represented by these units: it could be made from one unit per concept. In some systems units can be of three types—*input*, *output* and *invisible*. The invisible units provide communication links between input and output units, the task of the system being to translate the input patterns into output patterns.

The state of activation, a(t)

Each unit, at every point in time receives a composite signal from some pre-defined set of signals. This signal is said to be composite as it is made up of some combination of output signals for other nodes. The N-element vector of such signals is the state of activation. Different models make different assumptions about the set of values from which the signals may be drawn.

Output of the units: $o_i(t)$

Each unit performs some variable function between its input and its output if $a_i(t)$ is the subset of $\mathbf{a}(t)$ related to the input of unit i, the output is a function:

$$o_i(t) = f(a_i(t)).$$

Sometimes the output is assumed to be stochastic.

The pattern of connectivity, W

Units are connected to one another through multiplicative weights, w_{ij} connecting i to j. If unit i has output $o_i(t)$ and is connected to j via w_{ij}, j receives a signal $w_{ij} x o_i(t)$; $\mathbf{W}$ is the complete matrix of such connections. Again different models make different assumptions about the range of values from which w_{ij} may be drawn. Negative values are seen as being inhibitory, and positive ones excitatory.

The rule of propagation

If net j is the total input (or net input [unfortunate choice]) arriving at unit j, then **net** is the vector of all such inputs. In simple cases

$$\text{net} = \mathbf{W} \cdot \mathbf{o}(t).$$

Activation rule, F
This seeks to compute the new $\mathbf{a}(t)$. In general

$$\mathbf{a}(t+1) = \mathbf{F}(\mathbf{a}(t), \text{net}(t)).$$

Modifying patterns of connectivity as a function of experience, Δw_{ij}
This mostly refers to rules for modifying $\mathbf{W}$ in order to achieve desired time sequences for $\mathbf{o}(t)$. Often this may be something like

$$\Delta w_{ij} = \eta a_j o_j.$$

η is a constant representing 'learning rate'.

Representing the environment
This is a representation of the probabilities of occurrence of certain inputs impinging on the whole net from outside the net. This could be some stationary probability distribution function.

Pattern association
This is the process of associating an *output* with given *inputs*. It usually involves a 'teaching input' which acts on the connectivity matrix in such a way as to obtain the desired output.

Auto-association
The process of creating stable patterns of $\mathbf{o}(t)$ is called auto-association. The usual way of using such a system is for it to re-create a complete $\mathbf{o}(t)$ from a set of such trained $\mathbf{o}(t)$s, given a frequent of $\mathbf{o}(t)$.

Bottom-up processing
This refers to a net structure which only allows signal flows from the input layer, through ordered layers *towards* the output layer.

Top-down processing
This is the reverse of the previous definition.

Interactive models
This, too, refers to layers and systems where each layer interacts with neighbouring layers but not those further afield.

Simple linear models
These communicate in real numbers without restriction, such that

$$o_j(t) = a_j(t).$$

They have the limitation of being single-layer systems only (as multi-layer schemes are equivalent to single-layer ones). This essentially removes the possibility of intermediate computations that are important in the systems which follow.

Linear threshold units
By adding a threshold to a linear summation of the input as part of the activation function, much of the strength and computational prowess of the PDP model is achieved (through the ability to take local decisions based on the state of activation of the entire net).

[Here the authors reply to the erroneous assessment made in 1969 by Minsky & Papert who missed the possibility of considering multi-layered systems.[2]]

Brain state in a box
This refers mainly to the work of Anderson & Mozer who limited the signalling between neurons to real number in the interval $(-1, 1)$.[3] The activation rule is

$$a_j(t+1) = a_j(t) + \sum w_{ij} a_i(t).$$

This is clamped to ± 1. Clearly, it implies feedback in each neuron. This ensures that a run ends with all the nodes with limit values, that is, at the corners of a state-space hypercube (hence the reference to a box).

Thermodynamic models
This refers to the elegant work by Hinton (Section 6 of this chapter) with the Boltzmann machine and Smolensky's *harmony theory* (Section 7 of this chapter). The activation function is stochastic as follows:

$$p(a_i(t) = 1) = \frac{1}{1 + e^{-(\sum_j w_{ij} a_j + \eta_i - \theta_i)/T}},$$

where η_i is an input from outside the system, θ_i is the threshold and T is the all-important parameter called temperature which, as T is reduced, fixes the logic of the unit which, as $T \neq 0$, endows the unit with a 'search' facility that can be at its highest during early stages of training or retrieval. This is discussed later.

Interactive activation
Specifically used to simulate a word-association task studied by Rumelhart & McClelland (Sections 17 and 18 of this chapter), this scheme is similar to the 'state in a box', but uses local feedback at nodes which decays with time.

Sigma–pi units
Here a node may receive a signal at a branch which is a *product* of another node output and then performs a usual weighted sum over several of these. This has the property of allowing a node output

effectively to alter the weight of a connection between two other nodes. [The logical formulation shown in Chapter 8 of this book is such as to include sigma and sigma–pi functions as part of its structure.]

3. Distributed representations (Hinton, McClelland & Rumelhart)

In a parallel distributed system, concepts may be represented in a *local* way (one concept per processing unit) or in a *distributed* way where a concept is represented by the combined firing patterns of several units. This chapter extols the virtues of the latter. Although this is less familiar to computer scientists than the local representation, it is responsible for some of the most powerful aspects of connectionism.

Connections = Microinferences
The language of AI engineering may be used to help the computer scientist understand the concept of a 'distributed representation'. Each node may be viewed as a 'microfeature' of an item, the connection strengths being microinferences between microfeatures. An 'item' is stored by adjusting the connection strengths to allow the microfeatures of that item to co-exist. This violates plausible microinferences less than distortion of this pattern. Several items may be stored by finding microinferences that support them all. Recall is, then, a process providing some microfeatures as cues, which force the net to find the rest as being the only ones that satisfy the given constraints and the stored inference–connection strengths.

By adjusting weights a little at a time and presenting the collection of items over and over again, a useful system will converge on meaningful inferences–connection strengths where these are supported by the entire collection. Contradictory inferences will cancel each other out. This gives the system a power of generalization akin to what seems to be happening in the human brain. New 'items' only alter some of the inferences. For example, two items such as

> *A chimpanzee is an ape and likes onions.*
> *A gorilla is an ape and likes onions.*

will set up inputs that allow the clues '*x* is an ape' to build up a pattern among the remaining microfeatures which has the meaning 'likes onions'. This does not prevent the possibility of building up other systems of microfeatures for

> *A baboon is an ape and does not like onions.*

and

> *A gibbon is an ape and does not like onions.*

Knowledge distributed in a network in this way can continuously be refined.

Coding

Part of the science of distributed representation is to assess the pros and cons of local versus distributed schemes. Distributed schemes win over local ones when it comes to adding new items to the net. In the local case a new unit needs to be found for every new item, whereas in the distributed case it is merely a matter of weight adjustment. Clearly, the latter must collapse at some stage by weakening the stability of the net to the point of uselessness, but the degradation is gentle.

The other side of this coin is the difficulty of selecting the appropriate coding, particularly, as the authors point out, because the idea of using a unit for each discriminable feature (eg position, orientation, etc.) leads to undesirable ambiguities.

Coarse coding schemes are proposed which essentially try to distribute the representations in state space so as to maximize the accuracy for a given number of units. A section on the encoding of non-continuous variables concludes that a target for learning schemes may well be the discovery of appropriate distributed representations.

Contrary to intuition ...

Much of the connectionist literature discusses word-association networks where input layers are sub-word units such as graphetics. Middle layers have a unit per word where a third layer has one unit per semantic feature (such as 'animate' 'hairy', etc.). These are clear examples of *local* coding in the middle layer and the thrust of the latter part of this chapter is to show that this is not necessary. A distributed representation in the central layer, although requiring a probabilistic assessment, is shown to provide arbitrary links between graphemes and semantic units. A successful experiment is described with 30 units in the graphemes layer, 30 units in the semantic layer and 20 units in the middle layer.

The chapter ends with a comment on the relationship between structured knowledge representations such as frames, schemas and semantic nets, which have emerged from the classical artificial intelligence paradigm, and the notion of a distributed representation. The message is the same as before: distributed representation *seems* to be unsuitable, because its function is not as obvious as that of local representation. There is encouragement to look at the greater detail at Chapter 14, as the distributed representations offers promise of rapid access to much knowledge, avoiding the search problems found in AI.

[Although this chapter contains some useful hints on how one could assess a given net in terms of its capacity for storing distributed representations, much fundamental work is still needed before concepts such as 'layering' and 'interaction' can become the tools for the design of a system of knowledge representation.]

4. PDP models and general issues cognitive science (Rumelhart & McClelland)

Naturally, the PDP approach has had its critics. This chapter aims to handle some of the criticisms, particularly on the appropriateness of choosing PDP as a modelling paradigm for cognitive science (that is, the science of information processing in human beings).

Perceptron limitations

Here the objections raised by Minsky & Papert in 1969[2] to neural computing are met fairly and squarely. The first objection was a mathematical demonstration of the limitations of a 'perceptron' (a single-layer neural net where each processing element has a partial view of the 'image' to be processed). The answer to this criticism is that it applies only to the single-layer class which, indeed, is limited. This is not so for the multi-layer and feedback systems which are the essence of the PDP approach. The second objection was probably Minsky & Papert's greatest error: they argued that there is no value in multi-layered systems—that they are as vacuous as a conventional computer and therefore working with conventional computers was the thing to do. The PDP reply is simple: this objection misses the two major sources of exciting emergent properties—self-organization of powerful internal representations and speed in answering queries without the need for engineering search rules. The third objection was a lack of suitable training methods where multilayered and feedback systems were to be created. Again, this is what PDP is all about: the discovery of general and powerful training schemes, some of which were being discovered but not appreciated in 1969 (Rosenblatt's & Widrow's work).

[The WISARD, an early commercial system loosely based on neural net principles, is constrained by the first limitation above (the others do not apply as it is a single-layer device). This does not prevent it from solving a large variety of practical image recognition tasks. See Chapter 2 of this book for references.]

Rotation and translation invariance

To a given net where each element has a limited view of an input stimulus, any change (eg rotation) in the input stimulus is a new stimulus. In conventional computing this is easily overcome by normalizing algorithms. Here it is argued that Hinton's four-net mode (net 1 for retino-centric images, net 2 for actions that represent translations and relations, net 3 for canonical features, and net 4 for the objects themselves) shows a way forward for a net to learn whether an input needs to be normalized to be recognized.

[Too much may be made of the human's automatic application of invariance 'an A is still an A if rotated through 45°. The rebuttal to this is that a + changes meaning if rotated through 45°. *So when to apply and not apply normalization is a learnt* function. This supports the PDP argument.]

Lack of recursion
Conventional computer models exist which will easily parse surface strings to considerable nesting depths. The objection that this cannot be done with neural net models is simply wrong.

[It is well known that neural nets are Turing Machine equivalent so many arguments of this kind can be demolished *ab initio.*] Indeed, the failure of conventional computing schemes to get to grips with natural language, which comes so easily to people equipped only with PDP systems in their heads, is an encouragement to pursue this task with artificial neural models (as in Chapter 19 of PDP and others in this book).

PDP models are not cognitive
AI methodology has strongly influenced cognitive scientists to cast their models of human thought processes around the following of explicit rules. That these cannot be found in PDP models is a false objection. PDP models adapt their behaviour to become regular and effective. In this sense it could be said that examining how *rules* emerge in such models may be closer to studying human cognitive processes than simply writing such rules into an AI programme.

The level of PDP theory
During the too-brief sojourn at MIT prior to his death, David Marr suggested that cognitive tasks must be understood at three levels: a computational analysis of the task itself; a set of algorithms that represent the task; and the hardware implementation of the algorithm. PDP has been criticized for develping cognitive theory at the third, implementation, level which does not easily map into higher levels. The authors, however, draw attention to the fact that PDP operates in a different computational domain that possesses the twin attributes of being more plausible than conventional computing as a model for living organisms, and of possessing emergent properties which, as in living things, and contrary to conventional computing, are a function of *structure*. Seeing this as *implementation* is missing the point: PDP simply offers an alternative, perhaps more appropriate, computational domain for discussing cognition.

There is another 'level' type of criticism in the sense that in conventional computing the process of compiling or interpreting creates a gulf between the language at the high level (say Pascal) and routine hardware behaviour at the lower level. Again, uninformed critics have argued that PDP is too concerned with the run-time behaviour of its hardware. The truth is, however, that the gap between the problem statement and network behaviour is much closer in PDP than in conventional computing. Another way of putting it is that the hardware is better attuned to the higher level and high-level PDP descriptions are approximations of what is happening at the lower level. This is an advantage.

[Old habits die hard—certainly those interested in functional programming are aware of the awkward gap between a statement of what needs to be done and what is actually being carried out at the hardware level. Had PDP been here first, conventional computing might look quite implausible and awkward. There is no virtue in having a heap of levels.]

Is PDP reductionist?

Another accusation is that talking about cognitive science in terms of units and connections is reductionist—it uses the wrong language to express ideas that should be expressed in language more relevant to psychology. The authors reject this in the sense that the object of the PDP science is to *understand* cognition right along the behaviour–network axis, in the same way as one *understands* transistors along the behaviour–atomic theory axis.

Is the brain too complex?

[J. Z. Young once said that on some days the brain seems to him to be a finely tuned, precise apparatus, while on other days it seems more like pea soup.]

The critical assertion here is that it is futile to try to define cognitive theory from the little that is known about the neurophysiology of the brain. But this is precisely the misconception that PDP puts right. What is known of the brain is intriguing enough to allow PDP scientists to build such knowledge into their models and to try and understand how this curtails or aids the experience of intelligent behaviour.

The list of important questions that PDP might answer is impressive:

- Neurons are slow, how is it that the brain is very fast?
- Although the brain has many neurons how does this number *limit* its capacity?
- Although the connectivity of neurons is high (about 10^4 on average), it is low with respect to the number of neurons (10^{11}). What are the computational implications of this?
- The brain learns through connection modification. How does information flow to cause such changes? [What are the limits of training algorithms?]

338

- Very little is communicated between neurons (excitation and inhibition). How does symbolic processing emerge from this sub-system level?
- The brain has a symmetrical and layered structure. What are the computational implications of this?
- The state variables of the brain (neuron outputs) continuously broadcast the level of their decisions. How does this affect emergent properties?
- Relaxation into a solution is the fundamental computational mode. Does this explain behavioural characteristics?

Clearly this list does not rely on discoveries from neuroscience—it forms the axioms for providing insight into *brain-like* computations.

Is too much known about the brain?

In contrast with the last few paragraphs, PDP scientists are sometimes accused of not building enough of what is known of the brain into the models, such as the exact nature of the firing intervals of neurons, the different kinds of neurons and the role of neurotransmitters. There is a degree of acceptance of these criticisms with the argument that one must start with the broader assumptions to begin building a theory and see how this might be modified by the addition of neurophysiological detail. [There are some highly pertinent objections here. It may well be that the early incorporation of the role of neurotransmitters may lead to interesting theories about the localization of learning. Approximations in PDP for the sake of mathematical tractability may drift a long way from observed fact leaving developed theories open to the accusation of being about things other than the brain.]

Nature of nurture?

Linguists are sceptical of PDP approaches, particularly if they are followers of the Chomskian tradition. Too much (they argue about PDP models as they argue about the brain) is left to learning by example. But, as the authors of this chapter point out, PDP stands to one side of the nurture–nature argument by allowing some of the structure of the net to be thought of as being determined by evolution and the rest by adaptation. It may be that PDP will help to resolve some of the issues of this controversy.

[It may be that some of the interconnections of the brain are due to the constraints of ways in which the brain can grow rather than the result of evolutionary modification. PDP would be capable of identifying the effects that such constrained structures have on a wide variety of human characteristics, varying from the structure of language to the appreciation of the arts.]

People and rats

PDP has been accused of not being capable of distinguishing people from rats. The authors argue that, on the contrary, PDP may be able to provide the analysis that explains how the larger cortex in people and areas such as the *angular gyrus* (that not even chimpanzees have) may have contributed to the development of language and intellectual faculties in people which distinguishes them from other species.

Explicit knowledge and reasoning

At the current level of development, PDP cannot explain extended step-by-step reasoning, as can be done by the AI paradigm. However, this is a crucial target and there is a likelihood that PDP may bridge the gap where AI has no chance at all. The authors are simply saying 'Watch this space'.

[If PDP is to be taken seriously as a prescription for systems design it may be that a system containing PDP to turn a fuzzy world into clear, symbolic concepts *and* an AI section which does the extended reasoning, would be a suitable target.]

Variety of models

The authors are aware of the differences between PDP models presented in the rest of the book, but they see this as an advantage. What they are offering is a set of explorations whose very diversity may assist future investigations.

Part II. Basic mechanisms

5. Feature discovery by competitive learning (Rumelhart & Zipser)

Some history

A most interesting summary of the history of neural net studies (dating back to McCulloch & Pitts in 1943) opens this chapter. The authors highlight the way in which Rosenblatt's exaggerated claims drove Minsky & Papert to put a dampener on the field in 1969, which the authors see as 'overkill'. Competitive learning picks up many of the threads left loose in 1969.

What is competitive learning?

Learning in artificial nets takes a variety of forms: pattern completion (part of the pattern causes a reconstruction of the rest); pattern association (like completion, but the distinction between preserved fields and recreated fields is clearer); classification (pattern classes are mapped into distinct output codes) and regularity detectors (classifications are not provided to the systems which discovers statstical features). Competitive learning falls into the latter category.

The net is layered, the first layer being the input. Each subsequent layer is partitioned into non-overlapping sets. Each unit receives inputs from all the units in the previous layer. The units in each non-overlapping set 'compete' with each other by inhibiting others in the set. The learning rule refers to one unit in a cluster (set) 'winning'. For the jth unit:

$$w_{ij} = g(c_{ik}/n_k - w_{ij}), j \text{ being the minimizing unit,}$$

$$w_{ij} = 0 \text{ for all other units in the cluster,}$$

where: g is a proportion that determines the rate of learning; w_{ij} is the weight between the ith unit at the previous layer and the jth unit; n_k is the number of 1s in the stimulus.

Effectively, each cluster specializes one of its units so that it responds to input stimuli that are clustered in the input space of the stimuli.

Main property

Each cluster forms a 1-in-M coding of the input stimuli, each message representing the presence of a feature of some structure. Stability and consistency depend on the representations of the features. The reason for having several clusters comes from the fact that due to different initial random settings of the weights, each cluster might settle to a different grouping of features in the stimuli.

Analysis

This assumes that the weights reach equilibrium, at which point it is shown that the weight w_{ij} becomes proportional to the probability that line i is active when unit j 'wins' the competition. This leads to the conclusion that the strongest response will be obtained for the strongest overlap with some 'prototype' stimulus on which the unit has specialized.

[In pattern recognition each unit would be seen as an adapted 'nearest neighbour' classifier.]

Results

(a) Dipoles

The stimuli are all the adjacent dipoles in a 4×4 grid of points. A two-unit cluster is shown to divide the input grid into roughly two continuous areas and, on settling down, indicates in which of the areas the stimulus is found. This is a predictable result as, initially, physically distant dipoles are likely to form the prototype for each unit. Then dipoles with one point in common with this prototype gravitate towards the appropriate unit.

(b) Letters and words

An alphabet of the letters A,B,S,E was constructed on 7×5 binary grids and presented in standard positions as letter pairs on a 14×7 grid. When the stimuli set consisted of the pairs

AA, AB, BA, BB,

the two-unit cluster always became a detector of two letter-position pairs. For example, unit 1 might respond to A in position 2 only, and unit 2 to B in position 2 only and so on. The six possible solutions appeared with equal probability with the stimulus set

AA, BA, SB, EB.

The two-unit cluster became a detector letter in the *second* position (A or B) B? But being given just the first letter the units responded appropriately, eg B? would say A and E? would say B [There are some ambiguities in the way that the end values of the weights are presented, making the exact nature of this experiment hard to access.]

(c) Vertical or horizontal lines?
This is a useful example of what one *cannot* hope for from competitive learning. Thin vertical lines have more features in common with thin horizontal lines than with other thin vertical lines. This makes it impossible for two units to specialize in these features. [Anyone who has tried to do nearest-neighbour computations on images in the stimulus space would anticipate this well-known weakness of such systems.]

The authors climb out of the hole by providing 'teaching' data on an extended input matrix: a fixed horizontal line with all horizontal lines, and so on. This is an interesting trick, but it abandons the concept of 'unsupervised learning'. [I would have liked more discussion on the limitations of this scheme, as limitations there are many, putting in doubt both its validity as a brain model and its engineering applicability.]

6. Information processing in dynamic systems: foundations of harmony theory (Smolensky)

This large (90-page) chapter is introduced as being motivated by the need to provide a mathematical expression of *sub-symbolic* reasoning which lies in the gap between the successful formulation of low-level perceptual processes and high-level reasoning through symbolic logic.

Section 1—overview

Schemata and self-consistency
This uses a familiar concept of activating script-like *schemata* to infer plans from situations (as in the work of Schank), with the difference that it seeks to structure such schemata in response to a situation from lower-order *knowledge atoms*. The knowledge atoms themselves are functions of

representative features rather in the way in which a word may be a function of its letters. A memory trace is the strength of the links between features and atoms.

Inference is seen as a process of *completion* in the sense that an incomplete set of features, by activating the appropriate atom, will activate (hence infer) the remaining features. Such a grouping of features and atoms is said to be *self-consistent*. This leads to the definition of a harmony function H which assigns a numerical value to any state based on active atoms and the state of their supporting features and weights. This is to be elaborated later.

Enter probability theory

The final feature of harmony theory is the making of the values of the variables of a schema probabilistic. Given dependency information [strength of links?], the eventual computation (inference) finds the most probable state of the environment [undefined] from a given partial set of variable values.

The object is to arrive at a situation where the probability of the environment being in some state is dependent on the harmony H of that state in proportion to $e^{H/T}$, where T is some 'activation' constant. This makes the theory parallel results in statistical mechanics, making H a kind of negative energy measure and T a computational temperature.

Section 2—the theory

[In many ways this is a re-statement of Section 1—we will concentrate on nomenclature and important results.]

Definitions

$$\mathbf{r} = [r_1, r_2, r_3, \ldots]$$

is called a *representation vector*, while r_1 is a representation variable with possible values of $+1$ and -1. The state of the environment is either fully or partially encoded by $\mathbf{r}$.

There is a set of knowledge atoms; for each knowledge atom α there is a *knowledge vector*:

$$\mathbf{k}_\alpha = [k_1, k_2, \ldots],$$

where $k_j = 0$, $+1$ or -1 depending on whether α is supported by r_j 0 or not supported $+1$ for possible support and -1 for the support.

Also for atom α there is an association variable α_α. This is 0 if α is not active and 1 if it is. The degrees between the two are represented by the *probability* of α being active.

The activation of the *entire system* is another vector, the *activation vector*:

$$\mathbf{a} = [\alpha_1, \alpha_2, \ldots].$$

Each atom is also associated with a *strength* σ_α which represents the relative frequency of occurrences and such an atomic sub-pattern in the environment [note the different use of the word *strength* as compared with the earlier parts of the book].

A distinctive feature of this scheme [distinguishing it, for example, from the Boltzmann machine of Section 7] is what the authors call 'architecture', which is always at two layers, the lower layer for r_j and the upper layer for α. A deviation is bi-directional and where the representations layer may contain letters and words as separate entities, these are atoms which combine them. So, say a *word* may be activated between a representation in a phrase, atom and in a letter-word atom. The harmony function is defined as

$$H_K(\mathbf{r}, \mathbf{a}) = \sum_\alpha \sigma_\alpha a_\alpha h_k(\mathbf{r}, \mathbf{k}_\alpha),$$

where

$$h_k(\mathbf{r}, \mathbf{k}_\alpha) = \frac{\mathbf{r} \cdot \mathbf{k}_\alpha}{|\mathbf{k}_\alpha|} - k$$

is the harmony contributed by activation atom α given $\mathbf{r} \cdot \mathbf{k}$ is a control parameter in the internal $(-1, 1)$ which offers some choice on the degree of matching that will be required to determine at what point the harmony of a node is affected.

Theorems
[I do not attempt to state these in full, merely point to their stated importance.]

Theorem 1: competence

> *This defines the target for how the system* **should** *perform given that* $\mathbf{k}_\alpha$ *patterns in the environment have been noted in terms of their frequency of occurrence.*

Theorem 2: realizability

> *Given that each node updates its value as:*

$$p\,(\text{value} = 1) = \frac{1}{1 + e^{-I/T}},$$

> *where I is a weighted input to the node and T starts at some higher*

value and falls to zero, then the 'best' completion with the given knowledge will be achieved.

Theorem 3: comparability

A procedure for modifying the strengths of the knowledge atoms for maximum competence exists.

An application: a simple electric circuit
The elements of the representation vector are voltages, currents, resistances, and so on. The knowledge atoms are laws expressed for groups of components. Allowed to run with some given parameters it retrieves the rest. Much space is devoted to a discussion of optimum cooling rates and other system parameters, all of which confirms that the theoretical structure holds. [Some of the performance figures seem to me to be uninteresting as the system was *given* the memory traces that *might* be left behind during exposure to many problems in this domain.] This section ends by using the last example in contrasting knowledge acquisition at the symbolic and sub-symbolic levels.

The chapter ends by returning to the question of being able to represent several levels of abstraction in a two-level system and an empirical account of how this might be learnt.

[This chapter underlines a motivation that has pervaded much PDP work: to stay in line with statistical mechanics in order to have both analytical tractability and ready-made results. I discuss the question as to whether this misses some general points in Chapter 8 of this book.]

7. Learning and relearning in Boltzmann machines (Hinton & Sejnowsky)

This is a more general approach to the finding of solutions in an interactive network than that discussed in Chapter 6. More general because no specific architecture is assumed and because the parallel with statistical mechanics emerges from the need to define a 'cost' function which is at a minimum for the state on which the network converges. The architecture is that used by Hopfield[17] where nodes are bidirectionally connected, weight w_{ij} being the connection from unit i to unit j and vice versa.

The cost function has a character of energy and, for the whole network, is

$$E = -\sum_{i<j} w_{ij} s_i s_j + \sum_i \theta_i s_i,$$

where s_i and s_j are the sets of units i and j (0 and 1) connected by input w_{ij} and $o_i i a$ threshold.

Locally, the *k*th unit being switched between 0 and 1 contributes an energy increment:

$$\Delta E_k = \sum_i w_{ki} s_i - \theta_k.$$

In a way similar to Chapter 6, PDP *simulated annealing* is introduced to allow the system to escape from local minima. This translates to an updating value, *v*, where unit *k* is switched to a 1 with a probability, p_k, given an energy, *q*, as ΔE_k

$$p_k = \frac{1}{1 + e^{-\Delta E_k / T}}.$$

As the 'temperature' is reduced to freeze the system into its found energy minimum, the probability of two global states ($\mathbf{P}_\alpha$ and $\mathbf{P}_\beta$) is determined solely by the energy difference:

$$\frac{\mathbf{P}_\alpha}{\mathbf{P}_\beta} = e^{-(E_\alpha - E_\beta)/T}.$$

A further distinction between this work and that of Chapter 6 is that it concerns mainly distributed representations as opposed to local ones.

Learning
If the network is run to equilibrium, a change of weight may be shown to control the probability of an unclamped (free running) net being in state α as:

$$\frac{\delta \ln \mathbf{P}_\alpha^-}{\delta w_{ij}} = \frac{1}{T}\left(s_i^\alpha s_j^\alpha - \sum_\beta \mathbf{P}_\beta^- s_i^\beta s_j^\beta \right)$$

(the superscript − indicates lack of clamping). This is good news because desired changes of probability may be achieved purely from local knowledge.

The bad news is that explicit knowledge about desired local states is not always available. This happens in all cases that go beyond the 'perceptron limitations'. In such 'hard learning' cases the task is to find appropriate feature detectors among the '*invisible*' units (ie those that are not part of the input, output or desired pattern used in pattern-completion exercises).

The learning algorithm
The key rule for adjusting weights is to try to provide among the visible units the same patterns and probability distributions of such patterns in an unclamped net, as occurs during training, ie when the environment

clamps the units. A measure of the distance between the clamped and unclamped probability is given by:

$$G = \sum_{\alpha} P^{+}(V_{\alpha}) \ln \frac{P^{+}(V_{\alpha})}{P^{-}(V_{\alpha})},$$

where $P^{+}(V_{\alpha})$ is the probability of the αth state and $P^{-}(V_{\alpha})$ is the corresponding probability of the free-running net delivering the same state.

The target for the learning algorithm is to effect weight changes to minimize G. It is shown that, at terminal equilibrium,

$$\frac{\partial G}{\partial w_{ij}} = \frac{1}{T}[p_{ij}^{+} - p_{ij}^{-}],$$

p_{ij}^{+} being the average probability that i and j are both on when *driven* from the environment and p_{ij} is that probability for a free-running system. Hence G may be reduced by altering the weights on the basis of local [albeit difficult] measurements.

As an aside, the authors suggest that the $+$ and $-$ phase alterations may be part of the mechanism of REM sleep in humans. This is a refinement of a comment by Crick & Mitchinson[4] who suggested that REM sleep caused synaptic changes. In this refinement no synaptic changes take place; it is postulated that sleep may be a time at which p_{ij} are measured so as to make them available for learning in the $+$ phase. Also there is a warning that the given algorithm is not always successful. The rate at which weights are changed remains to be determined. Also, it can generate large weights which lengthen the time-to-equilibrium beyond tolerable limits [many a research student must now be busy trying to find ways to overcome these difficulties].

An example of hard learning

This problem is chosen to demonstrate hard learning and consists of generating a sparse pattern of 1s in one field of eight visible units, and the same pattern in another field shifted to the left. Another group of three visible units detects which of the three shifts has taken place. Although the system demonstrated that it could recognize shifts with up to 89% correct evaluations, it proved to be 'extremely slow'.

Reliability

One of the advantages of PDP systems, in common with the brain, is that they should tolerate damage and recover from it. The grapheme–word association problems (mentioned in connection with Chapter 3) was used to discover the recovery of a system from damage. First the scheme was checked against the loss of intermediate units. The removal of one out of

20 intermediate units used led to a deterioration from 99.3% correct to 98.6%, which confirms that distributed representation are reliable, as one might expect. Also, recovery from reset weights was seen to be effective and shown to be rapid with respect to the original learning speed (this is due to a 'ravine effect' where weight disruptions cause G to climb down the sides of the ravine which is rapidly corrected, whereas in the original, G has to descend to the floor, which takes longer). One surprising result was the fact that re-learning after damage brings back associations not directly related to those practiced during re-learning.

[This is one of the key papers in this book—its line of reasoning is beautifully clear, its feel of curiosity for the failures as well as the successes is enticing and its lack of exaggeration of the potential of PDP systems in knowledge-based tasks appealing to the sceptical reader.]

8. Learning internal representations by error propagation (Rumelhart, Hinton & Williams)

The target again is 'hard learning', particularly rising to the challenge issued by Minsky & Papert,[2] that, because there is a need for hidden units, there is no general learning rule. The notion of error propagation is thought to overcome limitations in other PDP approaches. For example, competitive learning in Chapter 5 (PDP) does not generate the creation of appropriate hidden units and the Boltzmann machine carries undesirable overheads, stochastic processors, bidirectionally connected units and requires lengthy approaches to thermal equilibrium in two phases.

The generalized delta rule
Where there are *no hidden* units and using the relation and definition of an error,

$$E_p = \frac{1}{2}\sum_j (t_{pj} - o_{pj}),$$

where E_p is an error related to a particular input–output pair from a set of such pairs that define the problem; t_{pj} is the target output of the jth unit; o_{pj} is the actual output of the jth unit. It is shown that the delta rule

$$\Delta_p w_{ij} = \eta(t_{pj} - o_{pj})i_{pi},$$

where π is a learning rate constant of proportionality; and i_{pi} the state of the *input* unit to w_{ji}. This implies a gradient descent of the total error, E, for the entire set of examples given as a summation:

$$E = \sum_p E_p.$$

The thrust of this contribution is to show that despite the presence of local minima due to hidden units, the minima of error change for weight change may be computed and that, in practice, the presence of local minima does not matter in many practical cases.

Initially, linear, feedforward nets are considered where the input and output layers contain visible units. The intermediate layers are hidden. The analysis is directed towards semi-linear activation functions [see overview of Chapter 2].

If

$$net_{pj} = \sum_i w_{ji} o_{pi},$$

then if

$$o_{pj} = f_j(net_{pj}),$$

f_j is *semi-linear* if it is non-decreasing and differentiable.

It is shown that the generalized rule

$$\Delta_p w_{ji} = \eta \delta_{pj} o_{pi}$$

may be applied in straightforward fashion to output units as δ_{pj} is easily computed:

$$\delta_{pj} = (t_{pj} - o_{pj}) f'_j(net_{pj}),$$

f'_j being the derivative of the activation function at net_{pj}, for hidden units where f'_{pj} is not known.

$$\delta_{pj} = f'_j(net\ p_j) \sum_k \delta_{pk} \omega_{kj}.$$

The summation term is the error weight function over all the units to which unit j connects. This provides a training algorithm where, first, the actual responses are *fed forward*, and then the *errors* are *propagated back* to compute the weight changes of layers, one by one towards the input. Specific examples of the application of this method follows, using the activation function:

$$o_{pj} = \frac{1}{1 + e^{(\sum_j w_{ji} o_{pi} + \theta_j)}}$$

$$so \left(net_{pj} = \sum_j w_{ji} o_{pi} + \theta_j \right),$$

which has a simple $f'(net_{pj})$, ie $o_{pj}(1 - o_{pj})$.
The rate of learning is not only controlled by a constant of

proportionality, but also by the previous weight change, which handles the problem that gradient descent requires infinitesimally small steps. Initially, small random inputs are chosen to break a symmetry problem in the learning algorithm.

Only the bare essentials of the application results are mentioned below.

The exclusive OR problem
This is a two binary input node structure with one binary output node and one hidden unit. It reaches solutions on average after 558 sweeps. A learning rate of $\eta = 0.5$ was used and the discovery of false minima is reportedly low (one in 6600). It is reported that other experiments where the number of invisible units is increased follow a law:

$$\text{number of presentations} = 280 - 331 \log_2(I),$$

where I is the number of invisible units.

Parity
This is another well-known hard-learning problem raised by Minsky & Papert.[2] The output of a net with I inputs should be a 1 if and only if the number of inputs at 1 is odd. A four-input system was shown to converge after 2825 presentations with $\eta = 0.5$.

Encoding
A number of encoding problems have been solved. For example, a three-layer system with n input units, n output units and $\log_2 n$ hidden units, was trained to encode one-in-n codes into binary code at the hidden units and back to one-in-n at the output units.

Another example is to expand a 2-bit code into its one-in-n encoding by making the route through the network difficult: the input units feed just one hidden unit which then expands to four others.

Symmetry
A surprising result was found with the problem of discovering whether a string is symmetrical about its centre or not; only two hidden units are required irrespective of the number of inputs (string lengths). [This is a good example of the way in which hidden units, the singleton in particular, make use of real-number outputs in the interval $(0, 1)$.]

Addition
A minimal structure for the addition of two binary strings is suggested where the hidden units do the 'carry' computations. This scheme does regularly find local minima, but, it is shown, the addition of further hidden units reduces this possibility. Eventually a problem arises because both an output unit and a hidden unit are connected to the same pair of

input units. The carry unit starts solving the exclusive-OR problem, and, being a feed-forward net, the other unit doesn't get to know about it.

Negation
The input is $n + 1$ bits and the output is n bits. The extra bit in the input is the sign digit. The output produces the modules of the input digit which means inverting four bits when the sign bit is 1. For $n = 3$, three hidden units are used receiving inputs from an input digit and the sign bit. Each output receives inputs from input digits, hidden units and the sign digit. 5000 passes do the trick despite the presence of the exclusive-OR problem which is effectively broken down by the hidden units.

The T–C problem
The last simulation presented in this paper is again one highlighted by Minsky & Papert[2] T-patterns and C-patterns consisting of five bits in a 3×3 bit grid. These can appear anywhere in a larger (unspecified) grid [the retrieval grid]. The hidden units are in the next layer of the same dimensionality as the retrieval grid, each unit having a 3×3 receptive field. During training all the units are given the same weight input for output [this is nice in an engineering sense, but totally non-anthropomorphic]. Between 5000 and 10000 presentations of the eight representative patterns are required for a solution to be found.

Towards generality
This chapter ends with a return to the question of whether the generalized delta rule can be extended to schemes other than feedforward networks. This is done by first showing how it can be applied to sigma–pi nets (see overview of Chapter 2) and drawing attention to the fact that a system with feedback can always be decomposed into an iterative, feedforward net. Applying the generalized delta rule simply means that weights have to be copied to the iterative sections. An example on 'learning to be a shift register' shows that the scheme works.

The authors feel that they have risen to the challenge issued by Minsky & Papert[2], but more experience is needed with the methodology.

[This is another key chapter in the collection. It is important to note that the stochastic nature of the activation function has disappeared, to be replaced merely by a nicely differentionable function. The appearance and disappearance of local minima is something that is left unresolved. It may be that, if a sufficient number of examples with local minima appear, stochastic methodology will be incorporated. A major worry about this approach is the way that every example starts with a structured net, so sculptured because it is known to satisfy the information flows that are required, but also somewhat minimized in this respect. This raises the worry that an algorithm is loosely built into the structure and only its parameters set by the lengthy training process. More work needs to be done with general structures in which the discovery of specific structures is a task for the PDP system.]

Part III. Formal analyses

[As the focus of this part is analytical, I shall make the reports shorter, concentrating only on interesting or important discoveries.]

9. An introduction to linear algebra in parallel distributed processing (Jordan)

As the title suggests, this chapter provides a summary of important manipulations in linear algebra, which is the basis for the analysis of PDP systems. It covers vector and vector spaces, matrix analysis of linear systems, and representations of non-linearity. The examples are all drawn from PDP.

[Years ago, engineers and computer scientists used to be brought up on linear algebra and were not taught that computing is based on discrete, abstract algebra. It seems curious that the tables seem to be turning and that those used to the world of computing should have to be told what a matrix is.]

10. The logic of activation functions (Williams)

The aim of this chapter is to bring activation functions under one logical roof and explore some of their theoretical properties.

Examples of the activation rules used in PDP are initially described as *mappings* with specific characteristics. The value of this is a clear comparison.

The chapter focuses on activation functions where the activation is in the interval $(0, 1)$. It then concentrates on the limit values of such functions where the activations are precisely 0 or 1 and relates these to the underlying continuous function. Some of the results are familiar: linear functions cannot achieve all Boolean functions at their extremities, the ones they *can* achieve being the familiar *linearly separable* set. However, multi-linear functions can achieve arbitrary Boolean mappings. [This forms an interesting contrast to our own approach in Chapter 8 of this book where we are using units that *can* perform complete sets of Boolean functions and see narrowing this down as a task for the training algorithm.]

11. An analysis of the delta rule and the learning of statistical associations (Stone)

The author's aim is to provide a deeper understanding of the delta rule on which much **PDP** work relies, so that the science might rely less on simulation and more on prediction. The analysis is restricted to linear units and is based on the interaction between an activation vector and the weight matrix.

It is shown that a change of basis provides a pattern-based error function as opposed to the unit-based one used in previous chapters. This gives direct information about the degree of learning of the targets and the level of interference between them. The analysis is extended to the association of categories of input with categories of output where patterns within these categories are assumed to occur at random (eg dogs → bark, where no two dogs are the same and no two barks are the same). It is shown that the delta rule associates a particular input with a response which is the average of the target paired with that output.

The chapter ends by drawing an analogy between the delta rule and multiple linear regression without any strong implications, except that if linear regression is insufficient to model a particular system, that system will perform poorly.

12. Resource requirements of standard and programmable nets (McClelland)

This chapter centres on the 'hardware' requirements of PDP tasks: numbers of units, connections and weight (ie resources).

The first analysis uses a single PDP model proposed by Willshaw[5]. It consists of N_o output units each of which contains a threshold and is connected to each of a total of n_i binary input units. The system makes r associations each of which involves a random selection of n_i active input units. Thresholds are such that a unit fires if all its n_i input units fire.

The end result is

$$n_i n_o \geqslant 1.45 r m_i m_o$$

$n_i n_o$ being a direct measure of the amount of hardware in the system.

The analysis is extended to a statistical case of a square $n \times n$ network with an $m \times m$ level of activation. Each input has f outputs *randomly distributed* among the outputs. Another alteration is that a pre-defined threshold j is done away with, instead a sensitivity measure d' is defined, which is the ratio of activation of the output lines that *should* be activated to that of those that *should not*.

The end result is now

$$n^2 \geqslant \frac{2m^2 r}{[\log(mf/n - 2\log(d)]}.$$

This essentially shows that $m^2 r$ is still a crucial factor in determining the resources required by such nets.

Pursuing this further shows that the capacity r is proportional roughly to m^2/m^2, but increasing n eventually brings no further increase in r this happens as

$$(mf/n)^{\frac{1}{2}} \cong d'$$

hence the importance of f and d'.

Applying this analysis to known connectivities in the brain provides a curiously limited estimate of capacity (between 150 to 15 000 patterns). However, this pessimism is quickly corrected through the realization that the brain is unlikely to use an $n \times n$ structure. Re-doing the calculations assuming a *layered* scheme produces more likely predictions. The use of d' in the analysis also shows that the system is degradation tolerant.

The paper ends with a discussion of 'programmable' networks which are central to Chapter 16 and will be reviewed under that heading.

[The assessment of resource requirements is an important topic. It may be worth noting a paper by Mustafa & St Jaques[6] which shows that the information capacity of an N-neuron Hopfield model is of the order of N^3 bits.]

13. P3: A parallel network simulating system (Zipser, Rabin)

This describes an attempt at providing a software suite for PDP researchers. This is intended to supply the most commonly required parameter manipulation and structuring artefacts.

The system consists of:

- a *plan language* to define a structure;
- a *method language* (LISP-like) to define node functions;
- a *constructor* to run the system; and
- a *simulation environment* for interactive displays and extraction of results.

The system runs in LISP on a Symbolics 3600 machine. The chapter is vague about performance, but suggests that the system is best suited for early development work with small nets.

(In a review such as this, there is little point in giving details of systems that may not be available to readers, so I merely point out its existence. Much work needs to be done in this area particularly on fast architectures. It may be interesting to modify P3 to run on the connection machine (Hillis[7]) or to consider the design of special purpose systems which are directed towards the needs of PDP researchers but which allow the simulation of large units with realistic training times.)

Volume 2. Pyschological and biological models

[As this review is directed towards architectural and design issues in

PDP, the stated aim of the second volume '... to offer an alternative framework for viewing cognitive phenomena...' will be considered from the mechanistic standpoint. There is a wealth of material which is not only relevant to the understanding of human cognitive architecture, but also to ways of improving the cognitive powers of computing machinery. The review is angled towards the latter and merely attempts to dwell briefly on such points where they arise.]

Part IV. Psychological processes

14. Schemata and sequential thought processes in PDP models (Rumelhart, Sejnowsky, McClelland & Hinton)

PDP models = constraint satisfaction
The Necker cube illusion is chosen to some effect to argue that it is helpful to relate cognitive debates to constraint satisfaction. This is illuminated by showing how a network of conflicting interconnected labelling of the vertices of the cube, when 'run' leads to the two (sometimes three) coherent perceptions of the cube.

The factor *G* (goodness of fit of current state) seen in Chapter 7 [in inverse form?] is shown as a three-dimensional landscape which assesses thinking about the dynamics of such systems.

Constraint satisfaction and schemata
Traditionally in philosophy a schema is a vague notion of a *whole* thought or concept made up of parts. The authors point to the woolly way in which this concept has been used (perhaps more precisely in AI: frames, scripts and the like) and suggest that PDP is a methodology for revealing the true nature of such a concept.

In PDP a scheme is a stable state of the network of units. The units are distributed interacting parameters, which, on reaching a stable state of coexistence, define a schema. So a schema is not a 'thing' it is a distributed state of affairs of many parameters. [In fact, a schema is a *point* in *state space*. Not only philosophers have had difficulty with this concept, but some control engineers who, during the introduction of state-space analysis in the late 1950s, found it awkward to imagine all the things that go on in a control system as just *one* point in high-dimension spaces. This is now standard practice.]

Schema are not stored in any specific part of the system, but are learnt through judicious adjustments to distributed memory: another hard task for philosophers. A useful example is presented. There are 40 attributes such as 'large', 'oven', 'computer', 'bed', etc. *Knowledge* was elicited from volunteers who simply scored how important they thought each of the items might be to a small bathroom, a large kitchen, a large living room and an office. Instead of training the system, the weights of a 40-unit net were adjusted according to the known predicted outcomes of a training procedure. (The authors are careful to point out that a schema does not imply that each unit is an attribute, this was merely convenient for this experiment). Running the net showed clear goodness peaks for what could be identified as a prototype office, kitchen, etc.,... illustrating that schemata *emerge* through constraint satisfaction.

PDP and thinking

The remainder of the paper addresses some central but broad issues in cognitive science. *Consciousness* is seen as a sequence of schemata related to a single stimulus.

The criticism that such consciousness simply gets into a state from which it can't do anything is countered by arguing that the organism is in a feedback loop with its environment — the two develop by acting on one another [Kelly[8] would have argued that the organism acts in a *predictive* way with respect to the environment]. Indeed, the authors suggest a [almost Kellian] scheme of dividing the net into two parts, the first that has developed schemata which model the world, and the other which can play 'what if' games with the first before acting on the environment. The possibility of internal conversations, richer than external language can capture, is realized as an enticing point for discussion. [In Aleksander[9] these points were raised as a way of solving psycho/philosophical problems through the use of learning nets and automata theory.]

In answer to the difficult question of where our ability to do science, mathematics and logic comes from, the authors suggest that this is due to our ability to create *external* representations (ie pencil and paper) which are then internalized.

For example, teaching a child that

$$(A \supseteq B) \wedge (B \supseteq \bar{C}) \rightarrow (A \supseteq \bar{C})$$

is easy on a Venn diagram. Later the pencil-and-paper way of doing Venn diagrams becomes internalized as schemata, to enable the child to 'do in his head' (by internal conversation). Learning language (as a long shot) is seen as a related process of 'self-instruction' through the internal organization.

To bring the discussion to a concrete plane, an example of natural modelling of an opponent in the game of tic-tac-toe (noughts and crosses) is given.

15. Interactive processes in speech perception: the trace model (McClelland & Elman)

This is the first chapter in the collection which handles a problem in the time domain. It is probably one of the most elusive problems of this kind: speech recognition, TRACE (so named because the pattern of activation in the net left by a spoken input is a *trace* of the analysis that has been carried out).

There are three layers of units: *words* at the top, *phonemes* in the middle and signal features (acuteness, diffuseness, etc.) at the sound measurement level. At this lowest feature level there is one unit per feature per time slice. Higher units span several time slices of lower units. Connections between layers are excitatory, and within layers, inhibitory.

Interactive activation (as reviewed for Chapter 2) is used between the layers. There is no 'learning' as such—connections are prespecified. Multiplicative connections (Chapter 4) are used and the activation pattern at the end of an utterance should identify the words spoken. In TRACE II mock speech was used leading to detectors for 211 words made up of combinations of 14 phonemes.

Result

This is merely a telegraphic description of the properties of the model revealed by many experiments on the system described above. Most of these explain available data in human performance.

- There is on-going cooperation between the emergence of a plausible hypothesis of the word level and the emergence of supporting phonemes, even if some of the latter are ambiguous. This improves as the utterance progresses.
- The point of emergence of the lexical effect above on phoneme emergence is stronger for phonemes that come late in the word (simply because there is more cortex available).
- Language-permissible biases in ambiguous presentations (eg a sound between /l/ and /r/ in 's*ee p') are present through the presence of co-operation between word and phoneme level (/l/ wins over /r/ in this case).
- Purely at the phoneme level, trade-off between inputs cues in TRACE follow roughly the same pattern as that discovered in human perception.
- TRACE overcomes some of the difficulties of systems based on predicted word set reduction (eg COHORT, Marslen-Wilson & Tyler[13]) where the ambiguity comes early in the word (eg 'dwibble'). As TRACE integrates its activation over time, this problem does not occur as, indeed, it does not occur in human perception.
- *TRACE exhibits good word segmentation properties [this is generally the stumbling block for most artificial systems].

In their conclusions, the authors draw attention to the major deficiencies in TRACE: the need to replicate networks over and over again in time.

357

[This is a most impressive contribution to a problem that has normally been intractable through algorithmic methods. It may be that the major contribution of PDP technology will be to the design of speech understanding: an area where other computational methods have failed. See Chapters 3, 4, and 10 in this book for contributions to this topic.]

16. The programming blackboard model of reading (McClelland)

Part of the motivation of this work comes from the deficiency of the TRACE model discussed in Section 15: the knowledge hardware has to be replicated. Part of the inspiration for what to do comes from the BLACKBOARD section of the HEARSAY program (Reddy et al.[10]) where different domains of knowledge are stored (in a pseudo-geographical way) in different parts of the BLACKBOARD and may be accessed to aid understanding.

Programmability
In this PDP approach, knowledge is neither pre-programmed into the net *ab initio*, nor is it learnt: it becomes the responsibility of a special part of the system to adjust weights according to some knowledge possessed by this part. The programmability is achieved by multiplicative connections. Where in PDP it is conventional to have for a connection to unit i from j: $input_{ij}(t) = output_j(i) \times w_{ij}$; in a programmable scheme $input_{ij}(t) = output_j(t) \times output_k(t)$. So, it is unit k that processes the connection between units i and j.

The network
The connection information distribution (CID) model has the following features. It contains programmable modules which have letter–position inputs (eg A/2–A in position 2) and letter-group outputs. One such module is used for objects (such as letter-pairs) which are later combined to form higher-level objects (eg words). These modules are programmable in the sense that weights from inputs to outputs may be set by other parts of the system.

A *central module* (*CM*) is the key to the system (and is the distinguishing feature from TRACE in Chapter 15). It contains fixed-weight information about links between letters and letter-pair objects in the one physical location. This acts as a central activation (CA) system which feeds likely word-pair weights back from the programmable modules.

Simulations were carried out with a list of 32 4-letter words for which the first was fed to one programmable circuit and the second to another.

In essence, the notion for these cooperating units was shown to work with the somewhat restricted vocabulary. Two features were observed, for single-word recognition, the CID feedback mimics inhibitory connections in the bottom-up path which are not there. For word-pair work, errors similar to those of humans faced with the same task were observed (SANE-LANE confused with SANE-LAND).

Programmable blackboards

The target here is to recognize words from letter units which may be of different lengths and appear at different points in time. The problem here is that the positional information for letters is lost and must in some way be replaced for CID to work at all. To achieve this, *course coding* (mentioned under the review of Chapter 3) is used. Specifically, each letter is presented as a pattern of activation for several units, different word-centred roles for the letter giving just slightly different patterns. 'Role' represents such states as being the first letter, or the last letter of the word, etc.

Feedback through another set of programmable modules (also fed from CM/CA) is provided to enhance the creation of stable states related to known words. This is clearly distinguished from the feedback obtained for the connection strengths from CM/CA.

The notion of saccadic shifts in the focus of attention during reading is included in the mechanism in the sense that letters under the pre-point of fixation and those in a right 'formal' penumbra are fed into subsequent states of the programmable units.

The simulation

Nine letters were used and a lexicon of 92 words of 1–4 letters were made up of these chosen letters. Both simple and multiple fixations were studied. On the whole, the simulations furnished interesting results psychologically compatible with those of human readers. However, the crucial point is that connection information distribution has been added to the armoury of PDP tools. The central feature of this being the improved cost characteristics over TRACE-type modules.

[This too adds to the armoury of techniques needed to solve the speech understanding problem technologically. I find that statements such as 'we were unhappy about the results until we discovered that humans make the same mistakes', somewhat curious. It may be that PDP machines will have to be better than humans to be of use to humans. What then are the limitations?]

17. A distributed model of human learning and memory (McClelland & Rumelhart)

The dilemma, as the authors see it, is that psychological tests reveal that human memory appears to store both generalizations ('this thing has four legs and a woolly coat, so it's a sheep') and many specific facts

('Charlie is the fellow with long hair and a mole on his left cheek'). But storing such detail in the manner of a computer memory seems to be physically unlikely and the storing of rules as an AI program also seems limited and implausible. Can PDP help?

The model

Modularity
Each module may have thousands of millions of circuits that are totally interconnected. They receive inputs from similar modules and feed other modules. Modules may be categorized in terms of the more or less abstract nature of their task.

A mental state is interpreted as a pattern of activation over the module.

A memory trace is a change in connection weights either between modules or within modules.

Retrieval is the re-instatement of a previously 'fixed' pattern of activation, from some cue which may arise from a sensory input (but could be internal).

The simulation
Only one totally interconnected module is used with continuous activation function in the interval $(-1, +1)$. It has 24 units. Non-linear 'squashing' functions are used to update the activations in conjunction with a delay factor. It is felt that these details are not too important as other PDP modules would behave in a similar way.

When a stable activation pattern is achieved, the delta rule is applied (as discussed in Chapters, 2 8 and 11), the object being to minimize the distance between the output pattern and the internal pattern of the nets. *There are no hidden units.*

Examples
Three prototype objects are used (dog, cat and bagel) each allows eight outputs for the name and 16 for the 'visual' image. Either name or visual signal is used to retrieve the other. The following four technical points are made. *First*, given exemplars of a prototype and random distortions of it for training, the model extracts the prototype. *Second*, this can be done for different, not necessarily orthogonal, patterns (3 in this case). *Third*, there is no *teaching* information here, just the input patterns. *Fourth*, the same set of connections allows the co-existence of the exemplars.

Correlation with human memory
A recent model of word memory (Morton[11]) suggests that a 'logogen' becomes active in the brain (single unit?) for each word known. This looks implausible if the same unit is to be activated by different sensory aspects of a word: spoken, written, high-tone, low-tone, etc. It is argued

here that the *distributed* representation of a word in a net may serve the same purpose as a logogen; but this is consistent with PDP explanations of memory and overcomes some of the objection to arbitrariness of the logogen concept.

In particular, it is shown through a thorough series of experiments with distortions of familiar and unfamiliar words, that the model behaves in ways that are compatible with tests on humans and for which the logogen concept just has insufficient explanatory powers.

On the speculative side

Extensions of the model are discussed without experimental backing. Contrary to classical semantic network models of memory, the authors stress that PDP is compatible with more recent arguments where *episodic memory and semantic memory is not reported.* The latter is seen to emerge from the former.

Possibly the most significant speculation is that a PDP model can *develop* the kind of regularity the *linguists interpret as systems of rules*; more of this in the review of the Chapter 18 which follows.

Two effects found in amnesiacs may be explained through PDP: the retention of *learning and extraction ability* despite loss of episodic memory and secondly the distinction between domains that are and are not affected in annealing. More of this in the review of Chapter 25.

Psychological evidence is being gathered on the fact that people mix *indistinct memories* and report blends rather than correct facts from individual memories. This too is fodder for PDP explanations, or is what as known as the *jam effect*: propositions are harder to recognize the more facts about such propositions that have been learnt.

Hidden units

The main drawback is the fact that the model described does *not* have hidden units in its limited number of representational primitives. Also, flexibility for distinguishing similar events while collating different ones is missing. However, it is argued that adding hidden units only introduces minor changes to what has been said about PDP as a model of human memory, provided that learning schemes, such as that reviewed for Chapters 7 and 8 are used.

[Computer science has not been helpful to those who seek to model memory. There was a time when models where shown in the manner of computer organization which is bound to be wrong. Then the artificial intelligence era sent psychologists scurrying away to look for rules and structures. It must be true that PDP is the first computing paradigm that is of some use. This has also been argued in Aleksander[9] and Aleksander[12].]

18. On learning the past tense of English verbs (Rumelhart & McClelland)

Studies of language acquisition are based on the notion that the brain acquires explicit but inaccessible rules as part of the process. PDP provides an alternative paradigm: a system of acquisition in which the multiple stored constraints force lawful behaviour without requiring the need for an explicit memory site for rules.

The specific phenomenon of past tense acquisition as observed in children, is chosen to illustrate the PDP approach. This has been observed to exist in three phases:

(a) the acquisition of a small collection of often used verbs, most of which are irregular (eg came, got . . .);

(b) the apparent acquisition of a rule (eg pull → pulled) even to the extent of getting the known irregulars wrong (eg eat → eated);

(c) learning to distinguish between regular and irregular forms.

The change from one phase to another is generally gradual.

The PDP model

The intention is to build a model that learns from present–past word-pairs in their phonological form (rather than from everyday sentences which may not only be too ambitious, but might hide the point which is being made).

The network has four layers: the first the phonological root-form input, which is hand mixed to encode 'wickelfeatures' (context sensitive phoneme units consisting of the phone, its predecessor and successor). These are connected via *modifiable connections* to another set of wickelfeatures units representing the past form, which, in turn is fixed-wired to the output units representing the past tense.

A Boltzmann machine learning mechanism is employed (see review Chapter 7). A *fixed* temperature and the 'perceptron convergence procedure' are used. This is a discrete variant of the delta rule of Chapter 2.

A numerical example of an 8×8 network is used to illustrate that an association with the above properties will roughly follow the phases of blind mapping, rule-based mapping with incorrect interpretation of the exemptions as such. This provides the necessarily familiarity with the learning technique before going on to the model proper.

On the model proper, a modified set of wickelfeatures is used where phonemes are represented as an 11-unit binary vector of which ten bits are used to represent one of 36 groups of phonemes. This coding is slightly ambiguous (for six pairs of phonemes that are equally coded) and at the same time redundant in the sense that ten bits could encode 1024 messages. The 11th bit is used to indicate the first wickelphone in a string. This is further encoded to represent each verb as a pattern over 460 wickelfeature units, much in line with the philosophy of distributed representations. [One wonders how this model would work if the encoding were arbitrarily done rather than attempting to retain some phonetic meaning in parts of the representational code.]

The experiments

A standard set of verbs was used divided into frequency groups: 10 high-frequency verbs (two of which are regular), 410 medium-frequency (334 regular) and 86 low-frequency verbs (72 regular).

The training schedule was meant to have similarities to the exposures faced by a young child (in very broad terms). First, the high-frequency verbs were taught, and these were satisfactorily learnt, exhibiting the Phase 1 performance as in a child. Then the 410 medium-frequency were *added* to the training: early responses having much of the Phase 2 character and later ones as in Phase 3. The system was also tested on the low-frequency verbs *without additional learning* to check on transference.

The results also show that the dip in the performance on the irregular verbs, which characterizes Phase 2, is due to a regularization (eg gives → gived) and that this tendency is minimized in Phase 3.

A deep analysis of the results based on phonetic categorization of the verbs shows a sustained similarity to human performance.

Transfer

The overall transfer to the 86 low-frequency verbs was 91% correct. Particularly impressive was the transfer of 84% correct to previously unseen irregular word verbs.

Conclusion

The authors make some, as yet unproven, predictions (eg errors of the cut → cutted kind are likely to be more frequent than send–sended, the difference being in whether the past tense changes or not). But they rightly argue that evidence of regularization in children is *not* indicative of explicit rule learning. PDP can do it, and it doesn't learn explicit rules.

[This chapter, as the previous one, is important in correcting the distortion that computer science, through artificial intelligence, has brought to cognitive science. Even, if the proof provided by this work can be challenged in detail, it offers sufficient material to cast doubt on the notion that if an information processing task may be described by a set of rules, a mechanism performing the task must perforce employ such (or other) rules explicitly. Perhaps the era of such thinking is on its way out!]

19. Mechanism of sentence processing: assigning roles to constituents of sentences (McClelland & Kamamoto)

Role assignment is that activity in sentence processing which understands the effect of phrases in a sentence. For example:

> The boy broke the window with the rock.
> The boy broke the window with the tinted glass.

This requires an assignment of *instrument* to 'with the rock' whereas 'with the tinted glass' is a modifier of 'window'. A plethora of examples show that this task is neither purely mechanical, nor is it easily discernible as a task for rule-based computing. The authors suggest that it may be seen as based on the satisfaction of several simultaneous constraints, and is therefore a suitable case for a PDP solution.

The aims are to design a PDP model that *learns* to use word order and semantic cues as constraints in assigning roles by picking the correct meaning of ambiguous words, selecting appropriate verb frames based on patterns, filling in missing arguments and generalizing to previously unseen words.

The model

This is similar to the 'past tense' model in Chapter 18 where the verb model maps phonological representation of the root of a verb into phonological representations of the past tense. This model aims to map the surface structure (actual sentence) into the case structure (roles assigned to the main words). The input is not the raw sentence but a canonical representation as might be generated by a person and a lexicon which extracts microfeatures (the parser is not part of the system, but its implementation is easily imagined). The sentences have a verb and a subject noun-phrase and up to two object noun-phrases of which one is of the 'with' type.

The microfeatures

Words are represented by microfeatures, each of which is a choice of several options. An example for a noun is (chosen option italicized) boy: *human*/non-human; *soft*/hard; *male*/female/neuter; small/*medium*/ large; compact/1D/2D/*3D*; pointy/*rounded*; fragile/*sturdy*; food/toy/tool/ utensil/furniture/*animate*/natural inanimate;

A similar treatment is given to verbs. But to increase the redundancy of the representation, a unit is created for each *pair* of microfeatures. This outputs 1 for both microfeatures ON, 50% if only one is on, and zero if neither is. So the input representation for verbs has 240 units and nouns, 263 units.

Case role representation

Four matrices from the output of the network: one for each case role—
agent, patient, instrument modifier. Each matrix consists of 25 × 25 units
the horizontal rows being labelled in terms of verb microfeatures and the
columns as noun microfeatures. Therefore, in each case the group the
appropriate case triple may be activated. For example the correct output
for the sentence: 'The boy broke the window with the hammer' would be:

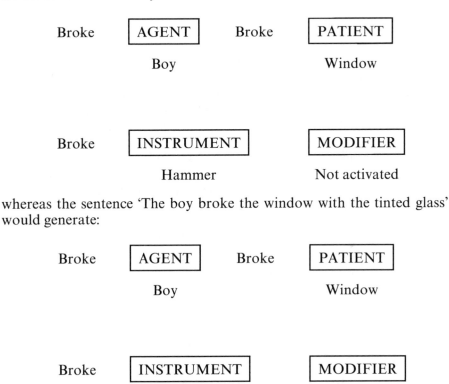

whereas the sentence 'The boy broke the window with the tinted glass'
would generate:

Learning

Again, the perceptron convergence rule is applied.

Experiments

General phrases such as 'The human broke the *fragile object* with the
breaker' were used for training.

In general, it was found that the system not only learnt familiar
sentences, but made less than 1% error on unfamiliar ones after 50 cycles
of learning. The correct verb frame was chosen. Also, given partial input
such as 'The boy broke', the features pointing to the set {plate, vase,

window, furniture} were activated, as plausible fillers, while 'bat' or 'lion' were made unlikely. It also showed the capacity to be sensitive to word-order cues and correct ambiguities. Generalization to totally novel, but properly encoded words, was also demonstrated.

Several suggestions for future modifications are made, particularly the use of backpropagation methods to correct output decisions back to the surface structure level. Also a distributed, rather than matrix-like representation of the role codes is a possible extension to current work.

Discussion

While being clear that the work reported here is only the beginning of a line of research which might lead to a language understanding system, the authors describe as myths some of the often quoted drawbacks of PDP in this area: the ability to do recursion in particular. Some of Hinton's ideas on the subject are evoked where a sub-net is a set of units that provides a distributed pattern over the rest of the net which is the equivalent of a stack-level counter.

On the whole, the basis now exists for building a PDP language processing mechanism that works iteratively along a sentence.

[Again the PDP philosophy is justified, this time in an area where the rule-based methods have not been properly applied. The worry is that the rather simple tasks simulated here required a very large number of units: my count is 1875 output units, and 1029 input units. Perhaps this work ought to be revised with the logical approach discussed in Chapter 8 of this book, to derive an implementation.]

PART V. Biological mechanisms

20. Certain aspects of the anatomy and physiology of the cerebral cortex (Crick & Asanuma)

The first of a group of chapters designed to bring PDP to bear on explanations of brain function is a sketch of the important features of the brain. This does not mean that PDP models that are not closely related to the way the brain is connected are invalid: they may well be recipes for designing competent machinery with human-like properties. But if PDP is to be seen as a form of theoretical neurophysiology, it must not assume degrees of function and connectedness that are *known* not to exist in the brain. On the other hand, it is perfectly plausible that PDP may suggest brain research that as yet has not been carried out, but this too must be related to the structure of the brain as it is known.

The neuron

Departures from the well-known and used synapse–soma–axon model are noted. Amacrine cells in the retina and some cells in the olefactory bulb (and *only* in these two sites) have no axons: they simply receive and transmit information. [This implies that one should not make the Hopfield assumption about bidirectionality except when talking about the two sites in question.]

Axons form synapses with the *individual* segments of other axons in certain cells of the cerebral cortex. [This may influence arguments about 'clamping' of neurons to certain states.]

Dendrites sometimes form synapses with the other dendrites (but not in the cerebral cortex. [The processing implications of this are not clear.]

In short axons (eg in the retina), graded potentials are output instead of the more common spikes. [So, models with continuous outputs make sense.] Such graded potentials could have a modulating effect effect on the input from longer axons which produce spikes [note the definition of sigma–pi units and models based on these.]

Synapses

Small stellate neurons usually receive about 10^2 inputs, larger pyramidal cells 10^3 and the largest pyramidal cells have about 10^4. Inhibitory and excitatory neurons appear to be physically distinct in terms of membrane thickening profiles. Other tentative statements may be made:

- Axons either make all excitatory or all inhibitory synapses on their contact sites.
- Axons generally transmit the same kind of (non-peptide: see later) neurotransmitter (the chemical which causes the excitation or in-hibition).

Peptides

These are recently discovered 'special' neurotransmitters. They appear to modulate synaptic functions rather than actually cause them. They do so over relatively long periods of time (seconds or minutes as opposed to milliseconds). They act over larger areas by the process of diffusion, and are thought to provide an alternative, slow, but broadcast-like means for neurons to communicate. A neuron can produce several peptides.

The cerebral cortex

The neo-cortex part (where, crudely, most of the 'clever' processing must be done) is organized in major layers: (a) a superficial layer which mainly receives axons from other layers; (b) an upper layer of small pyramidal neurons; (c) a middle layer that contains small stellate neurons; and (d) a deep layer where the larger neurons reside. Axons generally connect towards the surface (vertically) across layers. Horizontal structures appear to be much more local. The neo-cortex, besides being layered has (since the work of Brodmann[16]), been divided into more than 100 distinct areas on each side of the human brain, each being both anatomically and functionally distinct.

The input to the cortex comes mainly from the *thalamus* which acts as a 'gateway' for sensory data. The thalamus is divided into specialized nuclei (such as the lateral geniculate which is the relay centre for retinal input) which feed different areas of the cortex, usually through the middle layer. Architecturally, it seems important that the cortex also 'shouts back' returning connections to the thalamus. There also appears to be a special (thalamic reticular) nucleus in the thalamus which receives collaterals from outgoing axons and contains large neurons which have axons making inhibitory connections within the thalamus itself. This, too, has much strategic architectural importance.

Cortical areas *receive input* from a handful (rather than all) other areas: neighbouring neurons in one area connecting to neighbouring neurons in another. This topology is reasonably well documented for typical test animals such as the macaque monkey. But undue regularity should not be inferred: for example, the *striate cortex* receives inputs in interleaved stripe-like areas from each of the two eyes.

Cortical outputs are all excitatory and have been found to be similar for vertical orientations.

The nature of neo-cortical neurons
Descriptions are limited by all-but-perfect methodologies of microscopy. Much of the research has centred on defining types: they divide into pyramidal (of which there may be thousands of different types) and non-pyramidal. The latter appear to have only local connections and do not interconnect cortical areas. Another division appears to be into cells that are 'spiny' and those that are not. The latter are characterized by receiving both sorts of inputs (excitatory and inhibitory) on both body (soma) and dendrites, while the former receive non-excitatory somatic inputs.

Single neuron behaviour
There is much ignorance in this area. It is likely that dendrites are just passive collections of inputs. The weight changes merely seem due to the change of the synaptic *area*, but that, too, is conjecture. Even less is known about groups of neurons. Although many PDP models start as totally connected nets, there is virtually no evidence of this in a living neural net. Cells of one type generally tend not to connect to cells of the same type. Also, the direction of information flow in the neo-cortex is an uncharted area.

Average time between firing of a neuron is 10–20 ms. Bearing in mind how much processing the brain can do in 100 µs should influence PDP thinking away from processes that require many iterations.

Feature detection

Here the authors refer to the oft-quoted ability of 'simple cells' near sensory input to respond to simple features (such as edges). [Little is said about much current work that seeks to identify specialized cells (eg 'granny cells'). One of the results of PDP theory (the efficiency of distributed rather than local representations) would suggest that if the brain has evolved efficiently, the discovery of such cells would be unlikely.]

Warnings

The chapter ends by summarizing ways in which the cerebral cortex departs from some PDP models:

- Neurons excite or inhibit others, but not both.
- No neurons act as 'invertors' (excitation → inhibition).
- There is total connectivity within cell types.
- Elaborate synaptic computations (eg $\Sigma\Pi$) are rare.
- Single neurons rarely fire other single neurons.

On the other hand, attention is drawn to two features of the neo-cortex which are not used in PDP:

- veto cells that inhibit totally many other cells;
- diffuse inputs from the brain stem which have a global effect such as facilitating synaptic modifications.

[The last point is part of a major gap between PDP and brain studies. Central to PDP is the learning algorithm: computationally complex, carefully guided. Very little is known of such processes in the brain and much is assumed for PDP: this is a fruitful area into which research that might close the gap could be directed].

21. Open questions about computation in the cerebral cortex (Sejnowski)

Following from the last chapter, this is an attempt to summarize what is not known about the anatomy and physiology of the cerebral cortex. Although this area clearly uses the stored memory–processing characteristics found in PDP, several important questions still remain.

Representing information

Following the discoveries of Hubel & Wiesel[14] on the specificity of simple cells, much work in neurophysiology has been directed towards the discovery of single cells that identify complex percepts (eg 'the granny cell'). In view of what has been discovered about distributed representations in PDP (Chapters 3, 7, 18) it may be vital to look for such organizations in the brain.

Neuronal processing

The timing problem highlighted by Crick & Asanuma (Chapter 20 (PDP)), may be overcome by seeing the *probability of firing* (ie a stochastic variable) as being the carrier of information rather than average firing rates. This allows one to think of 40 or more net iterations within the 200 ms in which the cortex executes some visual tasks. This is enough for a cooperative algorithm to converge. (This has implications for neurophysiological measurement techniques.) Despite their rarity, sub-neuronal computations in dendritic branches may be crucial to the functioning of the cortex, and may deserve deeper experimental attention.

Temporal coincidence

There is no time discretization in the cortex as there is in most PDP models, but that may be to the advantage of the cortex where slight temporal differences between firing rates are significant. How significant, and whether applicable to PDP models, requires further attention.

Some recent suggestions (Crick[15]) that the thalamus may be sending 'searchlight signals' to groups of cells that represent a set of facts, and that these facilitate 'binding' through allowing rapid synaptic changes, are creating research attention. The result of this will be of value to PDP scientists.

Neuronal plasticity

That this exists there is no doubt, as verified by tests on somatotopic mappings of a monkey's hand into the cortex. These rearrange themselves after nerve section and ligation to make the best of the unused cortex. As this appeared to be due to the activation of previously dormant synapses, it raises questions about such spare capacity in neurons. On the whole, the potential dynamism of reconnection in neurons appears to be considerable, but an advance in multi-cell monitoring techniques is required to provide more information.

[There is a need to assess the plasticity of neurons on a simple-neuron basis. It may well be that most PDP models assume far too great a plasticity, putting them out of court.]

Computational models

The link between PDP and neuroscience should not be taken too literally. The interdependence between the two should not be based on the minutiae of neurophysiology. [Both the cortex and PDP models are capable of providing a bridge between low-level processing and higher level cognition. It is in this sense that PDP provides a theoretical framework within which neurophysiologists can explain their results and provide data that, in turn, increases the physiological reality of PDP models.]

22. Neural and conceptual interpretation of PDP models (Smolensky)

The target for this chapter is to relate distributed to local representations leading to a relationship between mind and brain. More pertinently, the centre of this question relates to the conceptual description of neural activity in mathematical terms.

Interpretations

Three interpretation domains come into play: the neural (eg spiking, frequency and synaptic contact,...) the mathematical (eg weight value, signoid activation function F,...) and the conceptual (hypothesis, inference,...). An *isomorphism hypothesis* enquires whether a state represented neurally has a conceptual partner such that if both models are run for the same length of time they will be in corresponding states at all times. The attack advocates a low-level Model 1 whose dynamics of patterns of activation may be described at a higher level by Model 2. It is pertinent to ask whether the two obey the same laws.

Networks and dynamical systems

Seeing the activation of a unit at time $t+1$ as a function of such activation of the other units at time t, defines a dynamic system where the activation of each unit is a state variable. [A well-trodden concept in state-space control theory and finite-state automata theory.]

Outside of the state variable, a state-space S of all possible state-variable values and state trajectories from some starting state to an end state, characterizes a dynamic analysis of such systems.

Kinematics concerns the geometrical relationships within S, while *dynamics* concerns itself with the shape of the trajectories in S. So, if one is trying to use such schemes to relate natural to conceptual issues, the discourse will be about kinematics rather than dynamics (related to specific cases of behaviour).

Taking each state variable as one coordinate in a hyperspace leads to a [classical] hypercube definition of S. A result of such kinematic consideration is that for linear activation functions, *vector addition holds*, each state being characterized as a vector. This also leads to a [dynamic] conclusion that

$$\mathbf{u}(t+1) = \mathbf{W} \cdot \mathbf{u}(t),$$

where $\mathbf{u}$ is the vector of activation values and $\mathbf{W}$ is the weight matrix.

A final theoretical consideration equates a state to a *pattern* view of kinematics, where a *pattern* is defined within a group of units. A state may then be defined as a superposition of such patterns, and leads to evolutionary equation of such patterns:

$$\mathbf{p}(t+1) = \mathbf{I}\mathbf{p}(t),$$

where $\mathbf{I}$ may be easily computed from $\mathbf{W}$.

The isomorphism hypothesis for linear systems

The sense in which isomorphism holds between low-level descriptions and high-level descriptions is that *unit* evolution equations are the same as *pattern* evolution equations. The two models started in the same state are in isomorphic states at any time.

An interesting characteristic of this isomorphism is that were one to damage a unit (a low-level statement) the linear will say what this does to the pattern space and vice versa.

Breakdown of the isomorphism

The isomorphism may only be proven for linear systems and break down for non-linear ones, although some interesting things can be said about incompatible hypotheses at the conceptual level and the low-level notion of inhibitory interaction between competing units.

Mind and body

As a final thought the authors speculate that mind may be the higher-level representation of body. If only one could find the algebra for the isomorphism...

[The author has stumbled upon the $64 000 question. It is sometimes called the structure–function problem which engineers designing logic systems grapple with every day of their working lives. Automata theory is in this state: only canonical structures may be mapped directly into the state-space representation. It is wrong, however, to see systems where a handle-turning algebra does not prove the isomorphism as inferior. One could argue that linear systems are *less* interesting because of the analytic isomorphism. It is possible to incorporate learning and the environment into the relationship, which at least enables one to *state* the problem in general terms. Arguing that the relationship has a bearing on mind–body is easy—I have often done it myself (Aleksander 1978).]

23. Biologically plausible models of place recognition and goal location (D. Zipser)

Although place location has been successfully tackled in classical AI methodology using rule-based methods, the object of this chapter is to discuss PDP models which provide the framework for experiments carried out with animals. For example, it has been shown that once a rat swimming randomly in cloudy water finds a slightly submerged platform and gets a view of the environment, it can later find the platform directly using environmental information. There is physiological evidence, too, that certain neurons in the hippocampus of a rat fire only when the animal is at a particular location relative to a set of digital landmarks. In particular, there appears to be a size-scaling of environmental features to the place-fields of the hippocampus.

The model

It is assumed that the apparatus exists which delivers data regarding a feature X_j and its distance from the observer d_j. The details of how this is done are not part of the model. There are two layers in the PDP model: the first has one unit for each feature which receives both X_j and d_j for the jth unit; The second layer receives inputs from all the first-layer units and acts like a place-field neuron. Initial tests showed that the performance of the system, on distance cues only, did not vary a great deal if the response function was:

$$R_1 = \begin{cases} 0 \text{ if } d_j - d_j^* > \sigma \\ 1 \text{ otherwise} \end{cases},$$

or

$$R_1 = exp-[(d_j - d_j^*)^2/\sigma^2],$$

d_j and d_j^* being the stored and observed distances respectively, and σ being a matching criterion. In each case the layer 2 computation was:

$$R_2 = \begin{cases} 0 \text{ if } \sum_j R_1(j) - \Theta \leqslant 0, \\ \sum_j R_1(j) - \Theta \text{ otherwise.} \end{cases}$$

But the crux of the problem is to compute position from landmark changes rather than given distance. Area has been chosen as the cue and, given four landmarks (both symmetrically and asymmetrically placed) and using a Gaussian matching function against stored values at layer 1 and a threshold function at layer 2, again the original location could be found depending on σ. Place-field displacements due to cue repositioning dilation roughly followed those found in physiological experiments, giving credence to the model.

Goal location

The above model lacks orientation information. In order to use place-field information to tell the organism where to go next, such information is required and two further models are proposed.

The first in the *distributed view-field* model where layer-one modules are replicated three times: left, right and centre gives a minimal directional cue. They all feed *view-field units* in layer 2. So layer 1: right unit j is only on when object j is in the right-hand field, and layer 2 unit for object j will fire only if object j is the correct orientation. Additional goal units modify the output of the view-field units to indicate the direction of some specified goal. This can drive a motor system.

The system is trained by storing information in layer 1 from 'visual data' and goal direction in the goal units form 'working memory'. This is done while the organism explores the field at random. The P3 system (reviewed under Chapter 13) is used to run the simulation which involves 100 view-field units. In general, the 'organism' when seeking the goal would head relatively rapidly towards it from a distance, but then would 'thrash about' for a 'great many steps' [number not specified] before hitting the goal. This, the author thinks, has sufficient biological plausibility to constitute a model. The main drawbacks of this model are the huge number of recordings (new position = new objects) and ambiguities that arise in the vicinity of the goal. The chapter ends with the presentation of a third model: *the β-coefficient model*. In this, direct computations are involved which merely recognize objects and compute goal location. Both the computational devices and the algorithms are a little less plausible biologically, although the model may provide a higher-level description of what the previous two models described at a finer grain.

[Obviously, a study of the fine grain models is heavily limited by current computational methods. This drives the researcher towards higher-level descriptions which are well within these limitations. But one should not miss the evolutionary pressure that this suggests for the development of novel hardware.]

24. State-dependent factors influencing neural plasticity: a partial account of the critical period (Munro)

Pitched at the single neuron-level and based on observations in the visual cortex, this chapter aims to suggest that the ability of a neural system to learn is a function of time rather than some global form of control. Particularly important is a 'critical period'.

Most of the physiological data come from single-cell experiments with kittens, where changes in neural responses resulting from blocking the input from one eye over long periods of time are observed (ocular dominance experiments).

Causes of plasticity modulation

In some physiological studies, modulation has simply been assumed to be age-related. This is unlikely in view of the fact that chemical effects, such as those of norpinephrine, have been shown to have a major (but complex) effect. Mechanical stimulation of extraocular muscles has also been shown to alter the plasticity of visual neurons.

The model pursued in this chapter is based on the idea that whatever the output that facilitates plasticity may be, it is controlled by the [functional] state of the neurons themselves.

State and plasticity

The model relies on evidence that in the newborn retino-cortical connectivities are weaker and more susceptible to change and become stronger as a result of experience. The weak connections are more *plastic* than the strong ones.

A semi-linear (see review of Chapter 2) neuron function is assumed. If **W** is the weight vector of a neuron, the object of the analysis is to show that for an initial **W** there are modification rules for which plasticity decreases 'naturally' [as learning progresses].

As most of the data for plasticity are obtained from ocular dominance, adaptations to eye blocking, cortical cells are represented as a two-dimensional plane with axes related to the ipsilateral and contra-lateral total weight. It is shown that the simple growth of these two values implies high plasticity (easy ocular dominance changes) when the weights are low, and low plasticity (large weight changes, hard ocular dominance change) when these are high. This is shown to be a sufficient mechanism for explaining empirical data.

Further experiments
The value of this type of analysis lies in the fact that it suggests sensible frameworks for future experiments. For example, comparing plasticity rates for dark-reared animals after dark-rearing with normally-reared animals, would separate environmental from maturitional effects. The analysis obviously predicts that the time of plasticity changes simply would be postponed by the dark-rearing.

On a more general point, whether a similar argument may be applied to plasticity in cortical areas which adapt to higher functions or not, the suggested regime of plasticity dependence on state is worth bearing in mind.

[The self-annealing behaviour of logical probabilistic neurons described in Chapter 8 of this book is akin to the above in the sense that *apparent* plasticity is a function of accuracy of learning (ie it is state-related). However, discovery of an error leads to an *increase in plasticity*: is this worth bearing in mind as a possible mechanism in biological systems?]

25. Amnesia and distributed memory (McClelland & Rumelhart)

A paradox motivates this chapter: some aspects of bi-temporal amnesia (such as a deficit in the ability to acquire new information) are consistent with distributed PDP representations, while others (the return of recently lost information) appear not to be. The object is to show that a particular distributed model can account for both findings.

Bitemporal amnesia
This is defined as resulting from 'insults' (damage due to a variety of reasons) to the medial portions of the temporal lobe in both halves of the brain.

Anterograde amnesia is the name given to a deficit in the ability to acquire new knowledge and the rapid loss of information once acquired. *Retrograde amnesia* is the loss of access to facts over a graded period of up to three years' duration. The latter loss diminishes with time and the information returns, at least partially. The two are sometimes coupled.

As the simple model (memory = state of weights, loss of memory = disrupted or damaged weights, weight change → a drive from experience) does not support the return phenomenon (new weights require new experience), the authors invent a hypothetical factor γ which is *necessary for consolidation* (stops weights from changing) and is *necessary for expression* (ie retrieval of the memory due to weight change).

A hypothetical neurochemistry suggests that the first step towards creating a memory is the addition of receptors at post-synaptic sites. The γ factor binds them in catalytic fashion. Once the binding is accomplished the γ factor is no longer required and the memory becomes functional. So an insult is seen as a loss of γ. New memories will never be bound and be forgotten, old ones will not acquire γ and so will be remembered, and in-between ones will be bound if γ (generated away from the site of the insult) returns. A by-product of this suggestion is that it may cast the hippocampus into the role of the γ producer.

Simulations
On the basis of quoting a binding probability ρ which depends on γ as

$$\rho = \frac{\gamma}{1 - \alpha},$$

simulation shows that amnesiac models behave in a manner similar to that observed in retrograde amnesiac patients in several aspects without the need to evoke mechanisms beyond γ. This is extended to *spared learning* (where amnesia does not affect *some* abilities to learn skills). This is based on an argument that amnesiacs merely have a limited capacity for making weight changes in their distributed nets. Again, simulations can be made to agree with measured effects.

Conclusion
The γ factor has, as yet, to be found or confirmed through biochemical experimentation.

[In some ways, the invention of a locally acting γ agent, globally produced, seems unnecessary. There are known transfer mechanisms in the brain where one part can exercise another (eg the cerebellum) and an alternative to the retrograde explanation is that a memory could shift from a non-explicitable site to an explicitable one.]

PART VI. Conclusion

26. Reflections on cognition and parallel distributed processing (Norman)

Cognitive science rather than being the focus for different disciplines has become compartmentalized; in particular, cognitive psychologists see brain studies as being interesting but too removed from their studies of thought and the behaviour of real, live human beings. Neuroscientists see cognitive models and psychological data as being based on speculation and description, and hence of little value to brain studies, while those in artificial intelligence are heavily involved in defining the type of representational and control structures demanded by current computing needs for which neurons and experimental results on living brains provide no input. PDP could change all that—it draws on evidence from all these three fields and is constrained by the findings in them.

The author [quite rightly in my view] suggests that the conventional von Neumann computer has had a distorting effect on those who work in cognitive science. Before its advent, the structure and 'engineering' of the brain were the unifying factors bringing psychologists, neuroscientists and mathematicians together. The break-up occurred because the computing exigencies dominated the modelling process. But a thread of neural-like thinking survived despite the criticisms of Minsky & Papert, which perhaps had a greater effect on decrying the approach than they themselves had intended.

Strengths of PDP

Rule-based systems appear to have boxed themselves into traps that simply increase (explosively sometimes) the number and complexity of rules required to capture even simple behaviours. PDP *starts* with an assumption of higher multiplicity in processing but centres on ways this is disciplined to produce simple, powerful cognitive behaviour. Its future does not seem to be overshadowed by the spectre of the combinatorial explosion.

The distributed *schema* at the centre of the PDP paradigm adds a useful tool to the brain modellers' armoury. It seems more flexible and uses neural circuitry more wisely than computationally better-known local representations such as semantic nets.

Human information processing systems are robust, and are insensitive to missing detail, erroneous data and damage. Ambiguities do not hold up the processing. The system is modified by descriptions and partial information and has a graceful degradation. All these properties come naturally to PDP schemes, while they are a puzzle and a nuisance in conventional rule-based computing.

PDP offers comfortable metaphors: local and global minima, adaptation stability, and so on. Although metaphors do not constitute a science, they facilitate an interaction between scientists and science.

Finally, is all this 'low-level' description useful? Undoubtedly, yes—it provides the cognitive scientists with a continuum of explanation down to microscopic levels where indeed some of the 'high-level' concepts are 'born'. [I have heard some systems designers in engineering argue that they do not care about physics, molecules, temperatures, and so on. All they need is a good data-sheet for their rule systems. Such designers are generally considered as being, at best, blinkered and, at worst, ignorant. Maybe the time has come to judge computer scientists interested in 'intelligence' in the same way.]

Weaknesses of PDP

PDP works well at the extremities of the perception-to-motor-output chain. Whether it moves towards providing essential links between these still remains to be seen. In PDP it is easy to handle concepts such as 'Harry likes a cream bun' and 'Mary likes a cream bun' as general classes, particularly with respect to the 'cream bun'. It is not easy to introduce the nuance implied by 'Harry eats a cream bun', and 'Mary eats a cream bun', where human knowledge and even semantic nets can represent the two cream buns as being different. This is the *type-token* problem.

PDP does not have *variables*, just instantiations of such. The author is uneasy about this as he has come to regard much of human thought as manipulating variables rather than instances. [I suspect that this will be solved in PDP as a variable is only a step in a set of linked representations. Not much work has been done as yet on such linking, but it is clearly not outside the PDP paradigm.]

PDP has been too concerned with modelling instances of problem solving. Whether it would be possible to link some of these together or not will determine its validity as an explanatory science in cognition. [Exactly the same criticism could be made with most rule-based models.] If PDP is to step into this multi-mode arena, the magnitude of the task may be such as to make the job impossible.

Learning and consciousness

A level of mental activity called direct conscious control (DCC) could be defined. It is argued that this is what is needed to control the more *sub-conscious* mechanisms implied by the PDP paradigm. Intraspection tells us of the existence of such mechanisms where consciously one 'places one's brains' into a particular state. The author suggests that the relationship between DCC and PDP still remains to be investigated.

The difference between the old and the new

In summary, where the old had to do with rules of thought, frame-based schema, inference mechanisms and production methods, the new has to do with changes in the system itself to best match what is required of it. Issues of learning are easier to contemplate in the new, while issues of control are more difficult.

In the old it seemed appropriate to ask the question 'why' did a particular processing event occur. The new neatly dispenses with that question by saying that at that moment a processing state is merely the best match to all constraints. This puts an end to years of argument in cognitive psychology.

Postscript
Future directions (Rumelhart & McClelland)

Despite the enormous progress documented in this book [the authors claim that it was not clear in 1982 as to how perceptron limitations might be overcome, although this has been repeatedly discussed in non-US publications, eg by Kohonen and Aleksander] a number of important unsolved questions have been uncovered.

Higher-level processes remain uncharted, learning theory is in its infancy, and the match between PDP and neuroscience is only weakly forged. More specifically the following are fruitful areas of research.

- Sequential symbol processing: clearly not all processing may be represented by neat stable states—some sequence relationships have to be established at some point.
- Language processing: the ground covered in these books is foundational. It has an overlapping approach to semantics with syntax and grammar as by-products—but it is only a beginning.
- Learning: this is the strength of PDP—more experience is required with methods such as error backpropagation.
- Neuropsychology: PDP offers a tool for deeper studies and predictions of damage effects.
- Physiology and anatomy: there is much scope for close modelling of brain structures which also reveals functions—this provides a much needed theoretical framework for psychologists.

[My feeling is that a *rapprochement* between rule-based methods and PDP should not be left off any list of work which still remains to be done.]

As a final word, it is the sense of excitement which pervades the rich ground for new discovery which is at the heart of the importance of *Parallel Distributed Processing*.

References

1. Marr, D. & Poggio, Z. Cooperative computation of stereo disparity, *Science* **194**, 283–287 (1976).
2. Minsky, M. & Papert, S. *Perceptrons: an Introduction to Computational Geometry* (Boston: MIT Press, 1969).
3. Anderson, J. A. & Mozer, M. C. Categorization and selective neurons. In Hinton, J. E. & Anderson, J. A. (eds.) *Parallel Models of Associative Memory*, pp. 213–236 (Hillsdale, NJ: Lawrence Erlbaum, 1981).
4. Crick, F. & Mitchinson, G. The function of dream sleep, *Nature* **304**, 111–114 (1983).
5. Willshaw, D. J. Holography, associative memory, and inductive generalization. In Hinton, J. E. & Anderson, J. E. (eds.) *Parallel Models of Associative Memory*, pp. 83–104 (Hillsdale, NJ: Lawrence Erlbaum, 1981).
6. Moustafa, Y. Abu and St. Jaques, J. Information capacity of the Hopfield Model *IEEE Trans Info Theory* **31**, 461–464 (1985).
7. Hillis, W. D. *The Connection Machine* (Cambridge Mass: MIT Press, 1986).
8. Kelly, G. *The Theory of Personal Constructs* (NY: Norton, 1955).
9. Aleksander, I. *The Human Machine* (St Saphorin, Switzerland, Georgi Publications, 1978).
10. Reddy, D. R., Erman, L. D., Fennell, R. D. & Neely, R. B. The HEARSAY speech understanding system: an example of the recognition process. *Proc. Int. Conf. on Artificial Intelligence*, pp. 185–194 (1973).
11. Morton, J. Facilitation in word recognition: experiments causing change in the logogen model. In Kholers *et al.* (eds.) *Processing Visible Language*, Vol. I (NY: Plenum, 1979).
12. Aleksander, I. Emergent properties of progressively structured pattern recognition nets, *Pattern Recognition Letters*, pp. 375–384 (1983).
13. Marslen-Wilson, W. D. & Tyler, L. K. The temporal structure of natural language understanding, *Cognition* **8**, 1–71, (1980).
14. Hubel, D. H. & Wiesel, T. N. Receptive fields, binocular interaction and functional architecture in the cat's visual cortex, *Journal of Physiology* **160**, 106–154 (1968).
15. Crick, F. H. C. The function of the thalamic reticular complex: The searchlight hypothesis. *Proc. of the National Academy of Sciences* USA, 81, 4586–4590 (1984).
16. Brodmann, K. *Vergleichende localisationslehre der grosshirnrinde in inren prinzipien dargestellt auf grund des Lellenbaues.* (*Principle of Comparative Localization in the Cerebral Cortex Presented on the Basis of Cytoarchitecture*) (Leipzig: Barth, 1909).
17. Hopfield, J. J. Neural networks and physical systems with emergent computational abilities, *Proceedings of the National Academy of Sciences*, USA **79**, 2554–2558 (1982).

Bibliography

Abbott, L. F. & Arian, Y. *Phys. Rev.* **A36**, 5091 (1987).

Abu Mustafa, Y. & St Jacques, J. M. Information capacity of the Hopfield model. *IEEE Trans. on Inf. Theory* Vol. IT-31, pp. 461–464 (1985).

Albus, J. S. A theory of cerebellar function. *Math. Biosci.* **10**, 15–61 (1971).

Albus, J. S. Mechanisms of planning and problem solving in the brain. *Math. Biosci.* **45**, 247–293 (1979).

Albus, J. S. *Brains Behaviour and Robotics* (Peterborough NH: Byte, 1981).

Aleksander, I. Fused adaptive circuit which learns by example. *Electronic Letters* **1**(6) (1965).

Aleksander, I. Brain cell to microcircuit. *Electronics and power* **16**, 48–51 (1970).

Aleksander, I. *Microcircuit Learning Computers* (London: Mills and Boon, 1971).

Aleksander, I. *The Human Machine* (St Saphorin, Switz.: Georgi Publ., 1978).

Aleksander, I. Emergent intelligent properties of progressively structured pattern recognition nets. *Pattern Recognition Letters* **1**, 375–384 (1983).

Aleksander, I. Adaptive vision systems and Boltzmann machines: a rapprochement. *Pattern Recognition Letters* **6**, 113–120 (1987).

Aleksander, I. & Atlas, P. Cyclic activity in nature: causes of stability. *Int. J. of Neuroscience* **6**, 45–50 (1973).

Aleksander, I. & Stonham, T. J. A guide to pattern recognition using random access memories. *IEEE Journal of Computers & Digital Techniques* **2**(1), 29–40 (1979).

Aleksander, I., Thomas, W. V. & Bowden, P. A. WISARD, a radical step forward in image recognition. *Sensor Review* **4**(3), 120–124 (1984).

Aleksander, I. & Wilson, M. Adaptive windows for image processing. *IEE Proc.* Vol. 132, Pt. E, No. 5 (1985).

Almeida, L. Backpropagation in perceptrons with feedback in neural computers. *Proc. of the NATO ARW on Neural Computers*, Dusseldorf (Heidelberg: Springer Verlag, 1987).

Almeida, L. A learning rule for asynchronous perceptrons with feedback in a combinatorial environment. *Proc. of 1987 IEEE First Ann. Int. Conf. on Neural Networks*, S. Diego (1987).

Bibliography

Amari, S. I. A theory of adaptive pattern classifiers. *IEEE Trans Electronic Computing* Vol. EC-16, pp. 299–302 (1967).

Amari, S. I. Characteristics of randomly connected threshold elements and network systems. *Proc. IEEE* Vol. 39, pp. 33–47 (1971).

Amari, S. I. Learning patterns and pattern sequences by self-organizing nets of threshold elements. *IEEE Trans. Compt.* Vol. C21, pp. 1197–1206 (1972).

Amari, S. I. Field theory of self-organizing neural nets. *IEEE Trans. Systems, Man and Cybernetics* pp. 741–748 (1983).

Amit, D. In *Proc. of the Heidelberg Colloquium in Glassy Dynamics and Optimization* (Heidelberg: Springer Verlag, 1987).

Amit, D. J., Gutfreund, H. & Sompolinsky, H. *Phys. Rev. Lett.* **55**, 1530 (1985).

Amit, D. J., Gutfreund, H. & Sompolinsky, H. *Phys. Rev.* **A32**, 1007 (1985).

Amit, D. J., Gutfreund, H. & Sompolinsky, H. *Ann. Phys.* **173**, 30 (1987).

Anderson, J. A. & Mozer, M. C. Categorization and selective neurons. In Hinton, J. E. & Anderson, J. A. *Parallel Models of Associative Memory*, pp. 213–236 (Hillsdale NJ: Lawrence Erlbaum, 1981).

Arbib, M. A. Perceptual structures and distributed motor control. In Brookhart, J. M., Mountcastle, V. B. & Brooks, V. B. *Handbook of Physiology*, pp. 1449–1480 (Baltimore MD: Williams & Wilkins, 1981).

Baldi, P. & Venkatesh, S. *Phys. Rev. Lett.* **58**, 913 (1987).

Barhen, J., Dress, W. B. & Jorgensen, C. C. Applications of concurrent neuromorphic algorithms for autonomous robots. In Eckmiller, R. & Malsburg, C. v. d. *Neural Computers*, pp. 321–333 (Heidelberg: Springer Verlag, 1988).

Baron, R. J. The high level control of movements. In Baron R. J. *The Cerebral Computer — An Introduction to the Computational Structure of the Human Brain*, pp. 402–452 (Hillsdale NJ: Lawrence Erlbaum, 1987).

Barto, A. G. & Sutton, R. S. *Goal Seeking Components for Adaptive Intelligence: An Initial Assessment* (Tech. Rep. AFWAL TR 81 1070, Univ. of Mass., 1981).

Bayley, J. S. & Fiddy, M. A. On the use of the Hopfield model for optical pattern recognition. *Optics Comm.* **64**, 105–110 (1987).

Bellezza, F. S. & Bower, G. H. Remembering script based text. *Poetics* **11**, 1–23 (1982).

Bellman, R. E. *Dynamic Programming* (Princeton Univ. Press 1957).

Berkinblit, M. B., Feldman, A. G. & Fukson, O. I. Adaptability of innate motor patterns and motor control mechanisms. *Behav. and Brain Sci.* **9**, 585–638 (1986).

Binstead, M. J. & Jones, A. J. A design technique for dynamically evolving N-tuple nets. *IEE Proc.* Vol. 134, Pt. E, No. 6, pp. 265–269 (1987).

Bledsoe, W. W. & Browning, I. Pattern recognition and reading by machine. *Proc. Eastern Joint Computer Conf.* Boston, Mass. (1959).

Bower, G. H., Black, J. B. & Turner, T. J. Scripts in memory for text. *Cog. Psych.* **11**, 177–220 (1979).

Brindle, A. Genetic algorithms for function optimization. Ph.D. thesis Univ. of Alberta (1980).

Broadbent, D. A. A question of levels: comment on McClelland & Rumelhart. *J. of Experimental Psychology* **114**, General 189–192 (1985).

Brodmann, K. *Principle of Comparative Localization in the Cerebral Cortex Presented on the Basis of Cytoarchitecture* (in German) (Leipzig: Barth, 1909).

Bruce, A. D., Canning, A., Forrest, B., Gardner, E. & Wallace, D. J. In Denker, J. S. (ed.) *Neural Networks for Computing.* AIP Conf. Proc. Snowbird Utah, Vol. 151 (Am. Inst of Phys.) (1987).

Bruce, A. D., Gardner, E. & Wallace, D. J. *J. Phys.* **A20**, 2909 (1987).

Caianello, E. Outline of a theory of thought-processes and thinking machines. *J. Theor. Biol.* **2**, 204 (1961).

Caianelo, E. Il sistema nervoso centrale. *Atti. Conv. Med. Eur.* 1st Angelis (1970).

Caianello, E. & De Luca, A. Decision equation for binary system-application to neural behaviour. *Kybernetik* 3 Band, 1 Helf 33–40 (1966).

Caianello, E. & Grimson, E. Synthesis of Boolean nets and time behaviour of a general mathematical neuron. *Biol. Cybern.* **18**, 111–117 (1975).

Caianello, E. & Marinaro, M. Linearization and synthesis of cellular automata. The additive case. *Physica Scripta* **34**, 444 (1986).

Caianello, E. & Marinaro, M. The inverse problem of neural nets and cellular automata. In *Computer Simulation in Brain Science* (Cambridge: CUP, 1987).

Caianello, E., Marinaro, M. & Tagliaferri, R. Associative memories as neural networks. *Proc. 9th European Meeting on Cybernetics and System Research*, Vienna (1988).

Caianello, E., Marinaro, M. & Tagliaferri, R. *Neural Computers* (Heidelberg: Springer Verlag, 1988).

Caianello, E. & Simoncelli, G. Polygonal inequalities as a key to neuronic equations. *Biol. Cybern.* **41**, 203–209 (1981).

Carnevali, P., Coletti, L. & Patarnello, S. *IBM J. of Res. & Dev.* **29**(6), 569 (1985).

Carnevali, P. & Patarnello, S. *Europhys. Letts.* **4**(10), 1199 (1987).

Cavicchio, D. J. Adaptive search using simulated evolution. Ph.D. thesis Univ. of Michigan (1970).

Chambers, W. G. *Basics of Communication and Coding,* pp. 101–103, (Clarendon Press 1985).

Chun, H. W. & Mimo, A. A massively parallel model of schema selection. *Proc. of 1st Ann. Int. Conf. on Neural Networks,* S. Diego (1987).

Clark, W. A. Aspects of integrated circuit hardware. In Aspinal, D. *The Microprocessor and its Applications,* pp. 1–39 (1978).

Cohen, M. & Grossberg, S. Absolute stability of global pattern formation and parallel memory storage by competitive neural networks. *IEEE Trans. Sys. Man & Cybern.* Vol. SMC-13, No. 5, pp. 815–826 (1983).

Cortes, C., Krogh, A. & Hertz, J. A. Hierarchical associative networks. *J. Phys.* **A20**, 449 (1987).

Cottrell, G. W. *A Connectionist Approach to Word Sense Disambiguation* (TR154 Dept. of Comp. Sci. Rochester, 1985).

Cottrell, G. W. & Fort, J. C. *Ann. Inst. Henri Poincare* **23**, 1–20 (1987).

Cover, T. M. *IEEE Trans.* **EC 14**, 326 (1965).

Crick, F. H. C. & Mitchinson, G. The function of dream sleep. *Nature* **304**, 111–114 (1983).

Crick, F. H. C. The function of the thalamic reticular complex: the searchlight hypothesis. *Proc. of Nat. Acad. Sci. USA* **81**, 4586–4590 (1984).

Crisanti, A., Amit, D. J. & Gutfreund, H. *Europhysics Lett.* **2**, 337 (1986).

Diederich, S. & Opper, M. *Phys. Rev. Lett.* **58**, 949 (1987).

Dobson, V. G. Pattern learning and the control of behaviour in all inhibitory neural network hierarchies. *Perception* **4**, 35–50 (1975).

Dobson, V. G. Towards a model of the development of adaptive behaviour in all inhibitory neural network hierarchies. Unpublished M. Phil. thesis. Brunel Univ. (1980).

Dobson, V. G. Superior accuracy of decrementing over incrementing associated networks in initially random connectivities. *J. of Inf. Sys.* **1**, 43–78 (1987).

Dolan, C. P. & Dyer, M. G. Symbolic schemata, role binding and the evolution of structure in connectionist memories. *Proc. of 1st Ann. Int. Conf. on Neural Networks.* S. Diego (1987).

Dotsenko, V. S. *J. Phys.* **C18**, L1017 (1985).

Eckmiller, R. Neural control of foveal pursuit versus saccadic eye movements in primates—single unit data and models. *IEEE Trans. on Systems, Man and Cybern.* **SMC-13**, 980–989 (1983).

Eckmiller, R. Neural control of pursuit eye movements. *Phys. Rev.* **67**, 797–857 (1987).

Eckmiller, R. Computational model of the motor program generator for pursuit. *J. Neurosci. Meth.* **21**, 127–138 (1987).

Eckmiller, R. Neural network mechanisms for generation and learning of motor programs. In *Proc. IEEE 1st Int. Conf. on Neural Networks,* S. Diego Vol. IV, pp. 545–550 SOS Publ. (1987).

Eckmiller, R. Neural networks for motor program generation. In Eckmiller, R. & Malsburg, C. v. d. *Neural Computers,* pp. 359–370 (Heidelberg: Springer Verlag, 1988).

Eckmiller, R. & Malsburg, C. v. d. *Neural Computers* (Heidelberg: Springer Verlag, 1988).

Edwards, S. F. & Anderson, P. W. *J. Phys.* **F5**, 965 (1975).

Eigen, M. & Schuster, P. *The Hypercycle Principle of Natural Self-organization* (Berlin: Springer Verlag, 1979).

Fanty, M. *Context Free Parsing in Connectionist Networks.* (TR174 Dept of Comp. Sci. Rochester, 1987).

Feigenbaum, M. J. Universal behaviour in non-linear systems. *Los Alamos Science* **1**, 4–27 (1986).

Feldman, J. A. & Ballard, D. H. Connectionist models and their properties. *Cognitive Science* **6**, 205–254 (1982).

Fish, A. N. The conformon—a synaptic model of learning. Ph. D. thesis Univ. Manchester. Dept of Psych. (1981).

Forrest, B. Content-addressability and learning in neural networks. Edinburgh preprint 87/413 (1987).

Frumkin, A. & Moses, E. *Phys. Rev.* **A34**, 714 (1986).

Fukunaga, K. & Koonz, W. L. G. *IEEETC* **19**, 311–318 (1970).

Galambos, J. A. & Rips, L. J. Memory for routines. *J. of Verbal Learning and Verbal Behaviour* **21**, 260–281 (1982).

Gardner, E. The phase space of interaction in neural network models. Edinburgh preprint 87/396 (1987).

Gardner, E. Maximum storage capacity of neural networks. *Europhys. Lett.* **4**, 481 (1987).

Gardner, E. *J. Phys.* **A20**, 3453 (1987).

Gardner, E. & Derrida, B. Optimal storage properties of neural network models. *J. Phys.* **A21**, 271 (1988).

Gardner, E., Stroud, N. & Wallace, D. J. Training with noise and the storage of correlated patterns in a neural network model. Edinburgh preprint 87/394 (1987).

Gardner–Medwin, A. R. The recall of events through learning associations between their parts. *Proc. of Royal Soc. London* **B194**, 375–402 (1976).

Geman, S. & Geman, D. *IEEE Trans. Pattn. Anal & Mach. Intell.* **6**, 721 (1984).

Gilbert, P. F. C. & Thach, W. T. Purkinje cell activity during motor learning. *Brain Research* **128**, 309–328 (1977).

Golden, R. M. Modelling causal schemata in human memory: a connectionist approach. Ph.D.thesis Brown Univ. (1987).

Graesser, A. C., Gordon, S. E. & Sawyer, J. D. Recognition memory for typical and atypical actions in scripted activities: tests of a script pointer and tag hypothesis. *J. of Verbal Learning and Verbal Behaviour* **18**, 319–332 (1979).

Grillner, S. & Wallen, P. Central pattern generators for locomotion with special reference to vertebrates. *Ann. Rev. Neurosci.* **8**, 233–261 (1985).

Groves, P. M. A theory of the functional organization of the neostiatum. *Brain Research Reviews* **5**, 109–132 (1983).

Gutfreund, H. & Stein, Y. In *Proc. of the Heidelberg Symposium on Glassy Dynamics* to be published (1987).

Haken, H., Kelso, J. A. S. & Bunz, H. A. A theoretical model of phase transitions in human hand movements. *Biol. Cybern.* **51**, 347–356 (1985).

Harris, B. Probability distributions related to random mappings. *Ann. Math. Stat.* **31**, 1045–1062 (1960).

Hemmen, J. L. v. *Rev. Lett.* **49**, 409 (1982).

Hemmen, J. L. v. *Phys. Rev.* **A36**, 1959 (1987).

Hemmen, J. L. v. & Kuhn, R. *Phys. Rev.* **57**, 913 (1986).

Hertz, J. A., Grinstein, G. & Solla, S. A. In *Proc. of the Heidelberg Symposium on Glassy Dynamics*. NORDITA preprint 86/18 (1986).

Hillis, W. D. *The Connection Machine* (Cambridge Mass: MIT Press, 1986).

Hinton, G. E. *Distributed Representation* (Tech. Rep. CMU CS 84 157, Dept. of Comp. Sci. Carnegie-Mellon Univ. 1984).

Hinton, G. E., Sejnowski, T. & Ackley, D. *Boltzmann Machines: Constraint Satisfaction Networks that Learn* (Tech. Rep. CMU CS 84 119, Carnegie-Mellon Univ. 1984).

Hogan, N. An organizing principle for a class of voluntary movements. *J. Neurosci.* **4**, 2745–2754 (1984).

Holland, J. H. *Adaptation in Natural and Artificial Systems* (Univ. of Michigan Press, 1975).

Holmes, J. N. The JSRU channel vocoder. *IEE Proc.* Vol. 127, Pt. F, No. 1, pp. 53–60 (1980).

Hopfield, J. Neural networks and physical systems with emergent collective comparabilities. *Proc. Nat. Acad. Sci. USA* **79**, 2554–2558 (1982).

Hopfield, J. Neurons with graded response have comparable properties like those of 2-state neurons. *Proc. Nat. Acad. Sci. USA* **81**, 3088–3092 (1984).

Hopfield, J. & Tank, D. W. *Biol. Cybern.* **52**, 141 (1985).

Horn, D. & Usher, M. Capacities of associative memory models. *J.*

Physique **49**, 389 (1988).

Hubel, D. H. & Wiesel, T. N. Receptive fields, binocular interaction and functional architecture in the cat's visual cortex. *J. of Physiology* **160**, 106–154 (1968).

Hutchinson, J., Koch, C., Luo, J. & Mead, C. To appear in *IEEE Comp. Mag.*

Ito, M., Miller, N. & Tongroach, P. Action of cerebellar climbing fibres during learning. *J. of Physiology* **324**, 113–134 (1982).

Jassem, W. Speech recognition work in Poland. In *Trends in Speech Recognition*, pp. 499–511 (Englewood Cliffs NJ: Prentice-Hall, 1980).

Jones, E. G. & Hendry, S. H. C. Co-localization of GABA and neuro-peptides in neocritical neurones. *Trends in Neuroscience* **9**, 71–76 (1986).

Jordan, M. I. Attractor dynamics and parallelism in a connectionist sequential machine. *8th Conf. of the Cognitive Science Soc.*, Amherst, Mass. pp. 531–546 (1986).

Kan, W. K. A probabilistic neural network for associative learning. Ph.D. thesis Imperial Col. London (1989).

Kanter, I. & Sompolinsky, H. *Phys. Rev.* **A35**, 380 (1987).

Kauffman, S. A. Metabolic stability and epigenesis in randomly connected genetic nets. *J. Theoret. Biol.* **22**, 437–467 (1969).

Kawato, M., Furukawa, K. & Suzuki, R. A hierarchical neural network model for control and learning of voluntary movement. *Biol. Cybern.* **56**, 1–17 (1987).

Kelly, G. *The Theory of Personal Constructs* (New York: W. W. Norton, 1955).

Kienker, P. K., Sejnowski, T. J., Hinton, G. E. & Schumacher, L. E. *Perception* **15**, 197 (1986).

Kirkpatrick, S., Gelatt, S. D. & Vecchi, M. P. *Science* **200**, 671 (1983).

Kirkpatrick, S. & Sherrington, D. *Phys. Rev.* **B17**, 4384 (1978).

Koch, C. & Poggio, T. The synaptic veto mechanism: does it underlie direction and orientation selectivity in the visual cortex. In Rose, D. & Dobson, V. G. *Models of Visual Cortex* (Chichester: J. Wiley, 1985).

Kohonen, T. *Proc. 2nd Scand. Conf. on Image Analysis*, pp. 214–220. Suomen Hahmontunnistustutkimuksen Seura r.y. Helsinki (1981).

Kohonen, T. In *Proc. 6th Int. Conf. on Pattern Recognition*, pp. 114–128. IEEE Comp. Soc. Press Washington DC (1982).

Kohonen, T. *Biol. Cybern.* **43**, 59–69 (1982).

Kohonen, T. *Biol. Cybern.* **44**, 135–140 (1982).

Kohonen, T. *Self-organization and Associative Memory* (Heidelberg: Springer Verlag, 1984), 2nd ed (1988).

Kohonen, T. In *Proc. 8th Int. Conf. on Pattern Recognition*, pp. 1148–1151. IEEE Comp. Soc. Press Washington DC (1986).

Kohonen, T. An introduction to neural computing. To be published in *Neural Networks*, Jan 1988.

Kohonen, T. *Learning Vector Quantization*. Helsinki Univ. TKK-F-A601 (1986).

Kohonen, T., Makisara, K. & Saramaki, T. In *Proc. 7th Int. Conf. on Pattern Recognition*, pp. 182–185. IEEE Comp. Soc. Press Silver Spring (1984).

Kohonen, T., Torkkola, K., Shozakai, M., Kangas, J. & Verta, O. In *Proc. Euro. Conf. on Speech Tech.*, pp. 377–380 (Edinburgh: CEP Consultants, 1987).

Krauth, W. & Mezard, M. *J. Phys.* **20**, L745 (1987).

Kuperstein, M. Adaptive visual-motor co-ordination in multi-joint robots using parallel architecture. In *IEEE Int. Conf. on Robotics and Automation* Vol. 3, pp. 1595–1602 (SOS Publ: S. Diego, 1987).

Lamb, G. L. *Elements of Soliton Theory*, (New York: J. Wiley, 1980).

Lansner, A. & Ekeberg, O. Reliability and speed of recall in an associative network. *IEEE Pattern Recognition and Machine Intelligence*-7 **4**, 490–499 (1985).

Lee, Y. C. *et al. Physica* **22D**, 276 (1986).

Leszek, K. A syntax-controlled segmentation of speech on the basis of dynamic spectra. *Int. Conf. on Acoustics, Speech and Signal Processing* 2015–2017 (1982).

Lippmann, R. P. *IEEE ASSP Magazine* **4**(2), 4 (1987).

Little, W. A. The existence of persistent stated in the brain. *Math. Biosci.* **19**, 101–120 (1974).

Little, W. & Shaw, G. *Math. Biosci.* **39**, 281 (1978).

Longuet-Higgins, H. C., Willshaw, D. J. & Buneman, O. P. Theories of associative recall. *Quarterly Reviews of Biophysics* **3**(2), 223–244 (1970).

Luttinger, J. M. *Phys. Rev. Lett.* **37**, 778 (1976).

Lynch, G. & Bemdry, M. The biochemistry of memory: a new and specific hypothesis. *Science* **224**, 1057–1063 (1984).

McCullough, W. S. & Pitts, W. A logical calculus of the ideas immanent in nervous activity. *Bull. Math. Biophys.* **5**, 115–133 (1943).

McEliece, R. J., Posner, E. C., Rodemich, E. R. & Ventakesh, S. S. The capacity of the Hopfield associative memory. Caltech preprint submitted to IEEE Trans. in IT.

McNaughton, B. L. & Morris, R. G. M. Hippocampal synaptic reinforcement and information storage. *Trends in Neuroscience* **10**, 408–415 (1987).

Marr, D. A theory of cerebellar function. *J. of Physiology* **202**, 437–470 (1969).

Marr, D. *Vision* (San Francisco: W. H. Freeman, 1982).

Marr, D. & Poggio, Z. Co-operative computation of stereo disparity. *Science* **194**, 283–287 (1976).

Marslen-Wilson, W. D. & Tyler, L. K. The temporal structure of natural language understanding. *Cognition* **8**, 1–71 (1980).

Martland, D. Behaviour of autonomous (synchronous) Boolean networks *Proc. 1st IEEE Conf. on Neural Networks*, S. Diego **II**, 243–250 (1987).

Martland, D. Auto-associative pattern storage using synchronous Boolean networks. *Proc. 1st IEEE Conf. on Neural Networks*, S. Diego. **III**, 355–366 (1987).

Mattis, D. C. *Phys. Lett.* **56A**, 421 (1976).

Maxwell, N. Methodological problems of neuroscience. In Rose, D. & Dobson, V. G. *Models of Visual Cortex*, pp. 11–22 (Chichester: J. Wiley, 1985).

Meddis, R. S. *J. Acoust. Soc. Am.* **79**, 703–711 (1986).

Mezard, M., Nadal, J. P. & Toulouse, G. *J. Physique* **47**, 1457 (1986).

Miles, F. A. & Evarts, E. V. Concepts of motor organization. *Ann. Rev. Psych.* **30**, 327–362 (1979).

Milligan, D. K. Annealing in RAM-based learning networks. Private (1986).

Minsky, M. & Papert, S. *Perceptrons: an Introduction to Computational Geometry* (Cambridge Mass: MIT Press, 1969).

Morasso, P. & Mussalvaldi, F. A. Trajectory formation and handwriting: a computational model. *Biol. Cybern.* **45**, 131–142 (1982).

Morton, J. Facilitation in word recognition: experiments causing change in the logogen model. In Kholens et al *Processing Visible Language* Vol. 1 (New York: Plenum, 1979).

Nadal, J. P., Toulouse, G., Changeux, J. P. & Delaene, S. *Europhys. Lett.* **1**, 535 (1986).

Oppenheim, A. & Schafer, R. *Digital Signal Processing* (Englewood Cliffs NJ: Prentice-Hall, 1975).

Orgel, L. E. & Crick, F. H. C. Selfish DND the ultimate parasite. *Nature* **284**, 604–607 (1980).

Palm, G. *Neural Assemblies* (Berlin: Springer Verlag, 1982).

Palm, G. & Aertsen, A. *Brain Theory* (Berlin: Springer, 1986).

Parga, N. & Virasoro, M. A. *J. Physique* **47**, 1857 (1986).

Parisi, J. *J. Phys.* **A19**, L617 (1986).

Parisi, J. *J. Phys.* **A19**, L675 (1986).

Parker, D. *Learning Logic: Casting the Cortex of the Human Brain in Silicon* (Tech. Rep. TR 47. Center for comp. res. in econ. and man. science. Cambridge Mass: MIT Press, 1985).

Patarnello, S. & Carnevali, P. *Europhys. Letts.* **4**(4), 503 (1981).

Pellionisz, A. & Llinas, R. Tensor network theory of the metaorganization of functional geometries in the central nervous system. *Neurosci.* **16**, 245–273 (1985).

Perretto, P. *Biol. Cybern.* **50**, 51 (1984).

Perretto, P. & Niez, J. J. *Biol. Cybern.* **54**, 53 (1986).

Personnaz, L., Guyan, I. & Dreyfus, G. *J. Physique Lett.* **46**, L359 (1985).

Pineda, J. Generalization of backpropagation to recurrent neural networks. *Proc. of IEEE Conf. on neural Inf. Processing Sys.- natural and synthetic* Boulder (1987).

Poppel, G. & Krey, U. *Europhys. Lett.* **4**, 979 (1987).

Provost, J. P. & Vallee, G. *Phys. Rev. Lett.* **50**, 598 (1983).

Psaltis, D. & Farhat, N. H. Optical information processing based upon an associative memory model of neural nets with threshold and feedback. *Opt. Letters* **10**, 98 (1985).

Rall, W. Core conductor theory and cable properties of neurons. In Kandel, E. *Handbook of Physiology, the Nervous System I*, pp. 39–97 (Baltimore: Williams and Wilkins, 1977).

Reddy, D. R., Erman, L. D., Fennell, R. D. & Neely, R. B. The HEARSAY speech understanding system: an example of the recognition process. *Proc. Int. Conf. on Artificial Intelligence*, pp. 185–194 (1973).

Ritter, H. & Schulten, K. *Biol. Cybern.* **54**, 99–106 (1986).

Ritter, H. & Schulten, K. Extending Kohonen's self-organizing mapping algorithm to learn ballistic movements. In Eckmiller, R. & Malsburg, C. v. d. *Neural Computers*, pp. 393–403 (Heidelberg: Springer Verlag, 1988).

Robbins, H. & Monro, S. *Ann. Math. Statistics* **22**, 400–407 (1951).

Rolls, E. T. Functions of neuronal networks in hippocampal cortex. In Byrne, J. H. & Berry, W. O. *Neural Models of Plasticity* (New York: Academic Press, 1988).

Rose, D. & Dobson, V. G. Methodological solutions for neuroscience. In *Models of Visual Cortex*, pp. 533–546 (Chichester: J. Wiley, 1985).

Rosenblatt, F. *Principles of Neurodynamics: Perceptrons and the Theory of Brain Mechanisms* (New York: Spartan Books, 1962).

Rubin, H. & Sitgreave, R. *Probability Distributions Related to Random Transformations on a Finite Set* (Tech. Rep. No. 19A Applied Maths and Stats Lab. Stanford Univ. 1954).

Rumelhart, D. E. & Hinton, G. Learning internal representations by error propagation. *ICS Rept 8506*. Univ. of California (1985).

Rumelhart, D. E. & McClelland, J. L. *Parallel Distributed Processing, Vol. 1 and 2* (Cambridge Mass: MIT Press, 1986).

Sakoe, H. & Chiba, S. A dynamic programming approach to continuous speech recognition. *Proc. of Int. Cong. of Acoustics* Budapest Hungary pp. 200–213 (1971).

Sammon, J. W. *IEEETC* **18**, 401–409 (1969).

Schank, R. C. *Dynamic Memory* (Cambridge: CUP, 1983).

Schank, R. C. & Abelson, R. P. *Scripts, Plans, Goals and Understanding* (Hillsdale NJ: Lawrence Erlbaum, 1977).

Sejnowski, T. J., Kienker, P. K. & Hinton, G. E. *Physica.* **22D**, 260 (1986).

Selman, B. *Rule-based Processing in a Connectionist System for Natural Language Understanding* (TR CSR1 168. Comp. Sys. Res. Inst. Univ. of Toronto, 1985).

Selviah, D. R. & Midwinter, J. E. Correlating matched filter model for analysis and optimization of neural networks. To be published in *IEE Proc. Pt. F.*

Selviah, D. R. & Midwinter, J. E. Unpublished results.

Selvertson, A. I. *Model Neural Networks and Behaviour* (New York: Plenum, 1985).

Sharkey, N. E. Neural network learning techniques. In McTear, M. (ed.) *An Introduction to Cognitive Science* (Chichester: Ellis Horwood, 1988).

Sharkey, N. E. A PDP system for goal-plan decisions. *Proc. of 9th Euro. Meeting on Cybernetics and Systems Research*, (1988).

Sharkey, N. E. & Bower, G. H. The integration of goals and actions in text understanding. *Proc. of Cognitive Science* **6** (1984).

Sharkey, N. E. & Bower, G. H. A model of memory organization for interacting goals. In Morris, P. E. (ed.) *Modelling Cognition* (New York: J. Wiley, 1987).

Sharkey, N. E. & Mitchell, D. C. Word recognition in a functional context: the use of scripts in reading. *J. of Memory and Language* **24**, 253–270 (1985).

Sharkey, N. E. & Sharkey, A. J. C. KAN—a knowledge access network model. In Reilly, R. (ed.) *Communication Failure in Dialogue & Discourse* (Amsterdam: Elsevier, 1987).

Sharkey, N. E. & Sharkey, A. J. C. What is the point of integration? The use of knowledge-based facilitation in sentence processing. *J. of Memory and Language* **26**, 255–276 (1987).

Sharkey, N. E. & Sutcliffe, R. F. E. Memory attraction: learning distributed schemata for language understanding. Paper to Edinburgh workshop on connectionism and memory.

Sharkey, N. E., Sutcliffe, R. F. E. & Wobcke, W. R. Mixing binary and continuous connection schemes for knowledge access. *Proc. of the Am. Assoc for Artificial Intelligence* (1986).

Shastri, L. & Feldman, J. A. Neural nets, routines and semantic networks. In Sharkey, N. E. (ed.) *Advances in Cognitive Science.* Vol. 1 (Chichester: Ellis Horwood, 1986).

Sherrington, D. & Kirkpatrick, S. *Phys. Rev. Lett.* **35**, 1792 (1975).

Shinomoto, S. *Biol. Cybern.* **57**, 197 (1987).

Singer, W. Activity-dependent self-organization in the mammalian visual cortex. In Rose, D. & Dobson, V. G. (eds.) *Models of Visual Cortex*, pp. 123–136 (Chichester: J. Wiley, 1985).

Soechting, J. F., Lacquanitu, F. & Terzuolo, C. A. Co-ordination of arm movements in three-dimensional space. Sensorimotor mapping during drawing movement. *Neurosci.* **17**, 295–311 (1986).

Somogyi, P. & Martin, K. A. C. Cortical circuitry underlying inhibitory processes in cat area 17. In Rose, D. & Dobson, V. G. (eds.) *Models of Visual Cortex*, pp. 504–513 (Chichester: J. Wiley, 1985).

Sompolinsky, H. *Phys. Rev.* **A34**, 2571 (1986).

Sompolinsky, H. In *Proc. of the Heidelberg Colloquium on Glassy Dynamics and Optimization* (Heidelberg: Springer Verlag, 1987).

Sompolinsky, H. & Kanter, I. Temporal association in asymmetric neural networks. *Phys. Rev. Lett.* **57**, 2861 (1986).

Steinbuch, K. Die Lernmatrix. *Kybernetica* **1**, 35–36 (1961).

Tattershall, G. D. & Johnson, R. D. Speech recognition based on N-tuple sampling. *Proc. Spring Conf. Inst. Acoustics* Swansea Vol. 9, No. 2 (1984).

Tanguay, A. R. Materials requirements for optical processing and computing devices. *Optical Eng.* **24**, 2 (1985).

Taylor, W. K. Machines that learn. *Science Journal* **102**(6), (1968).

Toffoli, T. & Margolus, N. *Cellular Automata Machines—a New Environment for Modelling* (Cambridge Mass: MIT Press, 1987).

Torkkola, K. Automatic alignment of speech with phonetic transcriptions in real time. *Proc. 1988 IEEE I C Assp.* NY (1988).

Venkatesh, S. In *Proc. of the Conf. on Neural Networks for Computing*, Snowbird Utah (1986).

Vintsyuk, T. K. Element by element recognition of continuous speech composed of the words of a given vocabulary. *Kybernetica* **2**, 133–143 (1971).

Walker, C. C. Behaviour of a class of complex systems: the effect of system size on properties of terminal cycles. *J. of Cybern.* **1**, 55–67 (1971).

Walker, C. C. Stability of equilibrial states and limit cycles in sparsely connected structurally complex Boolean nets. Submitted for publ. (1987).

Waltz, D. L. & Pollack, J. B. Massively parallel parsing: a strongly interactive model of natural language comprehension. *Cognitive Science* (1985).

Weisbuch, G. & Fogelman-Soulie, F. *J. Phys. Lett.* **46**, L623 (1985).

Werbos, P. Beyond regression: new tools for prediction and analysis in behavioural sciences. Ph.D. thesis Harvard Univ. (1984).

Wheatley, P. et al. A novel non-resonant optoelectronic logic device. *Electronic Letters* **23**, 92–93 (1987).

Widrow, B. & Holt, M. E. Adaptive switching networks. *IRE Wescon Convention Record* (1961).

Wiener, N. *Cybernetics* (Cambridge Mass: MIT Press, 1947).

Williams, J. *Stability Theory of Dynamical Systems* (London: Nelson, 1970).

Willshaw, D. J., Buneman, O. P. & Longuet-Higgins, H. C. Non-holographic associative memory. *Nature* **222**, 960–962 (1969).

Willshaw, D. J. Holography, associative memory and inductive generalization. In Hinton, J. E. & Anderson, J. E. *Parallel Models of Associative Memory* (Hillsdale NJ: Lawrence Erlbaum, 1981).

Index